BOND VIGILANTES

10th Anniversary Book

Published by M&G Investment Management Limited

Copyright M&G Investment Management Limited 2016

It shall not by way of trade or otherwise, be reproduced, stored in a retrieval system, transmitted in any form or by any means, lent, sold, hired out, or otherwise circulated without the publisher's prior consent or as expressly permitted by law. This book shall not be reproduced in any form of binding or cover other than that in which it is published and without the same conditions including this condition, being imposed on the subsequent purchaser or recipient.

ISBN: 978-1-5272-0044-9

Printed and bound in Great Britain by Pureprint Group Limited (incorporating Beacon Press)

Introduction

My first ever piece on the Bond Vigilantes blog, back in November 2006, reported that the Bank of England had just raised interest rates to 5%, and suggested that with inflation at 3.6% (the highest for 8 years) and house prices rising, nobody should have been surprised. We know what happened next though.

With the US Federal Reserve having also raised rates to 5.25%, earlier in the year, the American housing market began to cool rapidly, and after annual price gains of between 5% and 12% since the turn of the millennium and significant speculative overbuilding, boom turned to bust. Consumers sank underwater on housing loans, and delinquencies and defaults ballooned. Mortgages had always been regarded as "safe" loans, and financial institutions had not only taken on huge leverage themselves to finance them, but had also originated and repackaged these debts to sell to financial institutions globally. In what was then considered a low yielding world, Asset Backed Securities (ABS) and new financially engineered instruments such as Collateralised Debt Obligations (CDOs) offering potentially higher returns for theoretically low credit risk, became widely held. This meant that when the housing crash came, and US house prices fell by an average of 5% per year from 2007 to 2011, the distress was widespread and not confined to American banks.

Closures of ABS funds were followed by skyrocketing funding costs for banks in desperate need of liquidity, and collapsing bank equity prices. Eventually Lehman Brothers defaulted, and US financial institutions were bailed out by taxpayers and the Federal Reserve. Queues formed outside distressed banks in the UK, and Northern Rock and the Royal Bank of Scotland were nationalised as policymakers realised that what was happening had echoes of America's Great Depression. Bailouts and nationalisation were not the only emergency responses though. Monetary policy changed forever in response to the supply side shock of weak banks (lack of lending), poor consumer demand (over-leveraged and experiencing negative equity on housing loans), lack of business investment (low confidence in future growth) and deflation fears. Interest rates were slashed by central banks (0% – 0.25% by the end of 2008 in the US), and extraordinary policies such as subsidised lending to the banking sector were implemented. Most importantly, we also saw central banks print money to buy back government bonds from investors – Quantitative Easing (QE).

QE was designed to generate both growth and inflation. By lowering borrowing costs in capital markets, businesses would become more profitable and might invest more. Households would see interest costs reduced. And the so-called "portfolio rebalancing" effect would encourage investors such as ourselves to sell our expensive and low yielding government bonds to take riskier, higher yielding positions which would help finance the real economy. Did it work? Well the academic literature – much written by the central bankers themselves – says yes. Inflation and growth were both higher than they would have been without QE. But as a politician once said, "you can't put a counterfactual on a bumper sticker". We will never know how bad things would have got if QE hadn't happened, or indeed whether more "creative destruction" – letting failed institutions go bust, rather than limp on as bailed-out zombies – might have been a better outcome. Anyway, no feel good factor returned, and what started off as a financial sector crisis had, by the time the

Bond Vigilantes blog reached its 5th anniversary, become a sovereign debt crisis in Europe. Weak growth, poor demographics, badly capitalised banks, government indebtedness and imbalances within the Eurozone proved a toxic mix. Spanish, Italian, Irish and Portuguese government bond yields spiked. Greece had to be bailed out by creditors including the International Monetary Fund (IMF).

Government indebtedness became an economic football. On the one hand books like "This Time is Different" by Reinhart and Rogoff warned of dire consequences for nations that allowed government borrowing to hit 90% of GDP. This helped inspire a cult of austerity (for example in the UK under Chancellor George Osborne) where fiscal tightening was thought to be needed, despite the huge shock to growth that had been experienced. Others, like Olivier Blanchard of the IMF, warned that the negative multiplier effects from austerity would cause the downturn to persist, and that Keynesian stimulus was desirable. On the whole the austerians won, and monetary policy rather than fiscal policy was left to do the heavy lifting. Which brings us to the start of this book, covering the next five years of the ongoing Great Financial Crisis.

First the good news. Unemployment has fallen dramatically from the levels we saw in 2009. From 10% in the US, we now have just 4.9% of the American workforce out of work. We have a similar level of joblessness in the UK, and even in the Eurozone the unemployment rate is falling. Another reason to be cheerful is the relative stability in the financial sector. Having been forced to raise capital, been subjected to periodic regulatory "stress tests", and having access to cheap central bank money, banks are less of a threat to the economic system. But things still just don't feel "right", even though in December 2015 the Federal Reserve felt able to finally hike rates by 25 bps.

For although unemployment rates have fallen, workers have not seen the wage rises that we might have expected. Partly this could be due to lower participation rates in the US (people leaving the workforce because they are discouraged by fruitless job-seeking, flattering the unemployment numbers), but there are also good arguments to say that we now exist in a global labour market and that capital will move jobs to lower cost regions (for example emerging markets) rather than pay higher wages. "The Rise of the Robots" by Martin Ford makes the scary prediction that we are entering a period of rapid robotisation and use of artificial intelligence that will steal jobs and wages from not just manual workers, as has always been the case, but high skilled middle class jobs too. Unemployment will rise as a result, and because robots don't buy stuff, our consumer based economies will enter a negative spiral. The feeling that the average citizen has not seen incomes rise by much in real terms for many years now is likely to be a factor in both the lack of economic animal spirits and the rise of anti-establishment politics.

The Greek economic crisis (its unemployment rate hit nearly 30%) led to the rise of both far right (Golden Dawn) and far left (Syriza) political parties. Populist parties also emerged in Spain (for example Podemos who have suggested government debt forgiveness), and you could argue that the success of UKIP and Jeremy Corbyn, and the Front National in the UK and France respectively, as well as Trump and Sanders's popularity in the US, can be linked to the perception that incomes have stagnated for most workers whilst the "1%" have become richer as the result of QE and other post-crisis policies. The UK's two referendums, the first on

Scottish independence, the second on EU membership, also look like self-inflicted wounds from a purely economic standpoint, but may reflect voter dissatisfaction with remote "elites". Whilst most studies show that immigration may have only a marginal impact on wages (depressing them), globalisation is certainly no longer regarded as only a good thing. When China joined the World Trade Organisation in 2001, it felt like the movement towards global free trade was a one way street. No longer. Might we see the return of tariffs and trade barriers? And as monetary policy runs out of power, many nations have attempted to weaken their currencies in the hope that a competitive devaluation might stimulate their export trade in a way that lower rates couldn't. Currency wars are of course a zero sum game.

Five years ago, China was still a bright spot in an otherwise gloomy picture for global growth. Having bounced back from the Great Financial Crisis with some well-timed fiscal stimulus, its official GDP number was growing at around 10% per year. As an example of an investment-led economic miracle, China was a poster child. No other nation had invested a larger share of GDP for as big a boost to economic output as China had, and on a Purchasing Power Parity measure, it became the world's biggest economy in 2014. But not all investment is good investment, and the "bang for the buck" China was getting for each additional project started, has fallen dramatically in recent years. I remember attending an IMF meeting in Tokyo in 2012 where I heard Professor Michael Pettis speak. He told the audience that Chinese growth would average below 5% for many years as a result of over investment and bad loans, especially to the State Owned Enterprises (SOEs). I saw almost all the audience snigger and make "he's gone mad" faces to each other, and I realised that a China slowdown was not on anyone's investment radar. And with China being the biggest export market for many other emerging markets, and commodity producers such as Australia, when the continual slowdown began at the end of 2012, there was pain for countries like South Africa, as well as for metals and mining companies. Simultaneously oil prices were hit from the supply side. The opening up of shale oil fields in the lower American states led to oil prices halving, and then halving again, between 2014 and the end of 2015, provoking a new deflation scare as headline inflation rates (where direct energy contributions are around 10% to 15% of the basket) turned negative. And if inflation rates turn negative and central bank rates are already at zero, what can you do? Switzerland had briefly instated negative interest rates in the 1970s to deter foreign currency speculators, but aside from this the world entered new monetary policy territory in the past couple of years. Switzerland, Denmark, Japan, Sweden and the Eurozone now all have negative rates. Will they work to stimulate growth and inflation? There's little evidence so far to suggest it. Theoretically the impact of negative and positive rates should be symmetrical, but in a world where we can take our cash out of banks as notes, we can avoid paying a financial institution for the privilege of looking after our money. Safe deposit box sales have soared. Worse still for the central bankers, in a world where the banks realise that they can't pass on negative rates to depositors for fears that they'll withdraw all their money, they have to maintain their profits by increasing their lending rates. Swiss mortgage rates went up when the SNB cut rates. This is an unintended consequence that only the abolition of cash and a move to pure electronic money could prevent – the latter action would be intensely unpopular with populations. You should see the hate mail I got from the American Tea Party when I discussed the abolition of physical money in a newspaper article. It was almost as bad as that I received when I suggested that Scotland might not merit a AAA credit rating if it became independent. Given the adverse impact on the banking sector in particular, I suspect that global rates won't go much more negative than they already are. If that's the case is it time to suggest that we are also near the end of the bull market in government bonds that's run since the start of the 1980s when Paul Volker took over control of the Federal Reserve and set out to kill the inflation that had eroded returns for bond investors for two decades? We are now at record low government bond yields in virtually all developed markets, and there is over $11 trillion worth of negative yielding bonds outstanding worldwide.

If negative rates are not effective then, what do we do next if we have a new slowdown? Governments still seem reluctant to ease fiscal policy, and central bankers are running out of assets to buy as part of QE programmes. Having been seen as a crackpot idea even a few years ago, the idea that the authorities might use "Helicopter Money" to stimulate an economy is slowly edging into the mainstream of economic thinking. Rather than printing money to buy financial assets and hope that institutions use the cash they receive to make new loans and investments, central banks could print money to short circuit that transmission mechanism and give the money directly to individuals to spend (akin to dropping banknotes out of a helicopter) or they could directly finance infrastructure spending and other activities with high economic multiplier effects. Having been the first to suggest it might happen in a 2012 blog, I also wouldn't rule out some form of government debt cancellation involving the bonds held on central banks' balance sheets as part of QE. A cancellation of student debt owed to governments might however be far more powerful economically. The M&G bond team has covered all of the topics above on the Bond Vigilantes blog in recent years, and we've very much enjoyed doing it. We're obviously fund managers and investment specialists rather than journalists, and the "day job" comes first, but setting out our views and creating charts really does help us to challenge or crystallise our own thinking.

Thanks very much for continuing to support us by reading our articles, for following us on Twitter, watching our YouTube videos and coming to our events. It's much appreciated. As before all proceeds of the sale of this book will go to Cancer Research UK. Our last book raised over £10,000, so thanks also for your generous support.

If you'd like to, you can donate at our Just Giving page **www.justgiving.com/fundraising/bond-vigilantes-anniversary-book**. Also, as before we need to thank M&G for supporting the blog over the last decade, and all of the economists, strategists and experts who have helped us formulate our views. It's hard to imagine that the next five years can be as eventful as the past ten, but the whole global economic and political system just seems a little...odd, doesn't it? So I'm not ruling it out.

Jim Leaviss

Contents

2011

Chapter 1
European High Yield vs. Eurozone Tail Risk High Yield
James Tomlins — 16

2012

Chapter 2
Happy Hogmanay – would an independent Scotland still be rated AAA? And might the rest of the UK get downgraded too?
Jim Leaviss — 18

Chapter 3
German government bond yields may need to get very negative for the euro to weaken much further. And it could easily happen
Mike Riddell — 22

Chapter 4
The ECB's bazooka has hit the target
Mike Riddell — 24

Chapter 5
Competitiveness confusion reigns supreme
Anthony Doyle — 26

Chapter 6
4 Housing Markets, One Country
James Tomlins — 28

Chapter 7
Paying the locusts – what the PSI means for Greek bond investors
Richard Woolnough — 29

Chapter 8
The 5 things that bond investors have learnt from the Greek default
Jim Leaviss — 30

Chapter 9
The Bank of England should cut rates rather than make state run Halifax hike mortgage rates
Jim Leaviss — 32

Chapter 10
Central Bank Regime Change: who cares about 2% inflation targets anymore? A chart
Jim Leaviss — 33

Chapter 11
If the government simply cancelled the £300 bn+ of QE gilts held by the BoE, who would be unhappy?
Jim Leaviss — 35

Chapter 12
What should Mervyn do with his QE gilts? Free finance
Richard Woolnough — 36

Chapter 13
Should Europe let the single currency go to save the Union?
Markus Peters — 37

Chapter 14
The UK's AAA rating looks increasingly vulnerable. Growth negative, borrowing up. It might not matter though.
Jim Leaviss — 39

Chapter 15
UK gilts – "Whoah we're half way there, Whoah livin' on a prayer..."
Richard Woolnough — 40

Chapter 16
Peripheral corporate bonds and mass downgrade risk
Stefan Isaacs — 42

Chapter 17
Climate change – bzirc monetary policy
Richard Woolnough   44

Chapter 18
The toxic French economic cocktail: weak growth, poor competitiveness, fiscal tightening
Jim Leaviss   45

Chapter 19
Fallen Angel Delight – looking at returns from "junked" companies
Nicolo Carpaneda   49

Chapter 20
5 years on
Richard Woolnough   50

Chapter 21
Happy Halloween. Five scary charts. Boo!
Anthony Doyle   51

Chapter 22
Stress in the Eurozone – Day of action, years of reaction
Richard Woolnough   56

Chapter 23
The fiscal cliff is bad news, but is likely to be resolved – so don't ignore the extremely positive developments in the US housing market
Jim Leaviss   57

Chapter 24
Corporate bond market liquidity – flush or flushed?
Richard Woolnough   61

2013

Chapter 25
Should the people of Middle Earth have done Quantitative Easing to mitigate against Smaug's tight monetary policy?
Jim Leaviss   65

Chapter 26
Contingent capital notes – bank equity's best friend?
Stefan Isaacs   66

Chapter 27
Why we love the US dollar, and worry about EM currencies
Mike Riddell   67

Chapter 28
Europe, China and shale gas: euphoria or rejection?
Nicolo Carpaneda   72

Chapter 29
If China's economy rebalances and growth slows, as it surely must, then who's screwed?
Mike Riddell   76

Chapter 30
Insane in the brain. Dangerous precedents being set in Cyprus
Stefan Isaacs   78

Chapter 31
I predict a CypRIOT: Three major implications for the European and UK banking systems
Ben Lord   79

Chapter 32
Heinz: Beans, Buffett and the return of animal spirits
Stefan Isaacs   81

Chapter 33
Germany doesn't like its own fiscal union, so why would it ever agree upon a European one?
Markus Peters   83

Chapter 34
Old Lady sells her bonds
Richard Woolnough   86

Chapter 35
Funding for Lending – has the scheme achieved its goals?
Matthew Russell   87

Chapter 36
It's a new dawn, it's a new day. The ECB takes baby steps towards QE
Stefan Isaacs   89

Chapter 37
First home owner grants – a gift to new home buyers, or existing?
Anthony Doyle   91

Chapter 38
The arguments in favour of the Euro surviving
Anthony Doyle   94

Chapter 39
Monster Munch update – a victory for bondvigilantes.com
James Tomlins   97

Chapter 40
It's a knockout – why the gilt and currency markets have no love for Carney's forward guidance
Jim Leaviss   99

Chapter 41
How do house prices feed into inflation rates around the world? It's important for central banks, and for bond investors
Jim Leaviss   102

Chapter 42
Spain's answer to recession – the times they are a-changin'
Wolfgang Bauer   105

Chapter 43
Why the US Dollar now looks cheap against, well, basically everything
Mike Riddell   109

2014

Chapter 44
China's investment/GDP ratio soars to a totally unsustainable 54.4%. Be afraid.
Mike Riddell   113

Chapter 45
Deflating the deflation myth
Richard Woolnough   117

Chapter 46
Stand up for your rights! Covenant erosion in high yield bond documentation
James Tomlins   118

Chapter 47
The emerging markets rebalancing act
Claudia Calich   121

Chapter 48
5 Signs that the Bond Markets (rightly or wrongly) think the Eurozone Crisis is over
James Tomlins   122

Chapter 49
The Great Compression of peripheral to core European risk premiums
Wolfgang Bauer   124

Chapter 50
Playing Russian roulette
Claudia Calich — 127

Chapter 51
Sell in May and go away – does it work for European fixed income?
Anthony Doyle — 129

Chapter 52
Is Europe (still) turning Japanese? A lesson from the 90's
Stefan Isaacs — 132

Chapter 53
Why aren't bund yields negative again?
Jim Leaviss — 135

Chapter 54
Burrito Bonds – an example of the retail bond market
James Tomlins — 136

Chapter 55
The reliability of market and consumer inflation expectations
Ana Gil — 140

Chapter 56
Bondfire of the Maturities: how to improve credit market liquidity
Jim Leaviss — 142

Chapter 57
Falling soft commodity prices are a piece of cake
Anjulie Rusius — 144

Chapter 58
What is the collapse in the Baltic Dry shipping index telling us about global growth?
Jim Leaviss — 146

Chapter 59
Exceptional measures: Eurozone yields to stay low for quite some time
Stefan Isaacs — 148

Chapter 60
"Global greying" could mean getting used to ultra-low bond yields
Anthony Doyle — 150

Chapter 61
The lesson the Japanese economy has for the developed world
Richard Woolnough — 152

Chapter 62
Who's the biggest winner if ECB buys corporates? The French
Anjulie Rusius — 155

Chapter 63
"A grip on the public finances". Redeeming war loans as UK borrowing rises
Jim Leaviss — 157

Chapter 64
War Loan called. Yay. Quick thoughts…
Mike Riddell — 159

Chapter 65
Conservative QE and the zero bound
Richard Woolnough — 161

2015

Chapter 66
Long US Treasury bonds are overvalued by 250 bps. Discuss
Jim Leaviss — 163

Chapter 67
Europe needs a German fiscal stimulus package but won't get it
Anthony Doyle — 166

13

Chapter 68
Coming to a bond market near you: "A Brave New World: Zero Yield Corporate Bonds"
James Tomlins — 168

Chapter 69
The zero bound debate – are negative rates a tightening of policy?
Richard Woolnough — 170

Chapter 70
The falling US unemployment rate could benefit some emerging markets
Claudia Calich — 171

Chapter 71
What are index-linked corporate bonds telling us at the moment?
Ben Lord — 173

Chapter 72
Greece, the currency vigilantes and the Expulso solution
Richard Woolnough — 176

Chapter 73
Negative interest rates in European ABS
Anuj Babber — 178

Chapter 74
The downside of bonds
Anthony Doyle — 179

Chapter 75
Greece is not Argentina: don't expect exports to drive growth if Greece leaves the euro
Jim Leaviss — 185

Chapter 76
Mike Riddell's work here is done
Jim Leaviss — 188

Chapter 77
Greek debt forgiveness: Where there's a will, there's a way
Pierre Chartres — 189

Chapter 78
Covenant case study: Change of Control
James Tomlins — 192

Chapter 79
How bond investors should assess the opportunities in the US high yield energy sector
Luke Coha — 193

Chapter 80
Covenant case study – after the good, the bad
Charles de Quinsonas — 197

Chapter 81
Contrary to popular opinion, the Bank of England's next move will be a monetary easing
Matthew Russell — 199

Chapter 82
The ECB may lower rates, but the Swiss shouldn't follow suit
Mario Eisenegger — 200

Chapter 83
Three reasons why the UK will not raise rates anytime soon
Anjulie Rusius — 204

Chapter 84
High Yield Liquidity: 5 ways to help deal with it
James Tomlins — 207

2016

Chapter 85
Oil price slump is a drag on
emerging markets. But wait, why?
Charles de Quinsonas — 209

Chapter 86
Need motivation for your New Year diet?
M&G's cake index shows that cake
is getting more expensive
Anjulie Rusius — 211

Chapter 87
Investment grade credit spreads
spinning wider
Wolfgang Bauer — 213

Chapter 88
Why doesn't the ECB just buy oil?
Wolfgang Bauer — 217

Chapter 89
How long until China reaches the floor of
the recommended reserve adequacy range?
Claudia Calich — 219

Chapter 90
The ECB, negative rates, and the
Swiss experience
Mario Eisenegger — 220

Chapter 91
Has the ECB reached the limits of
monetary policy?
Stefan Isaacs — 223

Chapter 92
Negative Rate World (NRW) – a wiki of
unintended consequences
Jim Leaviss — 225

Chapter 93
Negative rates – a tax on saving?
Don't forget about actual tax
Richard Woolnough — 227

Chapter 94
The unintended consequences of
Negative Rate World Part II. An update
Jim Leaviss — 229

Chapter 95
What I am doing to protect against
Brexit... or Bremain
Ben Lord — 230

Chapter 96
Bond market reaction to UK "Leave" vote
Jim Leaviss — 232

Chapter 97
Four years of the ECB doing "whatever it
takes"
Anthony Doyle — 234

Chapter 98
The Bank of England could be about to
unveil a bumper monetary policy package
Anjulie Rusius — 236

Chapter 99
Should the Bank of England start
buying sterling corporate bonds again?
Jim Leaviss — 240

Chapter 100
Is QE unquestionably supportive
for risk assets? I think not
Richard Woolnough — 242

2011

Chapter 1

European High Yield vs. Eurozone Tail Risk High Yield
James Tomlins – Thursday, 22nd December 2011

As Eurozone concerns have dominated risk appetite within the market this year, a key question that faces many market participants is how to capture some of the attractive risk premiums that this weakness creates without exposing themselves unduly to the significant "tail risks" of a full blown Euro death spiral.

In this vein, a popular trade in recent months has been to add exposure to the US high yield market. The rationale is fairly simple (and one that we agree with): The US high yield market is trading at reasonably cheap levels, yielding 8.6% with a spread over treasuries of 754 bps*. Yet at the same time the US economy is performing much better than Europe, its government can borrow cheaply and you don't suffer from all the inherent tail risks of the European markets.

There is no doubt that issuers within the European high yield market are exposed to the economic headwinds that the Eurozone has created. However, is it fair to label the market as one that is riven with tail risks? We'd argue it isn't.

The chart on the next page splits the high yield market into different regions according to the geographic centre of gravity for each issuer. "Core Europe" encompasses German, French, Dutch, Austrian and any other current Eurozone country that has avoided the "Peripheral" tag. This area, arguably less exposed to true tail risk events (i.e. a Spanish and/or Italian exit from the Euro) accounts for just under half of the market at 47.58%. The "Peripheral Europe" issuers, or the real "tail risk" within the market, accounts for around 16% at current trading levels. Let's put this another way: 84% of the market is not directly exposed to a major tail risk event.

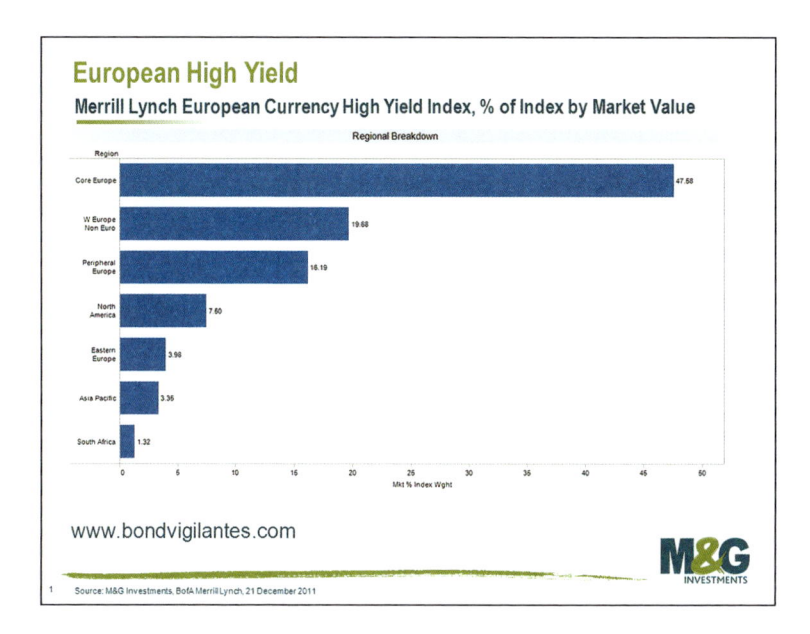

European High Yield

Merrill Lynch European Currency High Yield Index, % of Index by Market Value

Regional Breakdown:
- Core Europe: 47.60
- W Europe Non Euro: 19.68
- Peripheral Europe: 16.19
- North America: 7.60
- Eastern Europe: 3.98
- Asia Pacific: 3.36
- South Africa: 1.32

www.bondvigilantes.com

Source: M&G Investments, BofA Merrill Lynch, 21 December 2011

Probably more surprising is the proportion of the market that operates entirely outside of the Eurozone. Taken together, Western European Non Euro (i.e. Swiss, Swedish, Norwegian issuers), Eastern European, North American, South African and Asia Pacific issuers account for a little over 36% of the market.

Also, when we focus on the European map of issuance below, the country by country specifics of the market are easier to determine. Taken together German, French and British issuers account for 51% of the market.

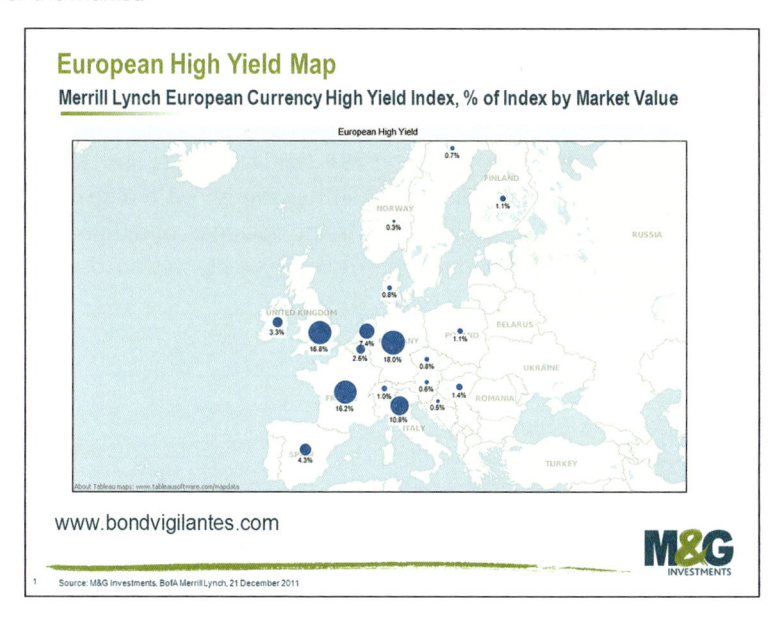

European High Yield Map

Merrill Lynch European Currency High Yield Index, % of Index by Market Value

European High Yield map values:
- Finland: 1.1%
- Sweden: 0.7%
- Norway: 0.3%
- Denmark: 0.8%
- United Kingdom: 3.3%
- Netherlands: 16.8%
- Germany: 18.0%
- Belgium: 2.4%
- Luxembourg: 2.5%
- Poland: 1.1%
- Czech: 0.8%
- France: 16.2%
- Switzerland: 1.0%
- Austria: 0.6%
- Romania: 1.4%
- Hungary: 0.5%
- Italy: 10.8%
- Spain: 4.3%

www.bondvigilantes.com

Source: M&G Investments, BofA Merrill Lynch, 21 December 2011

The point is this – there is no doubt that there are many risks within the European high yield market (volatility, economic headwinds, the likelihood of rising default rates), but we believe

17

there are still many pockets of opportunity where investors can capture some attractive risk premia without directly exposing themselves to catastrophic European "tail risks".

*Source: Bloomberg, Merrill Lynch US High Yield Master II Index, 20th December 2011

2012

Chapter 2

Happy Hogmanay – would an independent Scotland still be rated AAA? And might the rest of the UK get downgraded too?

Jim Leaviss – Wednesday, 4th January 2012

Happy Hogmanay – an independent Scotland looks AAA on the back of an envelope (as long as it gets all of the oil and none of the banks!), but would probably get rated lower. UK to get downgraded on uncertainty?

We've obviously been thinking a lot about the break-ups of currency areas lately, and it got us thinking about an Optimum Currency Area closer to home. What would happen if the UK broke up? We did talk about what might happen to the gilt market if Scotland left the Union back in 2007, but political events this year have made it less of a theoretical question, and one that outgoing cabinet secretary Sir Gus O'Donnell asked at the end of December.

First of all, is it likely? During 2011, the Scottish National Party gained a majority in the devolved Scottish Parliament. It is now able to call for a referendum on the issue of full Scottish independence. It will do this sometime in 2014 or 2015, in the second half of the Parliament, and can also determine the question to be asked (worth a handful of percentage points to the question setters' cause). If there is a "Yes to independence" vote, Scottish MSPs will need to pass a bill calling on the UK Parliament to negotiate terms for a break-up of the Union. That's where the fun starts, as we'll see. But will it happen? Back in October a YouGov poll put the "Yes" vote at 34%, with a decent number of "don't knows". But since the Eurozone problems began to accelerate, and UK growth prospects also slowed, it looks as if more recent polls have the "Yes" vote at around 28% (BBC November poll), with 17% "Don't know". The TNS opinion poll in the following chart however shows a much higher level of support for independence. The large differences in the outcomes of different polls reflects the wording of the question posed, and whether there is a simple "yes/no" or whether a third option for increased devolution within the UK is offered.

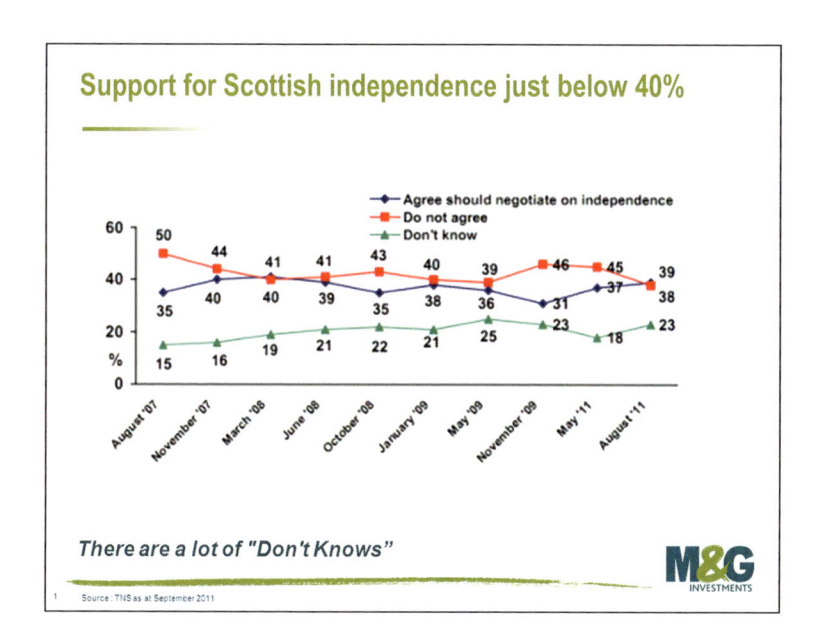

Support for Scottish independence just below 40%

There are a lot of "Don't Knows"

Source: TNS as at September 2011

M&G INVESTMENTS

The SNP independence cause may have been damaged somewhat by developments since Alex Salmond's 2006 "arc of prosperity" comments in which he favourably compared Scotland to Ireland and Iceland (now both with economies on life support – the "arc of insolvency" as Labour dubbed it) and also by their commitment to adopt the euro, at a time where peripheral economies which did adopt the euro are facing deflation, social unrest and default.

But let's assume that the "Yes" vote returns to its October levels, and that the "Don't knows" are converted to "Yes", so that the Scottish people vote for independence in 2014. What happens to the bond market? Is the UK ex Scotland still AAA, and what credit rating would Scotland have? AAA like Norway, or lower? Maybe a good starting point would be to share out the UK's national debt in terms of population. The UK population is 61.8 million, of which 5.2 million people live in Scotland. So Scotland becomes liable for 8.4% of the national debt, which equates to about £80 billion of the £940 billion debt.

To be a AAA rated economy, you would hope to have a debt/GDP ratio of about 60% or lower (although there are now AAA countries with ratios heading to 100%), and that your interest costs would run at under 12% of your state revenues. Scotland's GDP in 2009 was £143 billion (including all oil and gas produced in its waters), so its debt/GDP ratio would be 56% – respectable. The average interest rate on the existing stock of national debt is about 4%, so Scotland's debt servicing costs would be £3.2 billion per year. Scotland's revenues from taxes and duties in 2009-10 were £41.2 billion, so its interest payments to revenue metric would be just 8%.

Ah. But that's just the "ordinary" debt. What if we add in the government money committed to "Financial Interventions", which the headline numbers exclude nowadays. These financial interventions include the debts of the nationalised/part-nationalised banks (Northern Rock, Bradford & Bingley, Lloyds and RBS), and also money used in the bailouts of London Scottish Bank, and the Dunfermline Building Society, amongst others. The assumption of the debts of these nationalised/semi-nationalised banks onto the balance sheet of the UK takes the national debt from below £1 trillion to over £2.25 trillion. Because the government expects to sell these stakes back to the market, these are regarded as temporary liabilities and excluded from the headline numbers – the numbers also ignore that these debt liabilities fund assets so it's not the black hole it might seem to be. But if you were a bad tempered English MP negotiating the break-up of the Union, might you highlight that much of the banking sector interventions directly involve Scottish banks (mainly RBS, HBOS) and perhaps suggest that as well as 8.4% of the gilt market liabilities, independent Scotland might like to take its banks back too? The assets of Royal Bank of Scotland and (Halifax) Bank of Scotland alone dwarf the size of the Scottish economy (on the back of an envelope they amount to 1400% of Scottish GDP; Iceland's bank assets peaked at 1100% of GDP in 2008). Countries with relatively low public debt to GDP ratios still get into difficulty because of their private sector debt – at times of trouble, private debt often becomes public debt (the process where profits are privatised, and losses socialised).

Let's assume that Scotland doesn't have to support the banks. The bigger problem revolves around the sustainability of Scotland's strong credit position. The starting point for debt/GDP and revenues versus interest costs look good for Scotland on a headline basis (i.e. forgetting about the banks, if we're allowed to!); but is that relatively low debt burden maintainable? Oxford Economics produced a paper suggesting that of all the regions in the UK, Scotland made the biggest net negative contribution to the UK public finances. In 2004/05 Scottish revenues were about £35 billion, compared with government expenditures of £45 billion. In other words there was a net transfer of about £10 billion from 3 English regions of the UK (Greater London, the South East and Eastern regions – all other regions were net negative too). So Scotland would need to borrow this, plus its share of gilt interest at £3.2 billion each year to maintain a balanced budget. So £13.2 billion of deficit, compared with GDP of £143 billion is about 9% – about the same as the UK is running right now, but way above a sustainable number (for example the uniformly ignored Maastricht limit for Eurozone members is at 3%).

Now the elephant in the room. Oil. If Scotland were to receive its share of the revenues (North Sea Corporation Tax and Petroleum Revenue Tax) from the remaining North Sea oil, its position improves dramatically. In 2009/10 these totalled £6.5 billion, of which geographically Scotland is entitled to 91%, so £5.9 billion – although this is a volatile number which moves with the oil price. So on an annual basis the budget deficit falls from £13.2 billion to £7.3 billion – a deficit of 5%. Nice. On a present value basis, assuming these levels of revenue forever and a discount rate of 4% (to equate with its debt service costs) the oil revenues are worth £163 billion; but North Sea oil revenues are likely to fall aggressively from here – 1999 was probably "peak oil" for the North Sea, and by 2020, production will be a third of 1999 levels. So again, if I'm rating Scotland as a stand-alone entity, I worry what will happen going forwards. If you sold future revenues today you could wipe out Scotland's national debts – and even invest in a Sovereign Wealth Fund (SWF) like the Norwegians with the change (£80 billion or so)!

May I take a moment to rant about the lack of a UK SWF? In real terms the UK government has taken £270 billion out of the North Sea in tax revenues. Did we save it, like the Norwegian Statens pensjonsfond, now worth around £330 billion? Nope, after millions of years spent turning bracken into oil, we gave it away in a 20 year period to a population who just happened to be alive under a particular government's time in office and got a windfall gain which they used to buy avocado coloured plastic bathroom suites, now doomed to eternity in landfill across the nation. Bah.

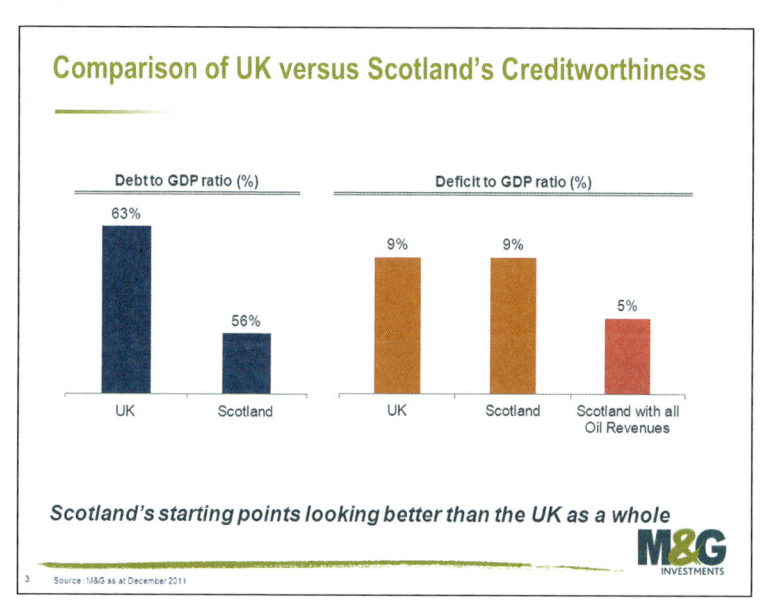

Comparison of UK versus Scotland's Creditworthiness

Debt to GDP ratio (%)
- UK: 63%
- Scotland: 56%

Deficit to GDP ratio (%)
- UK: 9%
- Scotland: 9%
- Scotland with all Oil Revenues: 5%

Scotland's starting points looking better than the UK as a whole

M&G INVESTMENTS

Source: M&G as at December 2011

What else would a rating agency consider when determining Scotland's credit rating? The US gets a massive boost to its rating due to its status as a global reserve currency, Japan has so much domestic saving that it can run a debt/GDP ratio of 200% and still be Aa3 rated, and the UK survives as AAA in part due to it being able to print its own currency. Additionally, ratings agencies favour big, systemic nations over smaller ones where there is an implied higher risk factor (rightly or wrongly) and given the experience of Iceland and Ireland which both held AAA ratings perhaps the agencies would err on the side of a lower rating. The currency point is interesting – the SNP position was to adopt the euro (a difficult one to get through the voters today I would guess), but Scotland could keep the pound (either officially with access to the Bank of England, or unofficially – Zimbabwe uses the US dollar without being part of the Federal Reserve System), or print its own currency (pegged to the Euro, pound, price of oil, nothing).

Also very important when considering debt servicing ability is the growth rate of the economy. Scotland performs relatively poorly on this measure (although one argument from those who want independence is that only when Scotland is separated from the UK will it be in charge of its own economic future, and its underlying growth rate can improve). Currently Scotland's average GDP growth rate is 0.6% per year behind the UK as a whole, and around 1% behind that of the other small European economies. The public sector represents 24% of Scottish employment – higher than in the rest of the UK, although it is falling as part of the recent austerity programmes. As well as being a drag on economic productivity, a disproportionate public sector also means a higher level of unfunded pension liabilities – a contingent liability, like the probable losses involved in the bank bailouts.

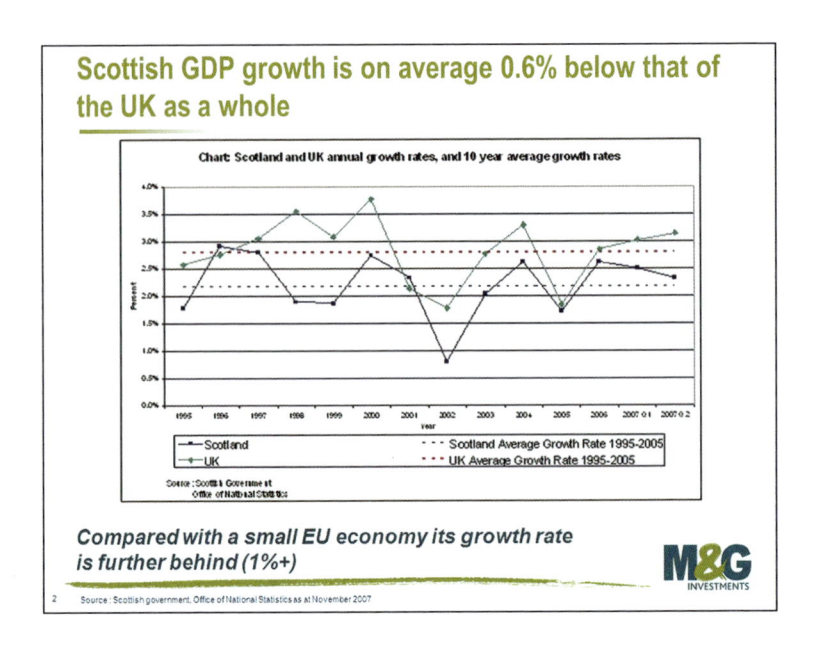

Scottish GDP growth is on average 0.6% below that of the UK as a whole

Chart: Scotland and UK annual growth rates, and 10 year average growth rates

- Scotland
- UK
- Scotland Average Growth Rate 1995-2005
- UK Average Growth Rate 1995-2005

Source: Scottish Government, Office of National Statistics

Compared with a small EU economy its growth rate is further behind (1%+)

M&G INVESTMENTS

Source: Scottish government, Office of National Statistics as at November 2007

So my guess is that a rating agency would not give Scotland a AAA rating, and that the market would trade any bonds it issued at a wider yield than the UK which still benefits from some reserve currency status. The next question we want to answer is how would a break-up impact the gilt market? Would I be given £8 of Scottish gilts and £92 of UK gilts for every £100 of gilts I own now? Can "they" do that to me? It would count as an event of default for the UK in CDS markets, and almost certainly also for the rating agencies, unless this was a voluntary exchange. Logistically nightmarish, so our UK sovereign credit analyst Mark Robinson suggests that the UK would keep all of the gilt liabilities, and Scotland and the UK would have a bilateral loan for an equivalent amount (the UK has a bilateral loan for about £7 billion to Ireland for example, albeit in very different circumstances). I doubt that the UK's credit rating would change as a result of any fundamental economics of Scottish independence – but international investors might worry about the instability, real or imagined, of the Union breaking up, so a downgrade for the UK is not out of the question. Mike Riddell has been doing some digging on what happened to assets and liabilities when states and unions dissolved (e.g. Russia assumed all of the USSR's debts, Yugoslavia's carve up was much more complicated) – he'll post up some thoughts some time soon I hope.

Chapter 3

German government bond yields may need to get very negative for the euro to weaken much further. And it could easily happen

Mike Riddell – Wednesday, 11th January 2012

In 2011 the euro underperformed the US dollar by 3.2%. Given everything that's occurred in Europe, many people have been surprised that the euro has not been weaker, and numerous commentators continue to call for a much weaker euro in this calendar year.

As usual with FX rates, most of the euro's behaviour versus the US dollar can be explained by changes in expectations of short-term interest rates, as seen by the relative differences between the regions' short-dated government bond yields. The euro's strength against the US dollar in the first half of last year was due to the contrasting approach of the Fed and the ECB. The Fed continued to state that it would maintain an exceptionally low Fed Funds rate for an extended period (and then in August went a step further by stating that "economic conditions….are likely to warrant exceptionally low levels for the federal funds rate until at least through mid-2013"). Meanwhile, despite almost the whole market telling them it was daft, the ECB merrily hiked rates in April and July last year. Very predictably, soon after the second hike, the markets promptly began to anticipate the ECB having to reverse its hikes (which it subsequently did in November and December) and the euro weakened over the remainder of the year.

The first of the two charts overleaf shows the yield on German and US government bonds maturing in October 2013. The bottom chart shows the difference in the two yields plotted against the EUR/USD exchange rate, and the correlation is strong as you'd expect. However, the euro is now at a 15 month low versus the US dollar, and for this weakening trend to continue, we need one of three things to happen. Firstly, the Fed needs to do the unlikely, have a big change of heart, and hike rate rates before mid-2013. Secondly, which is quite possible, the normal correlation between EUR/USD and short-term bond yields needs to completely break down. Or thirdly, German government bond yields need to get very negative.

Regarding the third point, Germany did indeed manage to issue six-month bills at a negative yield for the first time. If you eyeball the bottom chart, though, for EUR/USD to go to 1.15, you may need short-dated German government bond yields to be as much as 90 basis points below short-dated US government bond yields. Two year US government bonds currently yield +0.24%, so you'd be looking at German yields below -50 basis points. You'd end up with the interesting dynamic of investors going short of two year German government bond futures (the 'Schatz'), not rolling the contract, and making free money (if they can ride out the volatility) at maturity.

Could German government bond yields get very negative? Well, if investors increasingly doubt whether the euro can remain in existence, then negative German government bond yields are a totally rational outcome. Various analysts have had a stab at guessing where a new Deutschemark, Franc, Lira, Peseta or Drachma would trade versus the euro, and everyone seems to expect the new Deutschemark to strengthen against where the euro currently trades, although the range is huge with some going for 5% appreciation and some as much as 40% (for what it's worth I'm actually not convinced a new Deutschemark would necessarily trade higher than where the euro currently trades given the damage that a euro break-up would do to Germany's banking sector). It's all obviously a total guess though as nobody has any idea, however it's hard to argue against a new Deutschemark being a lot stronger than, say, a new French Franc and particularly a new Spanish Peseta, Italian Lira or Greek Drachma.

So increasingly negative German government bond yields, together with widening yield spreads between Germany and other countries, would be a rational response to the rising probability that the euro breaks up and the German government bond is redenominated into a new Deutschemark. Redenomination into a new Deutschemark could end up returning the holder of a -0.5% yielding short-dated German government bond perhaps a 40% capital gain, or maybe even a 90% gain if the investor is living in Greece. Negative German government bond yields can very easily become more negative as the risk of break-up increases, leading to the problems. And the euro could therefore weaken a lot further.

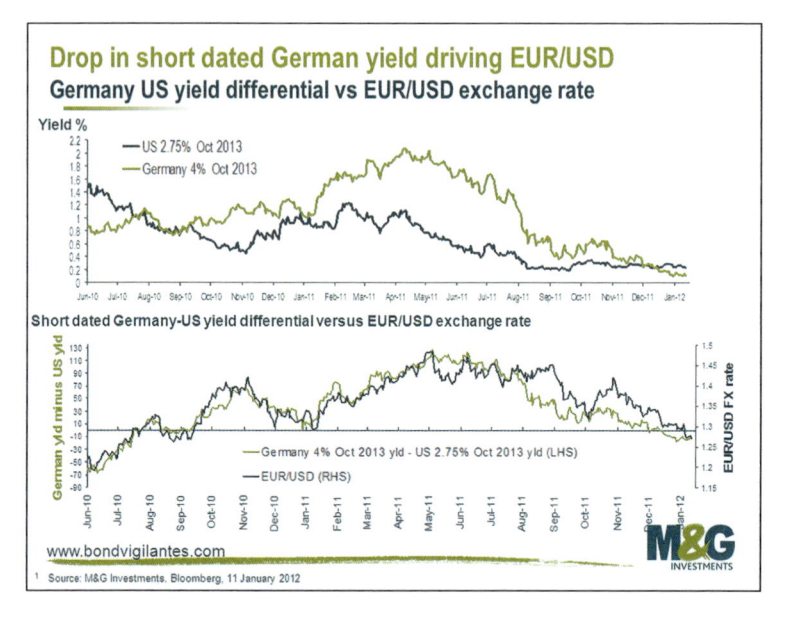

Drop in short dated German yield driving EUR/USD

Source: M&G Investments, Bloomberg, 11 January 2012

Chapter 4

The ECB's bazooka has hit the target
Mike Riddell – Tuesday, 24th January 2012

The ECB finally realised it had no choice and fired its bazooka in December. The impact has been huge. Two year Italian government bond yields have more than halved from the high of 7.5% seen at the end of November. Many hedge funds who were betting on Italian government bonds selling off have either changed views and taken profits or have been stopped out of their positions as the market has gone against them. Real money investors have been returning to the Eurozone sovereign bond market after a long absence. Just as Italian bank bond yields spiralled upwards with the Italian sovereign, so they have plummeted down too, and banks have been able to issue bonds to the market again this year (albeit almost solely covered bonds or senior bonds so far). The chart overleaf highlights just how much Italy's borrowing costs have fallen.

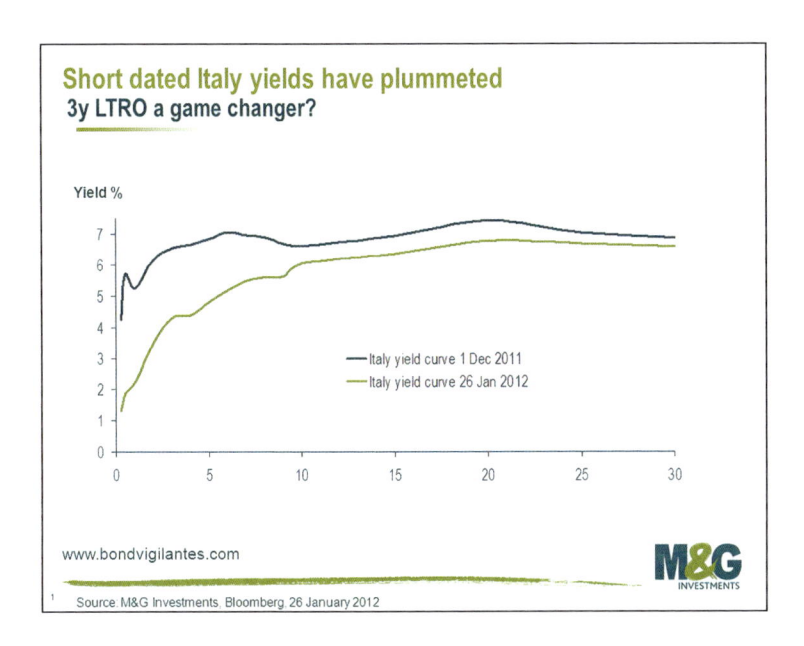

Short dated Italy yields have plummeted
3y LTRO a game changer?

Chart showing Italy yield curves — Italy yield curve 1 Dec 2011 and Italy yield curve 26 Jan 2012, with Yield % on y-axis (0-7) and maturity (0-30) on x-axis.

www.bondvigilantes.com

Source: M&G Investments, Bloomberg, 26 January 2012

Those who doubt the sustainability of the ECB's policies are entirely correct when they argue that hurling liquidity at the Eurozone debt crisis does nothing to solve the structural problems at the heart of the Eurozone. If you put lipstick on a zombie sovereign or zombie bank, it's still a zombie. The potentially terminal problems of huge competitive divergence between countries (ie current account imbalances) are still to be resolved. One answer is total fiscal union, which requires Northern Europe to take on Southern Europe's debts and Southern Europe to let Northern Europe tell it what to do (exceptionally unlikely). Alternatively, it requires Germany and the Netherlands to be willing to run consistently higher inflation rates than the rest of Europe (also unlikely). As Milton Friedman succinctly pointed out in 1999, "the various countries in the euro are not a natural currency trading group. They are not a currency area. There is very little mobility of people among the countries. They have extensive controls and regulations and rules, and so they need some kind of an adjustment mechanism to adjust to asynchronous shocks—and the floating exchange rate gave them one. They have no mechanism now".

But just because the ECB's policy response hasn't addressed the underlying problems, it doesn't mean the response is immaterial. Quite the opposite. We know from 2009 how powerful the effect on markets can be when central banks fully deploy their balance sheets. In light of this, the rally in the riskier fixed income assets that we've seen of late arguably has further to go, and in the past few weeks I've even bought Italian government bonds for the first time ever.

The flip side is that the current yield levels of core government bonds is a concern, and duration appears less attractive. In May last year, government bond yields were more than 1% higher than they are today and yield curves were much steeper. It was expensive to be short duration at the time. The situation has changed a bit since then, presumably because of Eurozone stress and perhaps also because of China. If Europe is no longer in a downward spiral (indeed the crucial Eurozone PMI data released this morning suggests there has been a bounce in economic activity in January) then government bonds really do look vulnerable.

Chapter 5

Competitiveness confusion reigns supreme
Anthony Doyle – Wednesday, 8th February 2012

Many question how the heavily indebted European nations will get out of the mess they are in. Absent a break-up of the single currency unit, most economists point to a significant reduction in unit labour costs (through a reduction in nominal wages) as the answer. In fact, Nicolas Sarkozy has stated that France has to bring down labour costs to improve its competitiveness like Germany did a decade ago. The question we are asking ourselves is if this so-called "internal devaluation" is the answer?

Competitiveness is a buzz word that gets thrown around a lot. But what is it exactly? The most widely used measure of competitiveness is unit labour costs (ULCs), the ratio of nominal wage growth to labour productivity. It is important to economists because they will deem an economy to be more competitive the lower the ULC is. This would suggest that an economy is more competitive the lower the share of the labour force's contribution to GDP. Thus, in order to close the "competitiveness gap" that exists between unproductive countries (like Greece) and productive countries (like Germany), countries need to implement policies that will result in downward adjustments in relative wages.

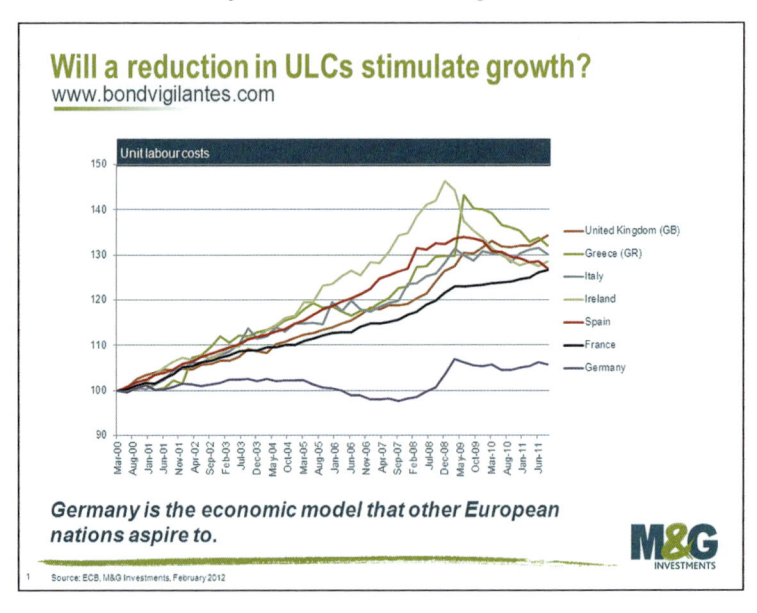

Will a reduction in ULCs stimulate growth?
www.bondvigilantes.com

Germany is the economic model that other European nations aspire to.

Source: ECB, M&G Investments, February 2012

In extremis, this means that the most competitive economy would have a labour share of GDP of zero (because wages are zero), and a capital share of GDP of 100%. Does this make sense? No. Reducing the income generated by labour by reducing nominal wages will be a drag on economic growth, and several economists have investigated the impact that ULCs have on an economy. Kaldor's paradox, put forward by Nicholas Kaldor in 1978, showed that the fastest growing economies in the post-war period also experienced faster growth in ULCs, and vice versa. This suggests that a higher labour share will not necessarily lead to a less competitive economy. The argument that many have been spouting that lower ULCs will lead to higher economic growth is a highly simplistic view, and may not reflect reality. Remember, those economies with the fastest growth rates in the 2000s, like Ireland and Spain, actually had the fastest rising ULCs over the same time period.

An increase in labour's share of income can have a number of effects. Firstly, it has been shown that the propensity to consume out of wages is higher than that of profits, so if you really want to get an economy going, the trick is to increase the amount of money that gets into people's pockets. And that is exactly what the central banks are trying to do, by flooding the financial system with cash. Of course, there is another way to reduce ULCs to become more competitive and that is to increase productivity, which means working more efficiently for the same amount of pay. If ULCs fall due to productivity gains, the benefits will largely accrue to the business owner and not the worker.

However, workers are getting poorer as shown by the chart below. It is very difficult to stimulate consumption when real wage growth is negative, as it has been for the last four years in the largest European nations. £100 in 2000 is now worth £68 in real terms, and €100 in 2000 is now worth €78 in Germany, €59 in Spain, €74 in France, and €67 in Italy (all in real terms). For the last four years wage increases across Europe and the UK have not kept up with the pace of inflation.

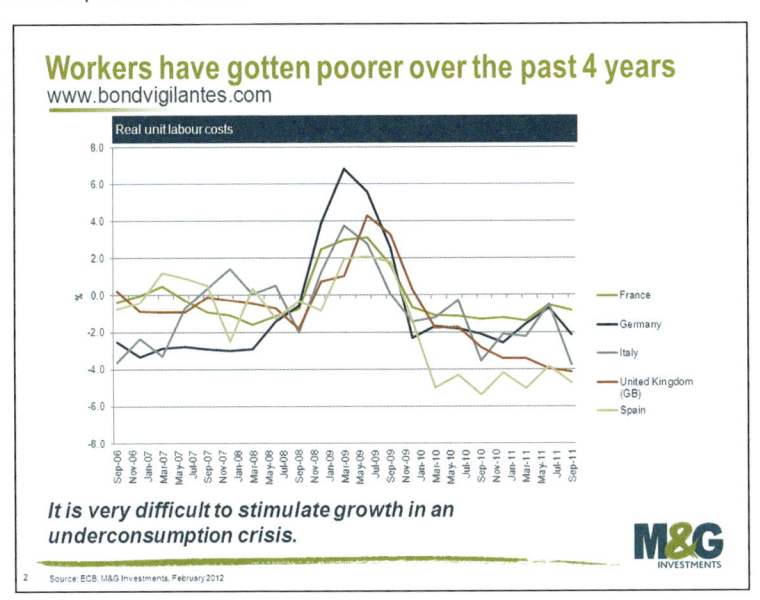

Workers have gotten poorer over the past 4 years
www.bondvigilantes.com

It is very difficult to stimulate growth in an underconsumption crisis.

Source: ECB, M&G Investments, February 2012

Secondly, if nominal wages are rising then prices for goods will also rise, though they will become less competitive in international markets. This will have a negative effect on growth. Would workers in countries like Spain, where unemployment is currently 22.9% and inflation is 2.4%, accept a reduction in nominal wages to maintain their firms' competitiveness and therefore keep their jobs? The point is, the overall result on GDP of a redistribution of income towards workers is ambiguous and depends on which of the two effects dominates.

Let's have a look at a shift in the distribution of income towards capital. Initially, an economy will probably experience an increase in investment causing GDP to increase. However, sooner or later prices will fall because of excess capacity caused by both an increase in investment and fall in consumption. Capacity utilisation will have to fall, followed by a reduction in investment, a decline in income will follow, and then a fall in production and employment.

The major challenge facing Europe is a lack of demand. This is an underconsumption crisis. Reducing ULCs will not solve this underconsumption crisis through either nominal wage falls or productivity gains. If a worker wakes up tomorrow and can do the job of two people, then the business owner could sack the second person to keep costs down and improve profitability. In this example, productivity gains will lead to rising unemployment and a further deterioration in government finances through reduced taxes and higher transfer payments.

It is true that the growth rate of an economy will depend on the growth rate of exports, but the problem is the growth rate of exports depends upon world demand and how competitive those exports are in the international marketplace. We doubt an internal devaluation is the answer to Europe's problems. To say that a reduction in ULCs will result in a rebound in growth numbers is wrong. You have to be producing stuff that people want to buy. Or you need your currency to devalue by enough to make your goods relatively cheap. This isn't going to happen in Europe, where the euro has been remarkably strong given the sovereign crisis. The growth answer lies in getting credit flowing through the economy again, and central banks recognise that. It is important to realise that sometimes the obvious solution – like "we need to be more competitive" – is not always the right solution.

Chapter 6

4 Housing Markets, One Country
James Tomlins – Thursday, 16th February 2012

The Eurozone has become a very extreme example of the dangers inherent of creating a single currency area populated with a myriad of different countries and regions. There is little doubt that the right monetary policy for Germany is not necessarily the correct one for Portugal given the underlying structural differences and lack of fiscal coordination.

However, closer to home, there could be an argument that the same (albeit in a less extreme form) is true of the UK. Looking through the prism of the UK housing market over the past 30 years, it's possible to argue that there are 4 distinct regional markets within the UK. The UK is not an optimal currency area.

Using historical regional data from the Halifax House Price Index (see the next chart), there have been some very large and identifiable variations between different regions within the UK. Prices within Greater London have fared the best over the period, showing a strong bounce back from recent lows. Northern Ireland has suffered from an extreme boom and bust whereas the Scottish market has been the relative underperformer over the same period. In contrast, the other regions of the UK have, by and large, moved in lock step with each other.

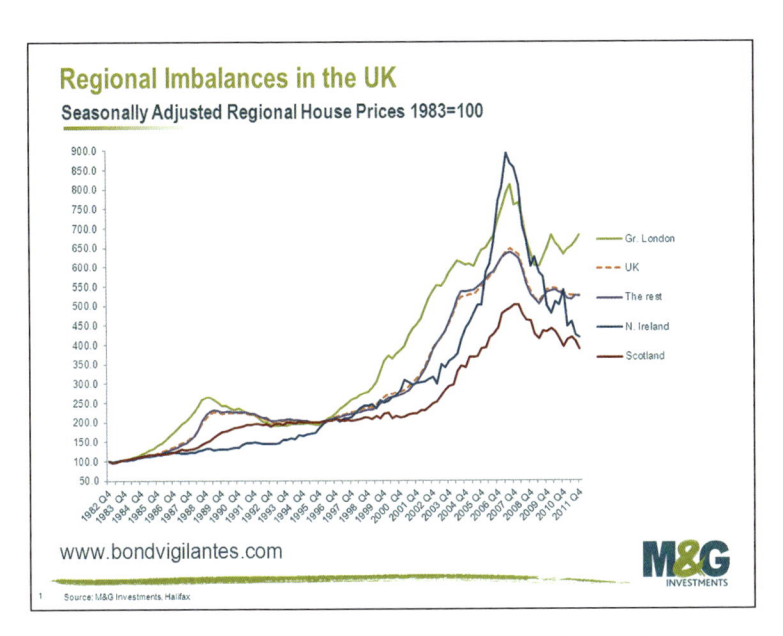

Regional Imbalances in the UK
Seasonally Adjusted Regional House Prices 1983=100

(Chart showing house price indices for Gr. London, UK, The rest, N. Ireland, and Scotland from 1982 Q4 to 2011 Q4)

www.bondvigilantes.com

Source: M&G Investments, Halifax

Given the fact that the Official Bank Rate is the same in Chelsea & Kensington as it is in Dundee, the potential to exacerbate structural imbalances between regions due to a common monetary policy is clear to see. Indeed there is a sense that as central London market prices rise to new highs in absolute and relative terms, we are witnessing a new liquidity fuelled bubble divorced from the economic fundamentals of the rest of the UK.

However, there are mitigating factors: existing within a single sovereign political entity, fiscal transfers and labour force mobility should all help redress these imbalances over time. The fact that the London and the South East contribute a greater proportion in tax revenue is a case in point. However, due to the foibles of negative equity, labour mobility has been greatly constrained in recent years. Differences in regional unemployment bear witness to this fact. For example, the latest ONS data states that the unemployment rate in the North East is 12.0% compared to 6.4% in the South East.

Are we therefore condemned to a future of further economic stresses and strains within the UK? Maybe not. If the Scottish do eventually decide to leave the United Kingdom with their own central bank and currency, maybe the Northern Irish and Londoners should be given the same option too?

Chapter 7

Paying the locusts – what the PSI means for Greek bond investors
Richard Woolnough – Tuesday, 21st February 2012

Early this morning it appears that at last Greece and the European authorities are at the final stages of launching a bond swap with the private sector – known as the private sector involvement (PSI) procedure – which will aim to reduce Greece's debt-to-GDP ratio to 120.5 percent by 2020 (currently 160 percent). The deal will receive blanket press coverage; we are going to focus on the PSI element.

The PSI ensures that the private sector will suffer a real loss while the public sector (national European central banks and the ECB) will not suffer any losses. Central banks have this privileged position as they are prepared to provide further finance to Greece (akin to a rescue rights issue diluting existing shareholders). Of course, it is not in the politicians' interests for the central banks to bear any losses as a result of lending to Greece and of course it is the politicians that set the legal and regulatory framework. Not only can politicians change the goal posts, they can change the ball you are playing with. Politicians, and the authorities, are exercising their imbedded power.

This deal will cause the private sector to suffer a disproportionate level of losses both in absolute and relative terms to the public sector. This punishes the private sector investor in Greek debt relative to the private speculator who was short Greek debt. We noted in an earlier blog that governments perceived owners of their debt to be good investors, whilst investors holding short positions in government debt are evil speculators.

The problem with the PSI procedure is that it does not reward these economic agents accordingly. This PSI precedent means that in the future, should a government debt crisis occur, private investors will be less willing to support troubled government debt, and speculators will be rewarded for being short. Obviously this will impact the sustainability of government finances at precisely the time they would be seeking to generate confidence in their ability to service their debt obligations.

What does this PSI look like in pounds, shillings, and euro cents? Those investors that are short Greek debt will make money, the legal power of the state means the authorities suffer no damage, while the private sector will suffer losses. The locusts will feed well, the authorities will not eat less, and the private investor will waste away.

Chapter 8

The 5 things that bond investors have learnt from the Greek default
Jim Leaviss – Friday, 2nd March 2012

1. **The price charged by central banks for saving the world is seniority.** The ECB did not take haircuts on the Greek debt it had bought as part of its SMP bond buying programme. Did you spot the clause in your bond documents that said that you were buying the subordinate tranche of the government bond market? Of course it never existed – in extremis, which is exactly where we are – the law is torn up and rewritten (see point 2). Historically you wouldn't have worried too much about being subordinate to the authorities, but that was before the age where over a third of the gilt market is owned by the Bank of England, and where the Fed owns large portions of both the Treasury and mortgage markets. Given sovereign recoveries have been below 40 percent on average (in the world before QE) if 40 percent of the outstanding bonds are now senior to private sector holdings of government debt, that leaves much less for investors. Recoveries will be lower going forward.

2. **The ECB is an anti-democratic institution – thank goodness.** The Eurozone cannot cope with crises through its democratic structures. Treaty changes are needed for even modest increases to fiscal union, and treaty changes require referendums (Ireland's referendum on the Eurozone fiscal pact announced this week will take three months to

organise. It may well not pass, and hence any one member state can stop integration). The anti-democratic organisation can therefore be the boy with his finger in the dyke. But think of the ECB as the pain-killer, treating symptoms rather than dealing with the illness. Only democracy will be able to deliver the surgery that is fiscal union.

3. **It looks as if the sovereign CDS market might work!** For a long time it looked as if Greece would restructure in a "voluntary" arrangement with its creditors. Whilst the rating agencies would likely still have called this a default, the credit default swap market's committee (ISDA) might well have decided that this, because voluntary, was not an event of default, and thus not triggered the CDS contracts. If that had been the case, then buyers of protection (insurance) might have found that the hedges they had for their collapsing Greek government bond holdings were worthless. The fact that new laws were hastily written to allow for majority votes of bond holders to bind minority investors to the same actions means that these CACs (collective action clauses) can force investors to take losses on bonds, and so if a default is eventually declared by the committee, the sovereign CDS market remains credible. However, yesterday ISDA declared that we hadn't yet seen an event of default – but it looks like this is simply because the CAC hasn't formally been triggered itself yet. However, if we're wrong and vested interests succeed in not eventually triggering a CDS payout, this would be very negative both for the continued existence of the sovereign CDS market, and more importantly for peripheral bond prices. If your CDS hedge is useless you might well liquidate your long positions as soon as you can.

4. **Ken and Carmen were right.** I saw Ken Rogoff, who co-authored 'This Time is Different' with Carmen Rheinhart, speak again on Monday. Don't start getting all cheerful yet. The key points from that book were that the sovereign default rate was abnormally low, and that we should expect it to rise sharply, and that once debt to GDP gets above 90 percent growth slows and inflation rises. Rogoff expects more than one other Eurozone member state to default. But the 90 percent threshold approaches for even highly rated sovereigns. A deliberate policy of keeping real interest rates negative (as they are now), and a tolerance of inflation, will help get debt burdens down – at the expense of real returns for bond investors.

5. **The Greek population was the real loser, not the bond investor.** This was a bad deal, not because bond investors took losses, but because the losses they took were too small. Even under heroic growth assumptions Greek debt to GDP will barely get down to 120 percent. The population will live with austerity for years and Greece will probably default again anyway. And as others implement extreme austerity too, we'll see the rise of extreme politics across the Eurozone. One lesson that policy-makers across the world keep missing is that imposing punishment on moral hazard "sinners" is a luxury we don't have in the middle of this series of crises. There have rightly been comparisons made between the terms of the Greek restructuring and the reparation terms that Germany was forced to accept after the First World War. The biggest wave of defaults has yet to happen – not in the bond markets, but with the breaking of promises (retirement ages, pension entitlements, healthcare) made to complacent western populations.

Chapter 9

The Bank of England should cut rates rather than make state run Halifax hike mortgage rates

Jim Leaviss – Tuesday, 6th March 2012

I had lunch last week with a Bank of England MPC member, and I asked him why the Bank didn't cut rates below 0.5% in order to help the banking sector improve its Net Interest Margins (NIMs) and thus its capitalisation. The MPC member replied that it was a matter of record that the Bank had discussed a rate cut in the Autumn but rejected it because of some technical reasons around the operations of the money markets (which nobody seems able to fully explain) and because the feed through into the banks' funding costs would likely be limited.

I disagree that there would be no benefit in a Bank Rate cut, and the news this weekend that Halifax is raising its mortgage rate from 3.5% to 3.99% for 850,000 Standard Variable Rate (SVR) mortgage borrowers will help show why. Halifax (HBOS) needs to improve its margins and become profitable before it will be able to increase its lending to the UK economy and slow its delevering. The method it (the state?) has chosen to improve its margins is to raise the interest burden on UK consumers (by 14% to those on the SVR). This is a zero sum game to the UK economy (consumers lose by the amount that the banks gain – there might even be a negative multiplier effect as the banks use their gain to delever whilst the consumer stops spending to the extent of their loss?), whereas if the Bank of England cuts rates (to near zero) many of the funding costs that directly impact HBOS, including LIBOR and 5 year interest rate swap rates would also fall. HBOS wouldn't need to pass on these rate cuts to customers, but the mortgage borrowers are not worse off, and the banks have improved their margins. So the Bank of England should cut rates later this week – the impact will of course be relatively small as we reach the "zero bound", but it is probably more certain in its effectiveness than a theoretically equivalent amount of Quantitative Easing.

Finally, the papers I read this weekend talking about the Halifax SVR rate increase said that the reason for the hike was due to increased funding costs in the wholesale markets. But is that true? I've put 4 charts together here. They show that 3 month LIBOR rates (a measure of short-term money market costs) have fallen in the year to date (albeit marginally), that 5 year swap rates (a measure of fixed rate mortgage funding costs) remain around record lows, and that senior CDS spreads for both European banks in general and HBOS specifically are both much lower than their 2011 Q4 highs. So if anything, since the ECB announced its 3 year LTRO facilities, both the cost of funding and the availability of liquidity for the banking sector have improved – and mortgage rates in an ideal world should be falling.

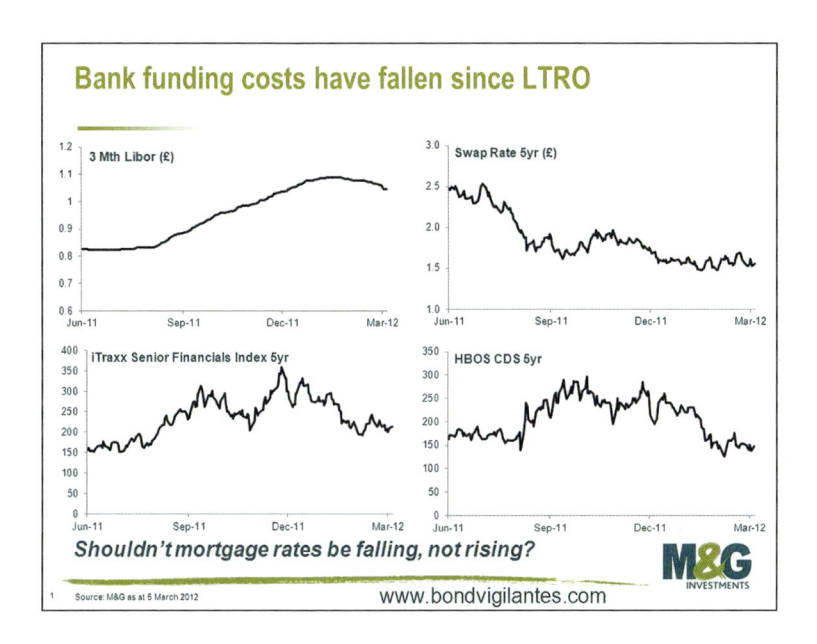

Chapter 10

Central Bank Regime Change: who cares about 2% inflation targets anymore? A chart

Jim Leaviss – Thursday, 15th March 2012

For those clients who received our Panoramic fixed interest newsletter in December (the latest edition is out now by the way, with a detailed analysis of the global high yield market), you will have seen that I talked about Central Bank Regime Change as one of the key issues for fixed interest investors in the coming years. What I meant by Central Bank Regime Change is this: the days of Central Banks caring too much about inflation are behind us. We've had three decades since Paul Volker took over at the Fed and set interest rates above the rate of inflation (a novelty at the time), and we've had independence granted to the Bank of England, and seen inflation targets of 2% become commonplace. From here on in though, Central Banks will care about two things – unemployment and debt.

Charles Evans of the Chicago Fed is the only person who will publicly say it (admitting you don't care about inflation anymore isn't such good news for your government bond markets), but getting the unemployment rate down aggressively must be the priority for the authorities, otherwise we are doomed to structurally low growth and social unrest. If this means inflation overshoots that 2% level, he is relatively relaxed about that (3% would be very acceptable). And an inflation overshoot helps the developed world's other big problem – debt. There are three ways to shrink an excessive debt burden. You can grow your way out of it (but with broken banks, austerity and high unemployment, below trend rather than above trend growth looks more likely – look at Greece). You can default on state liabilities to your populations (this is happening) or to your bondholders (less likely for regimes with their own currencies). Or you can set negative real interest rates and erode the debt burden through stealth inflation.

And this is the regime under which we are operating. The IMF put together part of the chart below – I've added the most recent period post the Great Financial Crisis. You can see that before the Second World War there was a wide range of real interest rates in the UK, with little pattern. For much of the period the UK was on the Gold Standard with fixed exchange rates. The period also includes the Great Depression where we experienced deflation. After the Second World War the UK emerged with a debt/GDP ratio of over 200%. You can see that most of the next three decades was spent in low real rate environments, with periods of negative real rates. With financial repression making UK banks hold gilts, and some modest growth, the debt burden was aggressively eroded. The Volker years show a step change in real interest rates to sharply positive rates.

The final normal distribution curve shows the world we live in now. Since 2008 real rates have been sharply negative (justifying the unusual negative real yields on virtually all inflation linked bonds). Remember that no person in authority will ever be able to admit to regime change, but all of us have to understand it's happening. What it might not automatically mean though is that we are in a big bond bear market. First we have to identify a regime (negative real rates), then understand whether the market is pricing that regime correctly (no, yields are too low) – but then you have to apply any structural overlays which might override your thoughts on fundamental valuation. And it's here that Quantitative Easing becomes important. As Charlie Bean of the Bank of England's MPC has stated, QE reduces "the cost of financing a given deficit". Here in the UK, the Eurozone and the US, Central Banks are keeping bond yields low enough to stop their governments from going bust – and that's not going to change for the foreseeable future.

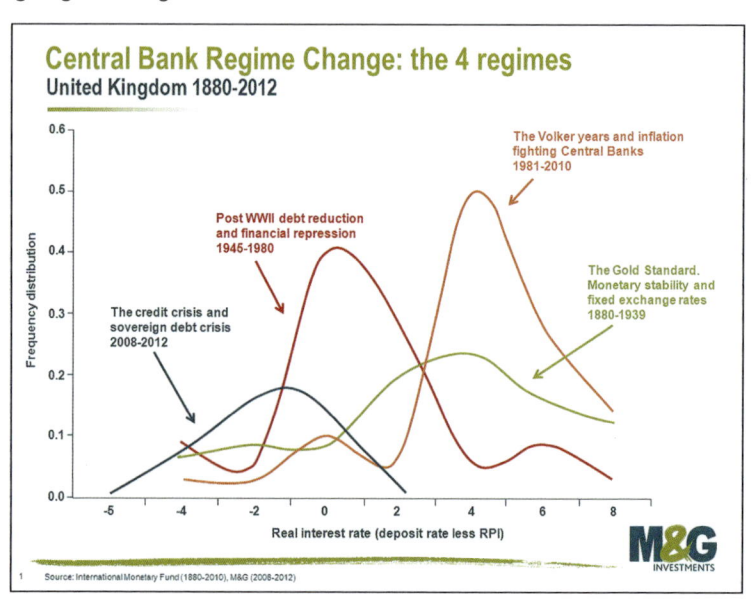

Chapter 11

If the government simply cancelled the £300 bn+ of QE gilts held by the BoE, who would be unhappy?
Jim Leaviss – Wednesday, 11th April 2012

The UK sits unhappily at the very boundary of what debt burden is acceptable for a AAA rated economy. If growth continues to disappoint, or if more austerity becomes socially impossible, the UK will be downgraded – and neither of these possibilities look very remote.

At the moment the UK public sector net debt to GDP ratio is about 63%, equivalent to about £1 trillion (these numbers exclude the debt of the part nationalised banks). Debt servicing costs are over £50 billion per year – a large chunk of our annual deficit. Additionally our debt position is likely to deteriorate before it improves.

But do we really need to be paying interest to the Bank of England on the £300 billion+ of gilts that it holds as part of the Quantitative Easing programme? In fact the Bank holds these gilts on behalf of the Treasury anyway, so the Treasury is effectively paying interest to itself on assets that it bought with "free" printed money. Could we decide that this is a waste of time, that we are unlikely to sell these gilts back to the market in any case, and that we may as well just cancel the gilts we bought for the nation? Gold bugs and inflationists will at this point be spluttering into cups of tea – what about all of the printed fivers that have been set free into the economy like in a modern day Weimar Republic? Well, how about this for a potential statement from the authorities on gilt cancellation announcement day:

"Today the Treasury announces the cancellation of £350 billion of gilt-edged stock held by the authorities. These gilts were bought as part of the Quantitative Easing programme started in the aftermath of the financial crisis. The purpose of Quantitative Easing was to boost nominal growth after what we thought was a temporary fall in UK output. Several years later it appears that this fall in output was permanent – the fall in UK GDP remains more severe than that experienced during the Great Depression. We will therefore make this liquidity injection permanent in order to boost UK growth and reduce unemployment. The Bank of England of course remains fully committed to its inflation target of 2% – a cornerstone of UK economic policy. Should inflation rise, or be forecast to rise above the target range, the Bank may raise interest rates, or sell Treasury Bills to the market in order to drain excess liquidity from the system and return inflation to its target. Today's action also reduces the UK's debt to GDP ratio from 63% to 41%, and slashes our interest bill from £50 billion to £32 billion per year. This prudent action safeguards the UK's AAA credit ratings and leaves holders of gilt-edged securities in a stronger position than before.

Note from the Debt Management Office: the gilt cancellation will take place using the same process and precedent set with the cancellation of £9 billion of UK gilt-edged securities acquired from the Post Office pension scheme in April 2012."

So who would be unhappy with this? No default has taken place (no CDS trigger, no D from the ratings agencies who are only interested in failure to pay private investors), the UK's public finances become sustainable, the economy gets a boost from the knowledge that the QE cash injected will stay there for the foreseeable future, and a mechanism exists to remove cash from the economy should inflation return. Apart from the fact it all feels a bit banana republicy everybody's a winner. In fact the genius of this idea is that it doesn't need to be done at all – if the Bank of England were to start paying gilt coupons and maturing gilt proceeds over to the Treasury automatically you would have an equivalent economic impact, without any of the awkward Zimbabwe comparisons.

Chapter 12

What should Mervyn do with his QE gilts? Free finance.
Richard Woolnough – Friday, 20th April 2012

Jim recently discussed the merits of officially cancelling the gilts bought back through QE, so I thought I would discuss another option that maintains the status quo through the Bank of England (BoE) simply rolling over the QE gilts into new gilts at maturity.

In order to understand the results of this process it is useful to re-examine how QE works.

Simply, QE is the willing exchange of gilts for cash between the BoE and the private sector.

What is the difference between a gilt and cash? Both are denominated in the same common currency; the main difference to the investor is that gilts pay a coupon, usually until a specified maturity date when they funge into cash on a one for one basis. Cash on the other hand has a zero return, unlike a gilt, and exists in perpetuity. Both cash and gilts can be lent to a third party in return for a payment. But that payment is simply a transfer payment for borrowing the asset (cash or gilt) with no extra intrinsic returns being embedded in the cash or the gilt.

Therefore as an investor you have the choice of owning a gilt that pays you extra return until a set date when it turns into a cash security that pays you no return forever, or investing straight away in cash that pays you no return forever.

The holding of a gilt looks intrinsically superior. A buy to hold investor of a gilt with a positive yield will always end up with a higher cash balance than the investor holding cash. Why do investors therefore choose cash over gilts? Mainly, it is due to the fact that the price of a gilt can go up or down, while the price of cash never varies. This risk aversion means investors are willing to forego a positive return in order for certainty when they decide to hold cash.

From an issuer's perspective this is wonderful and can be taken advantage of. If the government can exchange interest bearing securities for cash (QE) then they can swap interest bearing securities that need refinancing at maturity for non-interest bearing securities that never need refinancing.

If for example 25% of the national debt has been exchanged for zero coupon perpetual securities (cash), then an 80% debt to GDP ratio effectively gets transformed into a 60% debt to GDP ratio, as 20% costs nothing to finance, never has to be repaid, and so is therefore effectively free finance.

The more of your outstanding debt you can finance at zero cost forever, the more debt you can sustain. If this free financing is undertaken responsibly it can be used as a sensible economic tool. However, if the temptation of free finance results in a misallocation of resources via the state, then it can be very harmful to the economy. This is why many economies have introduced the concept of an independent central bank to remove some of the political process from the real economy.

So far, the BoE has convinced the market that QE is a responsible policy. The use of QE has neutered the bond vigilantes, whilst the next enemy of this policy, the currency vigilantes, remain dormant.

The BoE could officially cancel the gilts or could simply exchange its existing gilts at maturity for new gilts to maintain the windfall gain of free finance. This topsy turvy world of money printing, low bond yields and free financing is a new challenge for investors.

Chapter 13

Should Europe let the single currency go to save the Union?
Markus Peters – Friday, 22nd June 2012

Today is the day on which football is going to meet the Eurozone crisis when Germany and Greece compete in the Euro Cup's quarterfinal. Spectators will be watching closely any gestures by Angela Merkel sitting in the stadium next to other political and executive representatives, any behaviour (and banners) of both team's supporters inside and outside of the stadium, and any appearance and words of the squads on the pitch and during the post-match interviews. The fact that much of the recent news coverage has been centred on the political dimension of this match shows once more the polarised times in which we're currently living. A match that, frankly speaking, has never been a big deal for either nation before, suddenly has turned into a highly emotional act about success, respect and even dignity, according to some commentators and officials. Nowadays European integration looks more and more like a very complex theory whose (successful or unsuccessful?) proof might turn out to be one of the biggest challenges of the 21st century. Interestingly, I will have insider status tonight. Being a German watching this match in the European capital of Brussels, the main hub for European bureaucrats, politicians, enthusiasts and sceptics, this experience will be insightful. Let's see in which way, given that my past experiences in Brussels made it feel rather like a bubble than a true reflection of common sentiment.

Knowing that I'm going to be in Brussels this weekend and having spoken with many of my peers who work for institutions and companies closely related to the European Union, I couldn't really stop thinking about the political dimension of the Eurozone crisis. I asked myself the question "if the European Union is particularly a political project or even a political and economic project which was meant to develop both political stability and economic prosperity, can't one possibly argue that it does currently not only fail on the economic dimension, but also on the political dimension?"

Why is this? My first thought is this. If the euro is interpreted as a continuation of the European integration process which by nature was about:

- preventing a dominant state in Europe after the second world war which is able to dictate the fate of the continent

- enhancing social and economic mobility and establishing a European identity
- supporting democracy and, consequently, making democratic institutions an inevitable pre-condition to any membership,

Then don't we find ourselves currently in a situation in which the single currency union has led to a failure of delivery, given that:

- Germany appears to dictate the agenda and appears to be the elephant in the room
- we're seeing increasing nationalist tendencies in parts of Europe, and negatively polarised sentiment towards fellow member states
- Italy, founding member of the Union, empowered a non-democratically elected prime minister (incl. a technocrat government) to run the country for around 1.5 years, assuming that the next general elections will take place in April 2013?

My second thought is about the legitimacy of any further European integration (fiscal union, Eurobonds, political union) which is currently being discussed as part of the solution of the crisis. If the European project is also defined around the lines of democracy, a value which is primarily promoted, isn't there still a long way to go for politicians in order to convince the electorate that further integration is actually what they want, given that:

- the electorate in parts of Europe is not prepared for the idea to bail out other countries, i.e. share the burden
- a common European identity is apparently not reality
- social and economic mobility is far away from being fully fluid, and current political discussions at the national level across Europe rather suggest a decreasing tendency in the light of talks about the part suspension of the Schengen agreement.

The third thought to conclude the argument is about the nature of integration and, consequently, the European Union. Isn't European integration rather something ex post than ex ante? That is, it is not the idea that you force upon someone, but rather a process facilitated by institutions and paced by the electorate at whose end integration is concluded. Institutions and electorate interact closely during the process, and one cannot really deviate too far from the state of development, from the 'mind set' of the other because then it turns into an unhealthy relationship in which legitimacy and accountability become problematic. That is, the formalisation of political union may require a common sentiment, a common identity in this direction first before a new treaty should enact it.

But what could be the pre-requisite of further integration? Away from all the economics, I think that Wilhelm von Humboldt, the German philosopher, has a point by saying that a language draws a circle around a nation, deciding upon inclusion and exclusion. Going back in history, isn't one of the main differentiating factors between the United States of America and the idea of a United States of Europe that the separate states of North America emerged as satellite states of a single country – Britain – whose language, culture and legal system built the shared founding ground, as Tony Judt argues in 'Postwar'?

If the European integration process was to resume in political union at one point in the future, shouldn't we start to acknowledge that the electorate isn't ready for this step yet and, equally importantly, that we're currently jeopardising this prospect? There may be some valid economic arguments for steps to more integration, but the political arguments don't seem to be matching this. European integration has been on the fast track over the past decades, and much of it has shaped the interaction of states, companies and individuals across countries very positively. But the Eurozone crisis also seems to show that the electorate might not have kept up with the institutionalisation process. A full political union looks to me like something bigger than an emergency solution to a financial crisis. There is another dimension to it defined by identity and democratic legitimacy. If the Eurozone crisis jeopardises, rather than facilitates, further integration on both dimensions, politically and economically, wouldn't it be sensible to take a step back (euro break-up?) in order to overcome the structural imbalances, allow for slower, but more persistent structural alignment, and a less heated atmosphere in which a more shared identity can flourish? It is likely that a break-up will have adverse effects in the shorter term, but isn't there the possibility that it could lay the ground for a stronger subsequent economic, political and social recovery and, consequently, mark two steps forwards towards political stability and economic prosperity in the long term? That is, let one project go (optimists might argue here "put on hold") in order to ensure the survival of the bigger one.

Fingers crossed that Germany wins tonight – and Europe succeeds as a project in the long term.

Chapter 14

The UK's AAA rating looks increasingly vulnerable. Growth negative, borrowing up. It might not matter though.
Jim Leaviss – Thursday, 28th June 2012

On 14th February this year, Moody's put the UK's AAA credit rating on negative outlook. This means that the agency says there is a 30% chance of the UK being downgraded within the next 18 months (i.e. by mid-2013). A month later, Fitch moved the UK's AAA rating to negative too – for them this means a slightly greater than 50% chance that there is a downgrade within the next two years. At the time Moody's said that "any further abrupt economic or fiscal deterioration would put into question the government's ability to place the debt burden on a downward trajectory for fiscal year 2015-16".

Since that Moody's action, we have seen deterioration, both in economic growth and on the fiscal side. Q4 2011 GDP was revised down from -0.2% to -0.3%, and now today to -0.4%, and an official recession is now occurring with 2012 Q1 GDP growth coming in at -0.3%. Whilst the latest survey of economic forecasts has a median Q2 GDP growth of +0.1%, the impact of the extra bank holiday on economic activity has 35% of forecasters expecting a third consecutive negative quarter. At the same time, and as a direct result of that weak growth performance, government borrowing is overshooting. In May the UK borrowed £18 billion, compared with an expectation of £14.5 billion. This is £3 billion more than in May 2011 and was driven both by weakness in tax receipts (-7% year on year) and higher government spending (+8% year on year).

The government then came out and announced a freeze in petrol duty, postponing a planned 3p rise in the rate due to take place in August. The cost of this, whilst "only" £550 million, appears to be unfunded – there was talk of departmental underspends, although the monthly borrowing numbers don't seem to reflect such savings yet. As Treasury minister Chloe Smith said in "that" Newsnight interview, "it is not possible to give you a full breakdown (of the underspends)...because the figure is evolving somewhat". Whilst as a good Keynesian I'm all in favour of fiscal stimulus helping to support the existing monetary stimulus in the UK, this is not the implicit deal that Chancellor George Osborne made with the rating agencies – that being that he would deliver both growth and austerity together and thus get the UK's debt/GBP ratios down in coming years. Failing to both get government spending down, and to grow the economy means that that debt/GDP ratio will continue to grow, and it becomes increasingly likely that the UK will lose its prized AAA ratings. Whether this matters is a different question – our sovereign CDS spreads are lower than AAA Germany's (70 bps vs 103 bps), our bond yields are as low as they've ever been, and whilst the Eurozone crisis continues the UK remains a safe haven for capital. And as we know, when S&P downgraded the US last year its bond yields subsequently fell. It's also unlikely that gilts will sell off, as UK rates are pinned at 0.5% (or lower) for the foreseeable future, and more Quantitative Easing is on its way. A downgrade might therefore just be an embarrassment for the Chancellor, rather than the starting gun for a race out of UK bond markets.

Chapter 15

UK gilts – "Whoah we're half way there, Whoah livin' on a prayer..."
Richard Woolnough – Monday, 9th July 2012

Last week the Bank of England announced a further round of quantitative easing of £50bn, bringing the total to £375bn. It is obvious that the MPC thinks that monetary policy is still not sufficiently loose to create the desired economic effect and hence further stimulus is needed.

We have written numerous times on QE. When we started scribing on this novel experiment we focused on why it needed to be done, and how it was meant to work (like walking on custard) and the bizarre effect this may have on the bond market.

One thing we did not focus on was the length of time monetary policy would have to be kept super accommodative, though we did expect it to be for an extended period of time (certainly until we begin to see a meaningful recovery in employment outcomes).

Mervyn King appears surprised by the extent of the crisis. The MPC were slow in aggressively cutting rates after the onset of the credit crunch in 2007, but to his credit Mervyn and the UK authorities have been at the forefront of corrective action and have correctly realised the severity of the credit crisis. The MPC was correct to not interpret the inflation scare of 2008 or the economic rebound of 2009 as economic recovery. They have been spot on.

But how accurate is his current thinking?

The Governor is not one to pre-commit. However he did say something recently that shows how he feels about the potential long-term outlook for rates. At the latest Treasury Select

Committee he repeated that at this point in time – and he has said it at every committee meeting – he believes we are not yet halfway through the crisis.

"When this crisis began in 2007-2008, most people including ourselves did not believe that we would still be right in the thick of it, in the middle of it, quite this late. All the way through, I've said to this committee that I don't think we are yet halfway through – I've always said that and I'm still saying it." Mervyn King, June 26, 2012.

From the charts we can see that BoE base rate has been set at 0.5% since March 2009, and over £325bn has been pumped into the financial system through QE. If we are not yet halfway through this crisis, then this implies that rates will stay at these levels for at least another 3 years to 2015, and a further round of £375bn of QE is potentially on the agenda.

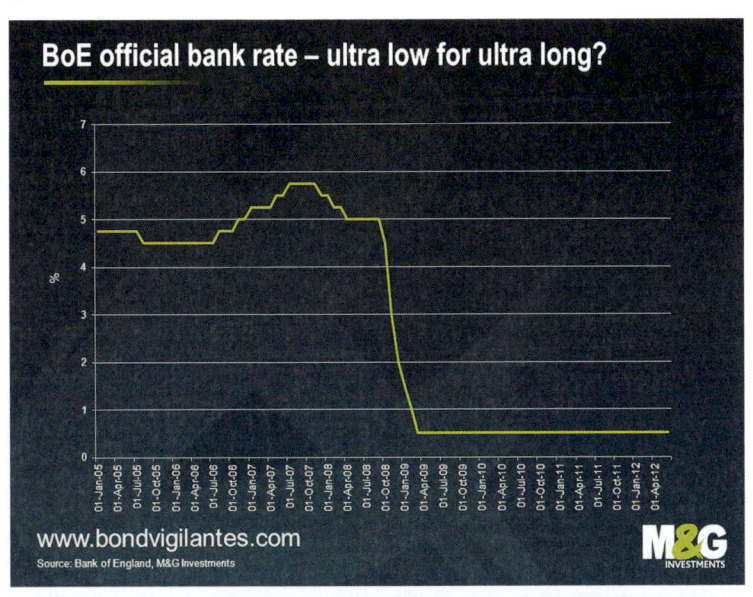

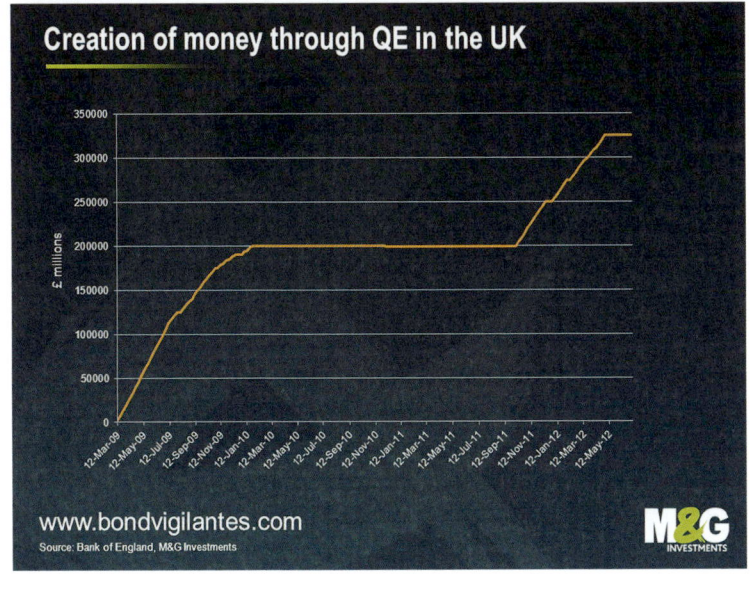

If this interpretation of the outlook turns out to be correct then these very low levels of short and long-term gilt yields begin to look more logical to gilt investors. And we can assume that the UK won't recover fully until the US and Europe does as well, which means that ultra-low yields on Treasuries and Bunds may also make sense.

Monetary policy is living on the edge, and if Mervyn King were to do a turn at a city karaoke machine, then the bar could well be ringing out to this Bon Jovi classic...

"Whoah we're half way there, Whoah livin' on a prayer..."

Naturally, his audience of gilt investors – despite the ultra-low yield they are currently receiving – will sing back "We got to hold on to what we've got".

Chapter 16

Peripheral corporate bonds and mass downgrade risk
Stefan Isaacs – Tuesday, 10th July 2012

Staying with the Bon Jovi theme, 'Ugly' was a track released by Jon Bon Jovi on his second solo album in 1998. It isn't well known, or any good for that matter, but it does aptly describe the price action of Spanish and Italian corporate paper of late.

Plenty of attention has been paid to the yield on Spanish and Italian govies – currently around 7% and 6% for 10 year bonds – but their bellwether non-financial corporate issuers have also seen their yields come under significant pressure. 5 year CDS levels for the likes of Iberdrola, Gas Natural, Repsol and Enel are trading near their all-time wides at 500, 525, 475 and 455 bps respectively. And it isn't just the utilities that have come under pressure: Telefonica and Telecom Italia have also seen their risk premia balloon to over 500 bps.

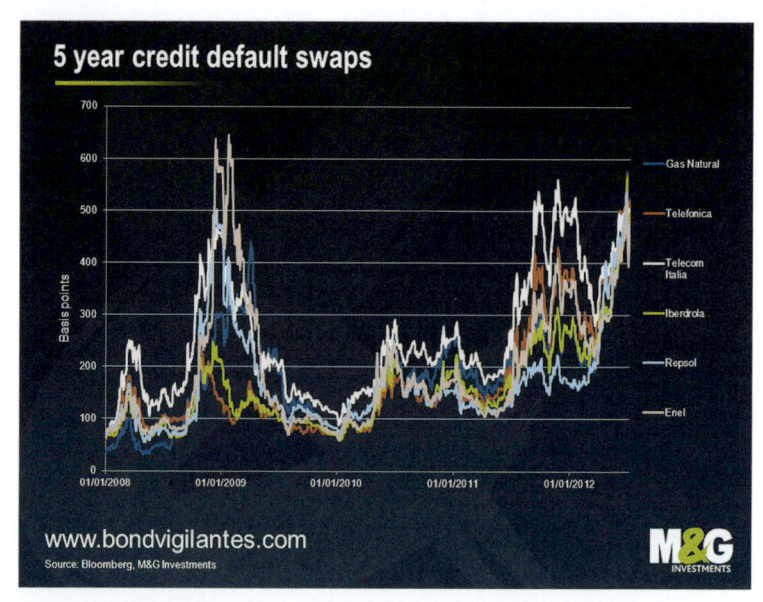

Whilst the aforementioned companies are still rated investment grade – some by many notches – they are actually trading wide of the Merrill Lynch BB Euro High Yield Non Financial

Index (current asset swap of +440). Put another way, the market does not believe that these businesses represent investment grade risks.

Such a view isn't without logic. The current ratings for the largest Spanish and Italian non-financial issuers (chart below) suggest that the market is right to be nervous. On average, the four largest Spanish issuers are only two notches above high yield status; for Italy's five largest issuers it's about three notches. That may seem like a fair bit of runway until you think about the pace of downgrades suffered by their sovereigns of late. Keep in mind that as late as July 2011 Moody's rated Spain at Aa2, seven notches higher than its current Baa3 rating. Italy has also seen its rating cut a full four notches between June 2011 and Feb 2012 by the agency. And S&P hasn't been much kinder, slashing Spain's rating from AA- to BBB+ in under a year and reducing Italy from A+ to BBB+.

Spanish and Italian corporate credit ratings

Issuer	Country	S&P rating	Moody's rating	S&P notches above HY	Moody's notches above HY
Gas Natural	Spain	BBB	Baa2	2	2
Iberdrola	Spain	BBB+	Baa1	3	3
Repsol	Spain	BBB-	Baa3	1	1
Telefonica	Spain	BBB	Baa2	2	2
Average notches above high yield				2	2
Enel	Italy	BBB+	Baa1	3	3
Eni	Italy	A+	A2	6	5
Finmeccanica	Italy	BBB-	Baa2	1	2
Telecom Italia	Italy	BBB	Baa2	2	2
Terna	Italy	A-	A3	4	4
Average notches above high yield				3	3

www.bondvigilantes.com
Source: Bloomberg, M&G Investments

Both Spanish and Italian corporates saw negative rating actions as a consequence of those sovereign downgrades. Moody's allows non-financial corporates a maximum two-notch rating uplift versus the sovereign, whereas S&P permits a maximum of six in extremis, with a couple of notches uplift far more common. The impact on Greek and Portuguese corporate bonds – such as EDP, OTE and Portugal Telecom – after their sovereigns lost their investment grade status serves to reinforce the potentially significant relationship between sovereign and corporate credit ratings.

So, in a hypothetical mass downgrade scenario what quantum of debt could be downgraded to high yield? If all Italian and Spanish non-financial paper were eventually to lose its investment grade status, we calculate that €47bn nominal of Spanish paper and €59bn nominal of Italian paper could fall into high yield territory. That would be a massive €106bn worth of paper – or 80% of the existing non-financial Euro High Yield Index – heading into the high yield market. That's a lot of paper for it to swallow.

Of course, the actual amount of debt that would end up for sale is difficult to quantify. This would depend, among other things, on index rules and investors' willingness and ability to hold high yield bonds. However, it seems reasonable to assume that over the coming months and even years a significant amount of paper will need to find a new home. Yields may well have to climb further, potentially a lot further, before traditional high yield investors see value in these names.

Chapter 17

Climate change – bzirc monetary policy
Richard Woolnough – Monday, 30th July 2012

As investors we get used to living within certain recognised bounds. For example, it has been commonly assumed that interest rates cannot be sub-zero. There has been the odd historical quirk when we've seen negative rates (Switzerland in the 1970s), but that's more for amusement than general investment consumption. However, there now appears to be the potential for a major investment climate change.

There are already plenty of bond markets now living in the sub-zero ice age, such as Switzerland, Denmark, Germany, Finland and the Netherlands. In these cases, the existence of negative rates could be down to the desire to express a currency or re-denomination view, so may be seen as a by-product of external factors and not of domestic monetary policy. However, there is now the potential for G7 monetary policy to enter the previously unbelievable reality of official sub-zero rates.

Many G7 economies have implemented very low rates and Quantitative Easing for a number of years, yet still appear to be in the economic doldrums with high unemployment, low growth and limited fiscal room. It could now be time for a significant change in the investment text book as central banks experiment with rates below zero.

Theoretically, a negative interest rate sounds simple – you put £100 in the bank and you get £99 back a year later if the rate is -1%. A rational investor would of course have the alternative of simply keeping their cash under the mattress and not suffering the negative rate, although the incentive to behave rationally would be limited by the administrative burden and security risk of holding cash. The central bank could simply limit this activity by basically not printing enough cash. Therefore the vast majority of money would have to be held electronically and could therefore suffer a penal negative rate. Implementation of sub-zero rates is possible.

From a central bank's point of view this should be stimulative, as it would discourage saving and encourage consumption like any traditional interest rate cut. At the extreme you could create exceptionally low, zero, or even negative borrowing rates.

The challenges faced by central banks and governments are still there despite traditional and unconventional policy action. Maybe it will soon be time to use the conventional tool of cutting interest rates in an unconventional way by making them negative. The next step to be taken by the authorities might mean economies working in a below zero interest rate climate (bzirc monetary policy).

Chapter 18

The toxic French economic cocktail: weak growth, poor competitiveness, fiscal tightening.

Jim Leaviss – Friday, 5th October 2012

Since the start of 2011 French economic growth has been extremely disappointing, falling from an annual rate of nearly 2.5% to just 0.3% in the second quarter of this year. Of course the whole Eurozone has seen weakness over the period, but French growth has lagged that of the "core" over the period. German GDP growth was at or above 2% for all but the last two quarters, and now stands at 1%. Purchasing Managers' surveys for September show more divergence, with more falls in French manufacturing and services, whilst the German surveys strengthened.

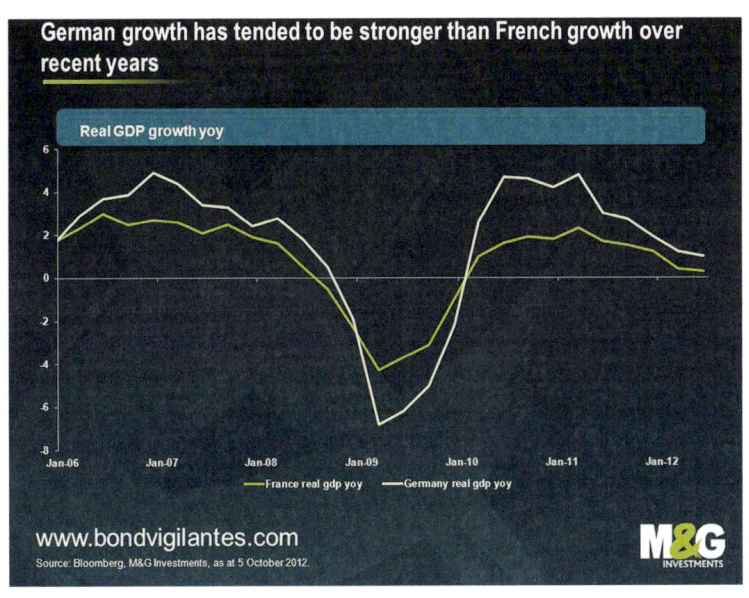

German growth has tended to be stronger than French growth over recent years

Real GDP growth yoy

Source: Bloomberg, M&G Investments, as at 5 October 2012.

Of course, it could be worse – Greece, Portugal, Spain, and Ireland have experienced much weaker economic growth and, perhaps most damaging, higher rates of unemployment. Spanish unemployment has risen from 8% in 2007 to 25% today, with youth unemployment over 50%. The French jobless total stands at "just" 10.3%. And the other big difference is that the bond markets believe that France is part of the core, not part of the periphery. Looking at 5 year CDS rates (the cost in basis points to insure a sovereign bond against the risk of default), France trades at 110 bps per year, compared with Ireland at 300 bps, Italy at 325 bps and Spain at 370 bps. And whilst this is still much wider than German CDS at 54 bps, since May the spread between German and French government bonds has narrowed significantly, from over 1.4% to 0.75%. Part of this reflects the perceived reduction in general Eurozone default/breakup risks following ECB president Draghi's assertion that he will do whatever it takes to save the Euro and his plan to buy short-dated government bonds of nations in distress, but this relative improvement also coincides with the election of Francois Hollande in May, when he became the first left-wing French president in two decades.

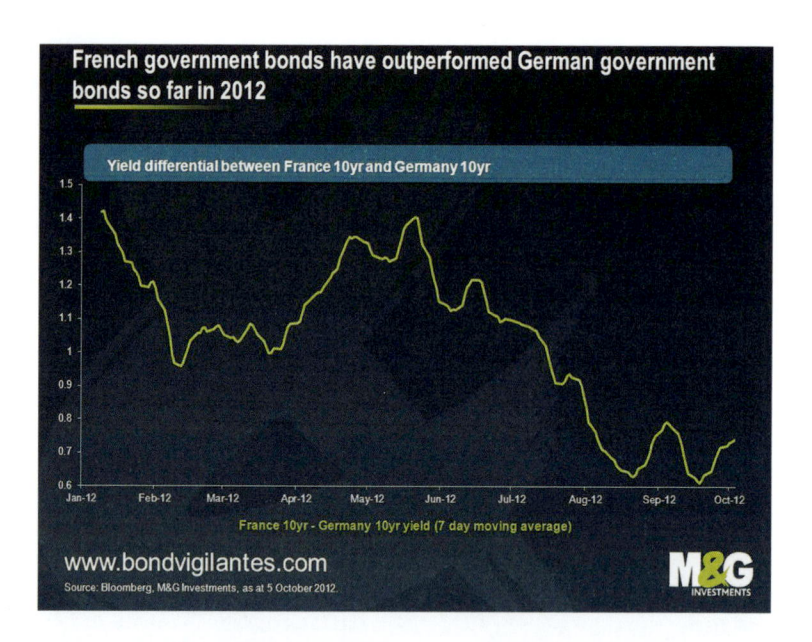

French government bonds have outperformed German government bonds so far in 2012

Yield differential between France 10yr and Germany 10yr

France 10yr - Germany 10yr yield (7 day moving average)

www.bondvigilantes.com
Source: Bloomberg, M&G Investments, as at 5 October 2012.

Hollande was elected on a platform of putting up taxes on the rich. He also pledged to cap France's budget deficit. As such last week's Draft Budget Law (PLF) for 2013 did not surprise the French population – there will be a fiscal tightening made up a third from household taxes, a third from corporate tax rises and a third from spending cuts. Goldman Sachs estimates that the tax take as a percentage of GDP will rise from 44.9% to 46.3%. But even this relatively aggressive tightening of fiscal policy (and the projections are based on GDP growth higher than many believe is possible, especially in light of that same fiscal tightening and a climate of austerity) doesn't prevent debt/GDP from rising above 90% in 2013. Remember that 90% is the level that Rogoff and Reinhart say delivers significant damage to an economy's ability to grow. But if the fiscal austerity "works", France should be moving towards a balanced budget within 3 or 4 years.

But back to the ability of France to grow its way out of a fiscal hole. Competitiveness is something that continues to worry us about the economy. The French current account is sharply in deficit, looking more like Spain or Italy than the "core" of Germany or the Netherlands (but not looking as bad as the UK's current account deficit of 5.4%, the most important reason we think that the pound is massively overvalued).

France looks more like periphery than core on its current account deficit

Current account balance as % of GDP

Netherlands — Germany — France — Italy — Spain

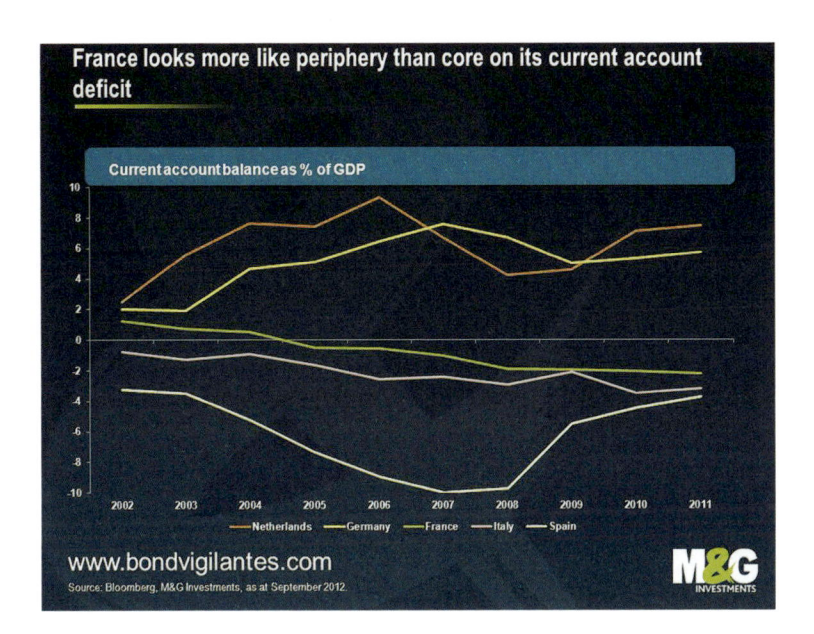

Source: Bloomberg, M&G Investments, as at September 2012.

www.bondvigilantes.com

M&G INVESTMENTS

In a typical economic model, a country with a current account deficit like this would devalue its currency to help its exporters. The single currency zone of the Eurozone doesn't allow this to happen, so instead an internal devaluation has to occur instead. Since the creation of the single currency, the German economy has outperformed, with strength in exported goods leading that success. This was no accident – post the collapse of the Iron Curtain, German companies had come to agreements with trade unions (a kind of neo-corporatism in which the government, companies and workers are social partners in a capitalist framework) to have wage restraint and thus keep German manufacturing from heading east to the cheaper labour supply. It meant that in the 12 years since the creation of the single currency, German labour costs rose by less than 25%. In Greece they rose by 65%, Spain 55% – and in France by 40%. Relative to Germany then, French labour costs had risen by 15% more, a significant deterioration of relative competitiveness within the core of Europe.

Spanish and Greek labour costs are adjusting, but France looks uncompetitive

Labour costs, rebased to 100 (base year 2000)

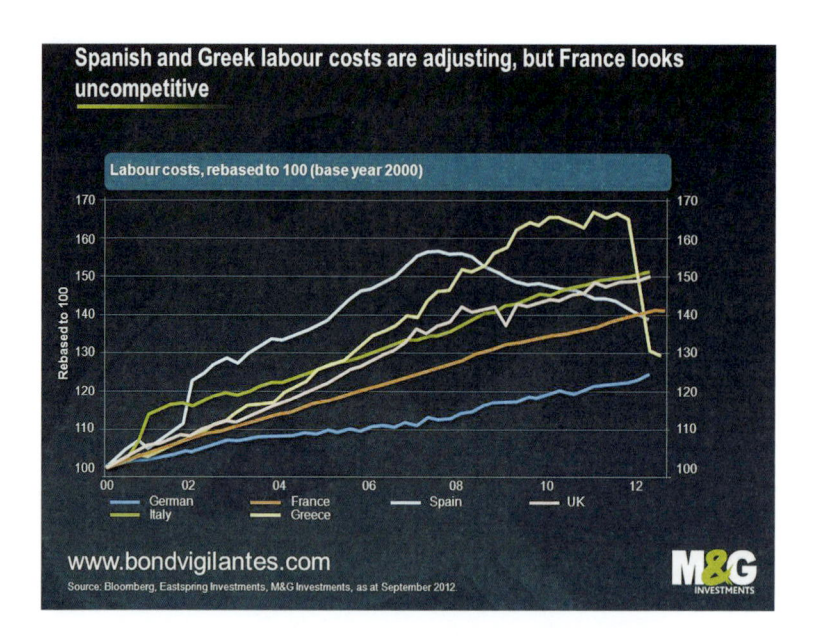

Legend: German, Italy, France, Greece, Spain, UK

www.bondvigilantes.com
Source: Bloomberg, Eastspring Investments, M&G Investments, as at September 2012.

It's clear that the "internal devaluation" is occurring in Greece and Spain, with labour costs falling sharply (as unemployment rockets). I'm not arguing this is positive – in the medium term it will stimulate exports as factories relocate in lower cost regions, but in the nearer term the drag this will have on Spanish and Greek growth could be medicine that kills its patient. But if there is capital to invest in plant, equipment and people in Europe once, and if, uncertainty fades, would it go to France, or to lower cost, restructured Spain?

And aggressive, publicly stated austerity doesn't appear to be a policy with great results – look at the UK where we've done less than 10% of the spending cuts that the coalition have planned, yet the psychological impact on the economy has been severe, and since the credit crisis began the UK economy has underperformed not just the US (where they did some good old Keynesian fiscal stimulus) but also the Eurozone, which is widely regarded as an economic disaster area here despite it having outperformed us by about 2% of GDP over the period (and having a lower debt/GDP level too, if you took the region together as a whole).

So the challenges to the French fiscal outlook are enormous – delivering growth (or defaulting) has always been the most successful method of reducing government indebtedness, and even an optimistic 2% per year real growth rate (pencilled in by the government from 2014) doesn't deliver a significant reduction in the debt to GDP ratio – certainly the 40% to 50% level that we used to associate with a AAA rated economy seems a long way away. It may be that the aggressive tightening in French government bond yields to those of AAA rated (for the time being) Germany has gone far enough. There are plenty of economic and social buy-in risks to come for France – let us not forget that Spain's Rajoy was also elected on a platform of fiscal consolidation, and it took less than a year for its population to change its mind about that.

Chapter 19

Fallen Angel Delight – looking at returns from "junked" companies
Nicolo Carpaneda – Monday, 8th October 2012

Earlier this year, Stefan highlighted the potential for sovereign debt downgrades to push big European companies into high yield territory becoming "fallen angels", issuers downgraded from investment grade to high yield. This is something the Financial Times has also recently picked up on. The chart below shows how near the average European sovereign ratings are to sub-investment grade.

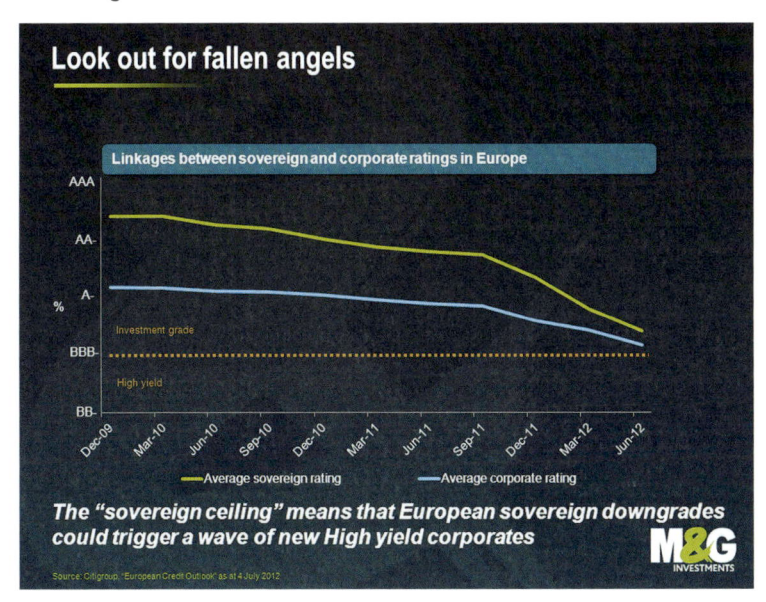

Look out for fallen angels

Linkages between sovereign and corporate ratings in Europe

The "sovereign ceiling" means that European sovereign downgrades could trigger a wave of new High yield corporates

Source: Citigroup, "European Credit Outlook" as at 4 July 2012

M&G INVESTMENTS

Rating agencies have flexibility in "capping" corporate ratings to the sovereign ratings of their respective home countries – the so-called sovereign ceiling. S&P for example has no strict limit on the number of notches by which an entity's rating can exceed the sovereign but Moody's is less generous, allowing a maximum two-notch rating uplift versus the sovereign for non-financials (the maximum is one notch above for financials). The reality is that a strong creditworthiness correlation tends to exist due to the likely exposure of companies to their domestic economy, and the ability of the sovereign to tax them (or worse) if necessary.

Where the market is not focusing enough is on the current role of existing fallen angels – companies that migrated from an investment grade index into a high yield index since the beginning of 2012. So far this year the fallen angels weighting in the Bank of America Merrill Lynch European Currency High Yield Index has increased by approximately 15% to 43.66%, the highest it has been in over two years.

Chapter 20

5 years on
Richard Woolnough – Wednesday, 10th October 2012

On the 9th October 2007 the totem pole of capitalism, the S&P 500, peaked at 1,565. Last night it closed at 1,441. So, five years into the crisis, where are we in terms of clearing up the banking crisis?

There's good news in the US. We have commented on the initial driver of the crisis in the world's largest economy – the boom and bust of the housing market – on many occasions. Recently, we've noted that we're beginning to see improvement here. This is an important sign that the US is moving on from the financial crisis. Although unemployment remains stubbornly high, it is moving in the right direction and the financial system is looking sound once again. The government's combination of supportive measures – such as taking equity stakes in banks – and allowing some pain to occur – in the case of Lehman Brothers and housing repossessions – seems to have been largely successful.

The UK economy and financial system have not yet returned to the same state of health and the government still holds legacy stakes in some of the bigger banks. It appears that the problems the country faced five years ago remain, even though they are not as severe as they were. These difficulties are highlighted by today's Financial Times where the two headline stories relate to the FSA easing bank rules further to encourage lending and help the financial system, and the governor of the Bank of England's speech at my old university last night where he talked about giving central banks greater flexibility with their inflation targets to help avoid financial crises.

Europe, the third major western financial system, faces its own particular problems. Five years on from the peak we had the strange situation of the German chancellor being taken in a convoy of cars through Athens past illegal demonstrators to try to sort out the continued funding of the Greek state. We have written many times about the questionable sustainability of a politically motivated single currency and the funding of states, individuals and corporates remains difficult in many parts of this system.

We believe financial systems need to be mended by a combination of government intervention and private sector responsibility. The US has led the way in this regard and the UK is trailing, hopefully successfully, behind it. However in Europe the problems have been exacerbated by the single currency regime, where the need for political intervention to solve the problem is relatively large versus the need for private sector adjustments. We are still concerned about whether the necessary political intervention will occur. So, five years on, it appears that the western world is still coming out of the credit crisis, albeit at different speeds and with different levels of success.

Chapter 21

Happy Halloween. Five scary charts. Boo!
Anthony Doyle – Wednesday, 31st October 2012

In the true spirit of October 31, today we thought we would try our best to try and scare you. Five charts, each more scary than the last.

1. Capital fright

Uncertainty in Europe is having a significant impact on investor and consumer confidence. This is manifesting itself in a flight to quality for capital, which the below chart highlights rather well. Most economists agree that capital flight may destabilise financial markets, raise a country's borrowing costs, reduces a country's tax base, and can have major ramifications for the domestic banking system. If capital is the lifeblood of an economy, then the blood is draining out of the peripheral economies.

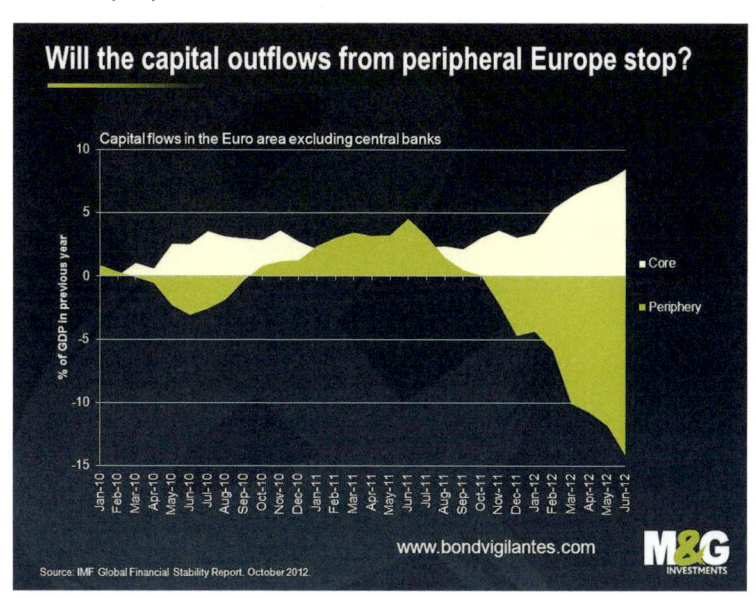

2. Ghostly foreign holdings of local sovereign bonds

On a related note, many emerging market countries have seen large capital inflows since 2007. We describe the percentage increase in foreign holdings of local sovereign bonds as ghostly. As quickly as the inflows appear, they can reverse again. This is a major risk in our opinion and is something we wrote about back in July.

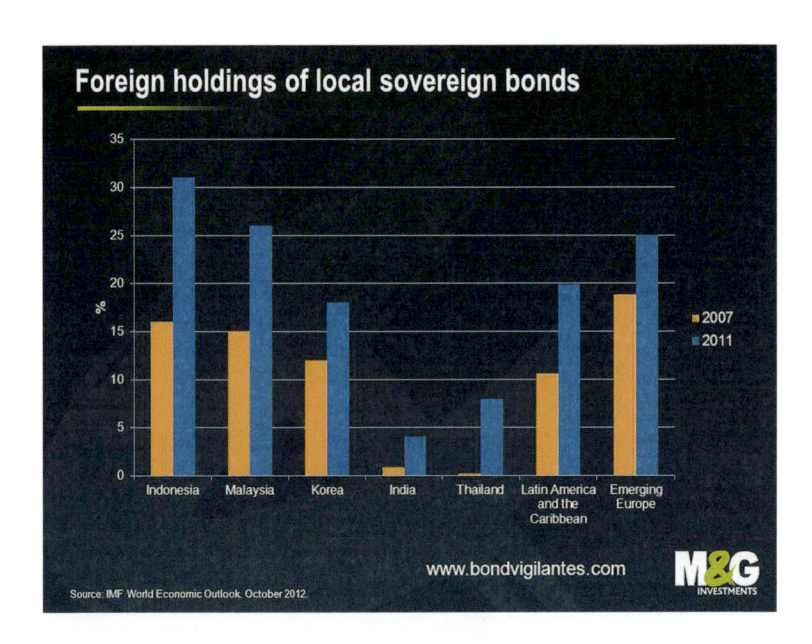

3. Country dependence on trick or treats and food

It remains the case that for a substantial proportion of the world's population, food remains the largest component of their consumption baskets. With global warming, rising populations, tightening supply dynamics and growing global demand, food prices and inflation will continue to have a large influence on the majority of us. How will governments and policymakers respond?

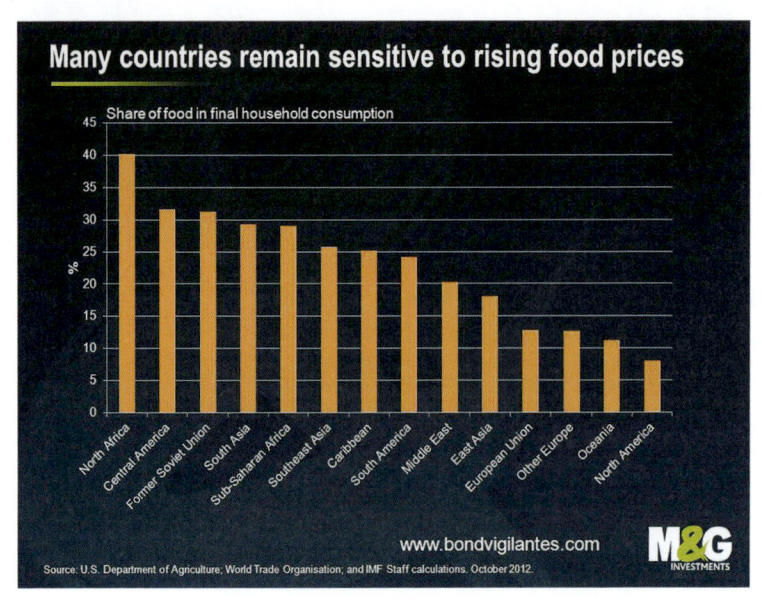

4. Growing public debt and zombie nations

Gross public debt as a percent of GDP in advanced economies is now near historical levels. There is significant debate about how policymakers will address the debt problems that many countries now face. If they don't, they risk being cut off from bond markets, rendering them as zombies. Is it better to implement fiscal austerity, or try and stimulate growth through further policy stimulus? What about financial repression? Whatever the answer, there is going to be a lot of structural pain in order for many countries to become competitive again.

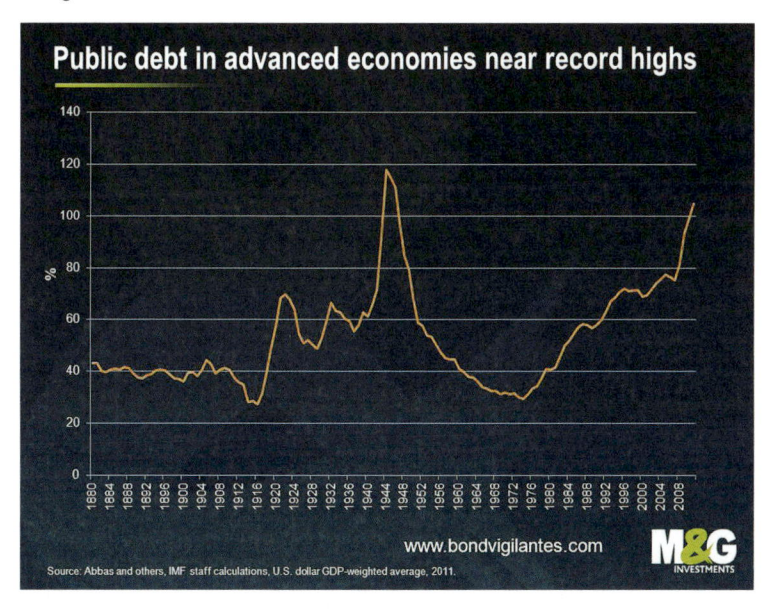

5. The global financial system is a monster

The global financial system can safely be classified as a monster. The global financial system is now valued at USD 255,855,541,100,000 (almost 256 trillion) in size. This is an increase of around 140% since 2002. To put this into context, the Milky Way galaxy is estimated to contain between 200-400 billion stars. As a per cent of GDP, the global financial system has grown to be worth around 367% of global GDP. Good luck to all the central bankers out there who are trying to tame the monster.

The monster financial system

Bar chart showing Stock market capitalisation, Debt securities, and Bank assets in Billions of U.S. dollars for 2002, 2007, and 2011.

Source: IMF Global Financial Stability Report, October 2012.

www.bondvigilantes.com

Fallen Angels weighting

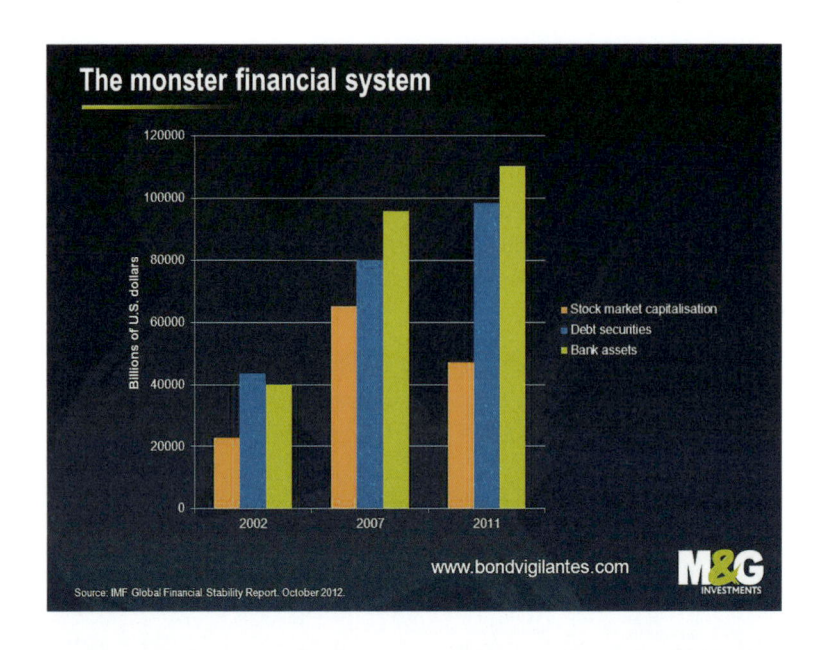

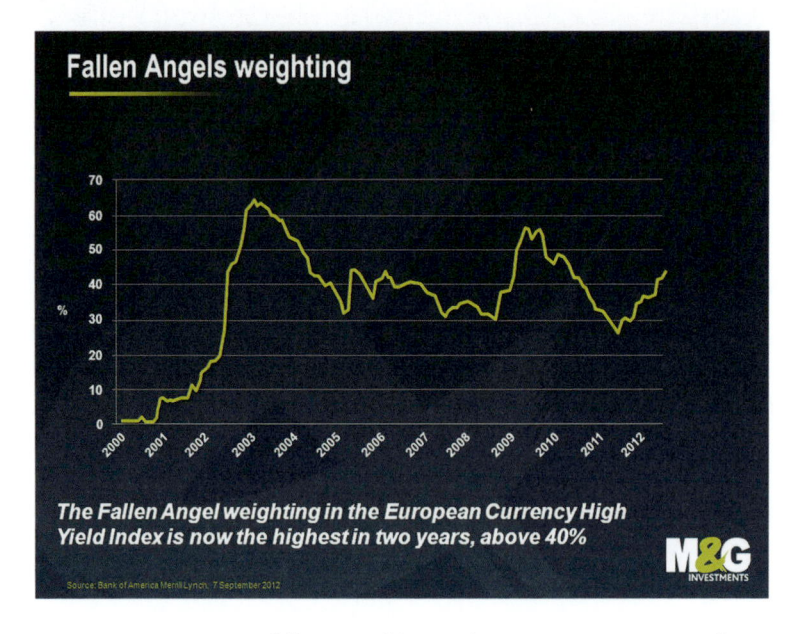

The Fallen Angel weighting in the European Currency High Yield Index is now the highest in two years, above 40%

Source: Bank of America Merrill Lynch, 7 September 2012

What is even more interesting is fallen angels' contribution over time to total return.

Total return of fallen angels...

...outperforms every rating segment

[Chart: ML European Currencies HY Index - BB, ML European Currencies HY Index - B, ML European Currencies HY Index - C, ML European Currencies HY Index - Fallen Angels, from Jan 01 to Jul 12, indexed to 100]

Source: M&G, Bloomberg as at 30 Sep 2012 (Total returns indexed to 100)

Fallen angels have significantly outperformed the original issue high yield portion of the index over time, whether you look at annualised returns over the last 3, 5, 7 or even 10 years (+2.59%, +3.70%, +2.87% and +3.24%, respectively).

Now, many future fallen angels may be different from their predecessors from a credit quality point of view. In the past, downgrades pushing corporates and banks down to high yield were mainly due to company-related issues: worsening balance sheets and poor revenue outlook. They were therefore as risky a bet as the rest of the universe.

Is this still true today? Well, reviewing the list of fallen angels in 2012, 41 out of the 110 European securities downgraded to high yield were due to sovereign downgrades (specifically from peripheral Europe – Spain, Italy and Portugal). This is equal to 37% of the total downgrades: more than one third of the total. This increase in the fallen angel population due to "externalities" (i.e. sovereign downgrades due to the eurozone debt crisis, rather than for the intrinsic worsening of their performance) has a potentially significant impact on the BB segment of the high yield market. Arguably, this increases the underlying quality of the market and, if historical risk/return characteristics hold, this could have a beneficial impact for high yield returns in general. On the other side, given the higher underlying quality of these downgraded issuers (lower leverage, better cashflows, global scale) their yields may be lower upon entering the high yield indices, and the potential for subsequent performance may be weaker than with "real" junk.

Chapter 22

Stress in the Eurozone – Day of action, years of reaction
Richard Woolnough – Wednesday, 14th November 2012

Today in Europe we have a day of action. The day of action means in reality a day of inaction, as the active protesting on the streets is outweighed by the inactive sectors such as transportation hit by the strike. Why are workers and, increasingly importantly, non-workers undertaking such protests?

Firstly let's look at the evidence. Below is a chart of unemployment in the Eurozone split by country. The chart shows who is protesting and why. The higher the unemployment the more concern there is in that nation's population over the current economic situation. Germany is not protesting; Southern Europe is.

Eurozone unemployment

Major structural issues in peripheral Europe
www.bondvigilantes.com
Source: Bloomberg, as at 31 October 2012

M&G INVESTMENTS

It can be seen from the chart that at various times over the last 10 years the sick and healthy economies of Europe have alternated, the strong core and the weak periphery were the weak core and the booming periphery in the middle of the last decade. Industry, labour skills, and structural shifts do not occur that quickly so what is causing this volatility in national economic outcomes?

We have commented before on the travails of the single currency concept. This is an economic construct, which has been constructed for the good of Europe. Let's look at how this current economic policy affects the Eurozone, and how the divergence in economic outcomes can be solved using economic theory.

The first economic lesson I learned from my excellent economics teacher, was the concept of the invisible hand (quite ironic as he had the biggest hands I've ever seen!). The introduction of a single currency causes the invisible hand as expressed via exchange rates to be metaphorically tied behind your back. Given the single currency is the root of the dislocation, disbanding it is an obvious solution. However the other ramifications of doing this are potentially large, and it is not an option European leaders are prepared to take. This is not because it is an ineffective policy option, but they are wedded to the political concept as well as the economic concept that comes with a single currency. The weak economies are therefore stuck with too high an exchange rate and the strong economies are left with too low an exchange rate. The economics of the invisible hand in foreign exchange markets is not allowed to work and therefore economic divergence not convergence becomes a more likely event.

Being educated in Britain, the next main economic lessons we learned were around the work of John Maynard Keynes, the principal point drummed into us being that governments should run counter cyclical budget deficits. Unfortunately in Europe the response that the weaker economies are being forced to take is more fiscal discipline through budget deficit reductions. The strong have room to undertake fiscal stimulus, the weak are being told to run pro-cyclical fiscal policy. So from this economic perspective the weak will get weaker and the strong stronger.....

The third basic lesson of economics was monetary policy. Lower interest rates stimulate consumption and growth. If you're the German state, a German company, or a German individual the transmission mechanism of borrowing substantial amounts of money at low rates is available and is working. Sadly if you're the state, a company, or an individual in the weaker economies the cost of borrowing is high and the physical quantity you can borrow is limited. The transmission mechanism is not working equally across Europe. The strong will get stronger the weak will get weaker.

The single currency is an economic construct that has come about through a political process. If that economic construct does not cause many economic ripples then politically it is relatively easy to take the political decisions to make the concept work. However if the economic construct becomes very destabilising as it appears to be doing then the political skills and policy options have to increase in size to offset its destabilising effects. The political day of action of launching a single currency was simple, the actions required to make it work long term are not.

Chapter 23

The fiscal cliff is bad news, but is likely to be resolved – so don't ignore the extremely positive developments in the US housing market
Jim Leaviss – Monday, 26th November 2012

There are some big risks to the US economy, but the potential for the US housing market to surprise on the upside, and deliver massive gains to US employment might well be the bigger story for 2013.

The real damage that the fiscal cliff is causing is mainly psychological at the moment, discouraging both capital investment and hiring. I'm not allowed to use the phrase that involves metal food containers being moved further along transport routes by means of the foot, as we have a "cliché box" at work, and saying it would cost me dearly – but that is both the obvious solution to the problem, and indeed the only solution. The size of the US debt is now too big for any politician to deal with decisively, and some sort of default (against bond holders if a default against the population's pension or healthcare expectations isn't possible) or devaluation (currency or inflation) sometime in the future will be likely.

The focus on the fiscal cliff has taken attention away from what we think are extremely positive developments elsewhere in the US economy – and particularly in the housing market, as alluded to in September. US housing became the centre of the global financial crisis from 2007 onwards, when the credit bubble burst as sub-prime mortgage loans started to go bad. Too many houses had been built, and the overhang of unsold inventory together with foreclosures and falling real incomes and unemployment led to a sharp fall in house prices. The banking system went bust, and a huge number of construction jobs were lost in the economy. From a peak of 7.7 million Americans employed in construction in 2006, by the start of 2010 the sector had lost 2.2 million jobs. But we're now seeing a large number of positive signs in the US housing market, and just as the negative multiplier effects spread through the economy when the sector tanked, the reverse might be true next year.

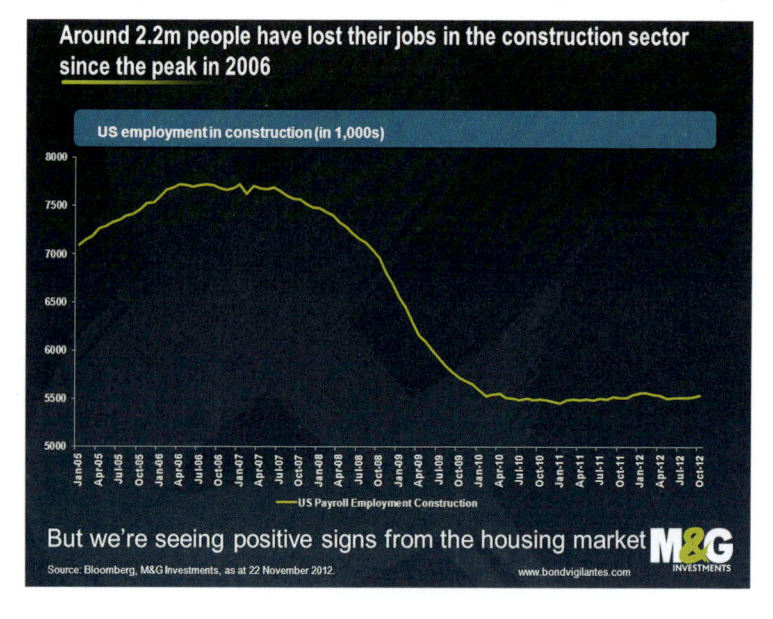

Around 2.2m people have lost their jobs in the construction sector since the peak in 2006

US employment in construction (in 1,000s)

But we're seeing positive signs from the housing market

Source: Bloomberg, M&G Investments, as at 22 November 2012.   www.bondvigilantes.com

The next chart was very important to us in 2007, when it led us to expect not just weak growth in the US, but an outright recession with huge damage to the banking sector. It showed that there had been so much overbuilding in US residential property that the supply of inventory had moved from about 4 months to over 7 months. This had historically been a leading indicator of recession. In fact unsold inventory moved much further than 7 months, hitting one year in 2008, presaging US GDP falling by 4% year on year. You can see that the available inventory of housing is now contracting sharply, to the extent that US growth should continue positive. It's also at a level where house-building should resume – and the multiplier effect from that will be extremely powerful.

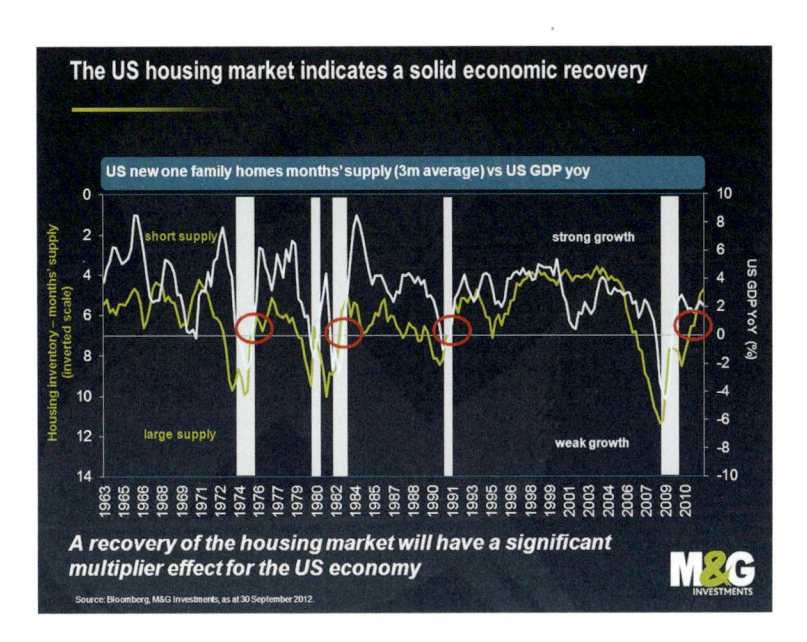

The US housing market indicates a solid economic recovery

US new one family homes months' supply (3m average) vs US GDP yoy

A recovery of the housing market will have a significant multiplier effect for the US economy

Source: Bloomberg, M&G Investments, as at 30 September 2012.

Other reasons to be cheerful about US housing? Well house prices have been rising, according to the S&P/Case-Shiller Index, since March this year (but remain "cheap", 30% below the peak in nominal terms, even weaker in real terms). So the negative sentiment around the sector will be fading somewhat – nobody wants to buy into a falling market. And the Federal Reserve has almost entirely moved its Quantitative Easing programme away from purchases of US Treasuries and towards the purchase of Mortgage Backed bonds. This should eventually help get the transmission mechanism working again. In theory American mortgage investors should be able to refinance existing mortgages at high rates into new lower rate loans. This hasn't been happening – banks have dragged their heels on paperwork (the time from agreeing a loan to it closing has anecdotally risen from a month to three months for example), and lending standards for the new mortgages are often higher than they were for the outstanding stock of mortgages. So new 30 year mortgage rates are around 3.31%, (a record low). But as at 2011 (it's probably lower now) 28 million Americans had outstanding mortgages with rates over 1% higher than the rate for new mortgages – in theory these are all refinanceable at lower levels. You could read this as bad news – but it represents a possible windfall gain for consumers if the transmission mechanism does start working again (lower interest payments equals more spending power). And the Fed is now focused on making the transmission mechanism work – it will get better.

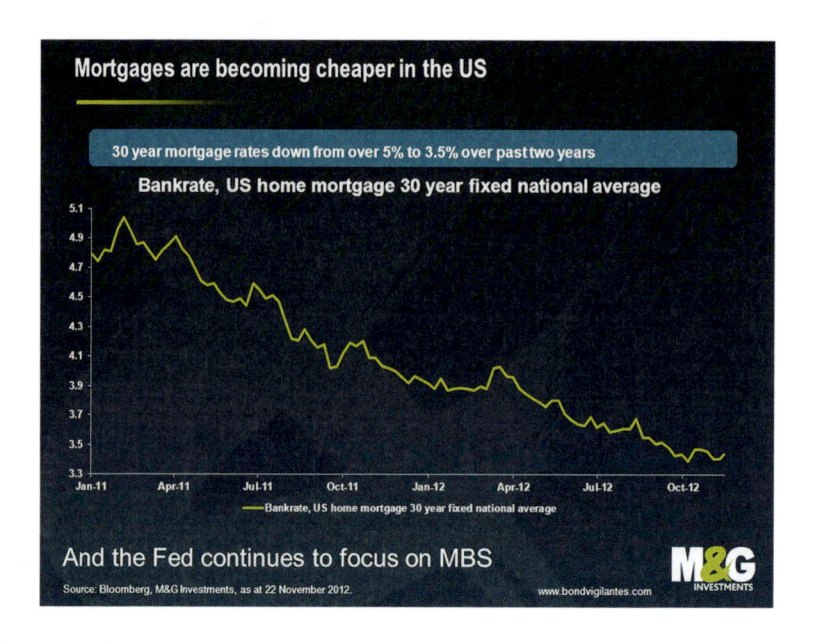

Mortgages are becoming cheaper in the US

30 year mortgage rates down from over 5% to 3.5% over past two years

Bankrate, US home mortgage 30 year fixed national average

And the Fed continues to focus on MBS

Source: Bloomberg, M&G Investments, as at 22 November 2012.

So if the price of US housing is attractive, and mortgage rates have fallen, and there's an increasing level of demand relative to low supply, how powerful can this be? Well we saw how powerful the negative impact was post 2007 – the multipliers involved with housing construction and household formation (people starting households for the first time, as a result of population growth and immigration, or moving out of a parental home) are very strong. A new housing construction project might result in a contractor hiring more workers, who buy pick-up trucks and power drills, and have wages to spend in their neighbourhoods. They buy cement (from Cemex hopefully, a high yield company we like!) and wood. And the people who move in buy carpets, chairs and flat screen TVs (is it time to stop saying flat screen when it comes to TVs? Probably). The Australian Bureau of Statistics calculated construction multipliers back in 2002. They found that there was an initial effect (the employment of construction workers and what they produce), a first round effect (the output and employment of those that produce the goods and services to the construction industry needs), an industrial support effect (the extra output impact on the suppliers to that first round effect), and a consumption induced effect (increased spending resulting from the wages resulting from all of those efforts). The ABS calculated that every US$1 million spent on construction output results in US$2.9 million of output in the economy as a whole. And, better still, gives rise to 13.5 jobs in construction and 55.5 jobs in the economy as a whole (I've pro-rated the jobs upwards from the Australian example, as their original calculations were using the Aussie $). The ABS did warn about the multiplier being overstated from the theory to the actuality, and Australia is obviously not America – but the numbers show the power of housing and construction, and could make you very bullish on the US economy over the next couple of years.

Which brings me on to my final, and tenuously related point – I had a coffee with George Trefgarne last week, the former economics editor of the Daily Telegraph, and the author of Metroboom, a paper about Britain's recovery from the 1930s slump. We can debate about whether it was austerity or currency devaluation that got the UK out of depression – but house building was certainly part of the solution. Between 1931 and 1939 we were building from 200,000 to (in 1936) over 350,000 new houses per year. Compare that to the UK today, where despite the much bigger population, we're building under 150,000 houses per year, whilst rents rise and affordability remains very poor for most. In some ways we are lucky – we have a potential solution to the UK's weak growth – allow house building to take off (by loosening planning restrictions, incentivising house builders to release land banks). If you are Spain, and you have a huge glut of housing, this is not a way out of the ongoing crisis – but for the UK, or the US, building homes could be the answer.

Chapter 24

Corporate bond market liquidity – flush or flushed?
Richard Woolnough – Tuesday, 4th December 2012

It has been a great few months for corporate bond issuance, as illustrated in the chart below. This huge flush of new transactions where buyer (investor) meets seller (issuer), shows that the primary market is in a historically healthy state, with buckets of liquidity. However, since the credit crunch there has been a great deal of discussion re the corporate bond market becoming less liquid, as dealers' ability to bid for bonds has gone down the pan. Which is right?

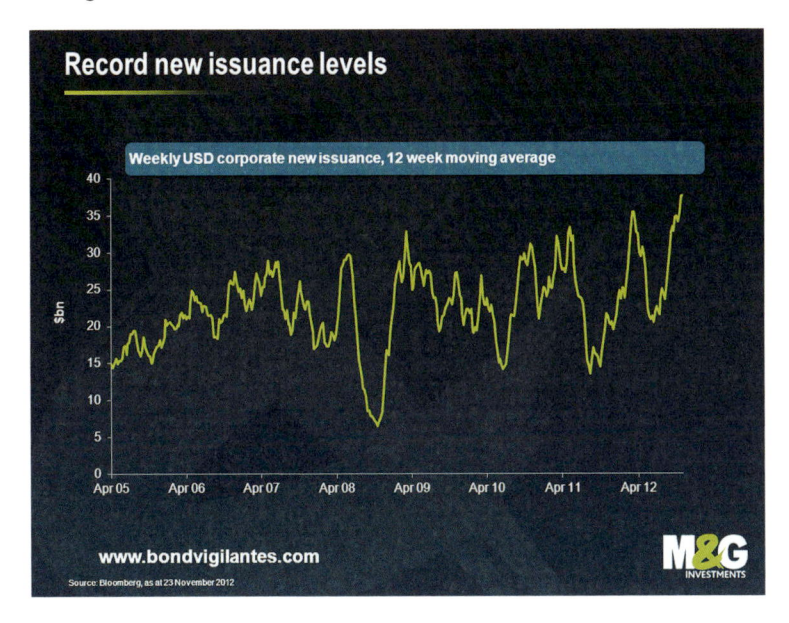

Record new issuance levels

Weekly USD corporate new issuance, 12 week moving average

Source: Bloomberg, as at 23 November 2012

Since the credit crunch began, the financial intermediaries who provide immediate liquidity for bond investors have been under a great deal of capital stress. Losses on securities, more conservative management, and reduced yet more expensive capital, have resulted in a shrinking of their market making balance sheets. This is illustrated in the following chart with data from the Federal Reserve showing primary dealer positions in corporates with maturities of more than a year.

Dealer inventories have collapsed

Source: Federal Reserve Bank of New York, Primary Dealer Positions - Corporate Securities Due in More Than 1 Year Net Outright Position as at 21 November 2012

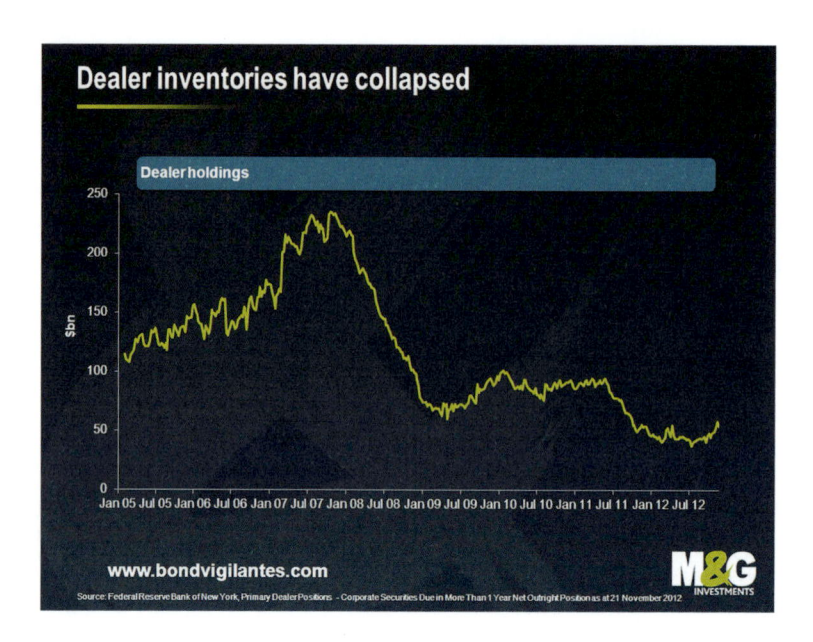

According to some market observers, the above indicates that traders' ability to take on risk has collapsed by roughly 80 percent, and therefore corporate bond market liquidity must have collapsed significantly in tandem, due to the disappearance of this historic pool of capital to bid for securities. However, we think this is a rather simplistic way for investors to explore what is going on. The chart overleaf shows a far more relevant number than the size of dealers' books – the actual historic trading volume in secondary corporate bonds, which gives a stronger indication of real, rather than hypothetical liquidity. This shows that turnover has not collapsed 80 percent in the same way as dealer inventory, and in fact daily volumes are on a par with where they were in 2007. It is also worth noting that investment banks', and their shadow bank counterparts' percentage of this volume will have fallen, and so it is likely that transactions between genuine end investors have increased substantially in real terms, and as a percentage of this turnover.

Volume is higher than pre-crisis

Average weekly IG trading volume

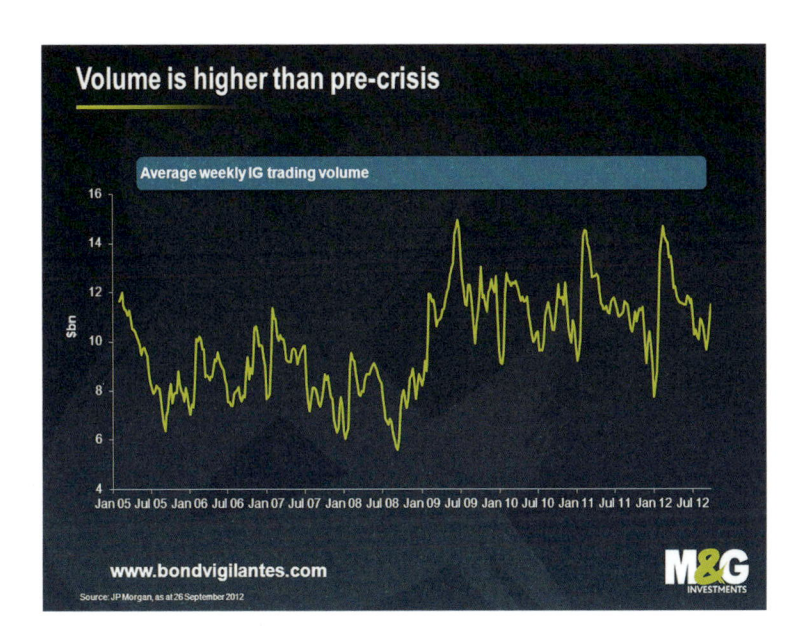

[Chart: $bn from 4 to 16, Jan 05 to Jul 12, Source: JP Morgan, as at 26 September 2012]

www.bondvigilantes.com

M&G INVESTMENTS

Back in 2007 the markets were exceptionally liquid. They were dominated by short-term players using cheap regulatory capital to take on enormous credit risk. This was done directly by investment banks on their own account, or to warehouse positions to be sold on to vehicles such as CDOs and CLOs as they were launched. This activity has collapsed. So, along with the more stringent capital environment, the size of their inventories has understandably shrunk considerably. However, making markets and operating in the corporate bond market remains an important source of revenue for these financial intermediaries. Despite less capital being deployed, total secondary volume has recovered to 2007 levels, which means they have become more efficient and turnover per unit of inventory has gone through the roof, as illustrated on the next page. The financial crisis has changed banks' and investors' appetites for and abilities to take risk.

Use of capital has become more efficient

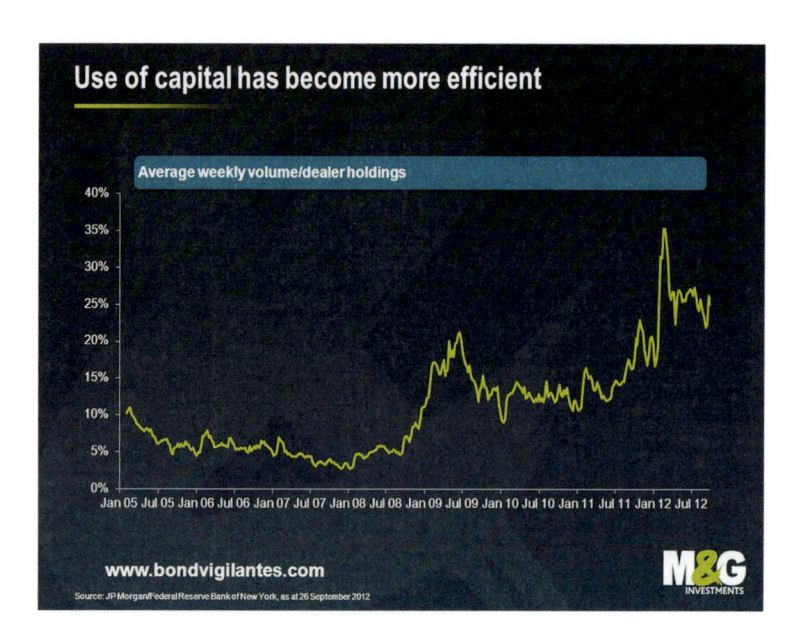

Average weekly volume/dealer holdings

Source: JP Morgan/Federal Reserve Bank of New York, as at 26 September 2012

www.bondvigilantes.com

M&G Investments

The financial crisis has also driven a significant fundamental shift in how capital markets work. The recycling of capital (through the mismatch of risk taken by banks that was the route of the credit crunch) by using short-term deposits to lend long term that dominated the landscape in 2007, is now morphing into a new, hopefully more stable process of borrowers being funded via the corporate bond market. Bank lending has shrunk, and the capital markets, led by the expanding bond market have attempted to fill the gap. As bank lending is replaced by more permanent term bond lending, then term mismatch and credit risk in the banking system is reduced, and that term and credit risk is assumed by the bond investor. The bond investor not only gets paid for assuming this risk but also has to work out what liquidity premium they need to be paid on top of the term and credit risk they have taken on board with their corporate bond position.

This premium will vary over the cycle like the other drivers of returns – credit and interest rates. It will expand when credit markets are weak, and liquidity poor (eg autumn 2009). It will contract when the credit outlook is great and liquidity high (spring 2007), and is something all investors need to be aware of when investing in the asset class. An investor in corporate bonds should examine where we are in the liquidity cycle, and should be aware that the perfect liquidity and huge dealer inventories of 2007 contributed to the ensuing rout in the asset class, while the illiquidity of the winter of 2008 was a great opportunity to buy and take advantage of the expanded liquidity premium. We know from the last 5 years that to an investor in corporate bonds, perfect liquidity can be a precursor to more dangerous times than illiquidity can.

Is corporate bond liquidity brilliant or is it at record lows? Well, it appears that daily volume of primary markets is at record levels, while secondary market liquidity has not grown in line with the size of the market place, but is not as low as a simple analysis of dealer inventory would imply. It is hard to know what average daily liquidity should be, as the market has been evolving in the recent dramatic economic conditions. However, the total liquidity of all transactions, both primary and secondary, indicates a growing, interesting market place as banks are being replaced by the corporate bond market as the funding vehicle of choice.

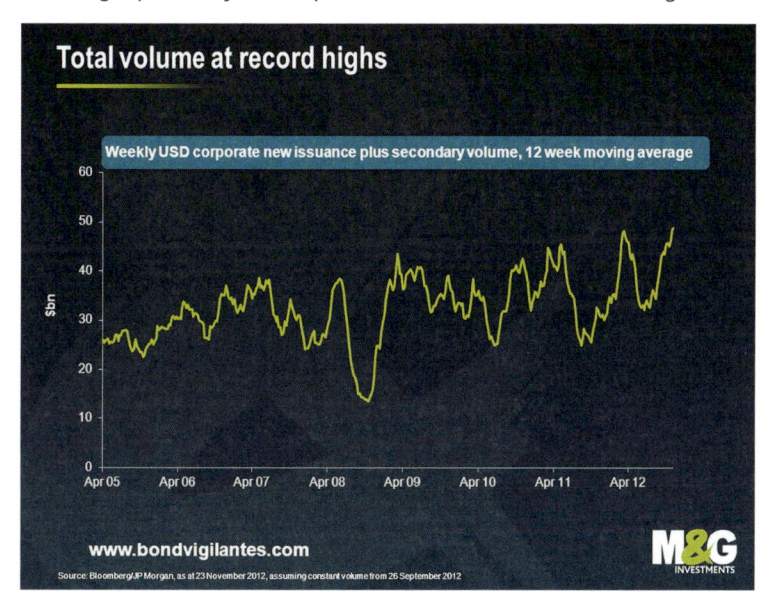

2013

Chapter 25

Should the people of Middle Earth have done Quantitative Easing to mitigate against Smaug's tight monetary policy?

Jim Leaviss – Wednesday, 2nd January 2013

Any blog that begins with the words "Smaug the dragon is typically viewed as a fiscal phenomenon..." has immediately got my attention. Please read The Macroeconomics of Middle Earth by Frances Woolley. Woolley compares the size of the dragon's hoard with a picture of the gold reserves at the Bank of England – although it is likely that Smaug is the beneficial owner of his gold, rather than a custodian of gold for richer dragons elsewhere in Middle Earth. He concludes by suggesting that the peoples of Middle Earth should have abandoned the gold specie standard and adopted paper currency to reduce the deflationary drag that Smaug's monetary tightness produced. Unfortunately though "the lack of a central bank, or indeed any but the most rudimentary monetary institutions, was a major obstacle to currency reform". The comments are worth reading too – was Middle Earth an Optimal Currency Area? Before Smaug arrived, were the Dwarves running Middle Earth like a petro-state?

SPOILER ALERT So Smaug dies in the end, and the gold was released into Middle Earth's money supply. Was there hyper-inflation as a result? Or did Nominal GDP return to trend (i.e. the "catching up" theory that has been talked about by Central Bankers like Mark Carney lately) without longer term inflation problems? If there was hyper-inflation perhaps the political instability that resulted allowed the rise of Sauron as a leader, and the subsequent world war between Men and Elves, and Orcs?

Chapter 26

Contingent capital notes – bank equity's best friend?
Stefan Isaacs – Tuesday, 15th January 2013

As investors, the majority of our time is spent pricing risk with an increasing amount of that spent trying to value optionality. We've always had to price the optionality inherent in owning certain bonds. For instance what's the likelihood of a call option sold to a bond issuer being exercised? What's the likelihood of an early refinancing, or perhaps a change of control? These and other options are both risks and opportunities that credit investors will regularly have to consider and reconsider.

Some of the more recent options that credit investors have been forced to consider are those embedded within contingent capital notes or CoCos. These aren't entirely new securities with Lloyds having exchanged bonds for CoCos back in 2009. Simplistically these 'first generation' CoCos are designed to behave like a traditional bond until a pre-defined trigger is breached. When triggered, first generation CoCo holders are forcibly converted into equity at pre-determined pricing, aiding the bank with its recapitalisation efforts. These instruments have found favour with the regulator not least because traditional subordinate capital instruments proved themselves almost entirely ineffective in providing loss absorbing capital.

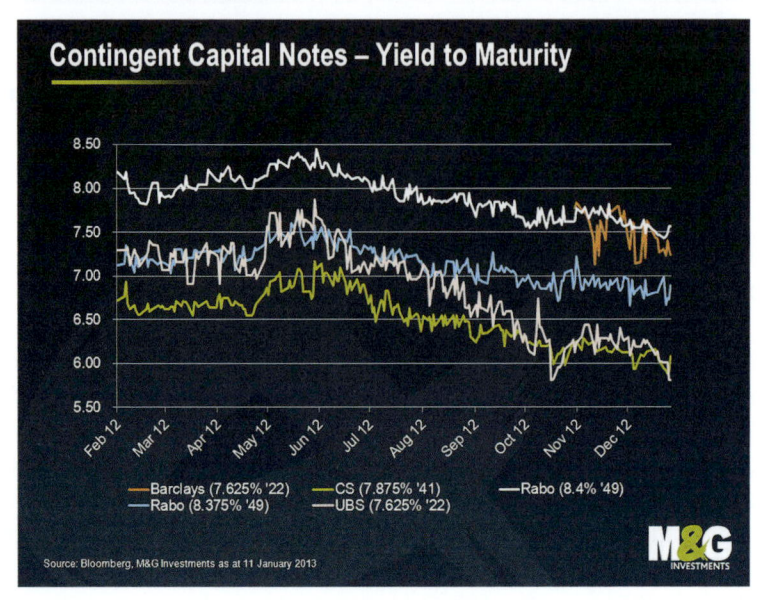

However, since the issuance in 2009 the market has moved on somewhat and a new breed of CoCo has since emerged. Many of these newer instruments (see previous chart) are designed to be written off entirely in the event of a trigger without the conversion into equity discussed here. This optionality has two obvious implications. Firstly, given that investors are written down to zero without equity conversion, any prospect of participating in a future recovery becomes null and void. Secondly (with the caveat that the quantum of issuance remains small for now), the prospect of a bond essentially performing the role of a non dilutive emergency rights issue has to be positive for all other stakeholders in the bank, not least common shareholders. And don't forget that the majority of these instruments will see their coupons paid before tax, further enhancing the relative value of said issuance.

Selling all this optionality does have its price, as do most things in life, but the current exuberance in credit markets may yet see CoCo investors fail to exact an adequate premium.

Chapter 27

Why we love the US dollar, and worry about EM currencies
Mike Riddell – Wednesday, 16th January 2013

The US dollar has been one of the worst performing currencies in the world in the last decade, but we think it is ripe for a rally. We expect the US dollar's correlation with risky assets to steadily change (in fact this is already happening). We believe that the US monetary policy transmission mechanism is actually working fine. We are bullish on US growth, particularly in relation to other regions. The Federal Reserve appears behind the curve, but a number of policymakers are increasingly realising this. And following a prolonged period of big underperformance, the US dollar is looking fundamentally cheap, especially in relation to some emerging market currencies.

The main push back we hear regarding our bullish US dollar view is that by being long US dollar you're basically being short of risky assets. Lately this has been true; the US dollar has tended to rally sharply when large banks are blowing up or the Eurozone is threatening to fall apart, and has tended to perform poorly when everything looks alright again.

However the US dollar has not always had this risk on/risk off ("RoRo") characteristic. The first chart on the next page plots the US Dollar Index (a general international value of the US Dollar) against the MSCI World equity Index, and the chart immediately following shows the rolling two year correlation of the two indices with some rough annotations (usual causation/correlation disclaimer applies).

It's noticeable that the RoRo qualities of the US Dollar have weakened in the last two years, presumably on the back of a broader risk rally at a time when investors and central banks have been dumping/diversifying away from euro denominated assets. Going further back, it's also apparent that the US dollar has not always been a 'risk off currency', where a major factor appears to be Fed Funds rate cycles.

The US dollar has definitely not always been a 'risk off' currency

MSCI World Index (log scale) vs US Dollar index, 1981-2013

2-year rolling correlation between MSCI World Index and US Dollar Index (DXY)

www.bondvigilantes.com

Source: Bloomberg, as at 8 January 2013.

M&G Investments

On the point of Fed Funds rate cycles, we think that the Federal Reserve continues to be behind the curve, or following the Federal Reserve's change in communication, it's perhaps more accurate to say that the market is behind the curve. We spent much of last year discussing how the US housing market was starting to take off, which is evidence that the monetary policy transmission mechanism is no longer broken. But it's interesting to consider the following chart – wherever the Fed Funds rate has gone in the last four decades, unemployment eventually follows. The shock to the US economy in 2008 was obviously huge, but this cycle doesn't actually look that different to previous ones.

The current trajectory suggests that the US unemployment rate could hit 6.5% sometime in the middle of next year, an eventuality that would surely see US Treasuries sell off violently. There are eerie echoes of 1994, when the Fed hiked rates from 3% in January 1994 to 6% in February 1995 with very little prior warning; investors were caught with their pants down and markets were given a jolly good spanking (the 10 year US Treasury yield had fallen to 5.2% in late 1993 but a year later peaked at 8%).

It's likely that the US dollar would appreciate as US yields jumped if you assume that hikes in the Fed Funds rate won't be replicated around the world. This seems a relatively safe assumption given the Japanese devaluation rhetoric and continuing mess in Europe (Eurozone unemployment recently hit a record high of 11.5%, while the UK is likely to have experienced negative growth in Q4). That said, the US dollar surprisingly depreciated versus the Japanese yen and a number of European currencies in 1994, prompting then Fed chairman Alan Greenspan to state that the US dollar was weaker than it should be – Greenspan's wish was granted from 1995-2000 though, as the US dollar was supported by factors such as high relative real interest rates, a US productivity surge, EM crises and Japanese stagnation.

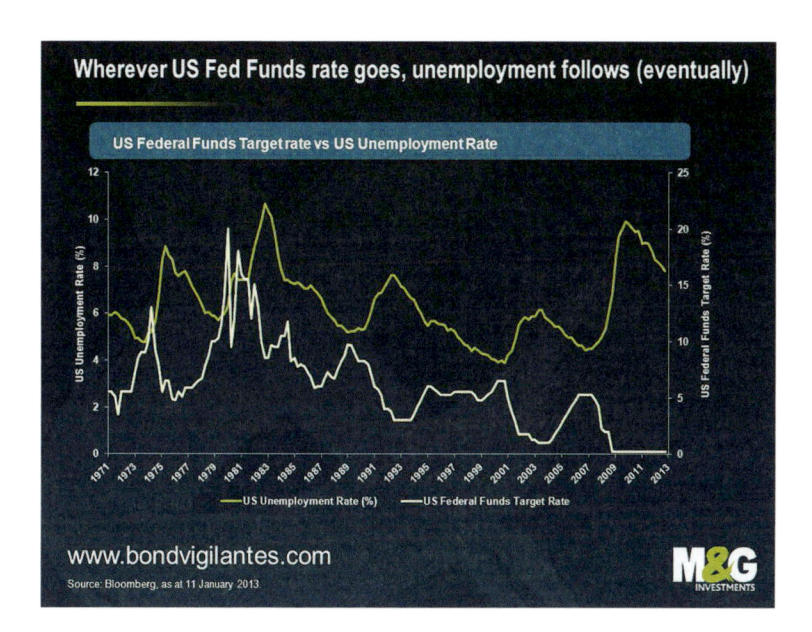

Wherever US Fed Funds rate goes, unemployment follows (eventually)

US Federal Funds Target rate vs US Unemployment Rate

www.bondvigilantes.com
Source: Bloomberg, as at 11 January 2013
M&G INVESTMENTS

Another plus point for the US dollar is that the horrendous performance of the currency over the last decade has left the US economy looking competitive. Last February I wrote about how some manufacturers were moving operations from China to Mexico to take advantage of the dramatic increase in Mexico's relative competitiveness. I've since heard a number of anecdotes – admittedly the weakest form of evidence – about manufacturers also relocating back to the US.

The conclusion from the next chart is that such behaviour makes a lot of sense. It shows the relative performance of real effective exchange rates, which is a measure of a country's trade weighted exchange rate adjusted for inflation. Real effective exchange rate measurement is imprecise since inflation data can be unreliable (eg Argentina) and calculations can vary depending upon the particular measure of inflation used (eg CPI, PPI, export price indices, core inflation, unit labour costs). The starting point can also make a lot of difference when using a time series – I've chosen 1994, which is immediately after China's 50% devaluation*, but before the Latin American and Asian financial crises.

But while the absolute level of some of the exchange rates in the next chart need to be treated with a pinch of salt, the direction of travel should give a relatively unbiased view. The US dollar (thick red line) is looking very competitive versus the majority of emerging market currencies.

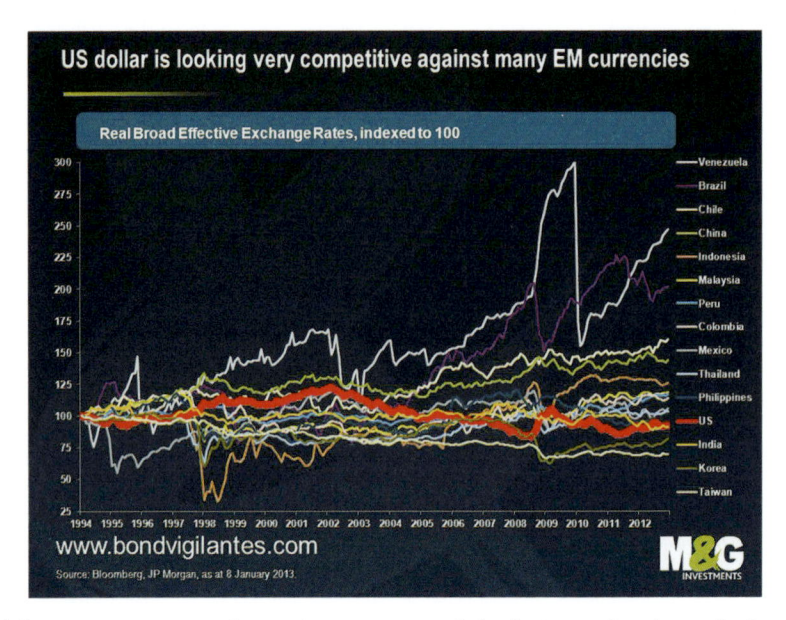

US dollar is looking very competitive against many EM currencies

Real Broad Effective Exchange Rates, indexed to 100

Venezuela, Brazil, Chile, China, Indonesia, Malaysia, Peru, Colombia, Mexico, Thailand, Philippines, US, India, Korea, Taiwan

www.bondvigilantes.com

Source: Bloomberg, JP Morgan, as at 8 January 2013.

M&G INVESTMENTS

Meanwhile a surprising – and worrying – aspect of the last year has been that emerging market FX reserve growth appears to have stalled. Part of this can be explained by weaker global demand resulting in weaker EM exports. Part of this can be explained by EM countries gradually rebalancing their growth models away from exports and towards domestic consumption, the result of which means a narrowing of the global current account imbalances.

However, lower FX reserve growth is not at all consistent with EM countries continuing to receive large Foreign Domestic Investment (FDI) and record portfolio inflows – you'd expect to see reserves jump. And neither is lower FX reserve growth consistent with the US dollar's performance over the past year – a slowdown in FX reserve accumulation is typically synonymous with US dollar strength because FX reserves are typically measured in US dollars, and non-US dollar denominated assets would fall in value when measured in US dollar terms. Yet the US dollar has been broadly flat and if anything weaker over this period.

It is a very dangerous combination to have flat or falling export growth combined with flat or falling FX reserve growth combined with a significant appreciation in real effective exchange rates. In a study of prior academic literature, Frankel and Saravelos (2009) find that measures of FX reserves and real effective exchange rates stand out as easily the most important lead indicators of financial crises. Note that other lead indicators with strong predictive powers were found to be credit growth, GDP and current account measures, and a number of EM countries are looking shaky on these measures too.

Concerns around stalling FX reserve growth are tempered by the fact that reserves in many countries are at or close to record highs. But while high levels of FX reserves do act as a cushion for the individual country during a crisis, FX reserve accumulation can also have significant downside risks for the individual country (eg real estate bubbles, credit bubbles, misallocation of domestic banks' lending – sound familiar?). Much has also been written about the risks to the global financial system** as a whole and I'd recommend this 2006 ECB paper for a good overview. I'd add that while countries with high levels of FX reserves allow countries to weather crises better, they don't make countries immune to crises; despite high levels of FX reserves, Taiwan still saw its currency slump 20% against the US dollar in 1997.

When is the US dollar likely to appreciate, or EM currencies depreciate? EM debt crises since the 1980s have tended to follow periods of rising Fed Funds rate and/or US dollar strength, so this would suggest it's not imminent. However I was presenting at a conference last month and found a kindred spirit in CLSA's Russell Napier, who has near identical concerns about EM debt, and his view is that there have been many examples where bubbles have burst before the risk free rate rises – domestic overinvestment, lending to poor credits, commodity price declines and capital exodus can cause debt crises independent of external factors.

Either way, the reason that EM FX reserves are not increasing (see the following charts) at a time when EM currencies aren't strengthening seems most likely to be because EM currencies are at best no longer cheap, and at worst have become overvalued. Which is another reason to like the US dollar right now.

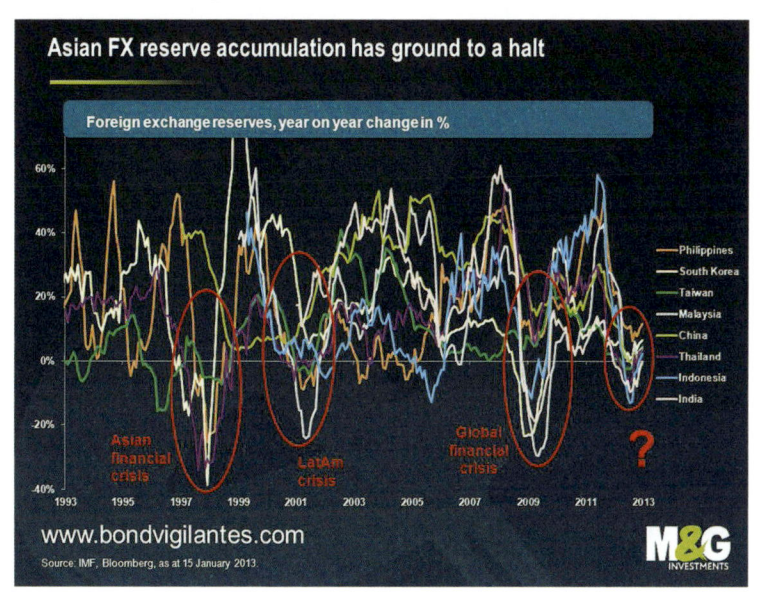

Latin America FX reserve growth has weakened

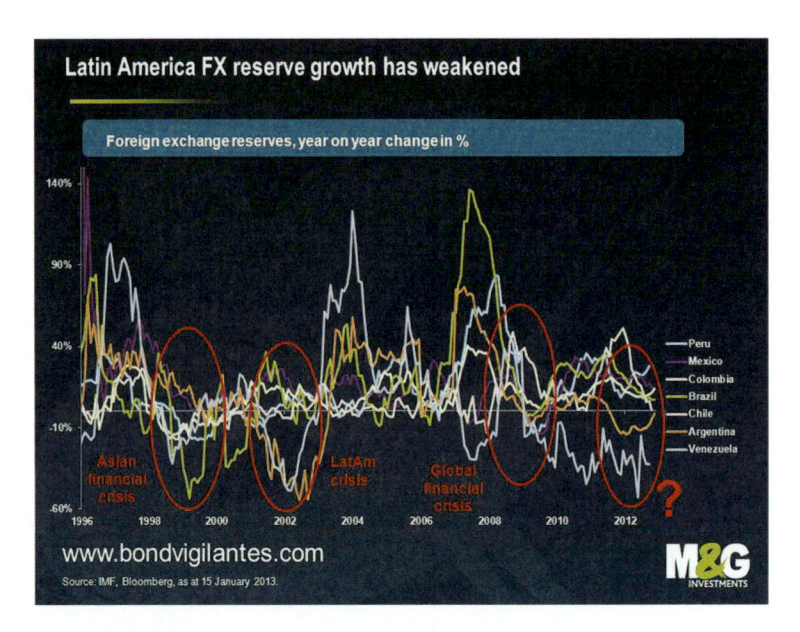

Foreign exchange reserves, year on year change in %

Source: IMF, Bloomberg, as at 15 January 2013.
www.bondvigilantes.com — M&G Investments

* China's devaluation in 1994 is widely cited as being one of the triggers for the 1997 Asian financial crisis. If you consider that Japan is currently more important to many Asian countries' trade now than China was in 1993, could a big yen devaluation wreak havoc on the region in the same way? A counterargument could be that a big yen sell-off would encourage Japanese savings to flood into its trade partners' capital markets – capital controls meant this wasn't possible following China's devaluation.

** Ben Bernanke's global savings glut hypothesis argues that excess global savings have been responsible for lower government bond yields. The fact that EM FX reserves have stalled suggests that these countries have not been net buyers of US Treasuries in the last year. The baton had been taken on by countries such as Switzerland and Denmark, whose FX interventions to maintain their respective currency pegs resulted in rapid FX reserve increases and strong support for core government bonds, but upwards pressure on these countries' exchange rates has recently greatly reduced and their reserves are no longer growing either. That really just leaves the GCC countries, whose FX reserves are largely a function of the oil price. Yields on core government bonds would presumably therefore be significantly higher were it not for large scale domestic central bank purchases.

Chapter 28

Europe, China and shale gas: euphoria or rejection?
Nicolo Carpaneda – Wednesday, 20th February 2013

It is commonly believed that – thanks to shale oil and gas discoveries in the US over the past couple of decades – the US is on a path towards energy self-sufficiency. Subsequent cheaper gas prices are boosting competitiveness in some domestic industries, starting from bulk chemicals and primary metals, by lowering the costs of both raw materials and energy.

Gas production in the US

The well known rise of shale gas in US – Trillion cubic feet (Tcf) per year

- Non-associated onshore
- Non-associated offshore
- Shale gas
- Associated with oil
- Alaska
- Coalbed methane
- Tight gas

www.bondvigilantes.com

Source: M&G, EIA as at 1 February 2013

Gas prices: a diverging trend

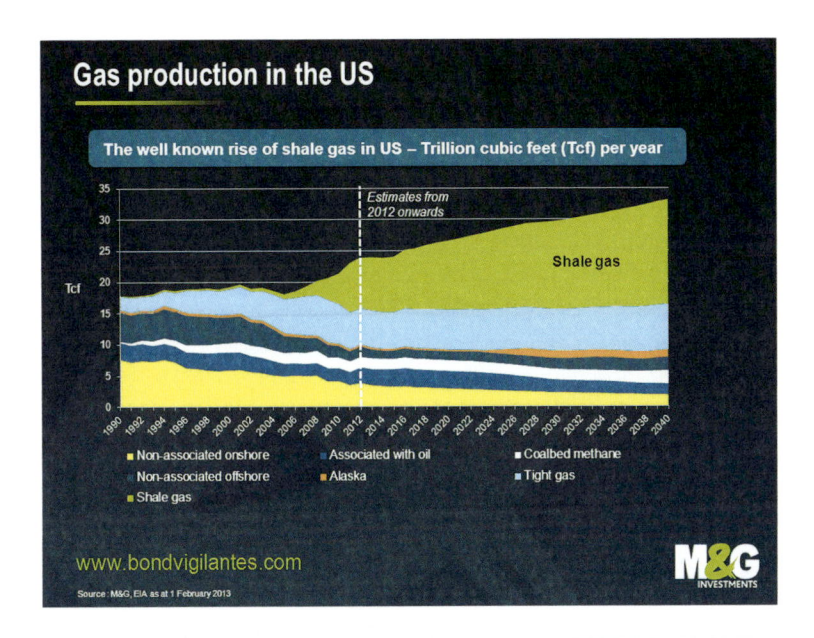

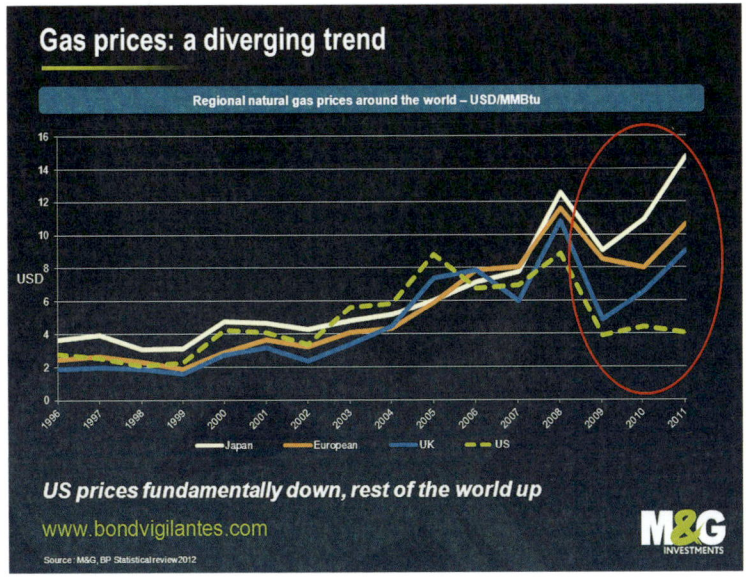

Regional natural gas prices around the world – USD/MMBtu

Japan — European — UK — US

US prices fundamentally down, rest of the world up

www.bondvigilantes.com

Source: M&G, BP Statistical review 2012

But will the US and its domestic companies be forever the only beneficiaries of cheap gas, as many believe? In Davos in January 2013, Royal Dutch Shell PLC signed a 50-year profit sharing deal with Ukraine to explore and drill for shale gas and oil. In fact, shale formations are not a prerogative of the US. Several countries in Europe and Africa have significant shale gas reserves (France, UK, Poland, Germany, Turkey, Ukraine, South Africa, Morocco, Libya, Algeria), and some other countries around the world too (Chile, Canada, Mexico, China, Australia, Argentina and Brazil). Preliminary research has shown that there are 32 countries with more than six times the amount of technically recoverable shale gas than the US. It will be key to understand which ones will prove of high "quality": in fact US shale basins tend to have rocks closer to the surface (easier to reach) and more porous (where gas is easier to extract), while foreign reserves tend to be deep and harder to reach (therefore more technically challenging and expensive).

Currently in Europe the shale gas debate is divided between euphoria and total rejection. A drilling procedure called "fracking" sees a cocktail of water, sand and some chemicals pumped into a well under high pressure to force the gas from the rocks. Early drillings in Netherlands and Luxembourg were suspended because of environmental fears and contrarian public opinion. In France, fracking is now banned, while in Germany opposition to Angela Merkel is creating a good deal of noise around this topic. In Poland, ExxonMobil just walked away from preliminary explorations that didn't deliver the expected results and, in Spain, the Basque local government has announced that there is 185 billion cubic meters of shale gas in the Gran Enara field with €40m invested in exploration.

No rapid breakthroughs are expected though. Exploiting shale gas reserves in Europe might be a long, technically difficult, politically tricky and also legally complex procedure, due to questions over property rights – determining who can drill and where. But the need to look for security of supply and cheaper energy sources remains. In particular, as Orlando Finzi – our M&G credit research director covering the energy sector – was telling me the other day, the latter is the subject of a key debate at the moment: EU long-term gas contracts which supply most of the gas to Europe have prices linked to oil, but this might all change with recent negotiations between buyers and sellers seeing a modest dilution of the oil linkage. RWE, the German utility, is seeking full removal of oil price linkage in its Gazprom contract via arbitration courts. Where will European prices head to then? If lower, the idea of extracting shale gas may become less attractive than the existing natural gas options. If prices continue to rise, who knows? Also, the need to reduce CO_2 emissions may push towards unexplored scenarios. Some think that the current CO_2 emissions "cap and trade" system is disappointing (see the chart below): too many permits in the market and therefore no incentives to cut emissions.

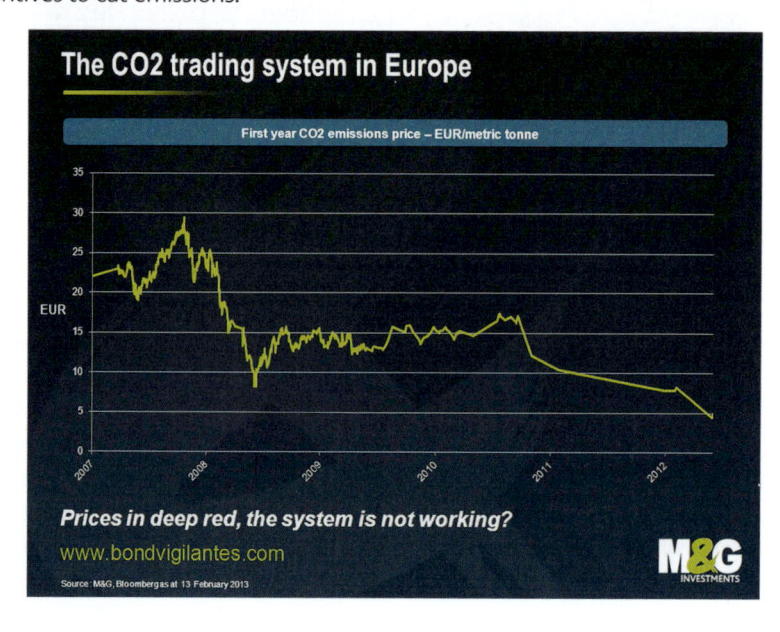

The CO_2 trading system in Europe

First year CO_2 emissions price – EUR/metric tonne

Prices in deep red, the system is not working?

www.bondvigilantes.com

Source: M&G, Bloomberg as at 13 February 2013

Gas is a great alternative to other fossil fuels (and coal specifically, but also oil) to both cut down emissions and potentially to cover when renewables do not generate (for example, wind turbines in a period of no wind). Will European countries, eventually strangled by economic stagnation, fearful of security of supply and in need to cut emissions, find a way to overcome multiple issues to give a boost to shale gas exploration? In a positive political climate, what if UK and Spain will be quick and successful in exploiting their shale gas resources? Will this new energy source support growth, help employment in weak economies and make local companies more competitive in certain industries?

More euphoria is engulfing China. China's revolution in shale gas is considered by some more a distant dream than a work-in-progress, but there are many new developments worth considering. Chinese public opinion has recently been shaken by the terrible air quality in many cities. China, estimated to have the biggest reserves in the world (50% more than the US as per an early research by EIA) is explicitly moving towards cleaner energy sources and has an incredible appetite for energy (and gas specifically, now fully imported). Even if little information exists, Petrochina, which is currently undertaking the development of shale gas in Alberta via a partnership with a Canadian company, has started shale gas drillings around China. Total is also preparing to sign an agreement, possibly within a few days, with a Chinese partner to explore for shale gas in the country. Furthermore, China just announced that 16 (only domestic) companies won a second round of bidding to explore 19 shale gas blocks around central China, agreeing to invest $2 bn over the coming years. The key issue also in China – and in some other countries such as Argentina and Mexico – will be to understand which technology to use and how to unlock reserves that are very difficult and expensive to reach for geological reasons: I would expect quicker progress only with foreign technology. But local energy needs, resolute politics and a more benign public opinion – now suffocated by smog – make the Chinese case stronger than Europe. If shale reserves are exploited quicker than expected, will China return to the good old days of double digit GDP growth? Will Chinese companies – which are losing their cost leadership position to neighbouring countries such as Vietnam and Indonesia or back to the US – find in local shale gas a new source of sustainable competitive advantage in the next ten years? Will the predicted shift of production and employment back to the US be a temporary adjustment only?

Reading the future of energy remains very complex. The prospects of shale gas developments outside North America will depend to a large extent on politics and developments in international gas markets, such as the future relationship between demand and supply, price relations (Liquified Natural Gas vs. pipelines for example) and movements, costs of production, shape of climate policies (it's difficult to see how other countries such as Argentina, for example, will be able to persuade foreign companies to help it develop its reserves while it has been busy expropriating assets) and specific local challenges. But imagine a not-so-remote scenario at this point: US shale gas may return less than expected over the long term (as the EIA always reports, the long-term production profiles of US shale wells and their estimated ultimate recovery of oil and natural gas are uncertain), while China and Europe may start exploiting shale reserves quicker, thus reshaping energy pricing dynamics or even the balance of world trade and geopolitics.

Chapter 29

If China's economy rebalances and growth slows, as it surely must, then who's screwed?
Mike Riddell – Friday, 1st March 2013

OK so that wasn't the exact title of the IMF's paper from the end of last year – it was Investment-Led Growth in China: Global Spillovers – but you get the gist.

First a little preamble. Many people who were China bears last year have become less bearish or even outright bullish, no doubt on the back of an improvement in Chinese economic data and a corresponding rally in China's equity markets. But I don't think the better data should inspire confidence, and you could actually argue the opposite; the growth rebound in China is likely due to yet more government-encouraged unproductive and unprofitable lending. The quality of China's growth has become increasingly poor, and the rate of growth is utterly unsustainable. The bigger the bubble, the bigger the eventual bust.

Morgan Stanley's Ruchir Sharma wrote a piece in the Wall Street Journal this week about how China's total and private debt has exploded to over 200% of GDP, and how the Bank of International Settlements has previously found that 'if private debt as a share of GDP accelerates to a level 6% higher than its trend over the previous decade, the acceleration is an early warning of serious financial distress. In China, private debt as a share of GDP is now 12% above its previous trend, and above the peak levels seen before credit crises hit Japan in 1989, Korea in 1997, the US in 2007 and Spain in 2008'. There's reference to this article among others in a good summary of China's near unprecedented credit binge at FT Alphaville.

The IMF has long been warning of the threat posed to global financial stability by the great Chinese credit bubble, and their study on global spillovers referenced above makes interesting reading. They estimate that for each percentage point deceleration in China's investment growth, 0.5-0.9% is subtracted from GDP growth in regional supply chain economies such as Taiwan, Korea and Malaysia. Commodity producers such as Chile and Saudi Arabia are also likely to suffer substantial growth declines while countries such as Canada and Brazil would experience 'somewhat significant output loss and slowdown'. There would be 'a substantial impact on capital goods manufacturing economies such as Germany and Japan', and one year after the shock, commodity prices, especially metal prices, could fall by 0.8-2.2% from the baseline levels for every 1% drop in China's investment rate.

So what kind of correction in China's investment growth rate is likely? China's growth in fixed investment from 2002-2011 was 13.5% per year, a rate that greatly exceeded China's GDP growth rate and meant that fixed investment is now running at about 50% of China's GDP. No major countries have sustained such a high investment rate as a percentage of GDP – since 1960, the only countries to have managed a ratio of more than 50% for at least two consecutive years are Republic of Congo 1960-61, Botswana 1971-73, Gabon 1974-77, Mongolia 1981-87, Kiribati 1982-83 and 1985-90, St Kitts & Nevis 1988-90, Lesotho 1989-97, Equatorial Guinea 1994-98 and 2000-01, Bhutan 2001-04, Azerbaijan 2003-04, Chad 2002-03, and Turkmenistan 2009-10.

Judging by other countries at China's stage of development, a more reasonable investment/GDP ratio is maybe 30-35%. Achieving this ratio will require a sharp drop in China's investment growth rate to perhaps mid-single digits, and if China's slowdown proves to be hard rather than soft, then the investment rate will likely fall even further (taking two other post bubble economies in the region, Japanese investment growth has been negligible since the early 1990s, while Korean investment growth has averaged low single digits since the mid-1990s). According to the IMF's model then, a drop in Chinese investment growth from 13.5% to 4.5% implies a 4%-7.2% hit to the GDP of countries such as Taiwan, Korea and Malaysia. Some commodity prices would fall almost 20%. Ouch. And if you want to get extra gloomy, you can also consider that such a large economic shock would also be accompanied by a reversal of the huge decade-long EM equity and bond inflows to the region, which is something else that the IMF has repeatedly warned about. It's quite easy to see how a Chinese rebalancing and slowdown can develop into an Asian/EM financial crisis.

Finally it's worth reproducing a chart I used in a note from last year demonstrating what happened to Japan's GDP growth rate as it rebalanced away from an investment-led model and towards more of a consumption based model in the 1970s-80s (countries such as Thailand and Korea followed a very similar path 20 years later). When investment as a percentage of GDP falls, then the GDP growth rate falls too. Everyone accepts that China must reduce investment and increase consumption, but few people acknowledge that this means that China's GDP growth rate will slow considerably.

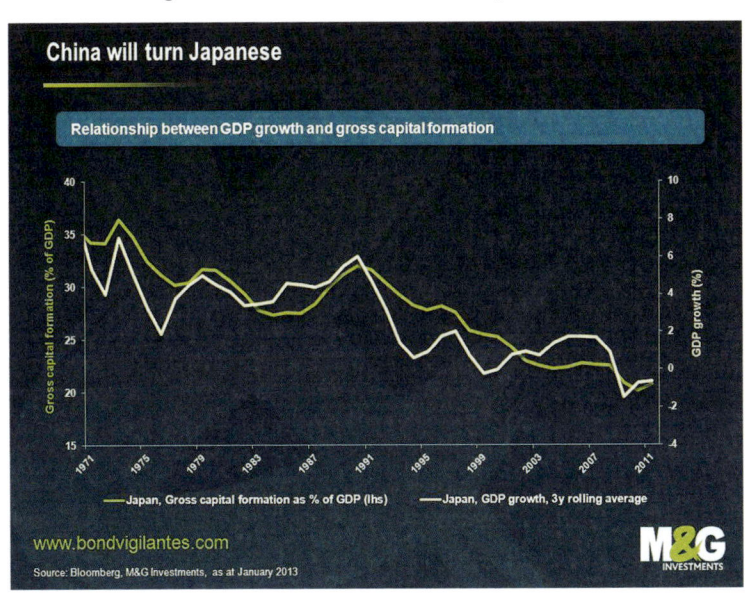

Chapter 30

Insane in the brain. Dangerous precedents being set in Cyprus
Stefan Isaacs – Monday, 18th March 2013

Depositors in Cypriot banks awoke on Saturday morning to learn a harsh lesson. A guarantee is only as strong as your counterparty. With the Cypriot banking system requiring €10-12 billion of bailout funds – some 60% of GDP – the government has been forced to accept burden sharing with depositors. Depositors who went to bed Friday night believing their savings were safe awoke Saturday to find that it has been proposed that those with deposits below €100k in the bank will be "taxed" at 6.75%; those with deposits above €100k will be "taxed" at 9.9%, contributing approximately €6bn to the bank bailout in total. This is regardless of supposed depositor insurance schemes. Depositors will receive equity in their respective banks by way of compensation and potentially bonds entitling those who leave their money in the banks for 2 years to a share of Cyprus' future gas revenues. The remaining €4-6 billion will likely come from the Troika.

If press reports are to be believed this was a 'take it or leave it offer' from the Troika with German and Finnish finance ministers unwilling to go to their respective parliaments without depositor burden sharing. This highlights the very real current challenges of domestic politics within the European Economic and Monetary Union and raises further issues.

Firstly, there are significant political challenges to be faced. Domestic opposition to this deal is likely to be significant, not least as it will be seen to be disproportionately harsh on domestic savers – who had believed their deposits were protected up to €100k, and favourable to wealthy non-Cypriot depositors who reportedly hold huge sums offshore in the banks. It can be argued that those with over €100k in deposits with the banks should bear the brunt of any proposed bail-in. With a small parliamentary majority, the Cypriot government may struggle to pass the necessary legislation. Approval will also need to be sought from Eurozone member states.

Secondly, alongside the recent expropriation of junior bond holders at SNS Reaal the attitude towards tax funded bailouts appears to be hardening. Whilst this crisis has already witnessed both equity and debt written down, the rubicon of depositor burden sharing has now been crossed. Precedent now exists for this approach over the socialisation of losses across the Eurozone as a whole. Whilst the Troika will endeavour to play its significance down, unintended consequences may still materialise.

Thirdly, the Cypriot situation serves as a reminder of the current fragmented approach of depositor guarantee schemes across Europe. Depositor guarantees are only as strong as the sovereigns providing them. In the case of Cyprus with a banking system seven times the size of its economy, clearly those guarantees were worth very little. With depositor rates currently paying very little across Europe it is unlikely to take much to prompt a change in investor behaviour.

Fourthly, it raises real questions about depositor preference. With only circa €2bn of Cypriot bank debt outstanding, policymakers have judged this too small in and of itself to recapitalise the banking system. That may be true. However by favouring senior debt over depositors it does beg the question whether the individual on the street is in theory better off owning higher yielding bank debt than depositing cash.

Fifthly, the ECB has apparently threatened that if the measures are not agreed, then it would withdraw European Liquidity Assistance (ELA) funding for Laiki Bank, Cyprus' second largest bank, leaving the Cypriot sovereign with the bill for the entire banking sector and having to pay out on deposit insurance in full. This highlights the extent to which a number of banks in Europe remain reliant on ECB funding, and that if that funding is withdrawn then their collapse is inevitable.

Finally, we have yet another example of a country being forced to face a stark choice between ceding sovereignty to Brussels or facing financial ruin. The Eurozone project continues to ask a great deal of its citizens. Bailouts don't – and won't – come cheap.

The Cyprus deal will be in the headlines for the next few days. We can't help but think that the markets will be listening to Cypress Hill – Insane In The Brain for the next week or so. Maybe the Troika should too.

Chapter 31

I predict a CypRIOT: Three major implications for the European and UK banking systems
Ben Lord – Wednesday 20th March 2013

Stefan blogged earlier this week about the landmark sovereign bailout occurring in Cyprus, and about some of the interesting issues this raises. Sure enough, the parliament did not approve the package in the form talked about at the weekend. The reason? The taxes were felt too painful for the poor and too lenient for the more wealthy. This harks back to a blog I wrote about a couple of years ago, and goes to reiterate the issues we discussed then. However, for now I wanted to highlight some of the issues that this raises more specifically for the European banking system at large.

Firstly, depositors were presumed to be guaranteed by governments up to at least €100,000 in Europe. Last weekend, that notion was dealt a brutal blow by the Cypriot situation. However, it feels to us as though the main reason for the parliamentary delays is that deposit guarantees could and should remain in place – or at least to a greater extent than was implied in the original bailout package. This package stated that those people with deposits of less than €100,000 would pay a 6.75% tax, whilst those with more than this amount would be taxed at 9.9%. The politicians that have delayed the approval of the rescue package want to see greater amounts of the burden borne by the wealthier (those with more than €100,000, and perhaps an even higher rate borne by those with greater amounts than, say, €500,000 in deposits), and so lesser amounts of the burden borne by those with small amounts of deposits.

My guess is that this is the key issue here. If the tax rates are not changed, then I would expect to see some significant moves in Spanish, Italian and other peripheral deposit flows and movements. As a risk, this must not be underestimated by the Troika. Why not maintain the deposit guarantee and generate the amount raised by the taxes, through taxing more on those with more than €100,000, more still on those with more than €250,000, and more still on those with more than €500,000?

Secondly, subordinated debt bail-in is a key part of the package, and without it one senses the Troika will not part with the bailout funds needed. We have expected weaker banks in weaker regions to have to use this as a necessary tool to break the sovereign-bank link for some time now. It is now official, and being used. I would expect more of these to come.

Thirdly and finally, sovereign bailouts of banking systems where the sovereign is already in an over-levered position will no longer be tolerated. It is time to break the sovereign-bank feedback loop (as we previously wrote about here). This has to be through bail-in and burden-sharing. However, the most unpalatable part of the proposed package to us (and I guess to many riotous Cypriots) is this: up until 2007 it was believed that senior bank bondholders ranked pari passu with depositors in the event of a bank failure. And now in 2013 we learn quite vividly that in actual fact in Cyprus depositors are likely to be subordinated to a bunch of wholesale and institutional (ie banks and insurance companies) investors?

The capital stack has been turned on its head in this regard. No one used to buy senior unsecured bank debt because they thought that depositors would take losses before them. Rather, it was because the markets believed 100% in the government guarantee of depositors. The pari passu relationship of depositors and bondholders supported high valuations on senior bank bonds. Thus to be pari passu with depositors, senior bank bonds need to take the same losses as depositors are. In my opinion, this part of the proposed deal is the most disgraceful.

So, I find myself wondering how on earth a deposit tax found its way into the package. The answer to me seems to be quite simple: contagion, or the avoidance thereof. We all know that in Europe and the UK in the future (as in the US already), senior bank bonds will be bail-in-able or writedownable if a bank fails or gets into difficulty. We were originally told that the date for senior bank bond bail-in in Europe would be 2018, although there has recently been much talk about bringing this forward to the beginning of 2015. It has long struck me that this should be the favoured route out of the bank-sovereign interconnectedness problem in Europe: continue to promote and enable senior issuance in Europe by banks, and then implement a higher level piece of legislation that at some date in the future makes all debt in the Eurozone and UK writedownable.

No matter how small Cyprus is relative to the rest of the Eurozone, if the Troika had forced senior bank bondholders to accept losses before 2018 – or is it 2015? – senior bank debt spreads would have suffered significantly across Europe. Given that this is the most attractive funding market for banks at the moment, as it is still cheap to issue from a bank's perspective, and as sovereigns do not want to have to (or cannot, in the Cyprus case) step in to take on more liabilities on behalf of their banks, the Troika has ripped up the rule book and done the insane.

I think parliamentarians in Cyprus should force a rethink on the sovereign-bank feedback loop, as well as forcing a more palatable (ie Robin Hood) sharing of the burden between smaller and larger depositors. After all, can anyone truly imagine the French, German or any core European government accepting losses for their depositors whilst a bunch of international senior bank bondholders get made whole? Our view is that depositors should be protected (at least to the guaranteed amount) over and above all wholesale creditors, whether senior or subordinated. This is the first step to break the sovereign-bank loop. The second step, only to be used in cases where there is not enough senior and subordinated debt to prevent the sovereign, and so tax-payers, from having to bail out the failed institutions, is to look at forcing losses on depositors, but with preserving the preceding guaranteed amounts of deposits. The final, most radical, and rarest, step is to have to renege on that deposit guarantee amount, so as to avoid tax-payer bailouts and increased probability of sovereign default.

Depositors across Europe are already watching Cyprus carefully. My guess is that many are starting to check the amounts they keep with any one institution or in any region. Subordinated bondholders are already aware of the risks if those banks get into difficulty, but senior bondholders in my opinion are not. These investors must ask whether the Cyprus package is likely to be copied in future cases. And they must also start to wonder if they still have until 2018 before senior bonds can be bailed in, or if it is significantly sooner.

Chapter 32

Heinz: Beans, Buffett and the return of animal spirits
Stefan Isaacs – Friday, 22nd March 2013

After years of inactivity, the combination of strong corporate balance sheets and cheap funding has sparked demand for takeover deals. The largest and highest profile deal this year has been the acquisition of H.J.Heinz by 3G Capital and Berkshire Hathaway. It is exactly the type of business that Berkshire Hathaway's Chairman and CEO Warren Buffett typically goes for: profitable growth; a very recognisable brand; and years of emerging market growth forecast in the future. Berkshire Hathaway and 3G Capital are buying Heinz for $72.50 per share, a 19 percent premium to the company's previous record high stock price at the time the deal was announced in mid-February. Including debt assumption, the transaction was valued at $28 billion. Berkshire and 3G will each put up $4.4bn in equity for the deal along with $12.2bn in debt financing. Berkshire is also buying $8bn of preferred equity that pays 9%.

Let's not beat around the bush. It's a great company. The business has seen thirty one consecutive quarters of organic growth, stable EBITDA margins, owns a number of globally recognised brands and should be well positioned for future emerging market led growth. Despite this, some are questioning whether Buffett is overpaying for Heinz. So is the price of the deal justified?

The answer, at least in part, lies with cost of debt. The pro-forma capital structure (per the offering memorandum) looks like this:

PF Capital Structure	Sources ($m)	Net Debt/PF EBITDA
Cash	-1,250	
1st Lien	10,500	3.87 x
2nd Lien	2,100	4.75 x
Rollover Notes	868	5.11 x
Total debt	12,218	5.11 x
Preferred Equity	8,000	8.46 x

Common Equity	8,240	
Total	**28,458**	

Current price talk on the first lien debt sits at $ LIBOR + 2.75% (floored at 1%) with the second lien at 4.5%. If this is finalised, the company will see an approximate blended interest cost of 3.9% on its new debt securities. Prior to the transaction, Heinz was rated as a solid investment grade business attracting a Baa2/BBB+ rating. Assuming the deal goes through, its new second lien notes are expected to be rated B1/BB-, some five notches lower than Heinz's current rating, reflecting the much higher financial leverage and structural subordination.

It's worth noting that through last year Heinz's 6.25% 2030 bonds traded in a range of 4–5%, despite the much higher rating and lower financial leverage at the time; albeit some term premium is warranted given the longer dated nature of the debt. The bonds have since sold off in recognition of the greater risk – as things stand they will remain in place.

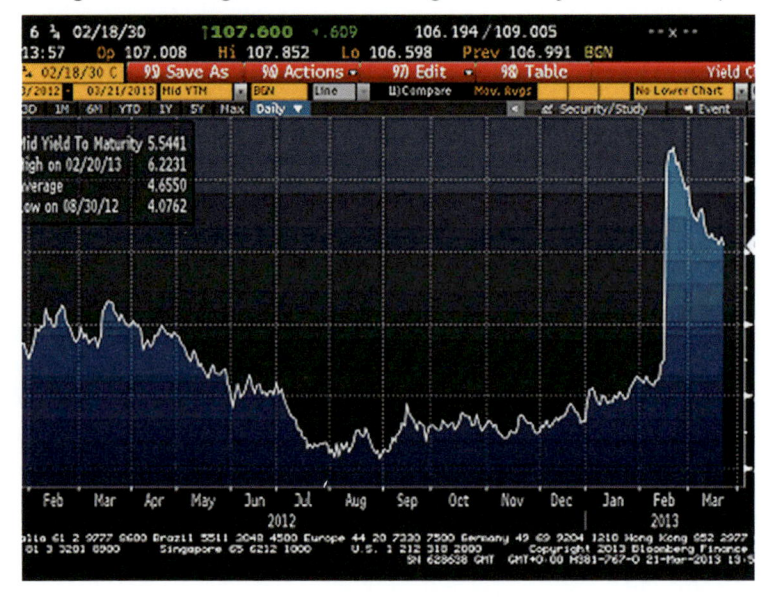

Now let's compare the price action of the proposed debt financing to the preferred equity to be owned by Berkshire Hathaway. Whilst the paper is structurally subordinate to all other debt, it still sits ahead of some $8,240bn of common equity and attracts a cash coupon (which can be deferred) of 9% vs the 3.9% weighted average above. It's also worth bearing in mind that the transaction has been structured to encourage the preferred equity to be retired, at least in part, ahead of both the first and second lien debt, potentially leaving bondholders with significantly less subordination than at day one. I'd argue that this is by far the most attractive (quasi) debt to invest in within the structure, though that is hardly surprising given that unlike Buffett, few of us can write a cheque of this magnitude.

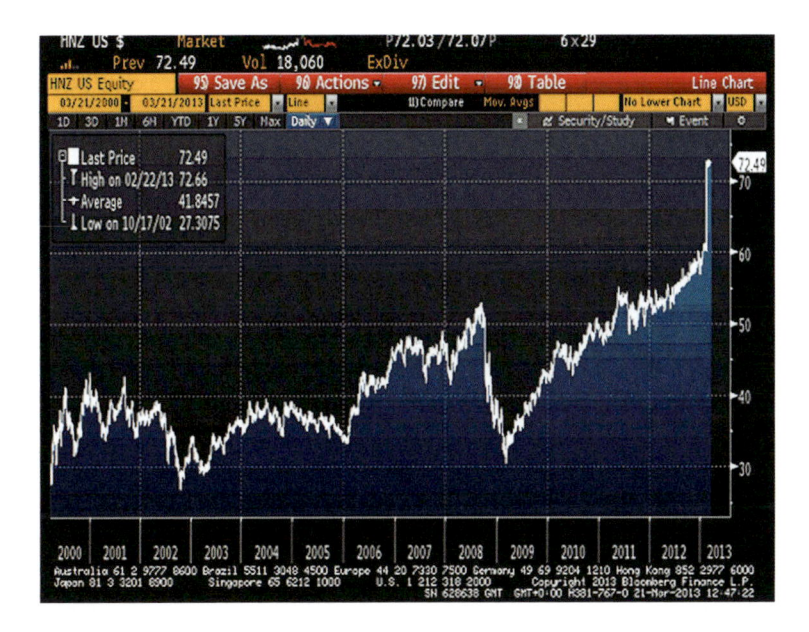

As animal spirits return and the leveraged finance community falls over itself to lend to well known companies, the likely winners in the space will be the private equity community. Whilst we are nowhere near the levels of the great private equity binge of 2004-07, the value of takeovers in 2013 is already running well ahead of 2012. After years of corporate deleveraging, we may now be entering into a period of increased M&A activity. Company managers may find that if they aren't willing to start leveraging up given the environment of extremely low borrowing costs, then investors like Buffett will do it for them.

The Heinz deal has been another recent shot across the bows of the bond market. Rising leverage has a longer term implication for credit markets, in that it is bad for credit quality. Bigger and bigger companies are clearly in play and this is something we will be keeping a very close eye on.

Chapter 33

Germany doesn't like its own fiscal union, so why would it ever agree upon a European one?
Markus Peters – Tuesday, 26th March 2013

If I asked you how the structural problems of the Eurozone may be resolved, I am sure that the suggestion of a fiscal union in which transfer payments will be made by the "rich" Northern member states to the "poor" ones in the South of Europe would rank amongst the top answers. I've been wondering for a while if the member states could ever agree upon major fiscal transfer payments and if it would indeed lead to a greater degree of convergence within the Eurozone. I feel that we have come closer to an answer to my questions this week. And I am not referring to the issues around Cyprus.

Yesterday the German federal states Hesse and Bavaria filed a lawsuit against the existing mechanism of fiscal transfer between the federal states of Germany, the so-called

"Länderfinanzausgleich". The German constitution states that the objective of this fiscal transfer mechanism is the convergence of the financial power across its federal states. The current system consists of vertical payments between the German state ("Bund") and the federal states ("Länder") as well as horizontal payments from federal state to federal state. The eligibility for transfer payment receipts is determined by an index ("Finanzkraftmesszahl") which indicates the relative financial power of the federal states. Bavaria, Baden-Württemberg and Hesse are currently the only net contributors, while Berlin is the biggest net recipient of these fiscal transfers.

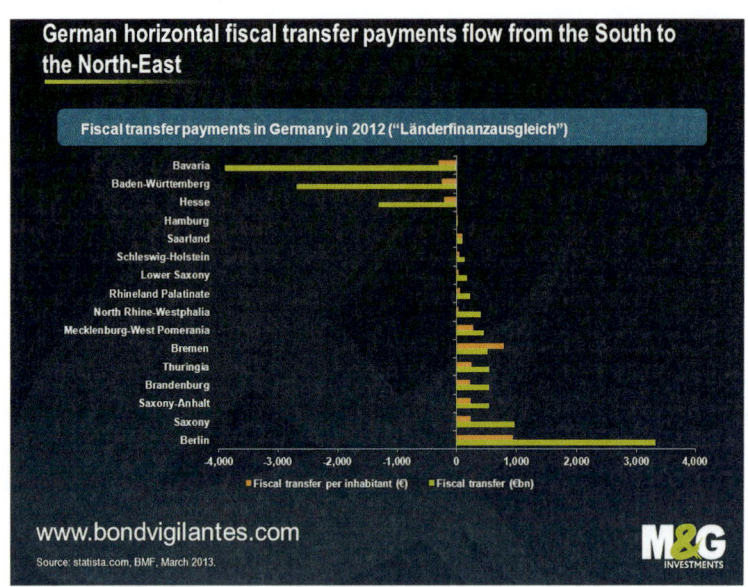

German horizontal fiscal transfer payments flow from the South to the North-East

Fiscal transfer payments in Germany in 2012 ("Länderfinanzausgleich")

- Bavaria
- Baden-Württemberg
- Hesse
- Hamburg
- Saarland
- Schleswig-Holstein
- Lower Saxony
- Rhineland Palatinate
- North Rhine-Westphalia
- Mecklenburg-West Pomerania
- Bremen
- Thuringia
- Brandenburg
- Saxony-Anhalt
- Saxony
- Berlin

■ Fiscal transfer per inhabitant (€)   ■ Fiscal transfer (€bn)

www.bondvigilantes.com

Source: statista.com, BMF, March 2013.

M&G Investments

Bavaria and Hesse argue that the current mechanism does not create any incentives for the net recipients to improve their financial position. It is said that sanctions for fiscal mismanagement are missing, while the net contributors are discouraged to consolidate their finances further as long as they have to redistribute their wealth. Basically, one rich German state is arguing why it should transfer its fiscal revenues to a poor (and arguably irresponsible) German federal state. If you already see significant opposition against a redistribution mechanism of wealth within a country, how is it possible to picture Germany, the Netherlands or Finland agreeing on major fiscal transfer payments to Southern Europe? Furthermore, the implication here is that the German Constitutional Court will have to decide if a stricter central enforcement of fiscal discipline has to be institutionalised and which set of sanctions can possibly be introduced to do so. Could you see anything like this being enacted in the Eurozone in the near future, including lawsuit files from Germany, the Netherlands and Finland in response to any agreement as well as the subsequent court rulings at national and European level? In this context, it might be worth noting that the German Constitutional Court indicated last year that any further European integration, e.g. fiscal union, would require a referendum. Ultimately, German taxpayers might get to decide whether they want their tax payments to be transferred to other parts of Europe.

There remains the question about the potential long-term effect of a fiscal union.

Would fiscal transfer payments from the North to the South lead to economic and social convergence in Europe? In Germany, fiscal transfers from the South to the North-East have certainly helped these federal states to converge in terms of their financial power and standard of living since the German unification in 1990. Nevertheless, after 23 years of fiscal transfer payments, the economic situation in these states remains highly unequal. For instance, the German unemployment rate varies significantly across federal states. While the unemployment rate in Mecklenburg-West Pomerania stands at around 14%, it is nearly as low as 4% in Bavaria and Baden-Württemberg. And the historic ties of companies, the geographical location and different geostructural fundamentals, infrastructure disparities, qualitative differences between educational and research institutions and many other factors might prevent them to ever fully converge.

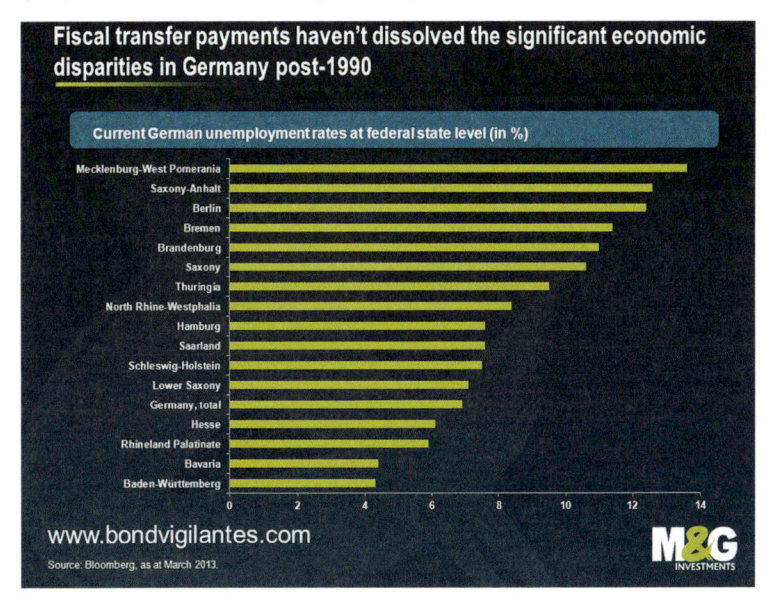

Fiscal transfer payments haven't dissolved the significant economic disparities in Germany post-1990

Current German unemployment rates at federal state level (in %)

Federal State	Unemployment Rate (%)
Mecklenburg-West Pomerania	~13.5
Saxony-Anhalt	~12.5
Berlin	~12
Bremen	~11.5
Brandenburg	~10.5
Saxony	~10
Thuringia	~9
North Rhine-Westphalia	~8.5
Hamburg	~7.5
Saarland	~7.5
Schleswig-Holstein	~7
Lower Saxony	~7
Germany, total	~7
Hesse	~6
Rhineland Palatinate	~5.5
Bavaria	~4
Baden-Württemberg	~4

www.bondvigilantes.com
Source: Bloomberg, as at March 2013.
M&G INVESTMENTS

This is the crux of the Eurozone matter for me. Only if we accept the fact that full convergence and homogeneity in Europe will not be achievable – even within a fiscal union – we may become sufficiently pragmatic to deal with the Eurozone issues. We might finally arrive at the conclusion that we could be able to improve the economic prosperity and dismantle some social stress in the periphery, but we will not make these economies as competitive and prosperous as Northern Europe as a whole. Take the US as an example. No one expects the standard of living, the average income level and economic competitiveness to be anyhow equal or homogenous across the country. Despite a long established currency and fiscal union, the economic situation and opportunity set still varies enormously depending on whether you live in New York, Detroit, Kentucky or Las Vegas. But you can reasonably move from Detroit to Kentucky if you want or have to because the same language is spoken and partly similar traditions are followed. You certainly won't be able to say that about your move from Athens to Munich. It has been taken as a given in the US that some degree of inequality and heterogeneity is the function of a free market economy (the rest is a function of bad policy-making), and that might be one of the reasons why the US model, including monetary and fiscal union, has managed to succeed.

This would be an inconvenient and unpopular insight in Europe which would fundamentally question the current ambitions of the European convergence project. If you discount the possible long-term return of the Eurozone to its member states because of a lack of German support for a fiscal union, you might want to ask where the Euro project is heading.

Chapter 34

Old Lady sells her bonds
Richard Woolnough – Monday, 15th April 2013

Back in 2009 the Bank of England (the Old Lady of Threadneedle Street) began buying a portfolio of investment grade bonds to provide funding to UK corporates, to aid liquidity in the corporate bond market and to supplement their QE purchases of gilts. Last Friday this investor sold its last corporate bonds.

This has been a great success from a profit point of view. The chart overleaf shows the total return of an index of non-financial corporate bonds over the period of the bank's purchases and sales as well as an indication of their total holdings.

I believe its actions helped stabilise the corporate bond market in the UK by providing a backstop bid, therefore helping to reduce the cost of funding at the margin for issuers, and would have added to the effects of QE. However, empirically measuring these effects is hard to do – corporate bond markets that experienced no domestic support from their central banks appear to have performed similarly, and the debate on the true effectiveness of QE remains.

What is the primary lesson we have learned? I think it is that state intervention can work where markets are priced inefficiently. This is illustrated by the large profits the bank has made by buying an out of favour asset class from the private sector. It is probably a good base to have the state intervene where markets are inefficient, for example in areas such as healthcare, defence, law and order, and infrastructure. The danger comes when the state interferes to the detriment of an efficient market. From an economic point of view, aggressive trade barriers are the first thing that comes to mind where there would be a great deal of consensus from the left and right side of politics. Other actions may depend on your economic or political view. The best current example of this is the single European currency experiment. Does it aid a free market via price transparency and low transaction costs, or does it hinder efficiency by having one single interest rate and exchange rate for such diverse economies ?

The Old Lady's portfolio of corporates has served her and the UK well because she bought them at cheap levels from distressed sellers. Unfortunately, this investor has a significantly bigger portfolio of gilts. The carry and mark to market on these looks great. However, turning this unrealised gain into a realised profit still remains a challenge. If she comes to sell, her position is likely to drive the market against her.

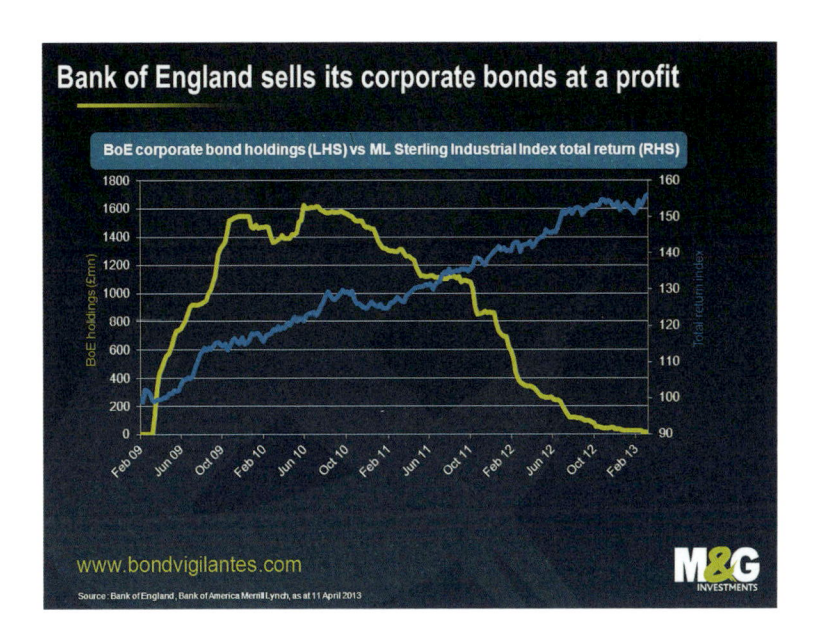

Bank of England sells its corporate bonds at a profit

BoE corporate bond holdings (LHS) vs ML Sterling Industrial Index total return (RHS)

Source: Bank of England, Bank of America Merrill Lynch, as at 11 April 2013

www.bondvigilantes.com — M&G Investments

Chapter 35

Funding for Lending – has the scheme achieved its goals?
Matthew Russell – Tuesday, 30th April 2013

As has been widely reported, last week the Bank of England and HM Treasury extended their Funding for Lending Scheme (FLS). The FLS was originally launched in July last year with the intention of stimulating lending in the real (non-financial) economy. Under this scheme a bank or building society borrows UK Treasury Bills and hands over eligible assets as collateral. The fee they are charged (effectively the interest rate) and the amount they can borrow are determined by how much they have increased their lending. The bank or building society can then either repo their T-Bills for cash or, more cheaply/likely, just use them to replace cash in their liquidity buffer. The more they lend the more they can borrow at the lower rate.

The BoE and HM Treasury have hailed the scheme as a success. But on what measure?

Today we received news that mortgage approvals had another weak month in March, increasing only slightly to 53,500. Mortgage approvals have been flat at around 50,000 per month since early 2010 and, considering last week's extension to the programme incentivises SME lending more, it doesn't look like the cheaper funding has spurred the desired increase in lending.

Mortgage lending barely changed

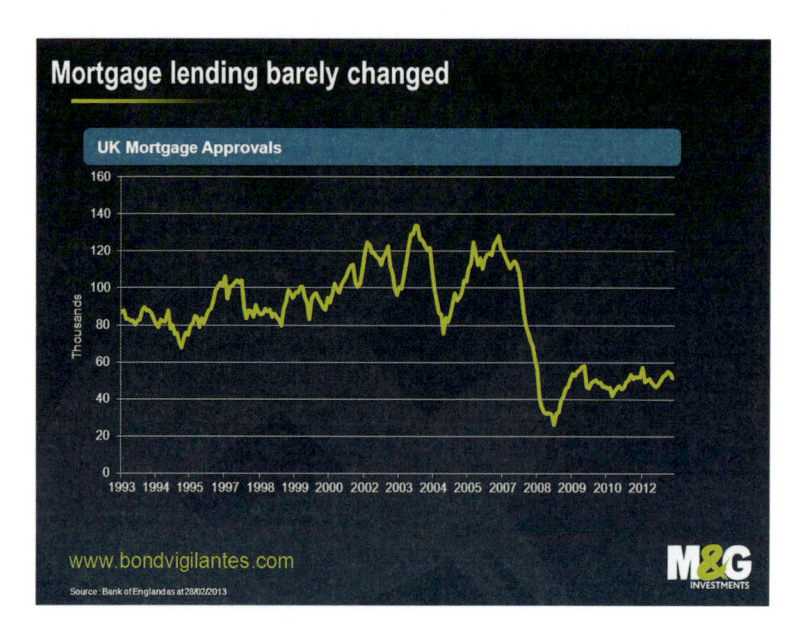

UK Mortgage Approvals (Thousands, 1993–2012)

Source: Bank of England as at 28/02/2013
www.bondvigilantes.com — M&G Investments

Further, with the average mortgage rate in the UK at around 4% and banks able to borrow at what the Bank of England estimates to be 0.75%, the lower rates clearly aren't being passed on to the man on the street either. Assuming banks' net interest margins aren't the measure on which this programme is judged I think it's fair to say it hasn't been a huge success.

Unless that is, you happen to be an investor in asset backed securities. The UK Residential Mortgage Backed Securities (RMBS) market has rallied significantly since the FLS was first announced. Granted, most risk assets have rallied since last summer – partly down to Mario Draghi's now famous speech – but I think that the UK RMBS sector has had an extra boost from the FLS.

Rather than issue RMBS, the banks and building societies have preferred to pledge their mortgage stock with the FLS which has provided a technical support for the market. The graph below shows the spread on an index of short-dated, AAA, UK prime mortgage deals. As you can see they began their rally last summer and have been hovering around 50 bps since the autumn. The lack of supply – we haven't had a new public deal since last November – has certainly been supportive for spreads.

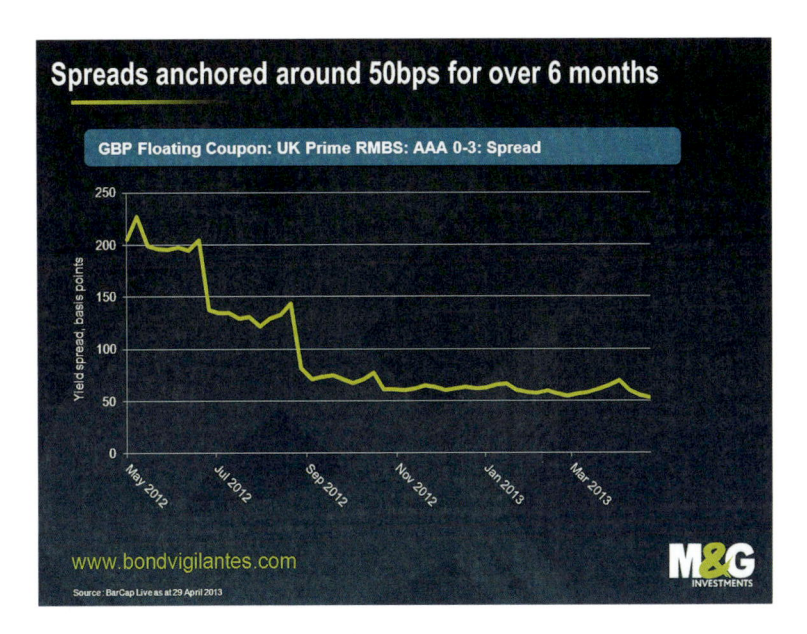

Spreads anchored around 50bps for over 6 months

GBP Floating Coupon: UK Prime RMBS: AAA 0-3: Spread

www.bondvigilantes.com

Source: BarCap Live as at 29 April 2013

The Bank of England and the Treasury claim that the scheme has been a success mainly on the grounds that things would have been worse without it. Clearly we'll never know. Whether things are better or not the FLS appears to have done almost exactly the opposite of what it set out to do. It was established to provide support to the non-financial sector, but as far as I can tell, to date it has actually made the financial sector marginally healthier and better off.

Chapter 36

It's a new dawn, it's a new day. The ECB takes baby steps towards QE

Stefan Isaacs – Friday, 5th July 2013

Just when you thought the Fed had well and truly killed the carry trade, a surprisingly dovish Mario Draghi reminded markets yesterday that Europe remains a very different place from the US. Having previously argued that the ECB never pre commits to forward guidance, yesterday marks something of a volte-face. 'The Governing Council expects the key ECB interest rates to remain at present or lower levels for an extended period of time.' The willingness to offer guidance brings the ECB closer to its UK and US peers, the latter having been in the guidance camp for some time. This firmly reinforces our view that the ECB retains an accommodative stance and an easing bias.

The willingness to offer forward guidance to the market no doubt came after some long and hard introspection within the Governing Council. So why the change? Firstly, the ECB is worried that it may miss its primary target of maintaining inflation at or close to 2% over the medium term. Secondly, Draghi indicated an increasing concern that the real economy continues to demonstrate 'broad based' weakness, and finally, as has been the case for some time, the Council worries that the Eurozone continues to labour with subdued monetary dynamics. This sounds increasingly like Fed talk of recent years.

Draghi also expressed his concern yesterday during his Q&A at the effective tightening of monetary conditions via higher government bond yields (see chart) since the Fed's tapering discussions. Frankly the last thing the Eurozone needs at this stage in its nascent recovery is higher borrowing costs.

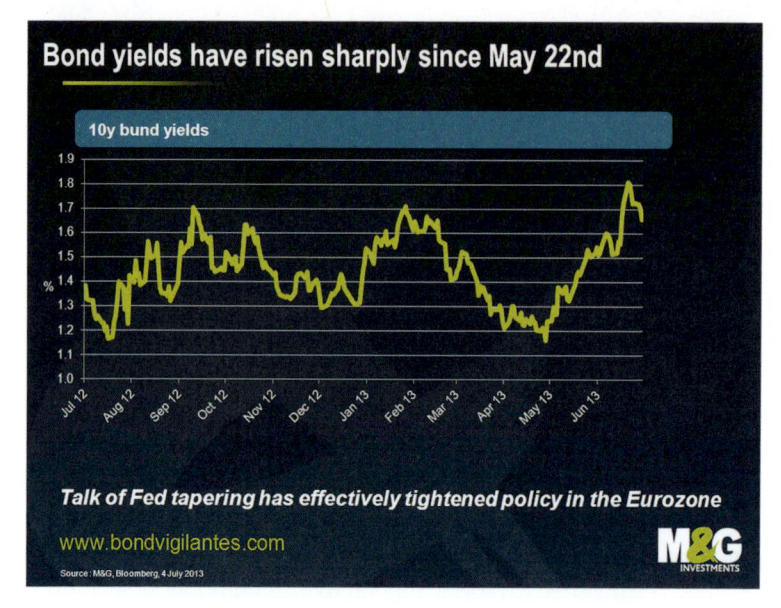

Bond yields have risen sharply since May 22nd

10y bund yields

Talk of Fed tapering has effectively tightened policy in the Eurozone

www.bondvigilantes.com

Source: M&G, Bloomberg, 4 July 2013

M&G INVESTMENTS

Draghi in communicating that the next likely move will be an easing of policy has attempted to talk bond yields down. European risk assets appear to have taken his comments positively but the bond market remains sceptical. At the time of writing only short to medium dated bonds are trading at lower yields.

In conjunction with revising down its 2013 Italian GDP forecast from -1.5% to -1.8%, the IMF has publicly urged the ECB to embark upon direct asset purchases. Is this a likely near-term response ? For now those calls will likely fall on deaf ears especially with German elections later this year. The ECB clearly believes that its next move would be to cut rates further in response to a weaker outlook. Buying time seems to be the current approach.

However, should Eurozone inflation expectations continue to undershoot (the market is currently pricing 1.36% and 1.66% over the next 5 & 10 years, see the next chart) and economic performance remain downright lacklustre across Europe, then the ECB will have to think very carefully about what impact it can expect from a 'traditional' monetary response. QE may be some way off, and would no doubt see massive objections from Berlin, but in the same way that the ECB never pre commits, maybe just maybe, QE will be on the table sooner than the market is currently anticipating.

Inflation expectations in Europe

German 5y and 10y breakeven rates

Will Eurozone inflation expectations continue to undershoot?

www.bondvigilantes.com

Source: M&G, Bloomberg, 4 July 2013

Chapter 37

First home owner grants – a gift to new home buyers, or existing?
Anthony Doyle – Wednesday, 10th July 2013

We aren't the first to have a look at George Osborne's "Help to Buy" scheme. It has been met by warnings far and wide. Sir Mervyn King stated that "there is no place in the long run for a scheme of this kind", whilst Albert Edwards from Societe Generale was a little more blunt when he wrote that it was "a moronic policy". Even the IMF and the OBR are getting in on the act, warning that the scheme may have more of an impact on the demand side of the house price equation, rather than fix the real issue which is a lack of supply.

What alternatives does Osborne have? Seeing as rising house prices do almost nothing to help the UK's biggest problem, the Government should target the bigger problem, which is the UK's dearth of investment. Construction is a very low productivity investment. The UK needs investment in infrastructure, education, plants and equipment. Without this the UK has very weak long run growth potential.

Now don't get us wrong. We can see what George Osborne is trying to do. By announcing the "Help to Buy" scheme in the latest budget, the Chancellor is doing his best to stimulate economic growth through construction which will hopefully encourage consumption through the multiplier effect in an economy that has been anaemic since the financial crisis. The Government coffers will start to look better too due to higher stamp duty and income tax receipts. Who knows, it might also help in the polls. And it will work. We know this because Australia and Canada – two of the most expensive countries for housing in the world – have been running schemes like this for years.

The UK's Help to Buy scheme will take two forms. The first part will offer buyers that qualify an interest-free loan (up to £120,000) from the Government. The second part will see the

Government act as guarantor for a proportion of the borrower's debt. In Australia, the "First Home Owner Grant" has been in existence in some form or another since 2000 and is a one-off grant to first home owners. It is not means tested and differs from state to state (in Sydney, the most expensive city in Australia, first home owners are currently entitled to $15,000 under the scheme). And in Canada, those looking at getting on the property ladder are entitled to a $5,000 tax credit and under the "Home Buyers Plan" can also withdraw up to $25,000 tax free out of their retirement savings to buy or build a home.

The problem is, these schemes have generally caused housing affordability to worsen in Australia and Canada. The chart below (courtesy of Torsten Slok at Deutsche Bank) highlights just how overvalued house prices are in parts of Australia and Canada. The fact that Wollongong ranks higher than New York on a house price to house income ratio seems like madness to me.

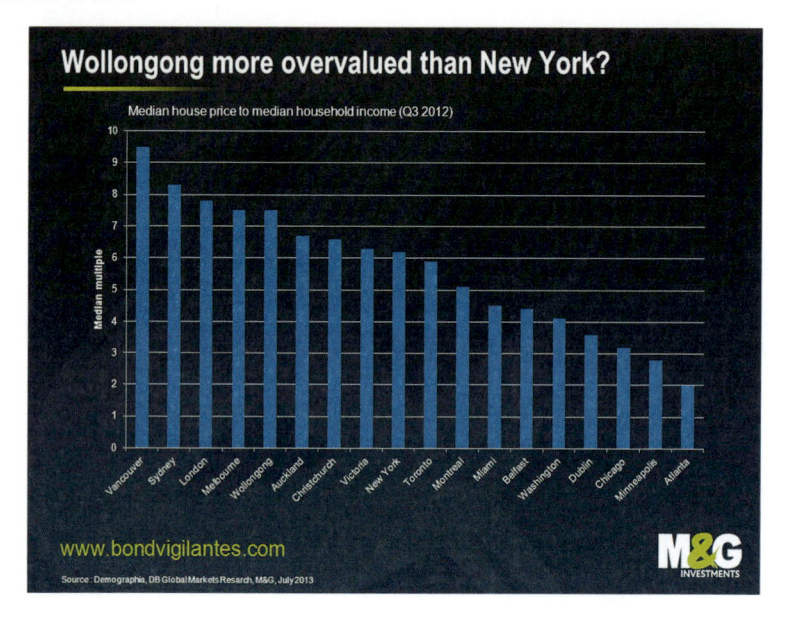

Wollongong more overvalued than New York?

Median house price to median household income (Q3 2012)

Source: Demographia, DB Global Markets Research, M&G, July 2013

www.bondvigilantes.com

M&G INVESTMENTS

Another interesting result of Torsten's affordability chart is the prevalence of New Zealand cities like Auckland and Christchurch. And you guessed right, New Zealand also has a form of the Help to Buy scheme, called the Welcome Home Loan. And if you are a New Zealander with some pension savings, you could be allowed access to your retirement savings to get on the housing ladder.

Home buyer schemes push up prices primarily through the accumulation of mortgage debt. Arguably financial companies have done the correct thing in tightening lending standards and reducing loan-to-value ratios. With the UK government now guaranteeing up to 20% of a new mortgage, those "riskier" types of borrowers that previously wouldn't have qualified for a mortgage now have the ability to enter into the housing market. Demand increases, supply may not respond to the same extent and prices rise. Additionally existing home owners may sell their home and acquire more debt in order to buy a more expensive home. Who knows, mortgage equity withdrawal levels might come back in a big way too. But sooner or later, the house of cards will come crashing down – as we are all very familiar with.

The following highlight the relationship between rising levels of mortgage debt and house prices in Australia, Canada and the UK. Australia is a very interesting example as the First Home Owners Grant has been increased and decreased over time with house prices suitably responding.

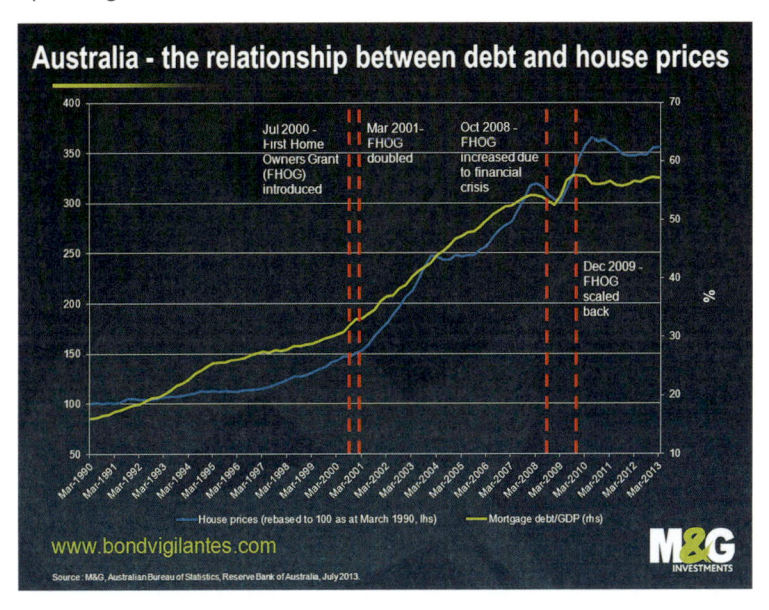

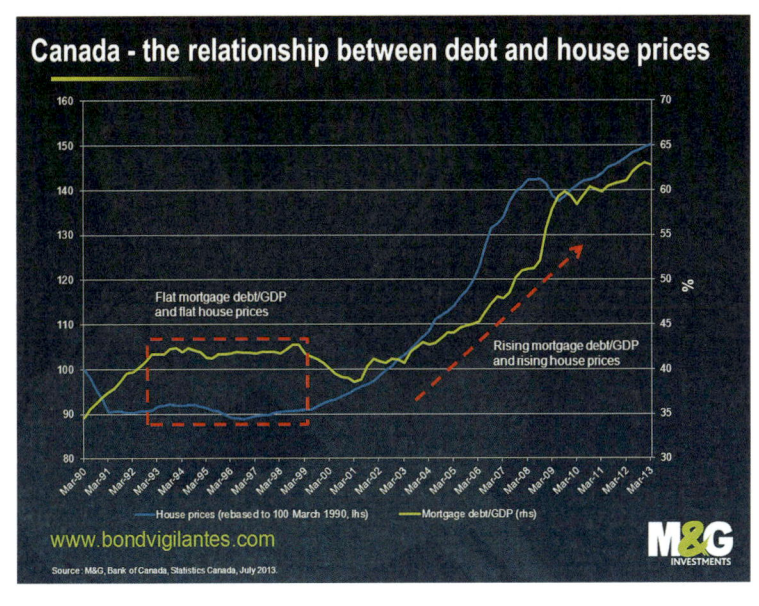

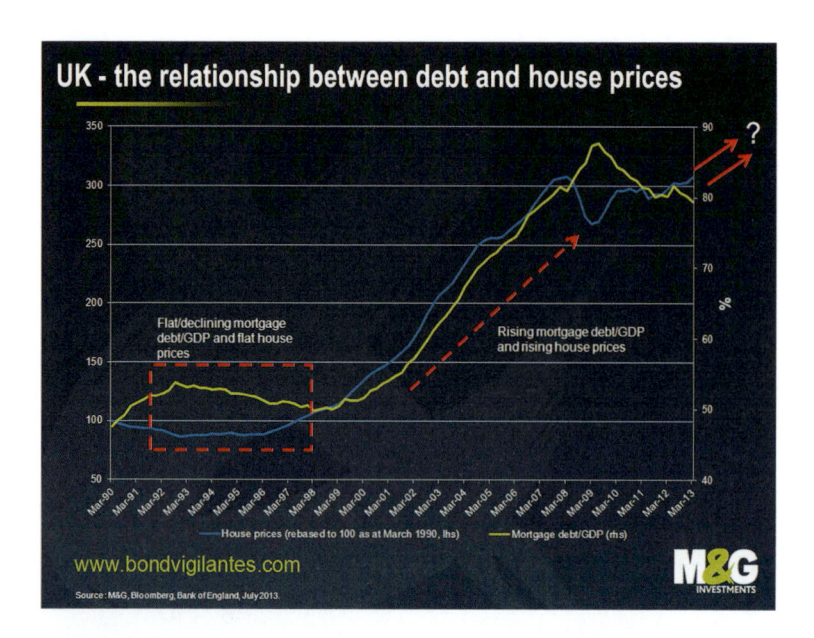

UK - the relationship between debt and house prices

Chart source: M&G, Bloomberg, Bank of England, July 2013. www.bondvigilantes.com

The UK's Help to Buy scheme is most likely going to encourage a further accumulation of mortgage debt, leading to higher house prices, causing housing affordability to worsen from current levels for those who don't have access to the scheme. Arguably, this scheme will also make income inequality much worse, so those who aren't in a financial position to buy a property will fall even further behind. It will also worsen the wealth age gap, i.e. it's the older, existing homeowners who are most likely to benefit, to the detriment of younger people who don't have a home and need somewhere to live.

We have already seen evidence of house prices increasing in the UK, with yesterday's RICS house price balance at levels not seen since January 2010. This data is consistent with the stronger house price data we have seen recently from mortgage lenders Halifax and Nationwide indicating that we are back at pre-crisis highs. One has to wonder whether a scheme encouraging financial companies to lend and consumers to borrow is the brightest thing to do in an economy with £1.26 trillion (or 80% of GDP) mortgage debt outstanding. Especially as it is designed to make an already expensive asset even more expensive, which could lead to financial instability if the economy wobbles and ultimately cost the taxpayer big time.

With house prices set to rise further in the short term, the question has to be asked – is this a help to buy or help to sell scheme?

Chapter 38

The arguments in favour of the Euro surviving
Anthony Doyle – Wednesday, 31st July 2013

Poor economic growth prospects, high unemployment, large debt burdens, poor public finances – it is all too easy for analysts and economists to say that the euro won't be around indefinitely. Yet here we are, coming up to the five year anniversary of the Lehman Brothers collapse and having lived through a number of sovereign debt crises, and the euro remains the single currency for the Economic and Monetary Union (EMU) after being established in 1999. Many will argue, as we have in the past, that a monetary union is unsustainable without a full and proper fiscal union and that to devalue internally through lower unit labour costs is too painful for countries like Ireland and Greece. This would likely result in a divergence of growth within the Eurozone. However, we have to acknowledge that the European Union members and European Central Bank have done a remarkable job of managing the short-term symptoms of the crisis and have met every challenge that having the monetary union in place has produced so far.

That said, the long-term challenge remains: convergence amongst the Eurozone members so that a single monetary policy based on some level of price stability is as relevant for Germany as it is for Greece. The difficulty in achieving this convergence is the main challenge facing the EMU today due to the difficulties in operating under a single monetary policy and a single exchange rate.

With this in mind, now is a good time to think about whether the most ambitious currency union in history has the legs to go the distance after all. What are the main reasons why the euro will survive and prosper in the future?

The Eurozone is on the cusp of recovery and there are signs of convergence amongst members

Leading indicators like the PMIs and industrial production are pointing toward positive growth in Q2. Consumer confidence is improving, while unemployment numbers are starting to slowly improve in some countries as well. Of course, Europe is not yet out of the woods and continues to face significant growth headwinds which we have written about before. Nonetheless, it may be that we are witnessing the some early signs that the substantial structural reforms in the periphery are starting to bear some fruit.

Importantly, the Eurozone is showing signs of rebalancing. Unit labour costs (ULC) rose too quickly during the boom years in peripheral Europe and in Germany they did not increase enough. This eventually resulted in a large difference in competitiveness within the Eurozone which has started to dissipate (though countries like Italy and France still have further work to do). Turning to current account balances, Italy and Ireland are running a surplus, Greece has reduced its large deficit and Spain and Portugal are running small deficits.

These are small, but necessary, steps toward ensuring the survival of the euro.

Germany is the China of Europe

In contrast to the southern European countries and Ireland, Germany has experienced an economic boom. Unemployment is low, exports are strong, inflation is low, the consumer sector is vibrant and we are starting to see some signs of house price appreciation in parts of Germany. A large reason Germany has done so well during the period of turmoil is because its external competitiveness has not been offset by a rising currency. For example, Germany's real exchange rate under the euro is around 40 per cent below where the deutschemark used to trade against the US dollar.

Germany is operating as the China of Europe (at least from a trade surplus perspective) – a massively undervalued exchange rate is generating the world's largest trade surplus of around €193bn a year (China's is running at around 150bn USD a year). This surplus is overwhelmingly being generated through trade with other Eurozone members (like Italy, Greece, Spain, Portugal and Ireland).

The surplus capital that Germany's improved international competitiveness generated has found its way into southern Europe and Ireland. German banks and investors were part of the international community that lent to the respective governments and businesses of the peripheral countries in search of higher yields than their own German bunds were offering. Of course, if this capital had not been provided, the southern European countries and Ireland would not have had the ability to build up so much debt (in 2008, around 80% of Greek, Irish and Portuguese government bonds were owned by foreign investors). Additionally, ULC growth could have been more constrained in these countries (particularly in the public sector) and the gulf in competitiveness between Germany and the peripheral countries would be less pronounced than it is today.

Germany has been the greatest beneficiary of the common currency. Any default would devastate its banking system and export industry. Germany is on the hook, so it is very difficult to see why it would abandon the euro.

The alternative for southern Europe and Ireland is way too painful

Germany currently benefits to a much larger degree from the euro than the heavily indebted countries. This is because the single currency has robbed these nations of the ability to become more competitive through currency devaluation (compare the experience of these countries against the UK for example). Additionally, interest rates are way too restrictive and deflationary forces have taken hold due to excess capacity and ultra high unemployment rates. Countries like Greece and Ireland have not had a recession, they have had a depression.

Because policymakers in southern Europe and Ireland have no access to the monetary policy or the currency lever, there remains only one possibility to gain competitiveness – painful austerity and internal devaluation through reduced wages. This is the only way that these countries can hope to compete with the likes of Germany in the globalised environment.

So why doesn't a country leave? Greece, Ireland and Cyprus have severely tested the euro in recent years yet remain in the union. The strongest argument that has been put forward is that the costs of leaving the EMU will be too painful relative to the gains. Capital outflows, skyrocketing inflation, bankruptcy on a national scale, mass unemployment and social unrest do not make the option particularly enticing. And just imagine what will happen if Italy or Spain decide to get out. To retain the euro is the least worst option for the debtor countries.

The European Central Bank will do "whatever it takes"

It has now been a year since ECB President Mario Draghi delivered one of the most important speeches in the history of Europe and stated: "Within our mandate, the ECB is ready to do whatever it takes to preserve the euro. And believe me, it will be enough." In stating these remarks, Draghi convinced the markets that the ECB had unlimited firepower to support its members and more specifically, Spain and Italy. Immediately, yields on peripheral European sovereign bonds fell from dangerously high levels that made borrowing unsustainable over the long term and are currently much lower than their levels a year ago. It is fair to say the market still believes Draghi and is now pricing risks more appropriately. With the ECB taking tentative steps towards forward guidance, it may not be long before we see further unconventional monetary policy measures like a new LTRO announcement.

Do not underestimate the political desire to keep the euro area intact

Despite the problems – the concerning outlook, the record levels of unemployment and debt, the proposed tax on savers in Cyprus – no country has left the EMU. The EMU has in fact added new members (Slovakia in 2009 and Estonia in 2011) and may add more (Latvia in 2014). European countries remain open for trade, have continued to enforce EU policies and have not resorted to protectionist policies. EU banking regulation has become stronger, the financial system has stabilised, and new bank capital requirements are in place.

It is true that Europe remains a huge concern for us. A successful monetary union requires not only political but also economic integration. European politicians must accept greater limits on their policy autonomy and this will be difficult to gain. Economic convergence is necessary. Perhaps most worryingly, a cocktail of lower domestic demand, austerity, reduced wages and high unemployment is normally politically costly and breeds social unrest. However, given the track record that the EU and ECB has shown and for the reasons listed above, perhaps the euro may be around much longer than some economic commentators currently expect.

Chapter 39

Monster Munch update – a victory for bondvigilantes.com
James Tomlins – Tuesday, 13th August 2013

One of our most popular posts of all time was written back in 2011. The subject was not the US losing its AAA rating, the impact of the default of Lehman Brothers or any other weighty matter of great economic import, but rather a quick look at how packets of Monster Munch were getting smaller over time and the associated inflationary impact.

Hence my surprise when I went into a shop last weekend and saw that Monster Munch packets have now been restored to their old 40g size, replacing the measly and frankly unsatisfying 22g version of recent times.

The new/old Monster Munch packet

www.bondvigilantes.com

Source: M&G, August 2013.

Further research on the manufacturer's website revealed that

" ... The re-launch comes in response to growing consumer demand and will take Monster Munch back to the original retro pack design and old texture, flavour and crunchiness that consumers remember and love ... Consumers have made it clear through both our own research and within online communities that they miss Monster Munch the way it used to be .."

I like to think that our blog was the spark that lit the fuse of this virtual nostalgia-laden fast food insurgency. A resounding victory for bondvigilantes.com fighting in the name of consumer activism!

But wait, it gets better. Back in October 2011, the M&G coffee shop charged 45p for 22g, or 2.05 pence per gram. Today, the same shop charges 65p (RRP 50p) for a 40g packet, or 1.63 pence per gram. This is a fall of 20.5% in nominal terms. Put simply, you are also getting more for your money.

However, before we applaud the manufacturer for their largesse, let's look at the main raw material. Back in October 2011, we pointed out that the headline cost of Monster Munch closely followed the corn price.

Deflationary impact of corn prices

Generic 1st corn future (cents per bushel)

www.bondvigilantes.com

Source: Bloomberg, M&G, August 2013.

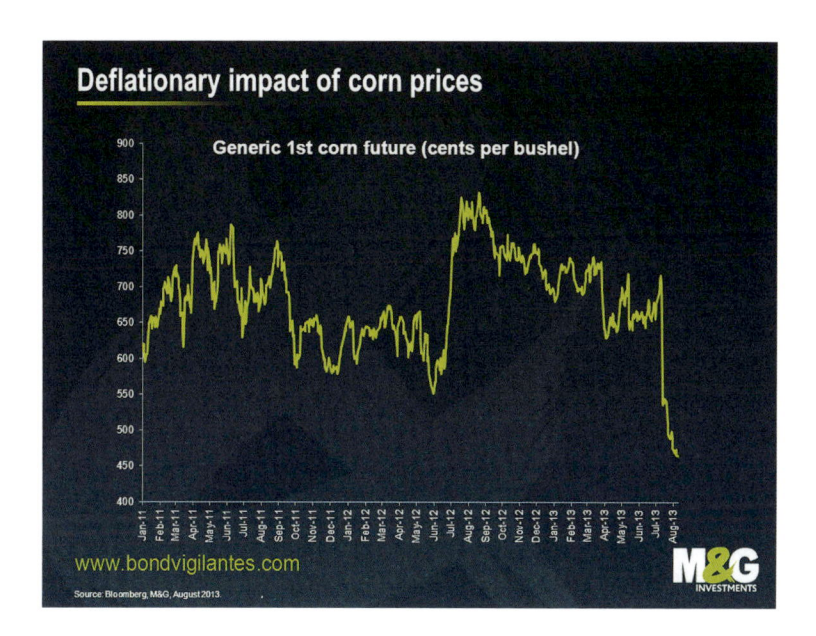

Since October 2011 the corn future has fallen by around 28.5% in price to $4.64 per bushel, a rare case of deflation in recent times. In sterling terms, the fall is around 25.5%. Accordingly, the dramatic fall off in corn prices has allowed the manufacturer to pass on part of this benefit to consumers, reducing the headline per gram price, but at the same time retaining some of the benefit in the form of an enhanced profit margin.

So whilst we cannot claim all the credit for this victory, this is a rare piece of welcome news for the consumer of corn based snacks.

Chapter 40

It's a knockout – why the gilt and currency markets have no love for Carney's forward guidance

Jim Leaviss – Thursday, 29th August 2013

Millwall FC wasn't the only team to trek up to Nottingham yesterday from London and to come back empty handed (at the hands of the mighty, mighty Forest). Team Carney from the Bank of England also had an unproductive time of it in the East Midlands as the new Governor gave his first speech in the role to the CBI, Chamber of Commerce and the Institute of Directors. Since the publication of the August Inflation Report, in which the Monetary Policy Committee delivered its framework for forward guidance, the markets have done the opposite of what the Bank had hoped for. The gilt market has sold off – not just at medium and long maturities, which are largely outside of direct Bank control and are more dependent on global bond market trends, but also at the short end, where 5-year gilt yields have risen by 20 bps in under a month. There has also been a de facto tightening of UK monetary conditions through the currency. Trade weighted sterling is 1% higher than it was before forward guidance came in. Both the gilt market and the pound went the "wrong" way as Carney discussed forward guidance yesterday afternoon. The Overnight Index Swaps market (OIS), which prices expectations of future official rate moves, fully prices a 25 bps Bank rate hike between 2 and 3 years' time.

Gilts softer, £ stronger since August Inflation Report

UK monetary policy is tighter, not looser, than it was before policy guidance

Source: M&G, Bloomberg August 2013

www.bondvigilantes.com

So why don't markets believe Mark Carney? In yesterday's speech he was clear that the UK's economic recovery was "fledgling", and weaker than recoveries elsewhere in the world. He spent some time discussing how a fall in unemployment to the 7% threshold would mean 750,000 new jobs having to be created, which would take some time, possibly three years or longer. And even if growth picked up, it didn't necessarily follow that jobs growth would be strong. But two things led gilts lower yesterday afternoon. Firstly there was the announcement that UK banks would be able to reduce the amount of government bonds that they hold as a liquidity buffer so long as their capital base is over 7% risk-weighted assets – potentially triggering sales of tens of billions of gilts over the next couple of years. But more importantly, Carney's attempted rollback from the "knockouts" stated in the Inflation Report was not strong enough.

On a recent Inflation Report, after detailing the forward guidance linking rates and asset purchases to the 7% unemployment rate, there are three "knockouts" which would cause the guidance to "cease to hold". The first knockout is the most important. If CPI inflation is, in the Bank's view, likely to be 2.5% or higher in 1 1/2 to 2 years' time then the unemployment trigger becomes irrelevant. The other two knockouts were that medium-term inflation expectations become unanchored, and that the Financial Policy Committee judges that the monetary policy stance is a significant threat to financial stability.

So for all the talk of the UK's weak economy, and the accommodative stance that the Bank will take to allow the unemployment rate to fall to 7%, perhaps over many years, don't forget that if CPI inflation looks likely to be at 2.5% or higher, the MPC will ignore the jobs market promise. Since the middle of 2005, UK CPI has been at or above 2.5% most of the time, through a strong economy and (for longer) the weak economy. Since the start of 2010 there have only been 3 months of sub 2.5% year-on-year CPI. And in 2008 and 2011 the year-on-year rates exceeded 5%.

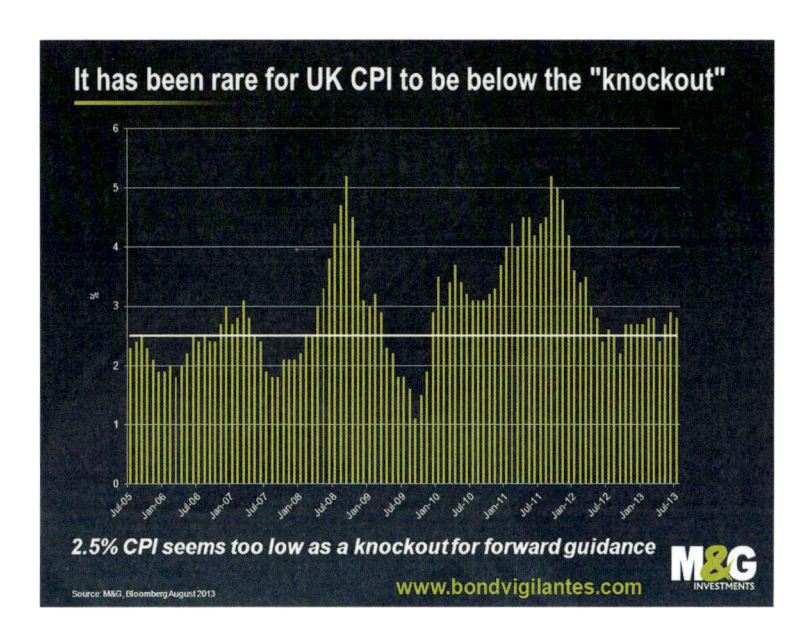

It has been rare for UK CPI to be below the "knockout"

2.5% CPI seems too low as a knockout for forward guidance

www.bondvigilantes.com

M&G INVESTMENTS

Source: M&G, Bloomberg August 2013

Of course, the Bank of England can forecast inflation to be whatever it likes over the next 1 1/2 to 2 years. Its inflation forecasts have famously been awful for years, always predicting inflation would return to 2% when it always was much higher than that. But it will be important for Carney to earn some credibility here in the UK, and the days of the Inflation Report's "delta of blood" inflation forecast always showing a mid point for future inflation of 2% must surely have ended when Mervyn King left. What does the outside world think about the prospects of UK inflation being below 2.5% in the future? Here the news is better – the consensus broker economic forecast is for CPI to fall to 2.4% in 2014 and 2.1% in 2015. And the implied inflation rate from the UK index-linked gilt market is for an average of 2.8% per year over the next five years on an RPI basis, which given the structural wedge between RPI and CPI suggests that the market's CPI forecast is somewhere below 2.5%. M&G has launched a new Inflation Expectations Survey, together with YouGov. We should have August results shortly, but in our last release we saw that one year ahead UK consumer expectations of inflation ran at 2.7% (a fall from 3% a quarter earlier) and 5 year ahead expectations were at 3%. Higher than the 2.5% target, but consumer expectations are often higher than the market, and the 3% level has been stable (well "anchored").

But as we have seen, UK inflation has been notoriously sticky. Not because consumers are demanding more goods than the shops can supply (although there has been some long awaited good news from the retail sector lately, with sales stronger), as in general real incomes have been squeezed and discretionary spending has been hit. But because non-discretionary items, like food and energy costs, have substantially exceeded the inflation rates of consumer goods. Add to this administered prices relating to public transport costs or university tuition fees and we can see that the UK's "inflation problem" is potentially something that a monetary policymaker can only influence by forcing discretionary spending into deflation. The following chart shows that so long as the non-discretionary basket of goods keeps inflating at around 5% per year, there must be virtually no inflation in discretionary goods in order to get below Carney's 2.5% knockout.

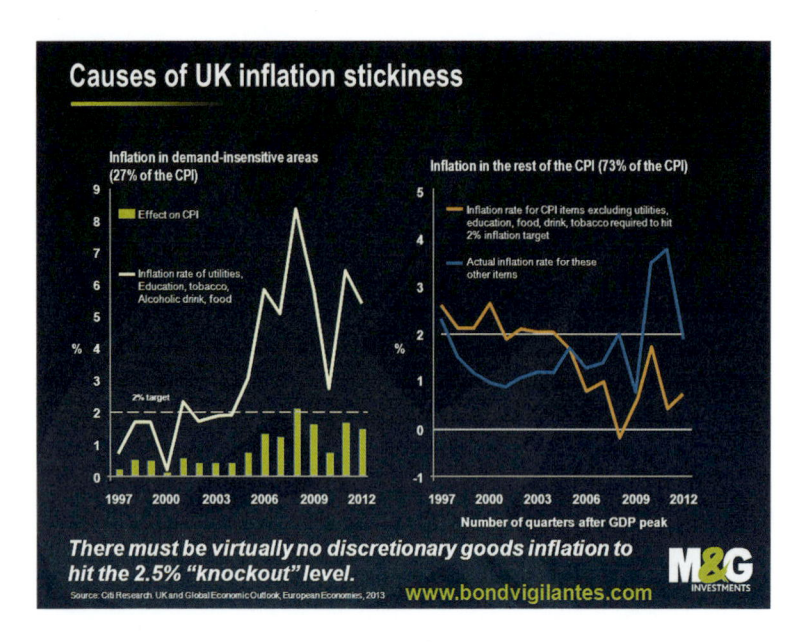

Causes of UK inflation stickiness

Inflation in demand-insensitive areas (27% of the CPI)
- Effect on CPI
- Inflation rate of utilities, Education, tobacco, Alcoholic drink, food
- 2% target

Inflation in the rest of the CPI (73% of the CPI)
- Inflation rate for CPI items excluding utilities, education, food, drink, tobacco required to hit 2% inflation target
- Actual inflation rate for these other items

Number of quarters after GDP peak

There must be virtually no discretionary goods inflation to hit the 2.5% "knockout" level.

Source: Citi Research, UK and Global Economic Outlook, European Economies, 2013
www.bondvigilantes.com
M&G INVESTMENTS

So it is going to be tough for the market to believe that the CPI inflation "knockout" won't have a decent chance of coming into play well before the 7% unemployment threshold is reached. I think Carney missed an opportunity to move away from the knockouts yesterday – he certainly didn't use the term again, and implied that the gilt market's move lower was driven by international developments and over-optimism about the prospects for a quick fall in UK unemployment. But the three knockouts were almost dismissed in the sentence "provided there are no material threats to either price or financial stability" rather than given the prominence that they were in the Inflation Report. So it looks as if the gilt and currency markets need something stronger if they are to produce the monetary easing that, from Carney's bearish analysis of the UK economy, it still needs.

Chapter 41

How do house prices feed into inflation rates around the world? It's important for central banks, and for bond investors
Jim Leaviss – Thursday, 3rd October 2013

After the collapse in real estate prices in many of the major developed nations during and after the Great Financial Crisis, housing is back in demand again. Strong house price appreciation is being seen in most areas of the US, in the UK (especially in London), and German property prices have started to move up. We're even seeing prices rise in parts of Ireland, the poster child for the property boom and bust cycle. I wanted to take a quick look at what rising house prices do for inflation rates. Not the second round effects of higher house prices feeding into wage demands, or the increased cost of plumbers and carpets, but the direct way that either house prices, mortgage costs and rents end up in our published inflation stats. Also, the question about whether central banks should target asset prices is another debate too.

House prices have started to recover post GFC

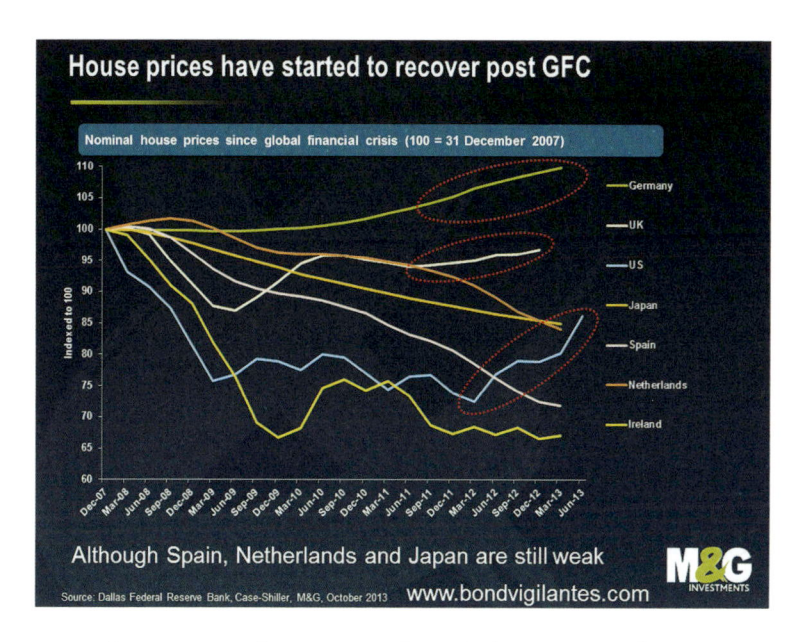

Nominal house prices since global financial crisis (100 = 31 December 2007)

Although Spain, Netherlands and Japan are still weak

Source: Dallas Federal Reserve Bank, Case-Shiller, M&G, October 2013 — www.bondvigilantes.com

There is no simple answer to the question "how do house prices feed into the inflation statistics". It varies not just from country to country, but also within the different measures of inflation within one geographical area. But given central banks' rate setting/QE behaviour is determined by the published inflation measures it's important to understand how house prices might, or might not, drive changes in those measures.

The US

"Shelter" is around 31% of the CPI which is used to determine the pricing of US inflation linked bonds (TIPS), but just 16% of the Core PCE Deflator, the measure that the Federal Reserve targets. The PCE is a broader measure, with much bigger weights to financial services and healthcare, so shelter measures therefore have to have a smaller weight in that measure. The CPI shelter weight looks high by international standards. For the Bureau of Labor Statistics (BLS), the purchase price of a house is not important except in how it influences the ongoing cost of providing shelter to its inhabitants. The method that the BLS uses to determine what those costs might be is "rental equivalence". It surveys actual market rents, and augments this data by asking a sample of homeowners to estimate what it would cost them to rent the property that they live in (excluding utility bills and furniture). In both the CPI and PCE, pure market rents are given around a quarter of the weight given to OER, Owners' Equivalent Rent. There are problems with this – and not just with the accuracy of the homeowners' rental guesses. Having rents and rental equivalence in the inflation data rather than a house price measure means that you can have – simultaneously – a house price bubble, and a falling impact from house prices in the inflation data. We've seen times when a speculative frenzy means house prices rise, but the impact of that speculation is overbuilding of property (just before the 2008 crash there was 12 months of excess inventory of houses in the US compared to a pre-bubble level of around 5 months) leading to falling rents. The reverse happened as the US recovered. House prices continued to tank, but because of a lack of mortgage finance more people were forced to rent, pushing up rents within the inflation data.

The UK

How house prices feed into the UK inflation data depends on whether you care about CPI inflation (which the Bank of England targets) or RPI inflation (which we bond investors care about as it's the statistic referenced by the UK index linked bond markets). House prices directly feed into the RPI, but because house prices have little direct input into the CPI, the recent trend higher in UK property will lead to a growing wedge between the two measures – good news for index linked bond investors! The RPI captures house price rises in two ways – through Mortgage Interest Payments (MIPs) and House Depreciation. Mortgage payments will increase as the price of property rises, but they will most quickly reflect changes in interest rates. For example Alan Clarke of Scotia estimates that a hike in Bank Rate of 150 bps would feed almost immediately into the RPI, adding 1% to the annual rate. This is despite the trend in the UK for people to fix their mortgage payments. Housing Depreciation linked to UK house prices with a lag, and is an attempt to measure the cost of ownership (a bit like the BLS's aim with rental equivalence) but has been criticized as overstating the cost of ownership in rising markets as house price inflation is almost always about land values accelerating rather than the bricks and mortar themselves. Land does not depreciate like other fixed assets (no wear and tear). Housing is very significant in the UK RPI, making up 17.3% of the basket (8.6% actual rents, 2.9% MIPs, 5.8% depreciation).

The UK's CPI is a European harmonised measure of inflation. It only takes account of housing costs through a 6% weight on actual rents. There has never been agreement within the EU about how wider housing costs should be measured! Countries with high levels of home ownership have different views from countries with a high proportion of renters. Housing is around 18% of the expenditure of a typical person in the UK, so the Office of National Statistics regards the current CPI weight as a "weakness". They therefore are now publishing CPIH, which includes housing on a rental equivalence basis (the same idea that the ONS measures "the price owner occupiers would need to rent their own home" as a dwelling is a "capital good, and therefore not consumed, but instead provides a flow of services that are consumed each period"). CPIH has a 17.7% weight to housing, but remains an experimental series, and plays no part in the official monetary targets.

The Eurozone

The European Central Bank targets CPI inflation, at or a little below 2%. As mentioned above the harmonised measure that Eurostat produces does not include any measure of housing other than actual rents, with a weight of 6%. If you think house price inflation (or deflation) is important for policymakers this low weighting has probably never mattered since the Eurozone came into existence. Although there have been pockets of very high house price inflation (Spain, Ireland, Netherlands) because the Big 3, Germany, France and Italy have had very little house price movement I doubt that a CPIH measure would be terribly different. We are, however, now seeing some upwards movements in the German residential property market in "prime" regions – albeit as Spanish and Dutch house prices continue to freefall. It's also important to note the range of importance of rents within the individual countries' CPI numbers. For Slovenians it makes up 0.7% of their inflation basket, but for the Germans it is 10.2%.

Japan

Housing makes up 21% of the headline CPI. Like the US CPI the Japanese statistical authorities use a measure of an "imputed rent of an owner-occupied house" as well as actual rental costs. Again the imputed rents from owner occupiers (15.6%) dwarf the actual numbers from renters (5.4%) – aren't these large weightings to imputed rents here and elsewhere a bit worrying? How would you homeowners reading this go about guessing a rent for your property? I'd only get close by looking at websites for similar places to mine up for rent nearby. Is that cheating?

Inflation statistics and housing weights

Rent and house price-related components of inflation baskets (in %)

	UK CPI	UK CPIH	UK RPI	US CPI	US PCE Deflator	Eurozone HICP	Japan CPI
Rental payments	6.2	5.5	8.6	6.5	3.4	6.0	3.1
Mortgage interest payments			2.9				
Depreciation			5.8				
Owners' equivalent rent/ housing costs		12.2		24.0	12.9		15.6
Total	6.2	17.7	17.3	30.5	16.3	6.0	18.7

US CPI housing % looks high relative to others

Source: BLS, ONS, Eurostat, Statistics Bureau Japan, M&G, October 2013 www.bondvigilantes.com

So why does this matter? Well if there is no correlation between house price inflation and consumer price inflation then it probably doesn't. But intuitively both the direct impact on wage demands of workers who see house prices going up, and the wealth effect on the consumption of those who see their biggest asset surging in value should be significant. Therefore central banks will be missing this if they use statistics where the relationship between house prices and their impact in those statistics is weak.

Chapter 42

Spain's answer to recession – the times they are a-changin'

Wolfgang Bauer – Tuesday, 8th October 2013

Times are changing in Spain, or at least they might – and I am not alluding to tentative signs of economic recovery, such as the recent upgrade of Spain's 2014 growth forecast from 0.5% to 0.7%. I am, quite literally, referring to a possible change of time in Spain. In late September, a Spanish parliamentary commission issued a report in favour of turning clocks back one hour in Spain. Being located in the wrong time zone, so the argument goes, had negative implications on eating, sleeping and working habits, and hence, a corrective time shift might improve public health as well as economic productivity. Interestingly, Spain had not always been in its current time zone but was moved one hour ahead in 1940 at General Franco's command to be in line with then fascist allies Germany and Italy. But does the commission have a point; should Spain return to its pre-war time zone?

Let's have a look at time zones in the European Union. Ignoring overseas territories, EU member countries use three time zones – Western European Time (WET, UTC+00:00), Central European Time (CET, UTC+01:00) and Eastern European Time (EET, UTC+02:00) – as well as the respective daylight saving time derivatives. In the following, only relative time differences between countries will be relevant. Therefore, to simplify matters, we can disregard daylight saving time since all EU member countries move clocks back and forth in sync anyway. Only three EU countries use WET: Portugal, Ireland and the UK. EET is used in the Baltics as well as in Finland, Romania, Bulgaria, Greece and Cyprus. Spain, except for the Canary Islands, is located in the CET zone together with the remaining EU countries.

In order to assess on a geographical basis whether Spain is placed in the wrong time zone or not, I took a look at the location of some of the largest Spanish and other major European cities using WET or CET. For each city I then calculated in degrees of longitude the difference between its actual location and the central axis of its time zone, i.e. the prime meridian for WET and the 15th meridian east for CET.

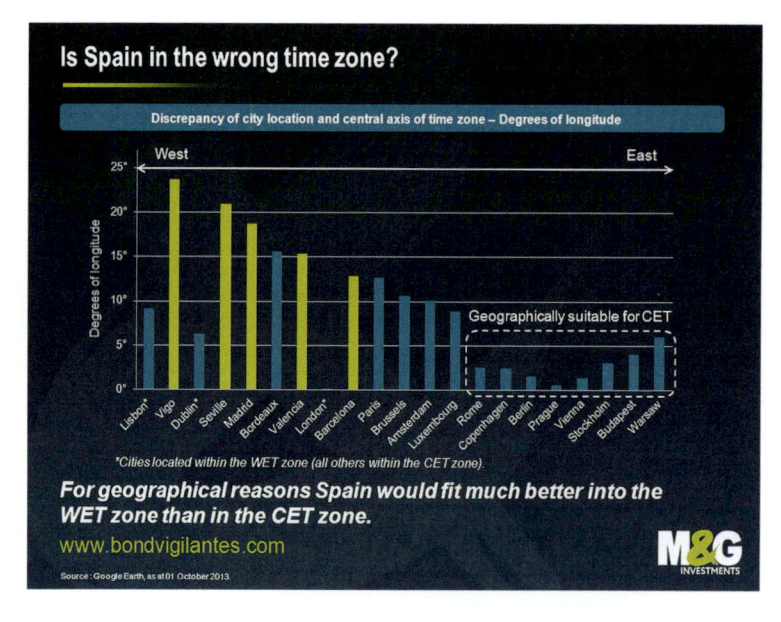

Is Spain in the wrong time zone?

Discrepancy of city location and central axis of time zone – Degrees of longitude

*Cities located within the WET zone (all others within the CET zone).

For geographical reasons Spain would fit much better into the WET zone than in the CET zone.

www.bondvigilantes.com

Source: Google Earth, as at 01 October 2013.

M&G INVESTMENTS

Amongst these European cities, sorted from west to east, Spanish towns (light green colour) exhibit the highest levels of misplacement. In particular Vigo, located in the north-west autonomous community of Galicia, features an impressive discrepancy of nearly 24°. Apart from Spain, cities in western France, such as Bordeaux, show very high displacement values. Western European cities using WET (marked with an asterisk), e.g. Lisbon, Dublin and London, have distinctly lower discrepancies, though, as their reference axis is the prime meridian rather than the 15th meridian east. Strictly speaking, only cities east of the Benelux countries, i.e. Rome onwards in the chart, are fitting geographically into the CET zone. Spain, in contrast, is clearly much more suitable for the WET zone. Sticking with

CET causes a permanent mismatch between official time and actually perceived solar time. But why has Spain not switched to WET long time ago?

One reason is that some of the effects of the time mismatch are actually considered desirable. For instance, an extra hour of sunshine in the evening might be beneficial for tourism in Spain. Another consideration to be taken into account is the effect a change from CET to WET would have on Spain's cross-border business. It is likely that in case of a switch to WET, business with CET countries would become more difficult. Due to a misalignment of daily schedules, business and trading hours, transaction costs could rise. Similarly business with EET countries might suffer as an additional hour of time difference would be added. In contrast, business with WET countries would most likely be facilitated. In order to evaluate these contrary effects, I grouped Spain's intra-EU exports and imports over the past five years into time zones. For the sake of simplicity, I did not include Spain's foreign trade outside of the EU. Major trading partners, such as China and the US, are separated from Spain by several time zones, and hence a shift of one hour would most likely have only negligible consequences.

Which time zone dominates Spain's EU exports and imports?

Spain's EU exports and imports over the past 5 years by time zone – EUR billion

Year	Exports WET	Exports CET	Exports EET	Imports WET	Imports CET	Imports EET
2008	24%	72%	4%	16%	81%	2%
2009	23%	74%	3%	18%	80%	2%
2010	23%	74%	3%	18%	80%	2%
2011	23%	73%	4%	17%	81%	2%
2012	22%	74%	4%	17%	81%	2%

Spain's EU exports and imports are clearly dominated by business with countries using CET.

www.bondvigilantes.com

Source: Eurostat, as at 01 October 2013.

M&G INVESTMENTS

Over the past five years the composition of Spain's EU exports and imports by time zone has remained remarkably stable. EET countries are only niche markets for Spain's exports and imports. Both sides of the balance of trade are clearly dominated by business with CET countries (72-74% of exports and 80-81% of imports). Exports to and imports from WET countries account for only 22-24% and 16-18%, respectively. This suggests that moving from CET to WET bears the risk of making the vast majority of Spain's EU trade more difficult.

But is there a way to reduce this risk and still enable Spain to switch to WET? Well, here is a thought: Spain could launch a lobbying campaign and convince France as well as the Benelux countries to switch together from CET to WET. As shown in Chart 1, cities in these countries, particularly in western France, would geographically fit much better into the WET zone. In addition, there is also a political argument to be put forward as CET was introduced at gunpoint in these countries during the German occupation in the Second World War. Therefore, a move to WET could be presented to the affected electorate as a long overdue measure to remove the legacy of fascist aggression in western Europe – and who could seriously question such an honourable pursuit? A large-scale move of several major EU countries from CET to WET would have significant implications for the composition of Spain's EU exports and imports as well as for the economic power balance of the EU in general. The below chart compares the actual 2012 percentage division of Spain's EU exports and imports as well as the EU's GDP into time zones with a hypothetical 2012 scenario in which Spain, France and the Benelux countries are located within the WET zone.

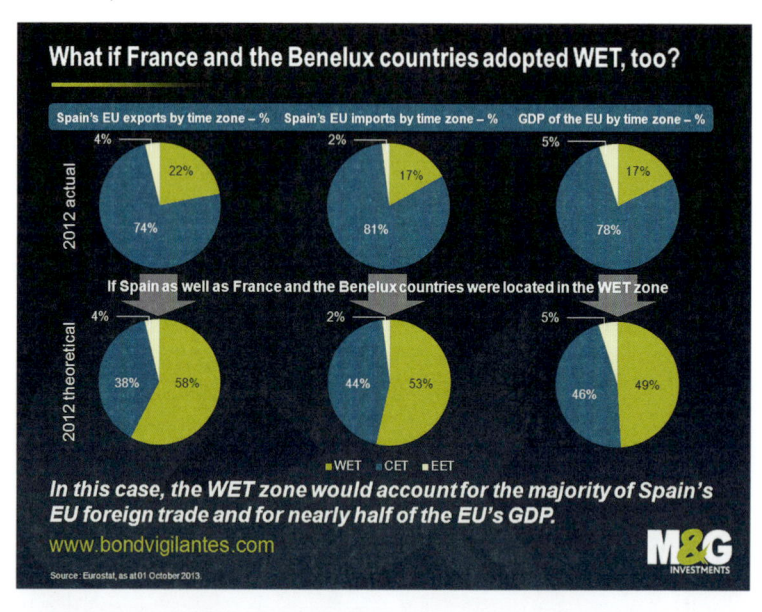

What if France and the Benelux countries adopted WET, too?

Spain's EU exports by time zone – % *Spain's EU imports by time zone – %* *GDP of the EU by time zone – %*

2012 actual:
- Exports: 4%, 22%, 74%
- Imports: 2%, 17%, 81%
- GDP: 5%, 17%, 78%

If Spain as well as France and the Benelux countries were located in the WET zone

2012 theoretical:
- Exports: 4%, 38%, 58%
- Imports: 2%, 44%, 53%
- GDP: 5%, 46%, 49%

■ WET   ■ CET   ■ EET

In this case, the WET zone would account for the majority of Spain's EU foreign trade and for nearly half of the EU's GDP.

www.bondvigilantes.com

Source: Eurostat, as at 01 October 2013.

M&G INVESTMENTS

As pointed out above, in terms of Spain's EU exports and imports CET countries currently dominate over WET countries. However, if other major western European countries moved together with Spain to WET this relationship would reverse, as indicated in the theoretical scenario. In this case, WET countries would account for 58% of Spain's EU exports and 53% of its EU imports. Furthermore, the economic weights of CET and WET within the EU would change drastically. The WET's share of the total EU GDP would rise from 17% to 49%, whereas the CET's share would drop accordingly from 78% to 46%.

In conclusion, it would make perfect sense for Spain to switch from CET to WET for geographical reasons. However, in order to guard against potential negative side effects on its cross-border business, Spain should lobby hard to convince France and the Benelux countries to copy its move. If this move is successful, then Portugal, Ireland and the UK will likely benefit as well.

Finally, if you think Spain has time-keeping issues, spare a thought for India and China. Indian Standard Time applies throughout India and Sri Lanka, and is confusingly GMT+ 5 hours 30 minutes. The time zone covers over 28 degrees of longitude, meaning the sun rises two hours earlier in the east of India than the west. Meanwhile, China has one official time zone spanning more than 60 degrees of longitude (the 48 contiguous US states cover 25 degrees of longitude), and while this problem is tempered by most of the Chinese population living on the east coast, sunrise in the western city of Kashgar can be as late as 10.17am!

Chapter 43

Why the US Dollar now looks cheap against, well, basically everything
Mike Riddell – Friday, 11th October 2013

Back in January I wrote about why we loved the US dollar and worry about EM currencies, and did an update on EM. Another EM piece will follow soon (the short version is that while it was 'just' a tremor, I'm increasingly worried that 'The Big One' is coming).

The US Dollar was strong through Q1 and Q2, but an interesting development in Q3 was that while the US Dollar held up OK against most EM currencies, it performed abysmally against other developed currencies. Below is a chart of the US Dollar Index, a gauge of US Dollar performance against a basket of major world currencies, where the basket contains EUR (57.6%) JPY (13.6%) GBP (11.9%) CAD (9.1%) SEK (4.2%) CHF (3.6%). The Dollar Index is back to where it was at the beginning of the year, and despite the relative strength of the US economy versus other developed countries, the Dollar Index has now returned to the average level of the last five years.

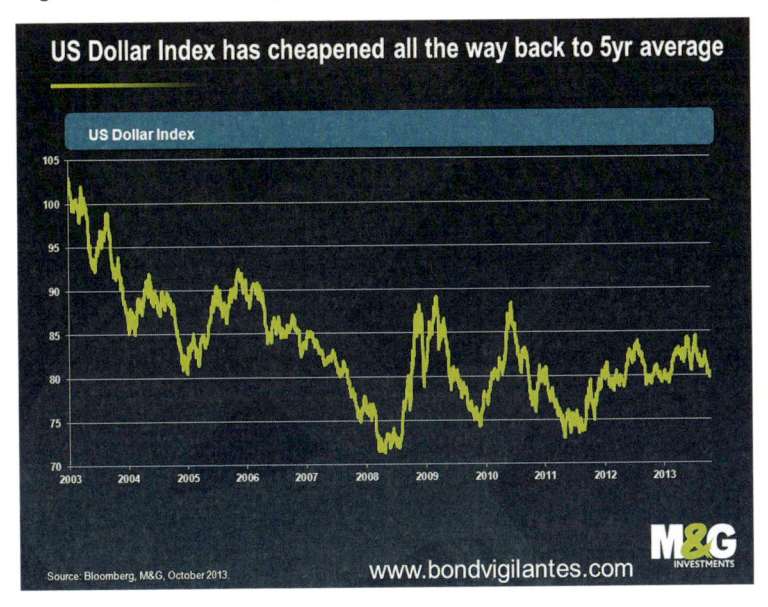

US Dollar Index has cheapened all the way back to 5yr average
Source: Bloomberg, M&G, October 2013

The reasons that led us (and an increasing number of others) to be so excited about the US dollar over the past 18 months were namely compelling USD valuations following a decade long slump, an improving current account balance, the rapid move towards energy independence, and a strengthening US economic recovery where a surging housing market and a steadily falling unemployment rate made it likely that the US would lead most of the world in the monetary policy tightening cycle.

The long term positives for the US dollar are still there, but have recently been overshadowed by negative ones. So what has changed? Recent US Dollar weakness is probably to do with the Fed's non-tapering in September, the ongoing budget nonsense, and a very big unwind in a whole heap of long USD positions.

It makes sense to be more bullish on the US dollar because these negative forces appear to be dissipating.

Firstly the non-tapering event. Treasury yields and the US dollar had already started to drop ahead of the non-tapering decision thanks to a slight weakening in US data, with US 10 year yields dropping from 3% on September 5th to 2.9% on September 18th and the Dollar Index falling 2%. Nevertheless markets were still taken by surprise, and Treasury yields and the US Dollar had another leg lower with US 10 year yields briefly dropping below 2.6% at the end of September, and the Dollar Index falling almost another 2%.

But then on Wednesday we had September's FOMC minutes, which were surprisingly hawkish. The decision not to taper was a close call, where most members still viewed it as appropriate for tapering to start this year and for asset purchases to be finished by the middle of next year. Yes, the US government shutdown that has occurred since the meeting took place appears to be already starting to hit US economic data (estimates vary enormously for the total hit to Q4 US GDP), and the weaker data is therefore likely to push the start date for tapering back a little. But if you assume that the US government shutdown is a one off event (admittedly not a particularly safe assumption), then the shutdown should merely slightly delay the tapering decision and the normalisation of US monetary policy, it should not result in a permanent postponement.

That said, something that was a little disconcerting from the minutes of the September FOMC meeting was that the jump in mortgage rates played a key role in the decision not to start tapering, with some members worrying that a reduction in asset purchases "might trigger an additional unwarranted tightening of financial conditions". HSBC's Kevin Logan makes the good point that higher mortgage rates present Fed policymakers with a dilemma; if rates rise because the markets expect a tapering of QE, and that in turn stops the Fed from tapering, then it makes any QE exit pretty tricky and it appears that the Fed now has an additional criterion for reducing QE – not only must the economy and labour market be doing better, but long-term interest rates cannot rise too much in advance, or even during, the tapering process. If the Fed's decision not to taper was heavily influenced by higher mortgage rates, though, then their fears should now be allayed given the chart on the next page. This chart, together with the effect that mortgage rates have on the US housing market, has clearly taken on added importance.

Mortgage rates now appear key to whether & when to taper

30y US Treasury Yield vs 30y US Home Mortgage Rate, Fixed National Average

Source: Bloomberg, Bankrate.com, M&G, October 2013.

What about the ongoing budget nonsense? This one takes a bit of a leap of faith, but markets are clearly starting to price in the risk of something going very badly wrong as demonstrated by the jump in T-bill yields and the surge in 1yr US CDS (i.e. the cost of insuring against a US default, see chart below). But market stresses should make the prospect of a deal more likely, and this appears to be starting to happen. It's dangerous reading too much into the headline tennis, but the latest news is that Republican and Democratic leaders are open to a short-term increase in the debt limit. And don't forget, the debt ceiling has been raised 74 times since March 1962 – past performance is no guide to the future as everyone knows, but while this episode is particularly chaotic, is this time really different?

Government shutdown is starting to cause market distress

1y CDS spread, United States of America, in EUR

Source: Bloomberg, M&G, October 2013.

Finally, the technicals for the US Dollar are now much more appealing. US Dollar positioning has seen a sharp reversal from earlier this year, and Deutsche Bank estimates the US dollar is the only substantial short in the market (see following charts). Does this matter? To finish with a quote from John Maynard Keynes* regarding investing, "It is the one sphere of life and activity where victory, security and success is always to the minority and never to the majority. When you find anyone agreeing with you, change your mind. When I can persuade the Board of my Insurance Company to buy a share, that, I am learning from experience, is the right moment for selling it'".

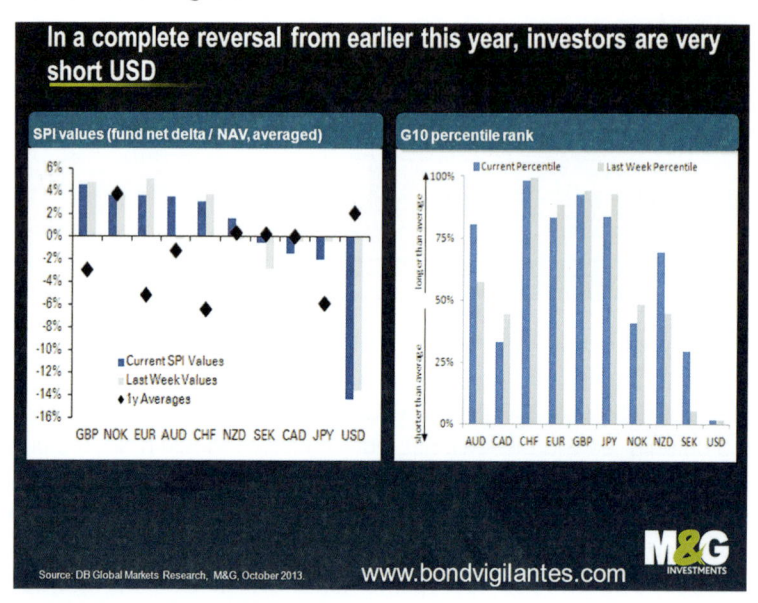

*Keynes is famous for amassing a fortune through investing, but in 1920 he had to be bailed out by his father together with an emergency loan from Sir Ernest Cassel, and he came very close to being wiped out in the 1929 and 1937 stockmarket crashes. So clearly the consensus can occasionally be right.

2014

Chapter 44

China's investment/GDP ratio soars to a totally unsustainable 54.4%. Be afraid.
Mike Riddell – Friday, 24th January 2014

"Once upon a time, Western opinion leaders found themselves both impressed and frightened by the extraordinary growth rates achieved by a set of Eastern economies. Although those economies were still substantially poorer and smaller than those of the West, the speed with which they had transformed themselves from peasant societies into industrial powerhouses, their continuing ability to achieve growth rates several times higher than the advanced nations, and their increasing ability to challenge or even surpass American and European technology in certain areas seemed to call into question the dominance not only of Western power but of Western ideology. The leaders of those nations did not share our faith in free markets of unlimited civil liberties. They asserted with increasing self-confidence that their system was superior: societies that accepted strong, even authoritarian governments and were willing to limit individual liberties in the interest of the common good, take charge of their economies, and sacrifice short-run consumer interests for the sake of long-run growth would eventually outperform the increasingly chaotic societies of the West. And a growing minority of Western intellectuals agreed.

"The gap between Western and Eastern economic performance eventually became a political issue. The Democrats recaptured the White House under the leadership of a young, energetic new president who pledged to "get the country moving again" – a pledge that, to him and his closest advisers, meant accelerating America's economic growth to meet the Eastern challenge."

The passage is the opening to the highly readable and hugely influential 1994 paper The Myth of Asia's Miracle. The period referenced is the early 1960s, the dynamic president was John F. Kennedy (read Bill Clinton), and the rapidly growing Eastern economies were the Soviet Union and its satellite nations (read East Asia). Author Paul Krugman took on the prevalent East Asian euphoria by drawing disturbing parallels between the unsustainable way that the Asian Tigers were managing to generate supersonic growth, and how the recently obsolete Soviet Union had also once achieved seemingly miraculous growth rates. Krugman's paper gained widespread attention at the time (even more so post the 1997 Asian crisis), and succeeded in refocusing attention on the concept of productivity. It mattered not what the growth rate was, but how it was achieved.

To explain this and briefly summarise, consider what actually drives economic growth. Growth accounting shows that GDP per capita growth comes from two main sources; inputs and efficiency. The 'inputs' can be split into labour (e.g. growth in employment) and capital (e.g. the accumulation of physical capital stock such as machines and buildings). But long-term, sustained per capita economic growth tends to come not from increases in the 'inputs', but from increases in efficiency, of which the main driver is technological progress. Nobel Laureate Robert Solow showed in his seminal 1956 paper that technological progress had accounted for 80% of US per capita growth between

1909 and 1949, although more recent studies have suggested a still substantial figure of more like 45-55% thereafter.

Krugman pointed to previous research showing that the Soviet Union's rapid growth had not been due to efficiency gains. Indeed, the USSR was considerably less efficient than the US, and showed no signs of closing the gap. Soviet growth had been solely due to the 'inputs', and input-driven growth has diminishing returns (e.g. there is a finite number of workers you can educate). The USSR's growth was largely 'built on perspiration rather than inspiration'.

In a similar way, the Asian Tigers' rapid growth was due to an ability to mobilise resources. There was no great improvement in efficiency, and no 'miracle' – it could be fully explained by the employed share of the population rocketing, education improving dramatically, and an enormous investment in physical capital (in Singapore, investment as a share of output jumped from 11% to more than 40% at its peak). But these were one time changes; they weren't repeatable.

Fast forward to 21st century China.

There is a perception that China's rocketing growth rate has always been reliant on heavy investment, but that's not the case. Investment, or capital formation, has of course been an important driver, but the 'pre 2008' China did achieve rapid productivity gains thanks to the rise of the private sector and technological catch-up as the economy slowly began to open its borders.

In the chart overleaf, I've looked at how much the world's biggest economies have invested as a percentage of their GDP, and compared this to the countries' GDP per capita growth rates. Countries with higher investment rates tend to have higher GDP growth rates and vice versa, which is intuitive and supports the discussion above. Since the 1990s, most (but not all) emerging/developing countries have been positioned towards the top right hand side with higher investment and higher growth rates, and the more advanced economies have typically been towards the bottom left with lower investment and lower growth rates. In one extreme you have China, where investment has averaged over 40% of GDP, and the GDP per capita growth has averaged a phenomenal 9.5%. The fact that China's growth rate is well above the trend line in the chart is indicative of the productivity gains that China has achieved over the period as a whole on average. The country with the weakest investment rate is the UK.

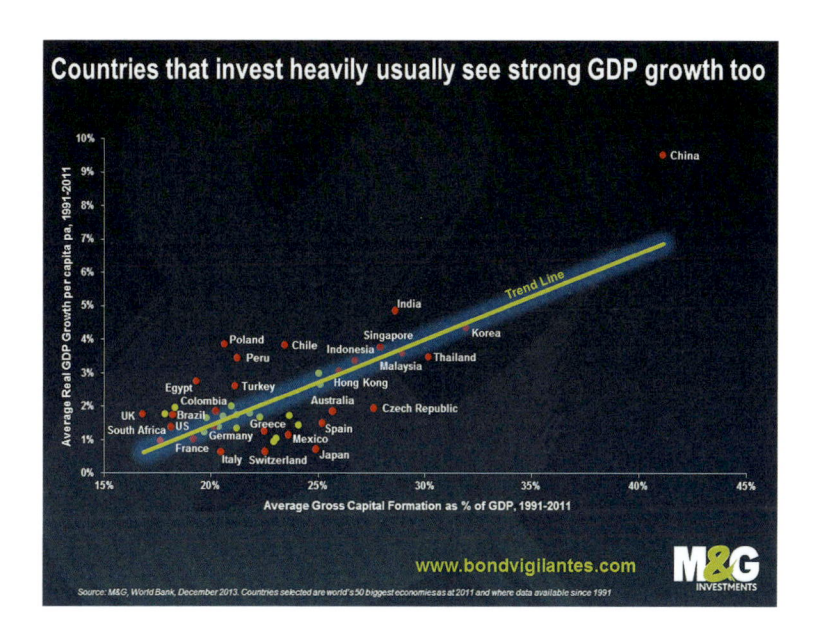

Countries that invest heavily usually see strong GDP growth too

[Scatter plot: Average Real GDP Growth per capita pa, 1991-2011 (y-axis, 0%-10%) vs Average Gross Capital Formation as % of GDP, 1991-2011 (x-axis, 15%-45%). Countries plotted include China (top right, ~9%, ~42%), India, Singapore, Korea, Poland, Chile, Indonesia, Peru, Turkey, Malaysia, Thailand, Egypt, Colombia, Hong Kong, Australia, Czech Republic, UK, Brazil, US, South Africa, Greece, Spain, Germany, Mexico, France, Italy, Switzerland, Japan. Trend line shown. Source: M&G, World Bank, December 2013. Countries selected are world's 50 biggest economies as at 2011 and where data available since 1991. www.bondvigilantes.com M&G INVESTMENTS]

'Post 2008' China looks a different animal. Productivity and efficiency seem to be plummeting, where GDP growth is becoming dangerously reliant on the 'inputs', namely soaring investment. We've all heard about how China's leaders desire a more sustainable growth model, featuring a rebalancing of China's economy away from investment and export dependence and towards one that is more reliant on domestic demand and consumer spending (e.g. see the 12th 5 year plan covering 2011-2015 or the Third Plennum). In practice, what we've instead consistently seen is an inability or unwillingness to meaningfully reform, where any dip in economic growth has been met with yet another wave of state-sponsored overinvestment. (Jim recently blogged about economist Michael Pettis' expectation that China's long-term growth could fall to 3-4%, a view with which I have a lot of sympathy.

It was widely reported earlier this week that China's 2013 GDP growth rate fell to a 13 year low of 7.7%, a slowdown that seems to have continued into 2014 with the release of weak PMI manufacturing reading yesterday. But much more alarming is how the makeup of China's growth has changed: last year investment leapt from 48% of China's GDP to over 54%, the biggest surge in the ratio since 1993.

The next chart puts China's problems into perspective. As already demonstrated, there is a strong correlation between different countries' investment rates and GDP growth rate. There also tends to be a reasonable correlation over time between an individual country's investment rate and its GDP growth rate (Japan's experience from 1971-2011 is a good example, as shown in a previous blog). Over time, therefore, a country should be broadly travelling between the bottom left and top right of the chart, with the precise location determined by the country's economic model, its stage of development and location in the business cycle.

It should be a concern if a country experiences a surge in its investment rate over a number of years, but has little or no accompanying improvement in its GDP growth rate, i.e. the historical time series would appear as a horizontal line in the chart below. This suggests that the investment surge is not productive, and if accompanied by a credit bubble (as is often the case), then the banking sector is at risk (e.g. Ireland and Croatia followed this pattern pre 2008, Indonesia pre 1997).

But it's more concerning still if there is an investment surge accompanied by a GDP growth rate that is falling. This is where China finds itself, as shown by the red arrow.

Part of China's growth rate decline is likely to be explained by declining labour productivity – the Conference Board, a think tank, has estimated that labour productivity growth slowed from 8.8% in 2011 to 7.4% in 2012 and 7.1% in 2013. Maybe this is due to rural-urban migration slowing to a trickle, meaning fewer workers are shifting from low productivity agriculture to higher productivity manufacturing, i.e. China is approaching or has arrived at the Lewis Turning Point (see more on this under China – much weaker long-term growth prospects from page 4 of our July 2012 Panoramic).

However the most likely explanation for China's surging investment being coupled with a weaker growth rate is that China is experiencing a major decline in capital efficiency. Countries that have made the rare move from the top left of the chart towards the bottom right include the Soviet Union (1973-1989), Spain (1997-2007), South Korea (1986-1996), Thailand (1988-1996) and Iceland (2004-2006). Needless to say, these investment bubbles didn't end well. In the face of a labour productivity slowdown, China is trying to hit unsustainably high GDP growth rates by generating bigger and bigger credit and investment bubbles. And as the IMF succinctly put it in its Global Financial Stability Report from October 2013, 'containing the risks to China's financial system is as important as it is challenging'. China's economy is becoming progressively unhinged, and it's hard to see how it won't end badly.

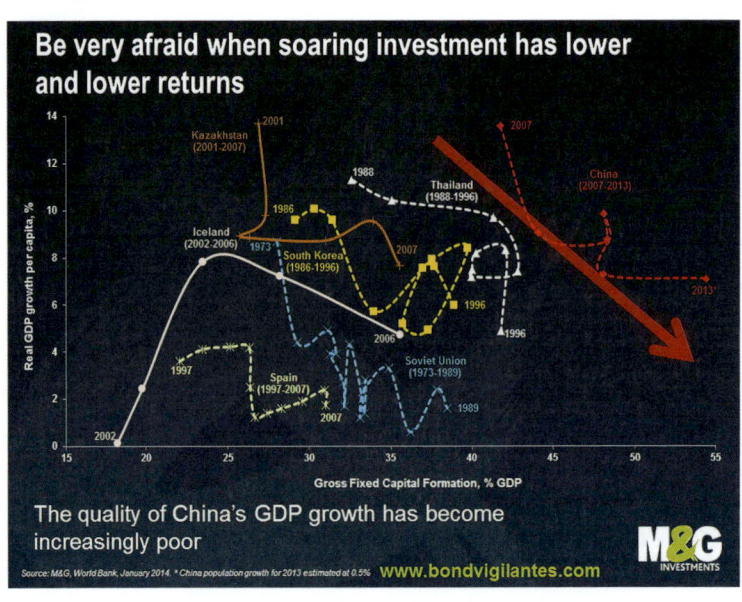

Chapter 45

Deflating the deflation myth
Richard Woolnough – Friday, 7th February 2014

There is currently a huge economic fear of deflation. This fear is basically built on the following three pillars.

First, that deflation would result in consumers delaying any purchases of goods and services as they will be cheaper tomorrow than they are today. Secondly, that debt will become unsustainable for borrowers as the debt will not be inflated away, creating defaults, recession and further deflation. And finally, that monetary policy will no longer be effective as interest rates have hit the zero bound, once again resulting in a deflationary spiral.

The first point is an example of economic theory not translating into economic practice. Individuals are not perfectly rational on timing when to buy discretionary goods. For example, people will borrow at a high interest rate to consume goods now that they could consume later at a cheaper price. One can also see how individuals constantly purchase discretionary consumer goods that are going to be cheaper and better quality in the future (for example: computers, phones, and televisions). Therefore the argument that deflation stops purchases does not hold up in the real world.

The second point that borrowers will go bust is also wrong. We have had a huge period of disinflation over the last 30 years in the G7 due to technological advances and globalisation. Yet individuals and corporates have not defaulted as their future earnings disappointed due to lower than expected inflation.

The third point that monetary policy becomes unworkable with negative inflation is harder to explore, as there are few recent real world examples. In a deflationary world, real interest rates will likely be positive which would limit the stimulatory effects of monetary policy. This is problematic, as monetary policy loses its potency at both the zero bound and if inflation is very high. This makes the job of targeting a particular inflation rate (normally 2%) much more difficult.

What should the central bank do if there is naturally low deflation, perhaps due to technological progress and globalisation? One response could be to head this off by running very loose monetary policy to stop the economy experiencing deflation, meaning the central bank would attempt to move GDP growth up from trend to hit an inflation goal. Consequences of this loose monetary policy may include a large increase in investment or an overly tight labour market. Such a policy stance would have dangers in itself, as we saw post 2001. Interest rates that were too low contributed to a credit bubble that exploded in 2008.

Price levels need to adjust relative to each other to allow the marketplace to move resources, innovate, and attempt to allocate labour and capital efficiently. We are used to this happening in a positive inflation world. If naturally good deflation is being generated maybe authorities should welcome a world of zero inflation or deflation if it is accompanied by acceptable economic growth. Central banks need to take into account real world inflationary and deflationary trends that are not a monetary phenomenon and set their policies around that. Central bankers should be as relaxed undershooting their inflation target as they are about overshooting.

Under certain circumstances central banks should be prepared to permit deflation. This includes an environment with a naturally deflating price level and acceptable economic growth. By accepting deflation, central banks may generate a more stable and efficient economic outcome in the long run.

Chapter 46

Stand up for your rights! Covenant erosion in high yield bond documentation
James Tomlins – Tuesday, 1st April 2014

2013 saw a record year for new issue volumes in the European high yield market. A total of $106bn equivalent was raised by non-investment grade companies according to data from Moodys. Whilst this is beneficial for the long-term diversification and growth of the market, there have been some negative trends. Given the intense demand for new issues, companies and their advisors have been able to perpetuate the erosion various bondholder rights to their own advantage. What form has this erosion taken and why are they potentially so costly for bondholders? Here we highlight some of the specific changes that have crept into bond documentation over the past 2 years and some examples that demonstrate the potential economic impact for investors.

1) Shorter call periods – high yield bonds often contain embedded call options which enable the issuer to repay the bonds at a certain price at a certain point in the future. The benefit for the issuer is that if their business performs well and becomes less financially risky, they can call their bonds early and re-finance at a cheaper rate. The quid pro quo for bond holders is that the call price is typically several percentage points above par, hence they share in some of the upside. However, the length of time until the next call is important too. The longer the period, the higher the potential capital return for any bond holder as the risk premium (credit spread falls). The shorter the call period, the less likely the issuer will be locked into paying a high coupon. Take for example the following situation: reducing the call period has an associated cost to the investor of 2.6% of capital appreciation.

Shorter call periods

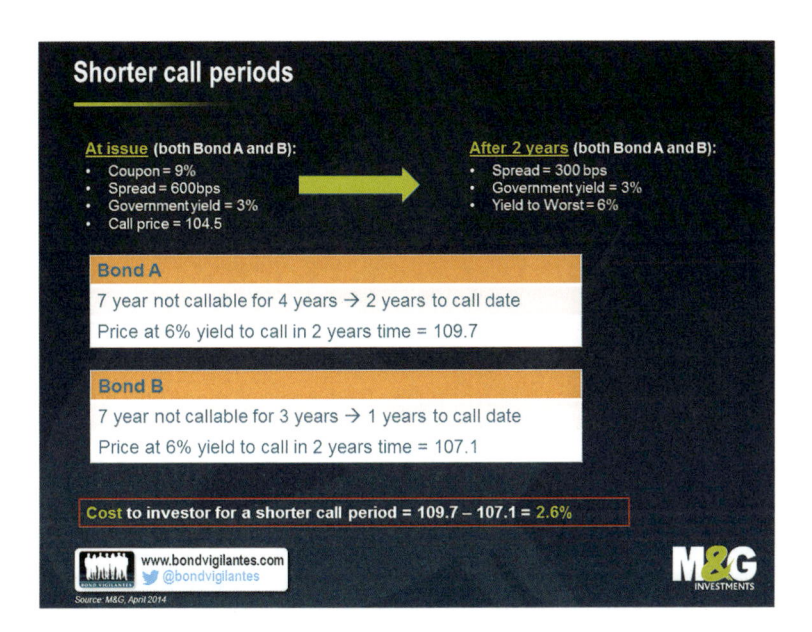

At issue (both Bond A and B):
- Coupon = 9%
- Spread = 600bps
- Government yield = 3%
- Call price = 104.5

After 2 years (both Bond A and B):
- Spread = 300 bps
- Government yield = 3%
- Yield to Worst = 6%

Bond A
7 year not callable for 4 years → 2 years to call date
Price at 6% yield to call in 2 years time = 109.7

Bond B
7 year not callable for 3 years → 1 years to call date
Price at 6% yield to call in 2 years time = 107.1

Cost to investor for a shorter call period = 109.7 – 107.1 = 2.6%

www.bondvigilantes.com
@bondvigilantes

Source: M&G, April 2014

2) 10% call per year at 103 – Similar to the example above, the ability to call a bond prior to maturity has the impact of reducing potential upside to investors. One innovation that favours issuer's has been the introduction of a call of 10% of the issue size every year within the so called "non call" period, usually at a preset price of 103% of par. So assuming a 3 year "non call" period, almost 1/3rd of an issuers bond can be retired at a relatively limited premium to par. Take for example the counterfactual scenario below. Here we see the inclusion of this extra call provision has reduced the potential return to bondholders by 3.3% over the holding period.

10% call per year at 103

At issue:
- Coupon = 8%
- Spread = 500bps
- Government yield = 3%

After 3 years:
- Price = 108.4
- Spread = 300bps
- Government yield = 3%

Bond A has a 10% called at 103% of par every year for 3 years. Bond B has no call. Both are sold at 108.4

Cash Flows	Bond A	Bond B
Year 0	-100	-100
Year 1	17.5	8
Year 2	16.7	8
Year 3	91.78	116.4
IRR p.a.	**9.4%**	**10.5%**

Cost = 1.1% per year (3.3% over the whole period)

www.bondvigilantes.com
@bondvigilantes

Source: M&G, April 2014

3) Portability – One of the most powerful bondholder protections is the so called "put on change of control". This gives the bondholder the right but not the obligation to sell their bonds back

to the issuer at 101% of face value in the event the company changes ownership. Crucially, this protects investors from the potential re-pricing downside of the issuer being purchased by a more leveraged or riskier entity. For the owners of companies, this has been a troublesome restriction as the need to refinance a complete capital structure can be a major impediment to any M&A transaction. However, a recent innovation has been to introduce a "portability" clause into the change of control language. This typically states that subject to a leverage test and time restriction, the put on change of control does not apply (and hence the bonds in issue become "portable", travelling with the company to any new owner removing the need to potentially re-finance the debt). With much of the market trading well above 101% of par, the value of the put on change of control is somewhat diminished so some investors have not seen this as an egregious erosion of rights. The owners of the issuers on the other hand enjoy a much higher degree of flexibility when it comes to buying and selling companies. There are costs to bondholders, however. In particular, as and when bonds trade below face value, this option can have significant value. In the example below we see that the inclusion of portability has an associated cost of 2.4%

Portability

Company owners announce deal to sell the bond issuer

	Bond A	Bond B
Coupon	5%	5%
Portable	Yes	No (put at 101 on change of control)
Price before announcement of sale	97.5	97.5
Maturity	5 year	5 year
Price after announced sale of business	98.7	101
Return	1.2%	3.6%

Cost to bondholders = 3.6% - 1.2% = 2.4%

www.bondvigilantes.com
@bondvigilantes

Source: M&G, April 2014

M&G INVESTMENTS

4) **Conditional Restricted Payment Basket** – Another protection for high yield bondholders has been the restrictions on dividends. This prevents owners of businesses from stripping out large amounts of cash leaving behind a more leveraged and riskier balance sheet. If a company was performing very well and the owners wished to take out a large dividend, they would usually be forced to re-finance the debt or come to a consensual agreement with bondholders to allow them to do so. Consequently, the call protections would apply and the bondholders would be able to share in some of the success of the issuer's business. However, another recent innovation has been the loosening of this "restricted payments" provision to allow a limitless upstreaming of dividend cash out of the business subject to a leverage test. This limits the ability of owners to load up the balance sheet

with debt at will, but without the need to re-finance the bonds bondholders lose some of their bargaining power and once more are likely to lose out in certain situations. In this example, we see an impact of 1.0%

Conditional Restricted Payment Basket

Company wishes to pay out $100 mln dividend

	Bond A	Bond B
Coupon	4.75%	4.75%
Restricted Payment Language	$100 mln dividend permissible	$100 mln dividend not permissible
Price pre-dividend announced	101	101
Price post-announcement	99.5	100.5*
Return	-1.5%	-0.5%

* The company announces it will pay a consent fee of 1% of notional to bond B bondholders to allow the payment of the dividend

Cost to bondholders of weaker restricted payment language = 1.0%

www.bondvigilantes.com
@bondvigilantes
Source: M&G, April 2014

What can investors do to cope with these unwelcome changes? Some sort of collective resistance would probably be the most effective tool – bondholders need to be prepared to stand up for their rights – but this is difficult to maintain in the face of inflows into the asset class and the need to invest cash. Until the market becomes weaker and negotiating power swings back toward the buyers of debt rather than the issuers, the most pragmatic course of action is for investors to asses any change on a case by case basis, then factor these in to their return requirements. This way investors can at least demand the appropriate risk premium for these changes and if they deem the risk premium insufficient they can simply elect to abstain. In the meantime, the old adage holds as true as ever – *caveat emptor*.

Chapter 47

The emerging markets rebalancing act
Claudia Calich – Wednesday, 2nd April 2014

Over the past year, investors' perception towards emerging market bonds changed from viewing the glass as being half full to half empty. The pricing-in of US 'tapering' and higher US Treasury yields largely drove this shift in sentiment due to concerns over sudden stops of capital flows and currency volatility. For sure, emerging market economies will need to adjust to lower capital flows, with this adjustment taking place on various fronts over several years.

Some emerging market countries are more advanced than others in the rebalancing process, while others may not need it at all. Also relevantly, the amount of rebalancing required should be assessed on a case-by-case basis, as the economic and political costs must be weighed against the potential benefits. Generally, the necessary actions include reducing external vulnerabilities such as large current account deficits (especially those financed by volatile capital flows), addressing hefty fiscal deficits and banking sector fragilities, or balancing the real economy between investment and credit and consumption.

In our latest issue of our Panoramic Outlook series, we examine the main channels of transmission, policy responses and asset price movements, as well as highlight the risks and opportunities we see in the asset class. Our focus in this analysis is on hard currency and local currency sovereign debt.

Chapter 48

5 Signs that the Bond Markets (rightly or wrongly) think the Eurozone Crisis is over
James Tomlins – Thursday, 10th April 2014

Regardless of your opinion on the merit of the ECB's policy, there is little doubt that the efficacy of Mario Draghi's various statements and comments over the past 2 years has been radical. Indeed there are several signs in the bond markets that investors believe the crisis is over. Here are some examples:

1) Spanish 10 yr yields have fallen to 3.2%, this is lower than at any time since 2006, well before the crisis hit, having peaked at around 6.9% in 2012. This is an impressive recovery, almost as impressive as...

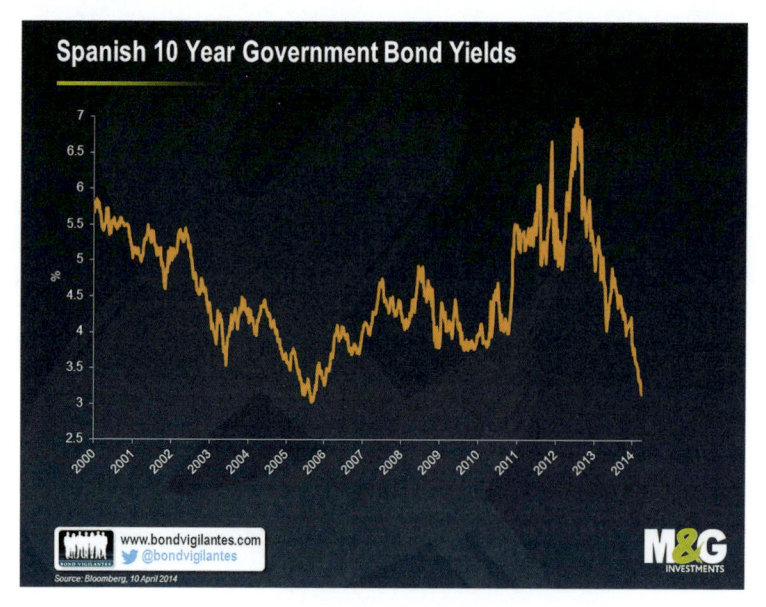

2) The fall in Italian 10 year bond yields, which have hit new 10 year lows of 3.15%, lower than any time since 2000. The peak was 7.1% in December 2011. To put this in context, US 10 year yields were at 3% as recently as January this year.

Italian 10 Year Government Bond Yields

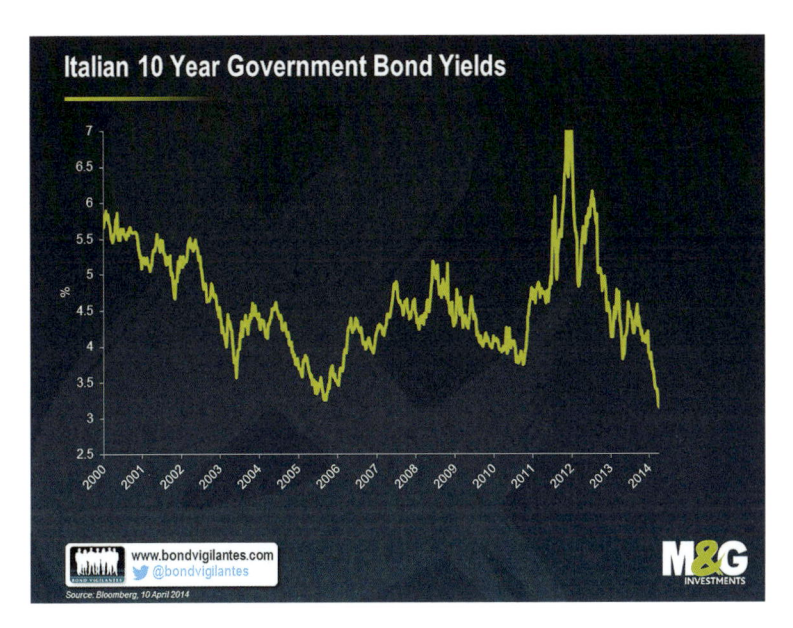

3) Last month, Bank of Ireland issued €750m of covered bonds (bonds backed by a collateral pool of mortgages), maturing in 2019 with a coupon of 1.75%. These bonds now trade above par, with a yield to maturity of 1.5%. The market is not pricing in any material risk premium relating to the Irish housing market.

4) There is no longer any risk premium within the high yield market for peripheral European risk. The chart below (published by Bank of America Merrill Lynch) shows that investors in non-investment grade corporates no longer discriminates between "core" and "peripheral" credits when it comes to credit spreads.

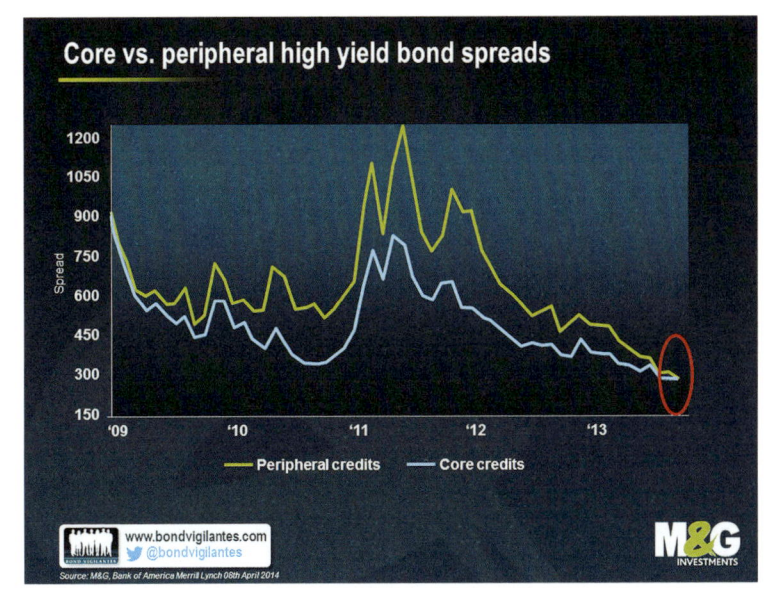

Core vs. peripheral high yield bond spreads

5) Probably the biggest sign of all, is that today Greece is re-entering the international bond markets. The country is expected to issue €3bn 5 year notes with a yield to maturity of 4.95%.

Chapter 49

The Great Compression of peripheral to core European risk premiums
Wolfgang Bauer – Thursday, 17th April 2014

Are investors still compensated adequately for investing in peripheral rather than core European debt, or has the ongoing convergence eroded debt valuation differentials altogether? In his latest blog entry, James highlighted five signs indicating that the bond markets consider the Eurozone crisis resolved. Inter alia, James pointed out that risk premiums for peripheral vs. core European high yield credit had essentially disappeared over the past two years. Here I would like to extend the periphery/core comparison by taking a look at investment grade (IG) credit and sovereign debt.

First, let's have a look at the spread evolution of peripheral and core European non-financial (i.e., industrials and utilities) IG indices over the past 10 years. In addition to the absolute asset swap (ASW) spread levels, we plotted the relative spread differentials between peripheral and core credit. The past ten years can be divided into three distinct phases. In the first phase, peripheral and core credit were trading closely in line with each other; differentials did not exceed 50 bps. The Lehman collapse in September 2008 and subsequent market shocks led to a steep increase in ASW spreads, but the strong correlation between peripheral and core credit remained intact. Only in the second phase, during the Eurozone crisis from late 2009 onwards, spreads decoupled with core spreads staying relatively flat while peripheral spreads increased drastically. Towards the end of this divergence period, spread differentials peaked at more than 280 bps. ECB President Draghi's much-cited "whatever it takes" speech in July 2012 rang in the third and still ongoing phase, i.e., spread convergence.

As at the end of March 2014, peripheral vs. core spread differentials for non-financial IG credit had come back down to only 18 bps, a value last seen four years ago. The potential for further spread convergence, and hence relative outperformance of peripheral vs. core IG credit going forward, appears rather limited. Within the data set covering the past 10 years, the current yield differential is in very good agreement with the median value of 17 bps. Over a 5-year time horizon, the current differential looks already very tight, falling into the first quartile (18th percentile).

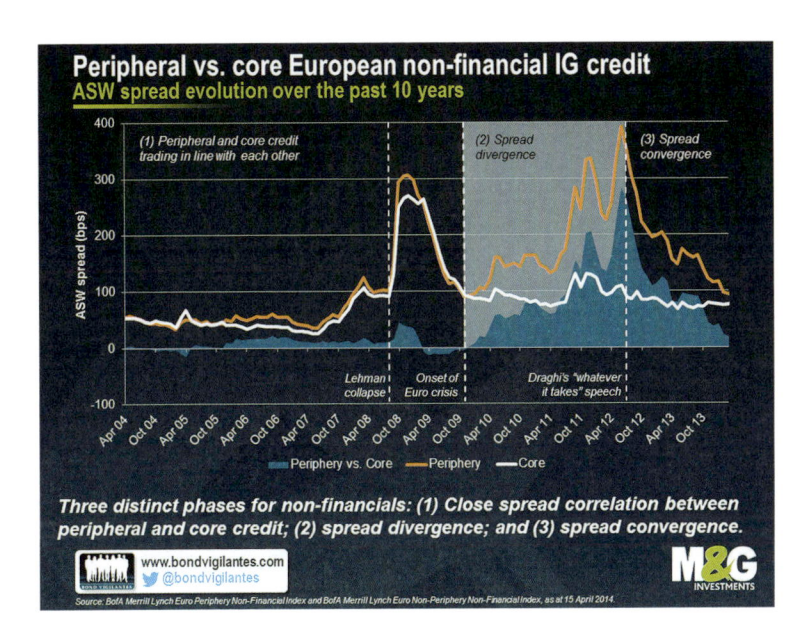

Peripheral vs. core European non-financial IG credit
ASW spread evolution over the past 10 years

Three distinct phases for non-financials: (1) Close spread correlation between peripheral and core credit; (2) spread divergence; and (3) spread convergence.

Moving on from IG credit to sovereign debt, we took a look at the development of peripheral and core European government bond yields over the past 10 years. As a proxy we used monthly generic 10 year yields for the largest economies in the periphery and the core (Italy and Germany, respectively). Again three phases are visible in the chart, but the transition from strong correlation to divergence occurred earlier, i.e., already in the wake of the Lehman collapse. At this point in time, due to their "safe haven" status German government bond yields declined faster than Italian yields. Both yields then trended downwards until the Eurozone crisis gained momentum, causing German yields to further decrease, whereas Italian yields peaked. Once again, Draghi's publicly announced commitment to the Euro marked the turning point towards ongoing core/periphery convergence.

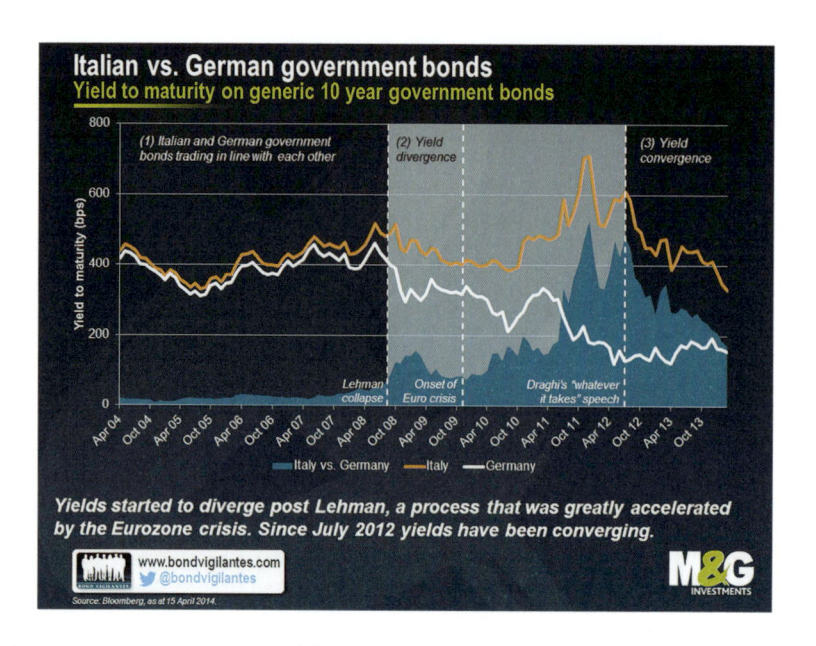

Italian vs. German government bonds
Yield to maturity on generic 10 year government bonds

(1) Italian and German government bonds trading in line with each other
(2) Yield divergence
(3) Yield convergence

Lehman collapse | Onset of Euro crisis | Draghi's "whatever it takes" speech

■ Italy vs. Germany   — Italy   — Germany

Yields started to diverge post Lehman, a process that was greatly accelerated by the Eurozone crisis. Since July 2012 yields have been converging.

www.bondvigilantes.com
@bondvigilantes

M&G INVESTMENTS

Source: Bloomberg, as at 15 April 2014.

Currently investors can earn an additional c. 170 bps when investing in 10 year Italian instead of 10 year German government bonds. This seems to be a decent yield pick-up, particularly when you compare it with the more than humble 18 bps of core/periphery IG spread differential mentioned above. As yield differentials have declined substantially from values beyond 450 bps over the past two years, the obvious question for bond investors at this point in time is: How low can you go? Well, the answer mainly depends on what the bond markets consider to be the appropriate reference period. If markets actually believe that the Eurozone crisis has been resolved once and for all, not much imagination is needed to expect yield differentials to disappear entirely, just like in the first phase in the chart above. When looking at the past 10 years as a reference period, there seems to be indeed some headroom left for further convergence as the current yield differential ranks high within the third quartile (69th percentile). However, if bond markets consider future flare-ups of Eurozone turbulences a realistic scenario, the past 5 years would probably provide a more suitable reference period. In this case, the current spread differential appears less generous, falling into the second quartile (39th percentile). The latter reading does not seem to reflect the prevailing market sentiment, though, as indicated by unabated yield convergence over the past months.

In summary, a large portion of peripheral to core European risk premiums have already been reaped, making current valuations of peripheral debt distinctly less attractive than two years ago. Compared to IG credit spreads, there seems to be more value in government bond yields, both in terms of current core/periphery differentials and regarding the potential for future relative outperformance of peripheral vs. core debt due to progressive convergence. But, of course, ongoing convergence would require bond markets to keep believing that the Eurozone crisis is indeed ancient history.

Chapter 50

Playing Russian roulette

Claudia Calich – Wednesday, 30th April 2014

The Russia and Ukraine geopolitical tensions have driven their asset prices since February. As the below research courtesy of BofA Merrill Lynch shows, investors' base case scenario is that a major escalation of the conflict, in the form of a direct Russian invasion of parts of Eastern Ukraine, is unlikely. The possibility of an invasion seems analogous to Russian roulette, a low probability but high impact game.

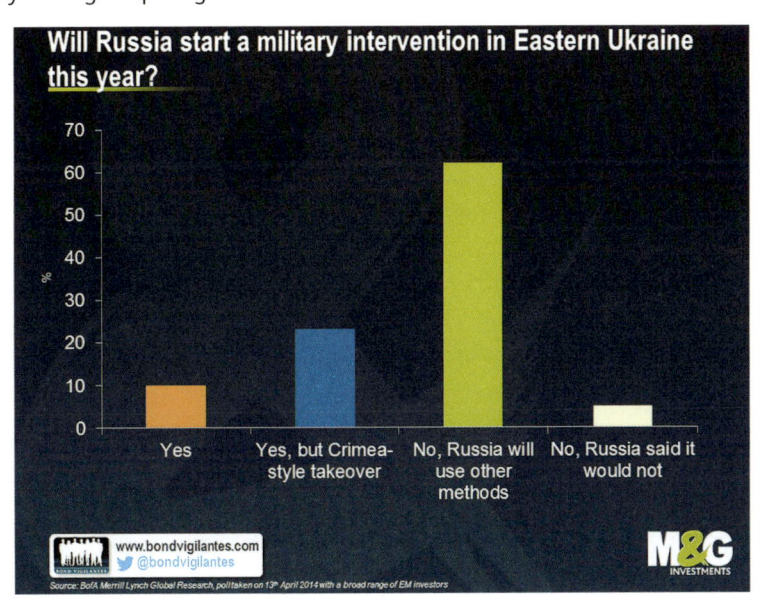

I just returned from a trip to Moscow. You would not know there is the possibility of a war going on next door by walking around the city, if you didn't turn to the news. Its picture perfect spring blue skies were in stark contrast to the dark clouds looming over the economy.

The transmission mechanism of the political impact into the economy is fairly predictable:

1. Political-related risk premia and volatility remaining elevated, translating into weakening pressure on the ruble;

2. Pressure for higher rates as the ruble weakens (the CBR has already hiked rates by 200 bps, including the unexpected 50 bps hike last week, but more will be needed if demand for hard currency remains at the Q1 2014 level and pressure on the currency increases further);

3. Downside pressure on growth as investment declines and through the impact of sanctions or expectation of additional sanctions (through higher cost of capital);

4. Downward pressures on international reserves as the capital account deteriorates and CBR smoothens the currency move;

5. Decline of the oil reserve fund should it be used for counter-cyclical fiscal purposes or refinancing of maturing debt (the $90 billion fund could theoretically cover one year of amortizations, but in that case, capital flight and dollarization would escalate further as the risk perception deteriorates).

All these elements are credit negative and it is not a surprise that S&P downgraded Russia's rating to BBB-, while keeping it on a negative outlook. What is less predictable, however, is the magnitude of the deterioration of each of these elements, which will be determined by political events and the extent of economic sanctions.

My impression was that the locals' perception of the geopolitical risks was not materially different from the foreigners' perception shown above – i.e. that a major escalation in the confrontation remains a tail risk. The truth is, there is a high degree of subjectivity in these numbers and an over-reaction from either side (Russia, Ukraine, the West) can escalate this fluid situation fairly quickly. The locals are taking precautionary measures, including channelling savings into hard currency (either onshore or offshore), some pre-emptive stocking of non-perishable consumer goods, considering alternative solutions should financial sanctions escalate – including creating an alternative payment system and evaluating redirecting trade into other currencies, to the extent it can. Locals believe that capital flight peaked in Q1, assuming that the geopolitical situation stabilizes. Additional escalations could occur around 1st and 9th of May (Victory Day), as well as around the Ukrainian elections on 25th of May.

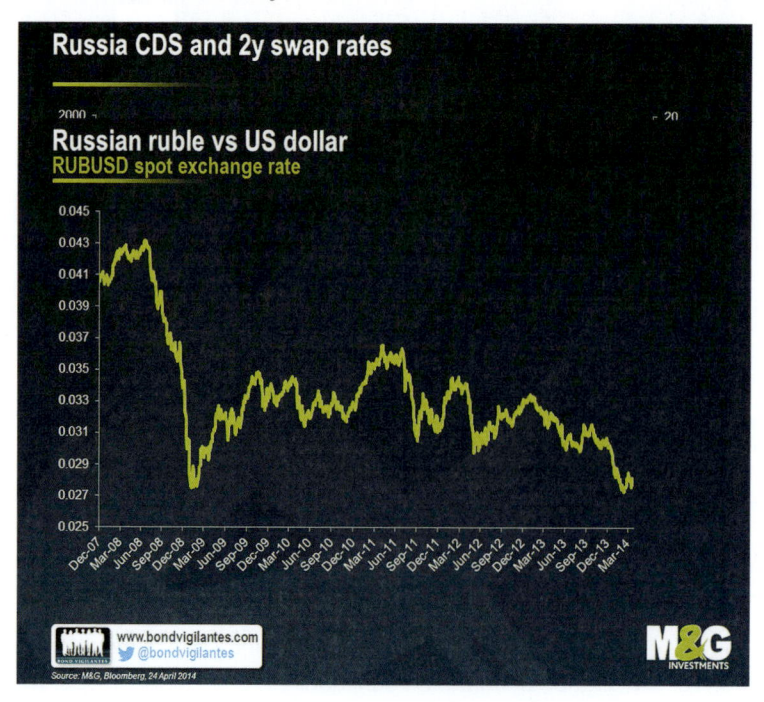

Russian ruble vs US dollar
RUBUSD spot exchange rate

Source: M&G, Bloomberg, 24 April 2014

The following table assigns various CDS spread levels for each of the scenarios, with the probabilities given per the earlier survey. The weighted probability average is still wider than current levels, though we have corrected by a fair amount last week. I used CDS only as it is the best proxy hedge for the quasi-sovereign and corporate risk. Also, the ruble would be heavily controlled by the CBR should risk premia increase further, and may not work as an optimal hedge for a while, while liquidity on local bonds and swaps would suffer should the sanctions directly target key Russian banks.

Russia 5 year CDS fair value

Russia invasion in Ukraine	Probability	5 yr CDS
Yes	10%	500
Yes, Crimea style	23%	375
No, other methods	62%	260
No	5%	190
	100%	307 → Weighted average
		270 → Current

www.bondvigilantes.com
@bondvigilantes

Source: M&G, Bloomberg, 25 April 2014

The risk-reward trade-off appears skewed to the downside in the near term.

Chapter 51

Sell in May and go away – does it work for European fixed income?
Anthony Doyle – Friday, 9th May 2014

As is usually the case on 1 May, there was a plethora of articles and commentary on the "sell in May and go away" effect. If you are unfamiliar with this highly sophisticated trading strategy, it involves closing out any equity exposure you may have on 30 April and re-investing on 1 November. Historically, U.S. equities have underperformed in the six-month period commencing May and ending in October, compared to the six-month period from November to April. No one knows why this seasonal pattern exists, but some theories include lower trading volumes in the summer holiday months and increased investment flows when investors come back from holidays.

With this in mind, we thought it might be interesting to see if the same effect exists in European fixed income markets. In order to identify the sell in May effect, we generated total returns on a monthly basis for a portfolio of European government, investment grade and high yield bonds. We then generated a total return for a portfolio that was invested between the months of November and April and compared this with a portfolio that was invested between the months of May and October. In order to generate the maximum number of observations possible, we went back to the inception of the respective Merrill Lynch Bank of America indices. The results are overleaf.

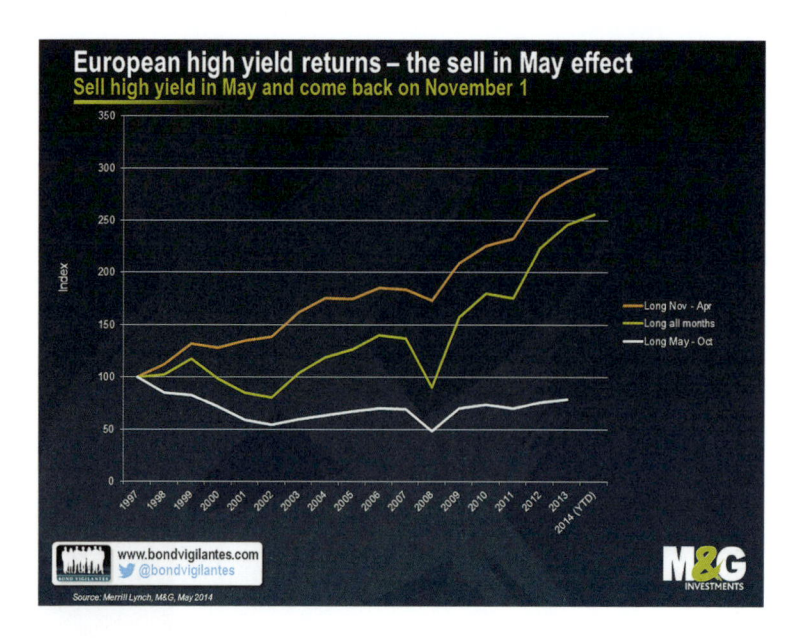

European high yield returns – the sell in May effect
Sell high yield in May and come back on November 1

There appears to be a seasonal effect in European high yield markets. This is the fixed income asset class that is most correlated to equity markets, and the analysis shows that a superior return was generated by only being invested between the months of November and April (199% total return). In fact, this strategy substantially outperformed a strategy of being invested over the whole period (1997 – April 2014). If an investor chose to only invest between the months of May and October, they would have suffered a 21% loss over the past 16 years.

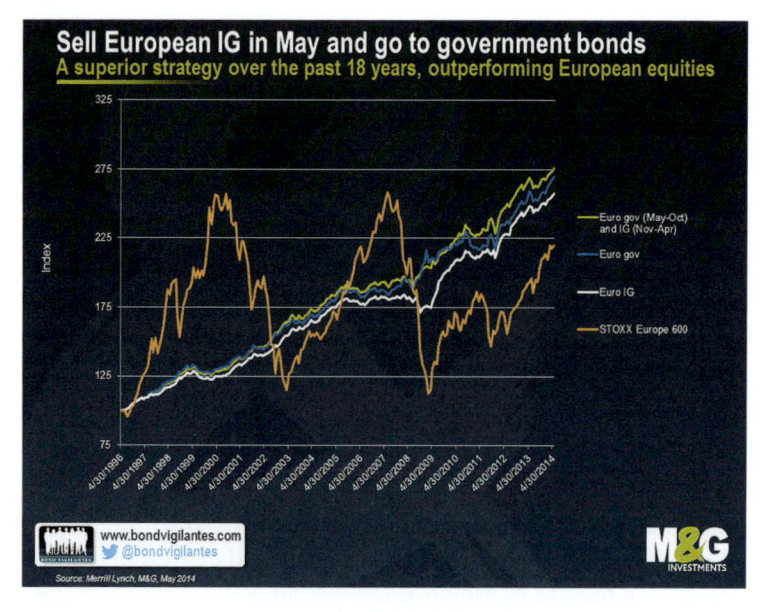

Sell European IG in May and go to government bonds
A superior strategy over the past 18 years, outperforming European equities

The natural extension of this analysis is to gauge how a trading strategy that was fully invested in European government bonds between the months of May and October and fully invested in European investment grade between November and April would have performed over the past 18 years. We can then assess how this strategy would have performed relative to portfolios that were fully invested in European government bonds, European investment grade corporate bonds and European equities only. The results show that a strategy of selling investment grade assets in May and buying government bonds has produced superior returns equal to 5.9% per annum, outperforming European equities by 56% in total or 2.5% p.a.

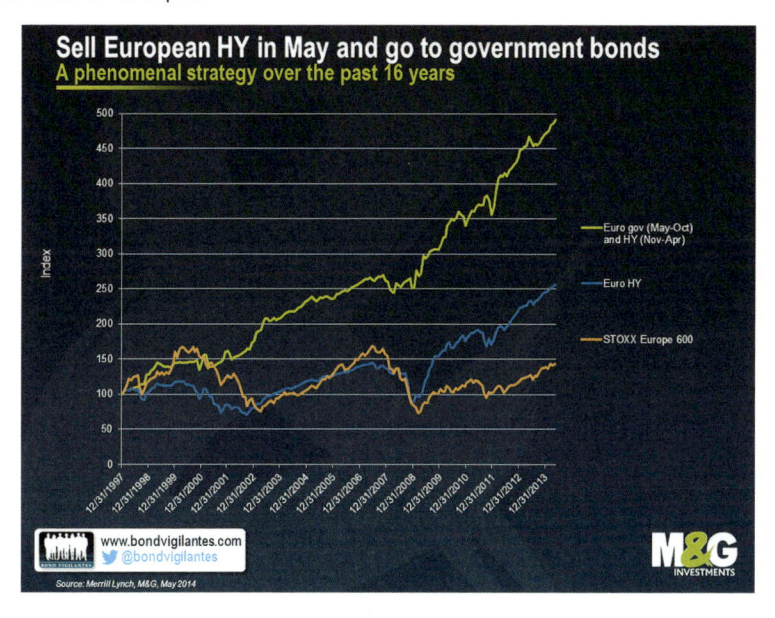

Sell European HY in May and go to government bonds
A phenomenal strategy over the past 16 years

[Chart showing index values from 12/31/1997 to 12/31/2013, comparing Euro gov (May-Oct) and HY (Nov-Apr), Euro HY, and STOXX Europe 600]

Source: Merrill Lynch, M&G, May 2014

The above chart shows the same analysis, this time looking at how the strategy would have performed in total return terms but we have replaced European investment grade exposure with European high yield. Following this strategy would have generated an annualised return of around 10.5% or 391% over 16 and a bit years. This is far superior to the returns on offer in the European high yield and European equity markets over the same time period, which were 155% and 43% respectively.

Our analysis shows that there is a strong seasonal effect evident in European high yield markets, where returns are more volatile and there can be large upside and downside contributions due to fluctuations in the capital value of high yield bonds. However, it should be acknowledged that the results have been biased by the fact that major risk-off events (like Lehman Brothers, the Asian financial crisis and the Russian financial crisis for example) have generally occurred between the months of May and October. Nonetheless, historical total returns suggest that there is a seasonal effect in European high yield markets that investors should probably be aware of. Ignoring transaction costs or tax implications which would eat into any total returns, a strategy of selling investment grade or high yield corporate bonds in May and buying government bonds until November would have produced superior returns relative to European government bonds, investment grade corporate bonds, high yield corporate bonds and European equities.

Whilst it is always dangerous to base a trading strategy around a nursery rhyme, based on historical total returns there does appear to be a bit of sense in selling risk assets in May, retreating into government bonds which would likely benefit most in a risk-off event, and adding risk back into fixed income portfolios in November. But of course, another old saying still rings true – past performance is not a guide to future performance.

Chapter 52

Is Europe (still) turning Japanese? A lesson from the 90's
Stefan Isaacs – Friday, 30th May 2014

Seven years since the start of the financial crisis and it's ever harder to dismiss the notion that Europe is turning Japanese.

Now this is far from a new comparison, and the suggestions made by many since 2008 that the developed world was on course to repeat Japan's experience now appear wide of the mark .The substantial pick-up in growth in many developed economies, notably the US and UK, instead indicates that many are escaping their liquidity traps and finding their own paths, rather than blindly following Japan's road to oblivion. Super-expansionary policy measures, it can be argued, have largely been successful.

Not so, though, in Europe, where Japan's lesson doesn't yet seem to have been taken on board. And here, the bond market is certainly taking the notion seriously. 10 year bund yields have collapsed from just shy of 2% at the turn of the year and the inflation market is pricing in a mere 1.4% inflation for the next 10 years; significantly below the ECB's quantitative definition of price stability.

So just how reasonable is the comparison with Japan and what could fixed income investors expect if history repeats itself?

The prelude to the recent European experience wasn't all that different to that of Japan in the late 1980s. Overly loose financial conditions resulted in a property boom, elevated stock markets and the usual fall from grace that typically follows. As is the case today in Europe, Japan was left with an oversized and weakened banking system, and an over-indebted and ageing population. Both Japan and Europe were either unable or unwilling to run countercyclical policies and found that the monetary transmission mechanism became impaired. Both also laboured under periods of strong currency appreciation – though the Japanese experience was the more extreme – and the constant reality of household and banking sector deleveraging. The failure to deal swiftly and decisively with its banking sector woes – unlike the example of the US – continues to limit lending to the wider Eurozone economy, much as was the case in Japan during the 1990s and beyond. And despite the fact that Japanese demographics may look much worse than Europe's do today, back in the 1990s they were far more comparable to those in Europe currently.

Probably the most glaring difference in the two experiences is centred around the labour market response. Whereas Eurozone unemployment has risen substantially post crisis, the Japanese experience involved greater downward pressure on wages with relatively fewer job losses and a more significant downward impact on prices.

With such obvious similarities between the two positions, and whilst acknowledging some notable differences, it's surely worthwhile looking at the Japanese bond market response.

As you would expect from an economy mired in deflation, Japan's experience over two decades has been characterised by extremely low bond yields (chart 1). Low government bond yields likely encouraged investors to chase yield and invest in corporate bonds, pushing spreads down (chart 2) and creating a virtuous circle that ensured low default rates and low bond yields – a situation that remains true some 23 years later.

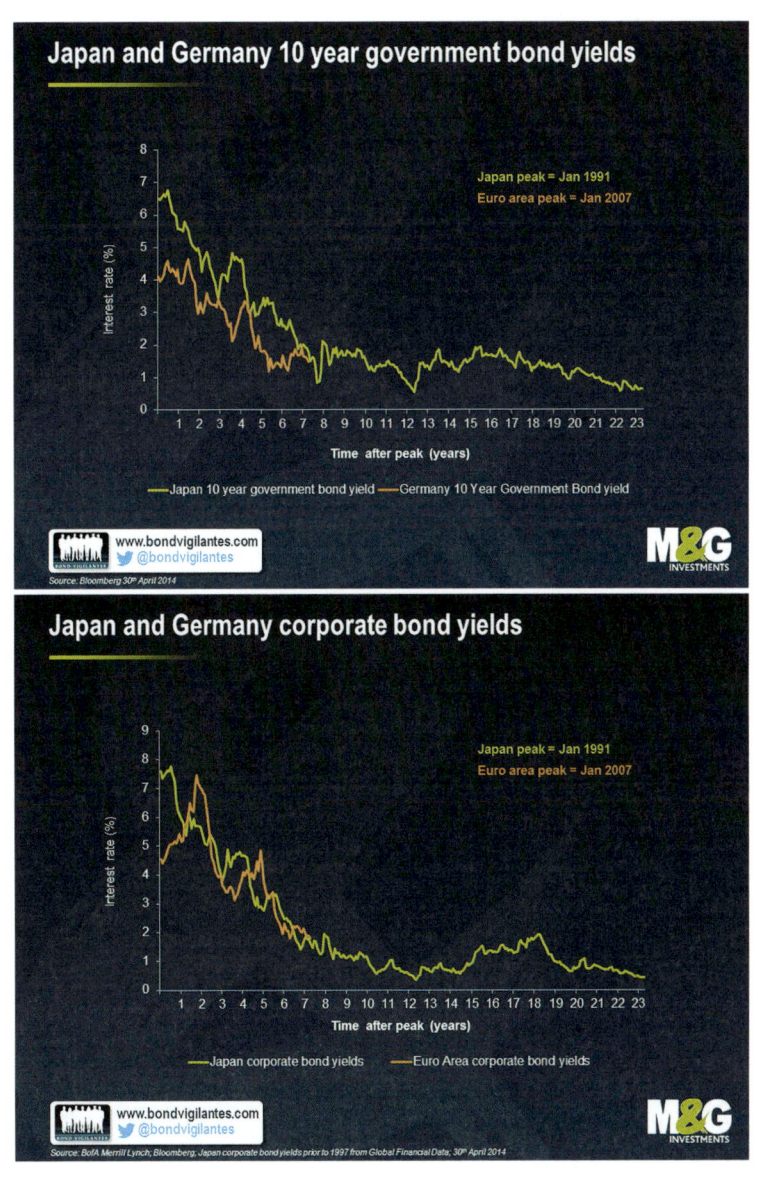

![Japan and Germany 10 year government bond yields]

![Japan and Germany corporate bond yields]

As an aside, Japanese default rates have remained exceptionally low, despite the country's two decades of stagnation. Low interest rates, high levels of liquidity, and the refusal to allow any issuers to default or restructure created a country overrun by zombie banks and companies. This has resulted in lower productivity and so lower long-term growth potential – far from ideal, but not a bad thing in the short-to-medium term for a corporate bond investor. With this in mind, European credit spreads approaching historically tight levels, as seen today, can be easily justified.

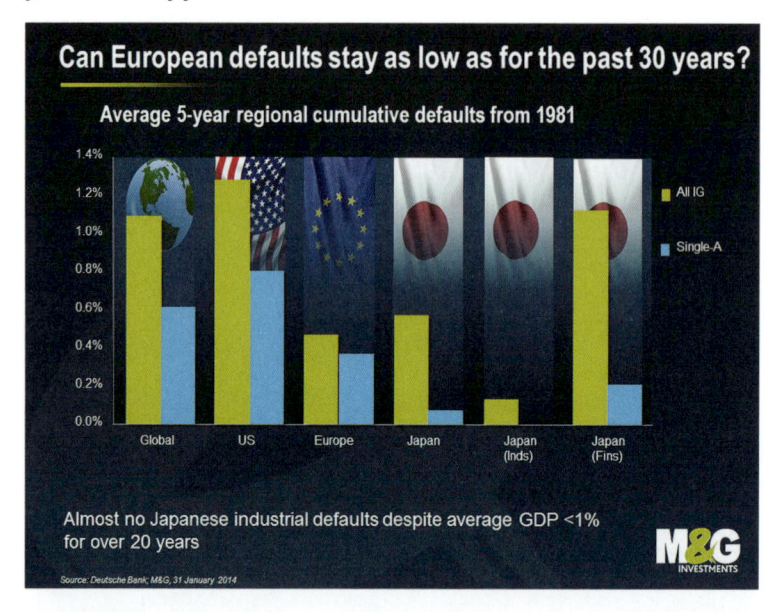

Can European defaults stay as low as for the past 30 years?

Average 5-year regional cumulative defaults from 1981

Almost no Japanese industrial defaults despite average GDP <1% for over 20 years

Source: Deutsche Bank; M&G, 31 January 2014

Europe currently finds itself in a similar position to that of Japan several years into its crisis. Outright deflation may seem some way off, although the risk of inflation expectations becoming unanchored clearly exists and has been much alluded to of late. Japan's biggest mistake was likely the relative lack of action on the part of the BOJ. It will be interesting to see what, if any response, the ECB sees as appropriate on June 5th and in subsequent months.

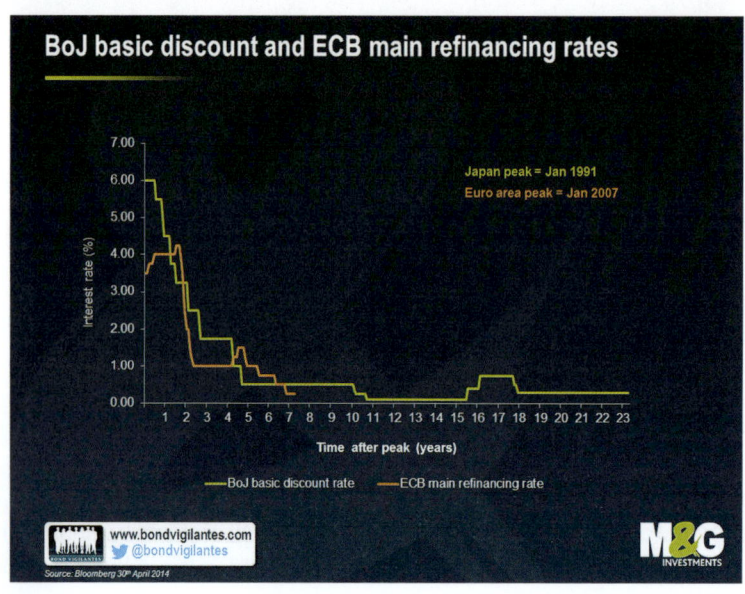

BoJ basic discount and ECB main refinancing rates

Japan peak = Jan 1991
Euro area peak = Jan 2007

Time after peak (years)

— BoJ basic discount rate   — ECB main refinancing rate

www.bondvigilantes.com
@bondvigilantes

Source: Bloomberg 30th April 2014

Though it is probably too early to call for the 'Japanification' of Europe, a long-term policy of ECB supported liquidity, low bond yields and tight spreads doesn't seem too far-fetched. The ECB have said they are ready to act. They should be. The warning signs are there for all to see.

Chapter 53

Why aren't bund yields negative again?
Jim Leaviss– Wednesday, 4th June 2014

Whether or not you believe that the ECB moves to full government bond purchase quantitative easing this week (and the market overwhelmingly says that it's only a remote possibility) the fact that German bund yields at the 2 year maturity remain positive is a bit surprising. The 2 year bund currently yields 0.05%, lower than the 0.2% it started the year at, but higher than you might have expected given that a) they have traded at negative yields in 2012 and 2013 and b) that the market's most likely expected outcome for Thursday's meeting is for a cut in the ECB's deposit rate to a negative level.

The chart below shows that in the second half of 2012, and again in the middle of 2013, the 2 year bund yield was negative (i.e. you would expect a negative nominal total return if you bought the bond at the prevailing market price and held it to maturity), hitting a low of -0.1% in July 2012.

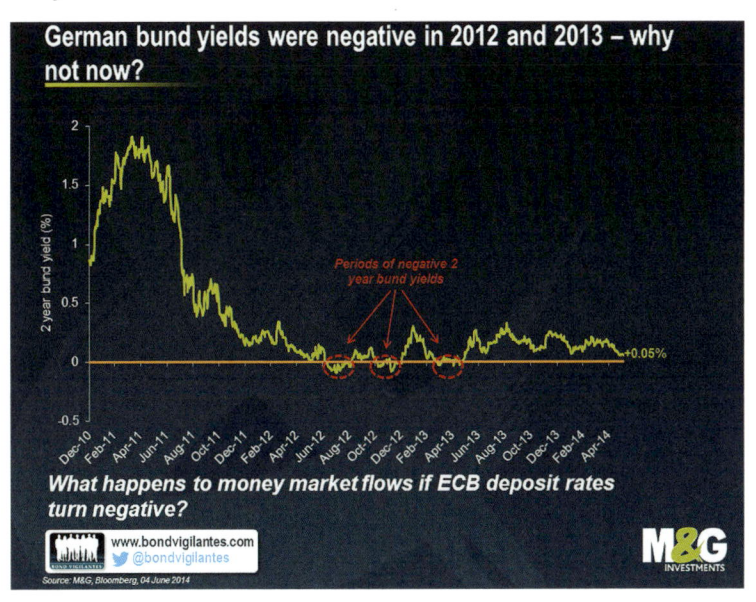

Obviously in 2012 in particular, the threat of a Eurozone breakup was at its height. Peripheral bond spreads had hit their widest levels (5 year Spanish CDS traded at over 600 bps in July 2012), and Target2 balances showed that in August 2012 German banks had taken Euro 750 billion of "safe haven" deposits from the rest of the euro area countries (mostly from Spain and Italy). So although the ECB refinancing rate was at 0.75% in July 2012 compared with 0.25% today, the demand for German government assets rather than peripheral government assets drove the prices of short-dated bunds to levels which produced negative yields.

This time though, whilst the threat of a euro area breakup is much lower – Spanish CDS now trades at 80 bps versus the 600 bps in 2012 – the prospect of negative deposit rates from the ECB might produce different dynamics which might have implications for short-dated government bonds. The market expects that the ECB will set a negative deposit rate, charging banks 0.1% to deposit money with it. Denmark successfully tried this in 2012 in an attempt to discourage speculators as money flowed into Denmark out of the euro area. Whilst the ECB refinancing rate is likely to remain positive, the cut in deposit rates might have significant implications for money market funds. David Owen of Jefferies says that there is Euro 843 billion sitting in money market funds in the euro area, equivalent to 8.5% of GDP. But what happens to this money if rates turn negative? In 2012, when the ECB cut its deposit rate to zero, several money market fund managers closed or restricted access to their money market funds (including JPM, BlackRock, Goldman Sachs). Many money market funds around the world guarantee, or at least imply, a constant or positive net asset value (NAV) – this is obviously not possible in a negative rate environment, so funds close, at least to new money. And if you are an investor why would you put cash into a money market fund, taking credit risk from the assets held by the vehicle, when you could own a "risk free" bund with a positive yield?

So whilst full blown QE may well be months off, if it ever happens, and whilst Draghi's "whatever it takes" statement means that euro area breakup risk is normalising credit risk and banking system imbalances, the huge amount of money held in money market funds that either wants to find positive yields, or is forced to find positive yields by fund closures, makes it a puzzle as to why the 2 year bund yield is still above zero.

Chapter 54

Burrito Bonds – an example of the retail bond market
James Tomlins – Monday, 23rd June 2014

One of our local burrito vendors has been advertising a new 8% bond to its customer base. The company, Chilango, wants to raise up to £3m to fund expansion of its chain in central London. This will be done via a crowd sourced retail offering that's already drawn some interesting coverage in the financial press. Having performed some extensive due diligence on the company's products as a team, we can safely say they make a pretty good burrito. However, when we compare the bond to the traditional institutional high yield market, we have some concerns that investors should be aware of.

1. **Disclosure** – a typical high yield bond offering memorandum (the document that sets out the rules of the issue, its risk and all the necessary historical financial disclosure) can be several hundred pages long. Producing this is a very time intensive and expensive process, but a valuable one for producing a host of useful information for potential investors. Additionally, a law firm and an accounting firm typically sign off on this document, effectively staking their reputation and incurring litigation risk based on the veracity of the information disclosed.

In contrast, the Chilango's document is 33 pages long, with some fairly superficial financial disclosure. The photos on the next page illustrates this comparative informational disadvantage and the relative lack of depth in financial information compared to a recent institutional high yield bond offering from Altice.

![Chilango vs. Altice Offering Memorandum - photograph comparing the slim Chilango Burrito Bond document with the much thicker Altice offering memorandum. Source: M&G, Chilango. www.bondvigilantes.com @bondvigilantes M&G Investments]

2. **Financial Risk** – there are two big potential concerns here. Firstly, the starting leverage for the bonds is potentially quite high. Using some admittedly finger in the air assumptions regarding the potential cashflow of each new outlet opened (a necessary approach given poor disclosure), leverage could be around 6.0x Net Debt/EBITDA in 2015. This is certainly at the riskier end of the high yield spectrum. The second major concern is that we don't know for certain how much debt the company will raise. Chilango state that they target at least £1m in this issue, but are willing to raise up to £3m, leverage is likely to be north of 10x (again this is a best guess). All this means the bonds would in our opinion get at best a CCC rating, right at the riskiest end of the credit rating spectrum for sub-investment grade bonds.

Chilango Financial Disclosure

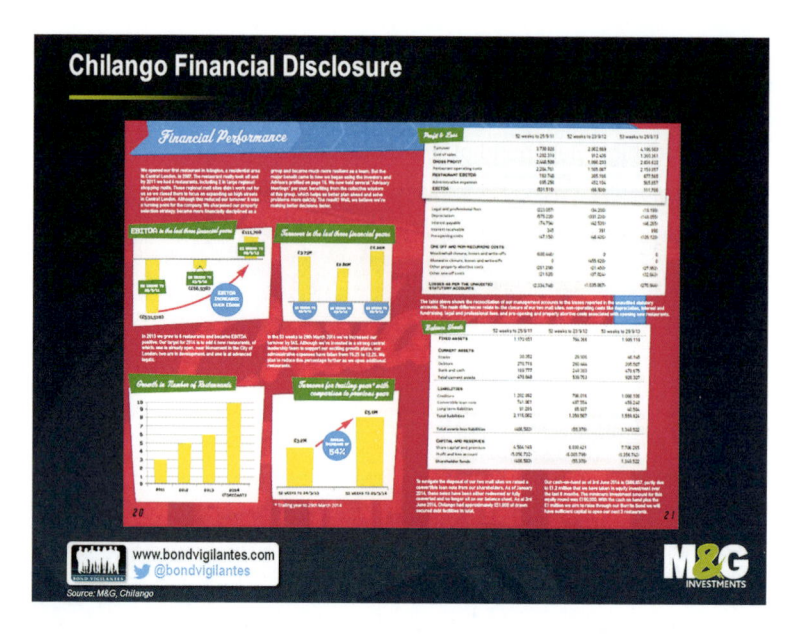

3. **Security** – Chilango state very clearly that these bonds will be unsecured instruments. This means that in the event of a default, the creditors will rank behind any secured creditors. There appears to be limited existing secured creditors, but we see nothing in the documentation to prevent a layer of new secured debt being raised ahead of these notes (something that is a common covenant in institutional bonds deals). Consequently, it's prudent to assume that in a default situation the recovery value of the bonds is likely to be significantly below face value. This equity-like downside means investors should demand an equity-like return in our view.

4. **Call Protection** – these bonds are redeemable at the option of the issuer at any time. Consequently, investor returns could be materially curtailed due to the lack of call protection. Call protection is the premium over face value the investors get when the issuing company redeems the debt early (their call option). Thus some of the benefit also accrues to the bondholder. Take the following return profile:

8% Bond, Callable at Par

Years Outstanding	Total Return
1	8%
2	17%
3	26%
4	36%

If the plan to open new branches goes well, the bond investor should be happy right? Wrong. If this happens, the company may well look like a less risky prospect and will be able to raise debt finance more cheaply. Let's say a bank offers them a loan at 5%, they could then redeem the 8% bond early, diminishing the total return to bondholders (as per above), and save £90,000 a year on interest costs per year (assuming they issued £3m bonds). Again, call protection is a common feature of the institutional high yield market which protects investors in these situations.

5. **Liquidity** – these are non-transferable bonds. This means that a) the company does not have to file a full offering memorandum hence the lack of disclosure and b) it will not be possible to buy or sell the bonds in a secondary market. This is more akin to a bilateral loan between an individual investor and the company, with the investor in it for the long haul. Consequently, an investor will neither be able to easily manage their risk exposure nor will they be able to take profits should they so wish before the bond is redeemed.

6. **Value** – we can see that there are many risks – but to be fair that is the nature of high yield investing. So the real question is, "is 8% sufficient compensation for this risk". The good news is that this bond has a unique bonus coupon in the form of a free burrito a week for anyone prepared to invest £10,000. At current prices, this equates to 3.63% additional coupon (a steak, prawn or pork burrito with extra guacamole is £6.99), so an all-in coupon of 11.63% (8% cash + 3.63% burrito). We'd argue that a "burrito fatigue factor" should be applied, simply because you may not want a burrito every week and you will probably not be physically near a Chilango every week to cash in this extra coupon. A 75% factor feels about right, which reduces the burrito coupon to 2.72% and the all-in return to 10.72%. So is 10.72% a fair price? To get a sense of this we can look at some GBP dominated CCC rated institutional bonds in other asset light industries.

Bond	Price	Yield
Phones 4 U 10% 2019	90.5	12.7%
Towergate 10.5% 2019	98.5	10.9%
Matalan 8.875% 2020	101.5	8.5%
	Average:	10.7%

7. By coincidence, the all in coupon of 10.7% is bang in line with the average of this (very limited) group of comparable bonds. However, I'd argue that the Chilango bonds should be significantly cheaper than the bonds above due to higher leverage, no liquidity, no call protection and the lack of disclosure. What should this differential be? Again, there is no scientific answer, but our starting point would probably be in the 15-20% range, and only then with some more certainty around the potential maturity of the bond and the ability to share in the future success of the company.

So, much as though we would all enjoy the tasty weekly coupons, our view is that like many of the so-called "retail" or "mini" bond offerings, the Chilango burrito bonds stack up poorly against some of the current opportunities in the institutional high yield market.

M&G has no financial interest in seeing this issue succeed or fail, either directly or indirectly.

Chapter 55

The reliability of market and consumer inflation expectations
Ana Gil – Thursday, 26th June 2014

After yesterday's poor U.S. GDP number and despite Mark Carney's seemingly dovish testimony before the Treasury Select Committee, the Bank of England is increasingly looking like it will be the first of the major central banks to hike rates. At this stage, the BoE can retain its dovish stance because inflation is not an issue. However, in an environment of falling unemployment, early signs of a pick-up in wage inflation, rising house prices and stronger economic growth, consumers and markets may increasingly begin to focus on inflation. In anticipation, we think now is a good time to compare the inflation forecasting performance of markets and consumers.

In the charts below we have compared UK RPI bond breakevens (a measure of market inflation expectations) with the Bank of England's Gfk NOP Inflation Attitudes Survey (i.e. a UK household survey with over 1900 respondents consisting of nine questions on expectations for interest rates and inflation). An important point to note is that the analysis compares realised inflation (% yoy) with what survey expectations and breakeven rates indicated 2 years before.

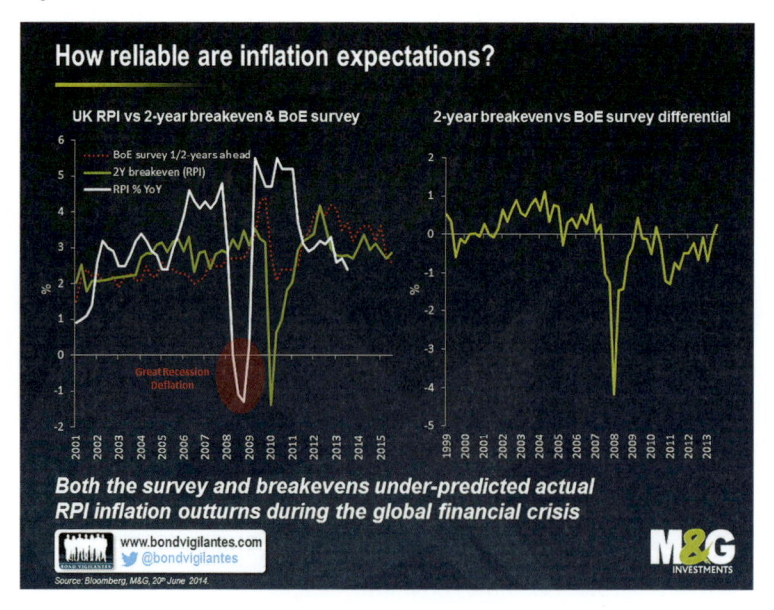

How reliable are inflation expectations?

Both the survey and breakevens under-predicted actual RPI inflation outturns during the global financial crisis

Source: Bloomberg, M&G, 20th June 2014.

The comparison presents a number of interesting results:

Unexpected deflation: Both the survey and breakevens underestimated actual RPI inflation outcomes between 2006-2008 (in other words, nobody anticipated the inflationary shock coming from higher commodity/energy prices). In 2008, UK RPI was rising at an annual rate of 5.2% as high oil prices were feeding through into higher energy bills. Market and consumer inflation expectations largely ignored the higher inflation numbers, a sign the central bank inflation targeting credibility remained strong.

UK RPI turned negative in 2009 as the world plunged into recession and the BOE cut interest rates. The market eventually began to price in deflation but only after RPI turned negative. For example, in November 2008 the 2 year breakeven was -1.4%, the actual RPI print in November 2010 was 4.7%. Owning 2 year gilt linkers relative to conventional 2 year gilts directly after the financial crisis was a great trade.

Deflation (and recessions) appear particularly hard to forecast, for consumers and markets alike. This is because consumers and markets tend to anchor their future expectations off current inflation (and growth) readings.

Post-crisis unanchoring: Consumer inflation expectations generally underestimated realised inflation up until the global financial crisis, and has overestimated it since then, a possible sign that the crisis-recession years may have affected consumer views on the BoE's commitment to fight inflation. Between 2000 and 2009, 2 year-ahead expected inflation averaged 2.5%. Since 2009, it has averaged 3.4%, almost one percentage point higher; suggesting a lower level of confidence that price stability will be achieved and also reflecting the higher RPI prints post 2009.

Surprisingly similar forecasts: Breakeven and survey rates differed only slightly over the sample period, with the largest gap (400 bps) opening up in October 2008 after the Lehman crash. This was probably caused by the forced unwind of leveraged long inflation trades combined with a huge flight to quality bid for nominal government bonds, which distorted the market implied inflation rate. The average differential through the period (excluding years 2008-09) is just 8 bps. Nevertheless, breakevens seem to track RPI better since consumer surveys are usually carried out on a quarterly basis whilst the former are traded and re-valued with higher frequency. This makes them better at capturing quick moves and turning points in inflation.

Future expectations: Over the next 2 years, both consumers and markets expect RPI to rise above the current level of 2.6%. With a 2.7% implied breakeven, 2-year gilt linkers look relatively inexpensive today.

Of course, breakevens are far from being a perfect measure of inflation, as they embed inflation and liquidity risks premia, but they do appear to be better predictors of future inflation relative to consumer surveys. That does not mean survey-based data does not provide us with useful information, and for this purpose we launched the M&G YouGov Inflation Expectations Survey last year. Consumer inflation expectations affect a number of economic variables, including consumer confidence, retail spending, and unit labour costs. However, during inflection points, such as the one we may be going through at present and in a world of approaching shifts in monetary policy, the timeliness of breakevens could represent an advantage that makes it worthwhile to follow them carefully.

Chapter 56

Bondfire of the Maturities: how to improve credit market liquidity
Jim Leaviss – Wednesday, 9th July 2014

Liquidity in credit markets has been a hot topic in recent months. The Bank of England has warned about low volatility in financial markets leading to excessive reaching for yield, the FT suggested that the US authorities are considering exit fees for bond funds in case of a run on the asset class, and you've all seen the charts showing how assets in corporate bond funds have risen sharply just as Wall Street's appetite for assigning capital to trade bonds has fallen. But why the worry about corporate bond market liquidity rather than that of equity markets? There are a couple of reasons. Firstly the corporate bond markets are incredibly fragmented, with companies issuing in multiple maturities, currencies and structures, unlike the stockmarkets where there are generally just one or two lines of shares per company. Secondly, stocks are traded on exchanges, and market makers have a commitment to buy and sell shares in all market conditions. No such commitment exists in the credit markets – after the new issue process you might see further offers or bids, but you might not – future liquidity can never be taken for granted.

So how can we make liquidity in corporate bond and credit markets as good as that in equity markets? First of all let's consider fragmentation. If I type RBS corp <Go> into Bloomberg there are 1011 results. That's 1011 different RBS bonds still outstanding. It's 19 pages of individual bonds, in currencies ranging from the Australian dollar to the South African rand. There are floating rate notes, fixed rate bonds with coupons ranging from below 1% to above 10%, maturities from now to infinity (perpetuals), inflation-linked bonds, bonds with callability (embedded options), and there are various seniorities in the capital structure (senior, lower tier 2, upper tier 2, tier 1, prefs). Some of these issues have virtually no bonds left outstanding and others are over a billion dollars in size. Each has a prospectus of hundreds of pages detailing the exact features, protections and risks of the instrument. Pity the poor RBS capital markets interns on 3am photocopying duty. The first way we can improve liquidity in bond markets is to have a bonfire of the bond issues. One corporate issuer, one equity, one bond.

Let's have a bonfire of the bonds (a bondfire?)
RBS has over 1000 different bond issues outstanding

Hugely fragmented corporate bond markets cause illiquidity

www.bondvigilantes.com
@bondvigilantes

M&G INVESTMENTS

Source: M&G, Bloomberg, 09 July 2014

How would this work? Well the only way that you could have a fully fungible, endlessly repeatable bond issue is to make it perpetual. The benchmark liquid bond for each corporate would have no redemption date. If a company wanted to increase its debt burden it would issue more of the same bond, and if it wanted to retire debt it would do exactly the same as it might do with its equity capital base – make an announcement to the market that it is doing a buyback and acquire and cancel those bonds that it purchases in the open market.

What about the coupon? Well you could decide that all bonds would have, say, a 5% coupon, although that would lead to long periods where bonds are priced significantly away from par (100) if the prevailing yields were in a high or low interest rate environment. But you see the problems that this causes in the bond futures market where there is a sporadic need to change the notional coupon on the future to reflect the changing rate environment. So, for this reason – and for a purpose I'll come on to in a while – all of these new perpetual bonds will pay a floating rate of interest. They'll be perpetual Floating Rate Notes (FRNs). And unlike the current FRN market where each bond pays, say Libor or Euribor plus a margin (occasionally minus a margin for extremely strong issuers), all bonds would pay Libor or Euribor flat. With all corporate bonds having exactly the same (non) maturity and paying exactly the same coupon, ranking perceived creditworthiness becomes a piece of cake – the price tells you everything. Weak high yield issues would trade well below par, AAA supranationals like the World Bank, above it.

So your immediate objection is likely to be this – what if I, the end investor, don't want perpetual floating rate cashflows? Well you can add duration (interest rate risk) in the deeply liquid government bond markets or similarly liquid bond futures market, and with corporate bonds now themselves highly liquid, a sale of the instrument would create "redemption proceeds" for an investor to fund a liability. And the real beauty of the new instruments all paying floating rates is that they can be combined with the most liquid financial derivative markets in the world, the swaps market. An investor would be able to swap floating rate cashflows for fixed rate cashflows. This happens already on a significant scale at most asset managers. Creating bigger and deeper corporate bond markets would make this even more commonplace – the swaps markets would become even more important and liquid as the one perpetual FRN for each company is transformed into the currency and duration of the end investor's requirement (or indeed the company itself can transform its funding requirements in the same way as many do already). Investors could even create inflation linked cashflows as that CPI swaps market deepened too.

So what are the problems and objections to all of this? Well loads I'm guessing, not least from paper mills, prospectus and tombstone manufacturers (the Perspex vanity bricks handed out to everyone who helped issue a new bond). But the huge increase in swapping activity will increase the need for collateral (cash, government bonds) in the system, as well as potentially increasing systemic risks as market complexity increases. Collateralisation and the move to exchanges should reduce those systemic risks. Another issue regards taxation – junky issuers will be selling their bonds at potentially big discounts to par. Tax authorities don't like this very much (they see it as a way of avoiding income tax) and it means that investors would have to be able to account for that pull to par to be treated as income rather than capital gain. Finally I reluctantly concede there might have to be 2 separate bond issues for banks and financials. One reflecting senior risk, and one reflecting subordinated contingent capital risk (CoCos). But if we must do this, the authorities should create a standard structure here too, with a common capital trigger and conversion. Presently there are various levels for the capital triggers, and some bonds convert into equity whilst others wipe you out entirely. There is so much complexity that it is no wonder that a recent RBS survey of bond investors showed that 90% of them rate themselves as having a higher understanding of CoCos than the market.

Addressing the second difference between bonds and equities, the other requirement would be for the investment banks to move fully to exchange trading of credit, and to assume a market making requirement for those brokers who lead manage bond transactions. This doesn't of course mean that bonds won't fall in price if investors decide to sell en masse – but it does mean that there will always be a price. This greater liquidity should mean lower borrowing costs for companies, and less concern about a systemic credit crisis in the future.

Chapter 57

Falling soft commodity prices are a piece of cake

Anjulie Rusius – Tuesday, 15th July 2014

Higher agricultural commodity prices at the start of the year raised concerns about the impact these could have on retail food prices, should the trend prove persistent. Fortunately, the price of soft commodities (coffee, sugar, wheat etc) appears to have decoupled from that of hard commodities (gold, silver, platinum etc) in recent months. Indeed, data from the last seven quarters indicate that the price of many agricultural commodities have actually fallen, as the chart overleaf shows.

Agricultural commodity prices have fallen in the last 2 years

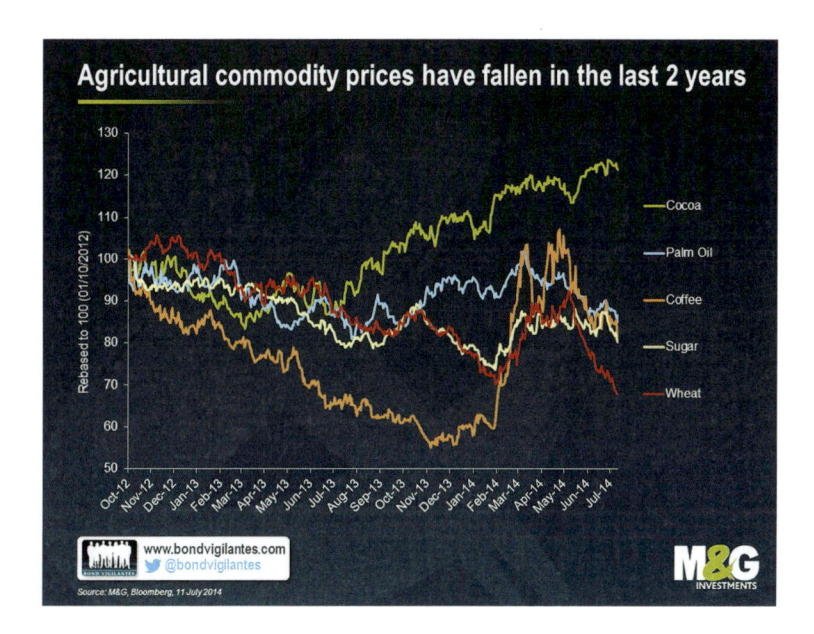

[Chart showing rebased prices (01/10/2012 = 100) from Oct-12 to Jul-14 for Cocoa, Palm Oil, Coffee, Sugar, and Wheat. Source: M&G, Bloomberg, 11 July 2014. www.bondvigilantes.com @bondvigilantes]

Coffee prices are now at a five month low, after fears of a shortage of coffee beans from Brazil have receded. The supply of sugar has increased year-on-year, while wheat prices have also fallen due to increased harvests and easing crop concerns.

In order to gauge the collective effect of these changing agricultural commodity prices and how they could potentially feed through into UK inflation, I have constructed a simple cake index, teaming up Global Commodity Price data with some basic recipes from the BBC Good Food website. Given that sponge and individual cakes are two of the representative items included in the CPI 2014 basket of goods — and that food and drink items make up 11.2% of the overall CPI index — combining the commodities in this way gives an indication of how future changes might affect the average consumer.

The next chart shows the results of the cake index, demonstrating the change in various cake costs (since October 2012) versus the UK CPI (yoy %). What's interesting is the generally downward trend of all cake indices in the last seven quarters. Sponge cake and plain scones look particularly good value in recent months, owing to the high proportion of wheat in their recipes. Apple cake unsurprisingly provides a price signal for its key ingredient (the price of apples has fallen 4% YTD), while coffee cake gives a less pronounced but similar effect. The good news — particularly for lovers of chocolate cake — is that despite the persistent increase in the cost of cocoa, the price of other cake constituents such as sugar, wheat and palm oil (used as a proxy for butter) have all fallen sufficiently to offset this, bringing the price of chocolate cake lower in recent months.

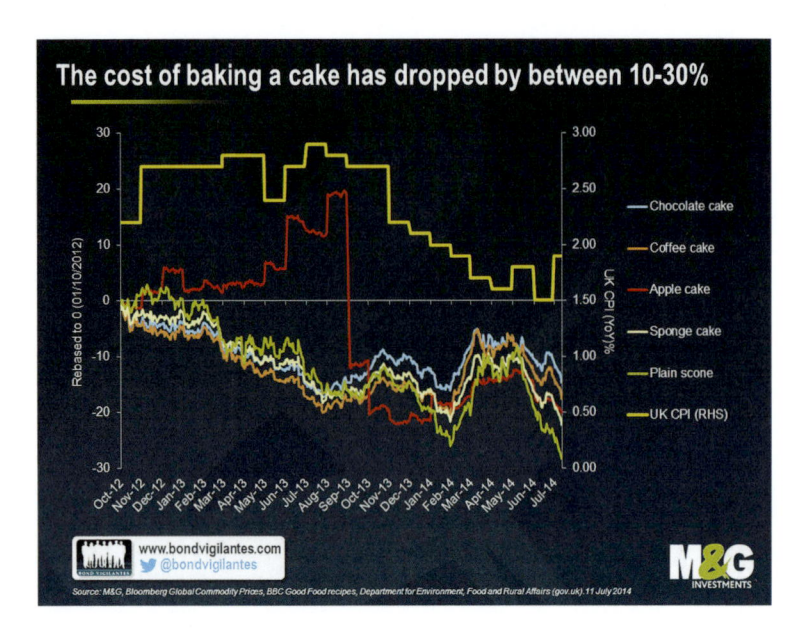

The cost of baking a cake has dropped by between 10-30%

Despite the recent June increase in CPI to 1.9% yoy, due to the lag between raw commodity prices and their general price level, we should perhaps expect to see deflation feeding into cake prices and the overall food constituent of CPI in the coming months. Therefore although it is unclear who exactly was the first to declare "let them eat cake!", this person may have been on to something. Personally, I'd recommend the (relatively cheap) scones.

Chapter 58

What is the collapse in the Baltic Dry shipping index telling us about global growth?

Jim Leaviss – Thursday, 31st July 2014

The Baltic Dry Index (BDI) is a daily priced indicator of the cost of shipping freight on various trade routes for dry bulk carriers, based on data submitted by shipbrokers to the Baltic Exchange in London. Since March this year the index has fallen by over 50%, and this has made economists worry that the fall reflects a generalized slowdown in global trade – dry bulk goods include cement, coal, ore as well as food stuffs like grain. A lot of it is the stuff that China imports to support its investment led growth model, so a collapse in demand for the ships that carry bulk dry goods to China might be telling us that China is slowing rapidly. And that obviously has significant impacts on those economies which are reliant on exporting to China for their own growth – for instance Australia, Chile, South Africa and South Korea all have between 21% and 36% of their exports going to China.

Obviously though demand for space on ships is only half of the equation. As expectations grew that the Great Financial Crisis was behind us, and as China kept publishing high single digit growth rates, there was a significant expansion in shipbuilding. Since 2010 annual growth in Dry Bulk supply has been anywhere from 5% to over 15% year on year – in most periods outstripping demand growth, and certainly depressing prices. It's not just dry bulk, there's also big excess supply in container ships. Shipping companies are trying to manage these supply problems – the average age of ships when scrapped has fallen from 28 years in 2011 to 21 years in Q1 2014, 4% of the fleet is "idle", ships are "slow steaming" (going slowly to save fuel and costs of being idle at port) and shipping companies are cancelling future orders for new ships (in 2013 32% of orders were not delivered as planned and were either postponed or cancelled). But for 2014 and 2015 at least the excess supply problem gets worse, not better.

So is the Baltic Dry Index telling us anything about global trade and growth? We started off from a position of scepticism – there used to be a good relationship, but since the massive shipping supply boom maybe it had lost its power as in indicator? But it turns out that the correlation between world trade and the BDI is EXTREMELY good. The CPB Netherlands Bureau for Economic Policy Analysis produces the monthly CPB World Trade Monitor. It's clear from these global trade data that the volume of trade has been weakening since the end months of 2013. Trade actually fell in May, by 0.6% month on month, although due to volatility and seasonals, a rolling 3 month versus previous 3 month measure is preferred. The chart below shows that after some strong momentum in global trade in 2010 it's fallen to a much more stagnant growth level in the past couple of years, and a brief recovery in mid-2013 has tailed away. In Q1 this year, world trade momentum turned negative. We have shown the Baltic Dry Index against this measure of world trade – it doesn't just look like a strong relationship optically, but it has a correlation coefficient of 0.74 (strong) with a t value of 7.83 (statistically significant at an extremely high level).

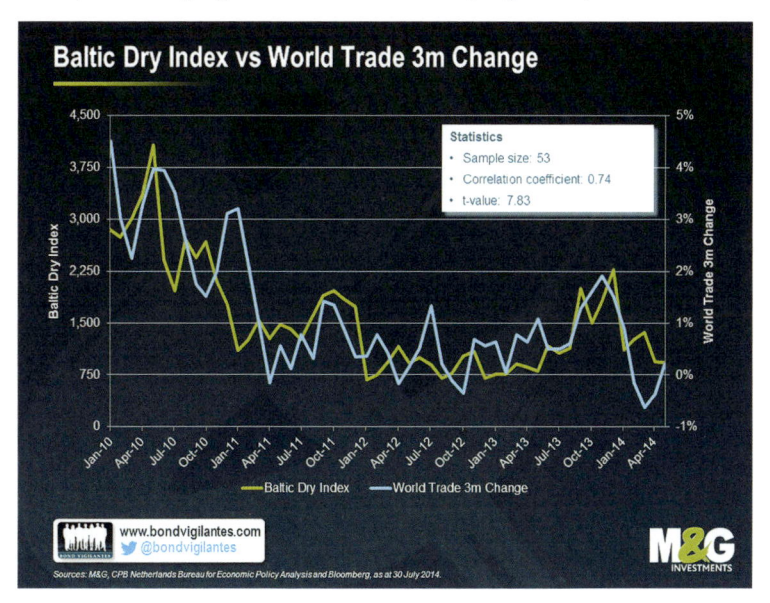

When we last wrote about the Baltic Dry Index we pointed out that it appeared to be a good lead indicator for 10 year US Treasury yields, the theory being that a fall in the BDI presaged falling GDP and therefore justified lower rates. And indeed the fall in the BDI in early 2011 did nicely predict the big Treasury rally 3 months later. There is still a relationship today, but sadly for us bond fund managers the better relationship is with UST yields predicting movements in the BDI (so ship-owners please feel free to make money on the back of this). Nevertheless, over the same time period as the earlier chart there is still a decent correlation if you use the BDI as a leading indicator and push it forward by 3 months, so it does appear to have some predictive powers.

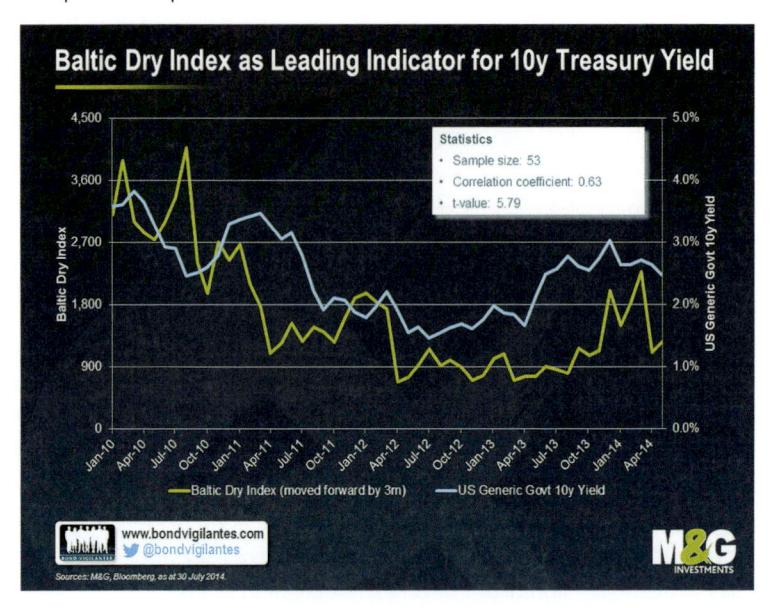

[Chart: Baltic Dry Index as Leading Indicator for 10y Treasury Yield. Statistics: Sample size: 53; Correlation coefficient: 0.63; t-value: 5.79. Sources: M&G, Bloomberg, as at 30 July 2014.]

So we'll keep looking at the Baltic Dry Index for the same reason that we like the Billion Prices Project for inflation. When you can find a daily priced, publicly available measure or statistic that comes out a month or more ahead of official data and is a strong proxy for that data it's very valuable.

Chapter 59

Exceptional measures: Eurozone yields to stay low for quite some time

Stefan Isaacs – Thursday, 4th September 2014

Richard recently wrote about the exceptional times in bond markets. Despite bond yields at multi-century lows and central banks across the developed world undertaking massive balance sheet expansions the global recovery remains uneven.

Whilst the macro data in the US and UK continues to point to a decent if unspectacular recovery, the same cannot be said for the Eurozone. Indeed finding data to be overly optimistic about is no easy task. Both consumer and business confidence indicators continue to point to a subdued recovery; parts of Europe are technically back in recession and inflation readings continues to disappoint to the downside. The most recent CPI reading came in at a mere 0.4%, German breakevens currently price five year inflation at 0.6% and longer term expectations have shown signs of questioning the ECB's ability to deliver on the inflation mandate.

Recognising the sheer size of the Eurozone banking system remains key to understanding the challenge Eurozone policymakers face. With a banking system over three times larger than the US (relative to GDP); significantly higher non-performing loans and massive pressure to deleverage as shown in the first chart below, it is unsurprising that the so called transmission mechanism appears damaged. The failure to pump credit into the Eurozone economy, especially into the periphery, continues to weigh on funding costs for SMEs & promote exceptionally high levels of unemployment. These are only now beginning to stabilise at elevated levels as shown in the second chart below.

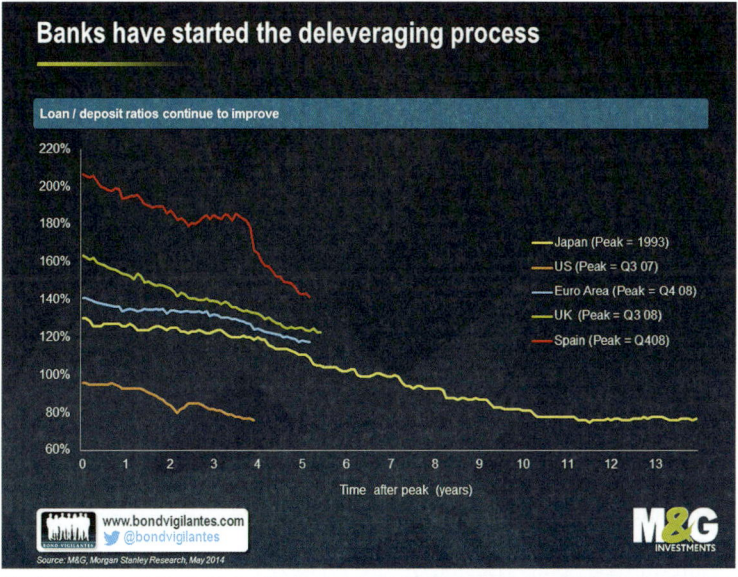

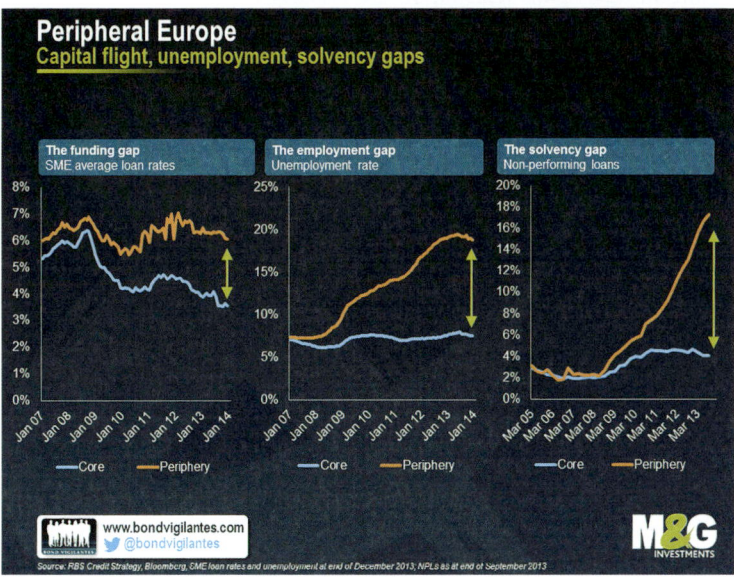

With previous demands for austerity in Europe preventing economies from running counter-cyclical fiscal policies and uneven progress in structural reform, the onus continues to fall on monetary policy and the ECB. And yet for a variety of reasons the response has fallen considerably short of that from the FED, BoE & BoJ, who have been happy to expand their balance sheets considerably.

Balance Sheets
FED, ECB, BoE

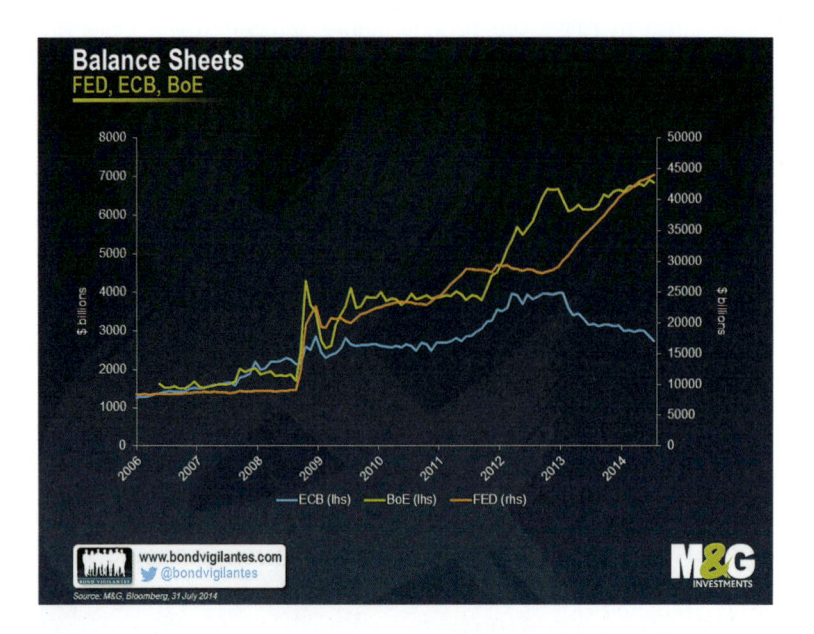

[Chart showing balance sheets of ECB (lhs), BoE (lhs), and FED (rhs) from 2006 to 2014, in $ billions. Source: M&G, Bloomberg, 31 July 2014. www.bondvigilantes.com @bondvigilantes]

The result has been, an overvalued Euro, imported disinflation and a lack of investment. Having offered re-financing cuts, forward guidance, massive liquidity in the form of the LTRO & TLTRO, the ECB will ultimately be forced to follow other central banks in undertaking broad asset purchases.

Whilst these broad asset purchases or QE are unlikely to be unveiled today, they are the only likely means in the near term, of ensuring that the banking system in Europe is able to extend significantly more credit to the real economy. This in turn should help to raise inflation expectations, boost potential growth and allow the ECB to fulfil its mandate.

In Europe exceptional times call for exceptional measures. The ECB isn't done, even if certain members will have to be dragged kicking and screaming to the QE party. I expect European bond yields to stay low for quite some time.

Chapter 60

"Global greying" could mean getting used to ultra-low bond yields
Anthony Doyle – Monday, 22nd September 2014

The developed world is going through an unprecedented demographic change – "global greying". This change is having a massive impact on asset prices and resources as populations around the world get older and live longer. It is also having an impact on the effectiveness of monetary policy. We would typically expect older populations to be less sensitive to interest rate changes as they are largely creditors. Younger populations will generally accumulate debt as they set themselves up in life and are therefore more interest rate sensitive. The impact of demographics implies that to generate the same impact on growth and inflation, interest rate changes will need to become larger in older societies relative to younger societies.

Turning to the impact of demographics on inflation, labour force growth may provide some insight into the potential path of future inflation or at least give us some guide as to the long-term structural impact of an aging population on inflation dynamics. The theory is that a large, young generation is less productive than a smaller, older generation. As the large, young generation enters into the economy after leaving school/university the fall in productivity causes costs to rise and therefore inflation increases. Additionally, the younger generation is consumption and debt hungry as they start a family and buy homes. Eventually, the investment in the younger generation comes good and there is a large increase in productivity due to technological change and innovation. As consumers become savers, inflationary pressures in the economy start to subside.

The long-term interplay between US labour force growth and inflation is shown below. Inflation lags labour force growth by around two years as it takes some time for the economy to begin to benefit from productivity gains. As US labour force growth rises and falls over time, inflation generally follows a similar trend.

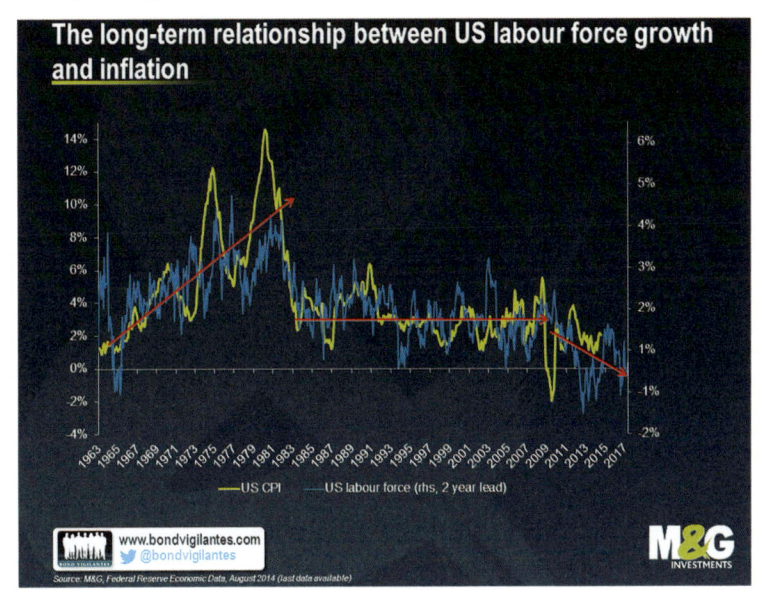

The next chart looks at the same economic indicators, this time looking at 10 year growth in the labour force against inflation. Interestingly, this chart seems to show that the baby boomers entered into the workforce around the same time as the global economy experienced a supply-side oil price shock. The influx of new workers into the US economy is likely to have contributed to the great inflation of the 1970s. For the next thirty years or so, inflation fell as the economy enjoyed the technological advantages and productivity gains generated by the baby boomers. Looking forward, it appears that long-term deteriorating labour force growth may contribute to deflationary pressures within the US economy.

10 year US labour force growth and inflation

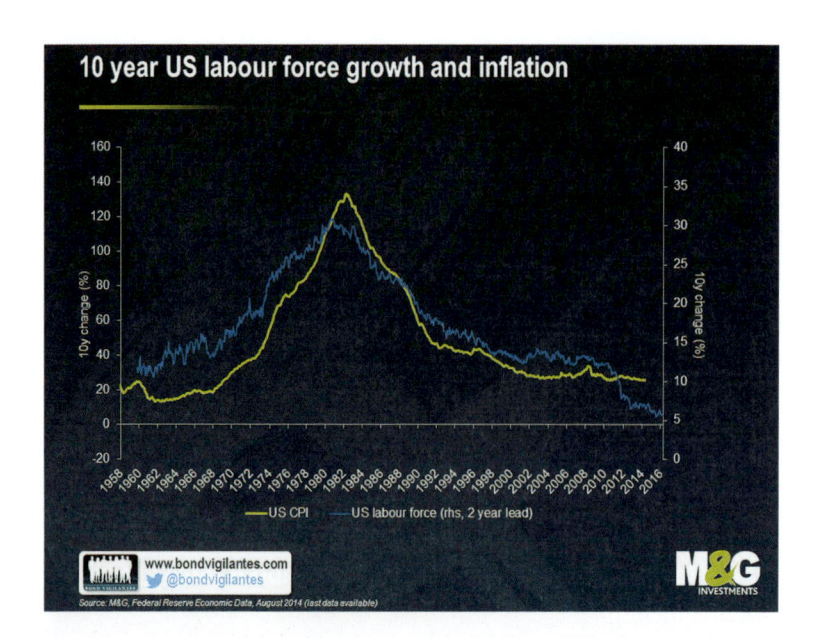

I am not saying that demographics are the only reason that inflation has fallen in recent years. The massive accumulation of private and public sector debt, globalisation and technological change are also secular trends worth monitoring. Rather I believe "global greying" and the impact of demographics on inflation and the real economy is an additional secular trend worth monitoring. Can central banks do anything in the face of this great generational shift should deflation become a reality? Interest rates are at record lows, quantitative easing has been implemented and we are yet to see the large impact on inflation that many economists expected.

Lower interest rates and the yield-dampening forces that exist in the global economy is a topic I previously covered here. In terms of bond markets, deflationary pressures are a "yield-dampener" and another reason why bond yields could remain low for some time and fall further from current levels over the longer-term.

Chapter 61

The lesson the Japanese economy has for the developed world

Richard Woolnough – Tuesday, 7th October 2014

One of the most commonly reported themes in financial markets today is the fear of disinflation/deflation, and how monetary authorities need to take economic action to avoid becoming the "next Japan". In February I commented on the fact that the fear of disinflation and deflation is not as logically straight forward as you may think. I think the common assumption that developed economies do not want to end up like Japan is also worth investigating.

Japan is commonly seen as the modern poster child of ineffective monetary and government policy. The policy errors of the Japanese authorities in the 1990s are seen as having resulted in a depressed economy that has stood still over the last 25 years. This view has partly come about as financial markets often simply judge an economy by observing how its equity market performs. Given the crash in the Nikkei from over 40,000 in the early 1990s to around 16,000 today, equity market performance as a measure of Japanese economic health has become engrained in the market's psyche.

In reality the strength of economies should be measured by their economic output and not equity market performance. In this regard, at first glance the national data bear out that Japan has lagged most countries in terms of nominal and real economic growth.

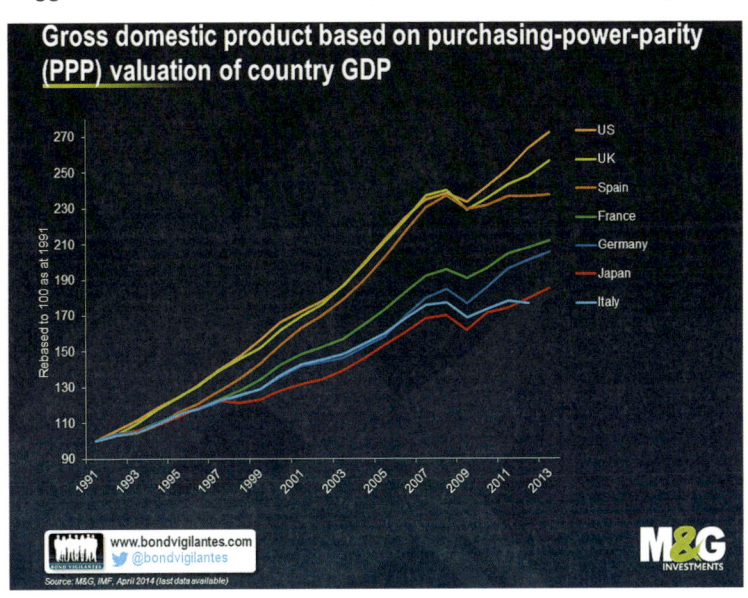

Gross domestic product based on purchasing-power-parity (PPP) valuation of country GDP

Source: M&G, IMF, April 2014 (last data available)

The simple measures of nominal and real GDP are often regurgitated as to why we do not want to end up like Japan. But from an economist's point of view, what matters most is GDP per head. The fact that one country grows more than another is not to be celebrated economically if it is in fact engendered solely by an increase in population.

On the next page is a chart of real GDP per capita. It shows that Japan has not been an economic failure from a local point of view. Rather, the Japanese economic experience has actually been quite positive in terms of increasing living standards for the average Japanese citizen over the last 25 years.

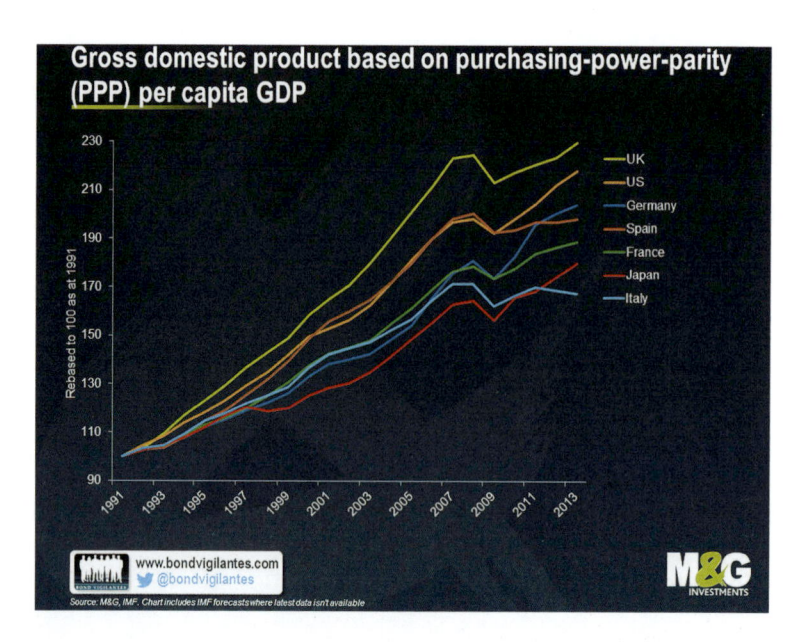

Gross domestic product based on purchasing-power-parity (PPP) per capita GDP

However the chart above shows Japan still lagging; no wonder economists still fear a Japanese outcome. Nevertheless I believe that a truer measure of GDP should not only be correlated to the number of people in its national boundaries, but should be seen in the context of the shifting function of the long-term demographics of the population. A country with a baby boom will experience strong GDP in the boom, and weaker GDP at the end of a population bulge. Workers retire; consumption and investment fall. In order to take into account the true GDP per head, one has to put this into context, by looking at the size of the working population, not just the size of the actual population. Below we chart GDP per head of working population. This adjustment allows a fairer reflection of GDP per head, with the Japanese situation improving on a relative basis again.

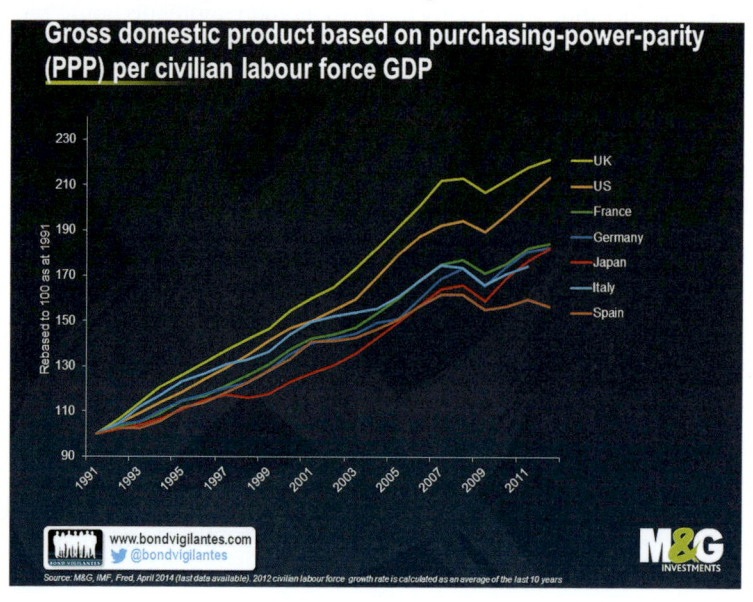

Gross domestic product based on purchasing-power-parity (PPP) per civilian labour force GDP

What lessons can we learn from Japan? Firstly it is not as bad as it looks given the true potential GDP per head of population. In fact monetary and fiscal policy has worked in Japan. Low inflation and the zero bound of monetary policy is something we and policymakers naturally fear. Maybe we fear it too much based on simple analysis of headline numbers.

Chapter 62

Who's the biggest winner if ECB buys corporates? The French

Anjulie Rusius – Wednesday, 29th October 2014

With the European Central Bank (ECB) purchasing €1.7bn of covered bonds last week, the Eurozone's "QE-lite" programme has well and truly begun. Although the focus to date has been on covered and asset backed bonds, an article from Reuters last week spurred the market, due to a rumour that the ECB would soon be considering an extension to include secondary market corporate bond purchases. Although quickly dismissed by officials, considering that the ECB has previously stated that it wants to return its balance sheet to where it was in 2012 to boost demand (which in doing so would approximately equate to €1 trillion of asset purchases), many dispute that this can be achieved via covered bond and asset backed purchases alone. Given the notion that sovereign bond QE would essentially amount to central bank financing of governments, the next best alternative is likely to be corporate bonds i.e. "QE-plus".

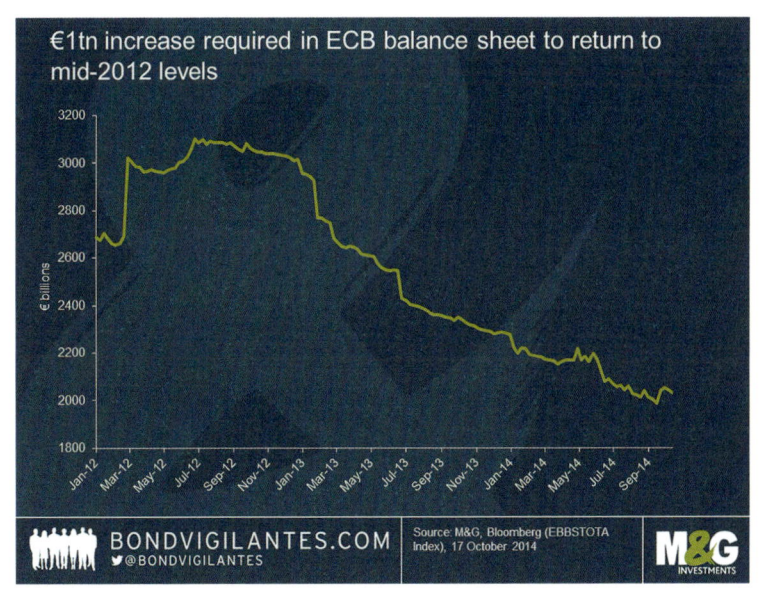

If QE-plus were to occur, which Eurozone countries would benefit the most? Assuming that the ECB will aim to purchase an equal spread of EUR denominated debt issued by Eurozone companies, I have filtered the Merrill Lynch Euro Non-Financial Index for these and re-weighted to get a proxy for a theoretical ECB corporate bond buying universe. Next, I calculated a Eurozone GDP contribution for each individual country (note: Cyprus, Greece, Latvia and Malta have been excluded from the analysis as they were not included in the original index)

and the difference between the two (i.e. the demand pick-up) has been measured in order to determine who could be the main winners and losers in a QE-plus world. Although this is a highly hypothetical approach, the results are nevertheless interesting. Constituting 21.7% of Eurozone GDP, but potentially representing 39% of all ECB corporate bond purchases, the 17.5% demand pick-up for France makes it the clear winner. The Netherlands is the only other country to witness a demand for its bonds in excess of its contribution to Eurozone GDP. All other member countries appear to suffer, especially Germany which represents over a quarter of Eurozone GDP, but ends up at the bottom of the table. For Estonia and Luxembourg the balance looks roughly correct. The periphery all witness less than proportional demand pick-ups, but Italy and Portugal look to suffer the most.

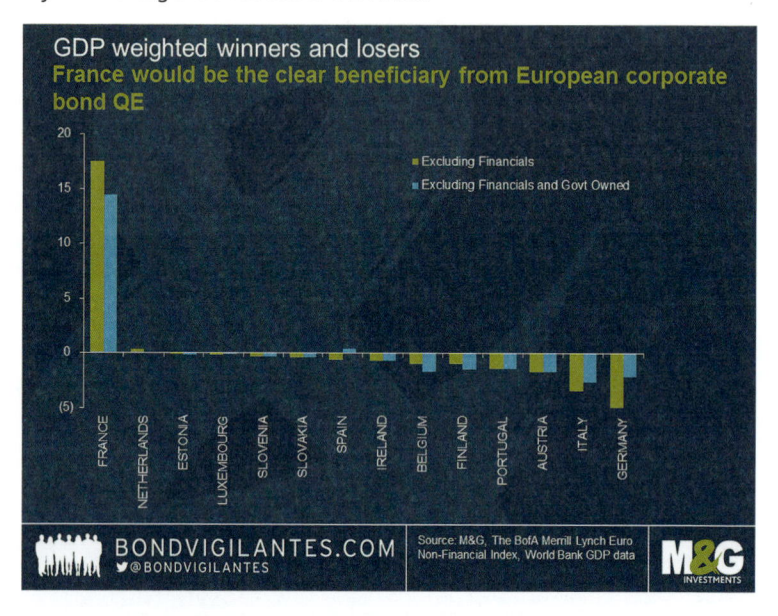

GDP weighted winners and losers
France would be the clear beneficiary from European corporate bond QE

Source: M&G, The BofA Merrill Lynch Euro Non-Financial Index, World Bank GDP data

Adding a layer and assuming that the ECB would rule out the purchase of government owned entities – e.g. utility and industrial companies – in line with its opposing stance on central bank financing governments, gives us a further refined universe. Most countries continue to benefit less than they're due (owing to France's gain) but on a smaller scale, excluding Belgium and Finland who are worse off. The main exception to this is Spain, which joins France and the Netherlands as a net beneficiary from ECB corporate bond purchases. The other key outlier is Estonia which previously was deemed just-right, but now loses out due to it no longer having any qualifying bonds in the new bond universe (its previous contribution to the index was via a government owned utility company).

Again I warn that this blog is highly theoretical in its approach, however the findings do provide food for thought. Though the ECB may aim for a uniform and decentralised approach, there will undoubtedly be political winners and losers (and this is not a clear-cut core versus periphery debate). This is especially true if the ECB continue to caveat their QE programme which acts only to reduce their potential investment universe. If the ECB are serious about overcoming the prospect of years of deflation, they should do away with QE-lite or even QE-plus and target the biggest, most liquid bond market via full-scale sovereign bond QE.

Chapter 63

"A grip on the public finances". Redeeming war loans as UK borrowing rises
Jim Leaviss – Monday, 3rd November 2014

As you know, we've always been fascinated by the UK's War Loans and have written about them repeatedly on this blog when we suggested that they should be redeemed. Bonds and war go together hand in hand, and for most of history rising government debt levels have been directly caused by the cost of financing conflicts, or the reparations afterwards. The several outstanding War Loans also tell the story of the UK's extreme fiscal distress in the 1930s, and the quasi default that lead to a patriotic (and on the face of it voluntary) reduction in the coupon of the 5% loan down to 3.5%, and of the inflations of the 1970s and 1980s which saw the value of these undated, long duration bonds collapse to levels where their yields were higher than their prices. British Pathé has a series of great clips around the time of the £2 billion debt conversion (coupon reduction) mentioned above, including Neville Chamberlain presenting his plan on the deck of a ship. At the time he was regarded as a media genius and newsreel gold apparently – the Russell Brand of his day.

On Friday HM Treasury announced that £218 million of one of the smaller, and higher couponed, War Loans will be repaid at par (100). This bond was issued in 1927 to refinance some WW1 debt. There's obvious speculation that the rest of the War Loans, including the £2 billion 3.5% issue, might also be redeemed if yields stay low (disclaimer: we own that, and other similar gilts, and it would be nice if it happened!).

The thing that struck me from the announcement though was the Chancellor's comment that "we are only able to take this action today thanks to the difficult decisions that this government has taken to get a grip on the public finances … (and) the fact that we will no longer have to pay the high rate of interest on these gilts means that most important of all, today's decision represents great value for money for the taxpayer".

I guess the bonds have indeed been a pretty sweet deal for the taxpayer – FT Alphaville calculated that in real terms the debt was inflated away such that it is effectively being redeemed at £1.82 per £100 issued (even defaulted junk bonds typically return 40p in the pound to investors!). But it is also the case that for all the talk about creating savings for the taxpayer, if this bond is refinanced at, say, 3% per year, the Exchequer benefits by just £2 million per year, in the context of a budget deficit of nearly £100 billion per year.

Also, has the UK government really been able to repay this bond because of the "tough grip" on the public finances? Not only did the UK lose its prized AAA credit rating under the current government, but even now growth has come back, the UK's deficit has been overshooting in most months this year, thanks to poor income tax receipts in particular. The Institute of Fiscal Studies (IFS) suggests that £37 billion of new austerity is required to get to a position of even balancing the books in the next 3 years or so. The following chart shows that the UK has actually seen much less improvement in its deficit as a percentage of GDP than its biggest economic peers. In fact, the UK national debt is £100 billion larger than it was a year ago and is heading towards £1.5 trillion.

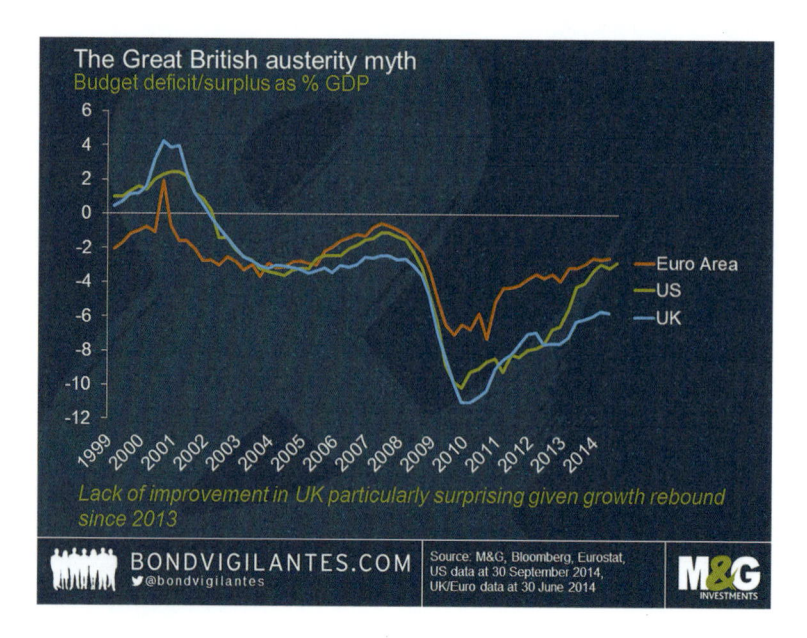

The Great British austerity myth
Budget deficit/surplus as % GDP

Lack of improvement in UK particularly surprising given growth rebound since 2013

BONDVIGILANTES.COM
@bondvigilantes
Source: M&G, Bloomberg, Eurostat, US data at 30 September 2014, UK/Euro data at 30 June 2014

So there hasn't been a significant improvement in the public finances in the UK. In fact, looking at the next chart you can see that the ability to refinance old perpetual bonds at low yields is nothing to do with UK specific factors. All developed market bonds have fallen in yield since the credit crisis and its aftermath. The collapse in bond yields is nothing to do with creditworthiness and all to do with a global savings glut, quantitative easing (or expectations of it in the case of Germany) and fears of secular stagnation and deflation.

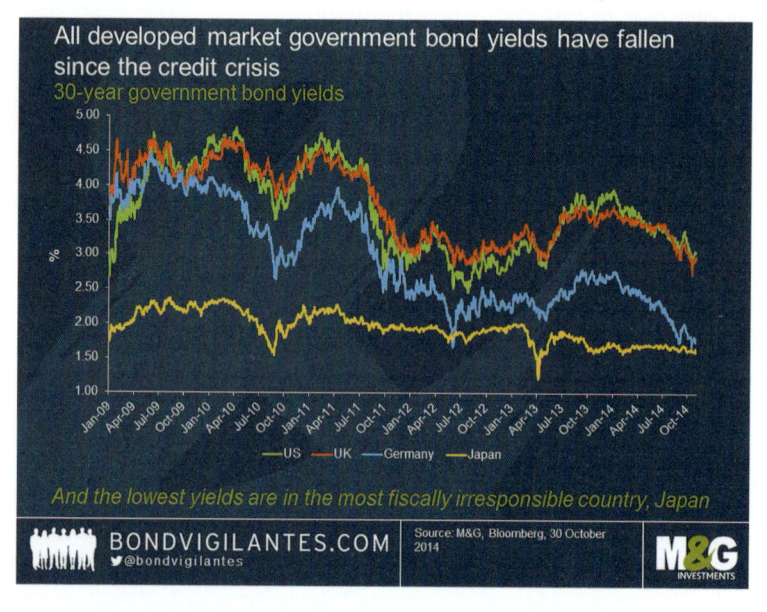

All developed market government bond yields have fallen since the credit crisis
30-year government bond yields

And the lowest yields are in the most fiscally irresponsible country, Japan

BONDVIGILANTES.COM
@bondvigilantes
Source: M&G, Bloomberg, 30 October 2014

Some of the lowest bond yields in the world are in Japan – 40 year government JGBs yield 1.77%. At the same time, Japan has been one of the most fiscally irresponsible countries, with a budget deficit averaging more than 6% each year in the last 20 years, a deficit in

2013 of 9.3% of GDP, and its gross public debt/GDP ratio having soared from something like 60% in the early 1990s to more than 200% now. Very low bond yields arguably say much less about fiscal discipline, and much more about the market's view on long-term nominal growth rates – if anything, you could argue that rather than something to celebrate, low bond yields – and the redemption of the War Loans – are a worrying signal since they suggest very low economic growth potential.

Will the 3.5% War Loan go the same way as the Consol 4s? Obviously the lower coupon sets the bar a bit higher for its redemption, and the bond price at just under 92 means that investors would be gifted 8 points of capital return. The other concern that the Debt Management Office has is that bond yields could rise substantially between an announcement like Friday's and the date when they repay the money next year, such that it looks like the bonds should have been left outstanding. So there is an "avoidance of embarrassment" factor too which means that the economic decision needs to be clear cut rather than borderline. The timing of 3.5% War Loan's coupon payments might make an announcement in an early pre-election Budget attractive for the government if yields remain around current levels as repayment would likely be on a coupon date, redemption requires 90 days' notice and therefore 1st June could be achievable.

Chapter 64

War Loan called. Yay. Quick thoughts...
Mike Riddell – Wednesday, 3rd December 2014

It has finally happened: the DMO has elected to call and refinance the 3 ½% War Loan, which at almost £2bn in size is by far the largest perpetual gilt outstanding. We've been banging on about this for years and Jim is worried he hasn't got anything to write about anymore. Jim typed up a few thoughts after the much smaller 4% Consol was called in October, here are mine.

Calling the 3.5% War Loan is a much bigger deal than the 4% Consol that was called just over a month ago. The 4% Consol is only £218.5m in size, while the 3.5% war loan is £1.938.8bn in size so is almost 10 times larger. [It's still not exactly big though – by way of comparison, the biggest gilt outstanding, the 4.75% 2015, is £38.3bn in size].

Refinancing the 3.5% war loan and 4% consol makes a lot of economic sense, as we and others have argued. But the political rhetoric that accompanied the first announcement in particular makes far less sense (today's announcement has been toned down as bit). The stark reality is that the effect on the UK's finances is negligible – depending upon where the gilts that refinance these bonds are issued, the decision in October to call the 4% Consol will be a saving to the taxpayer of between £2m and £3m per year, while calling the 3.5% War Loan will save around £15m per year. It's still worth doing, but to put these numbers in context, the UK's budget deficit this year is likely to be a bit above £90bn. Refinancing these perpetual gilts will trim the deficit by less than 0.02%.

Despite today's toned down announcement, we'd still take issue with both the Treasury statement that the "very low interest rate environment...in part reflects confidence in the plan the government has put in place to cut borrowing and create a resilient economy" and George Osbourne's comment that calling the war loan "is a sign of our fiscal credibility". Government bond yields have hit record lows around the world – this is a global phenomenon, not a UK one. If bond yields were a measure of economic strength, then why are Spain's 10 year bond yields lower than the UK's? Why did almost every country in the Eurozone see record low bond yields earlier this week (Greece is the major exception)? And why does Japan, one of the most indebted countries in the world, currently have 10 year bond yields at just 0.44%?

You can take the argument above further. If anything, very low government bond yields could be the market signalling its concern about very weak long-term growth prospects. Below is a chart showing long-dated gilt yields going back a very long way. Note the correlation with nominal GDP. So given that nominal GDP is equal to real GDP plus the inflation rate, low gilt yields today are telling us that either real GDP is expected to be very low, or inflation is expected to be very low, or a combination of the two. Looking at the index-linked gilt market, it appears that a lot of what's driving nominal gilt yields lower is the poor growth outlook, given that very long term UK inflation expectations are almost bang in line with the average of the last 5 years (30 year breakeven inflation rates, which are priced off RPI, are 3.34%).

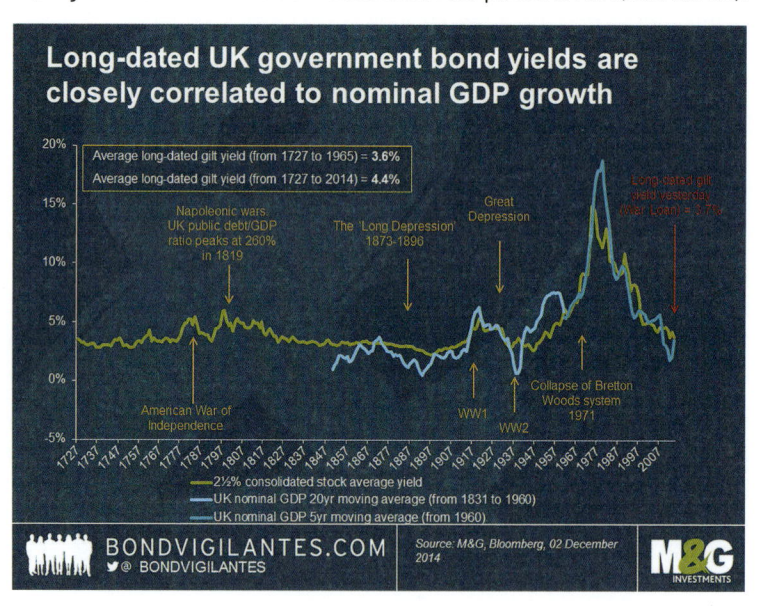

And finally are the UK's finances really that strong? Beware the Great British Austerity Myth, as I've argued previously. Updated chart below.

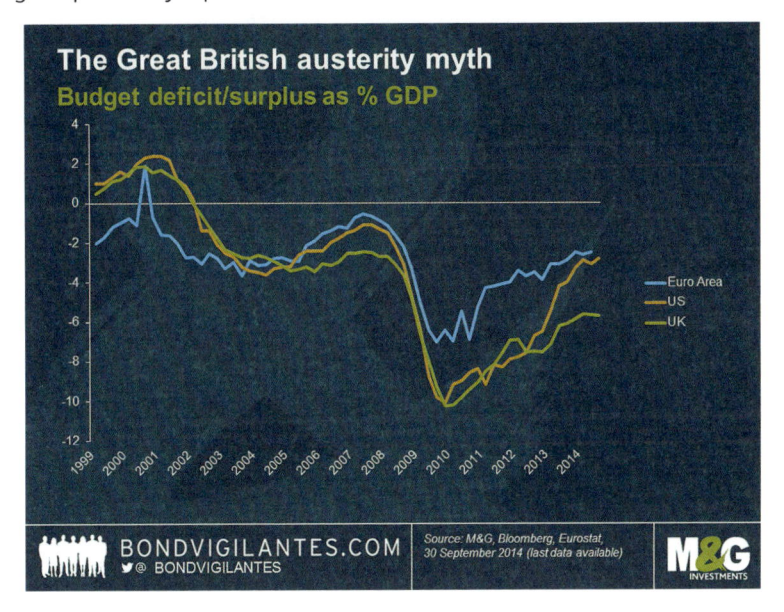

The Great British austerity myth
Budget deficit/surplus as % GDP
Source: M&G, Bloomberg, Eurostat, 30 September 2014 (last data available)

Chapter 65

Conservative QE and the zero bound.

Richard Woolnough – Wednesday, 10th December 2014

It has been a while since we talked about QE, but we covered this substantially in the past (see for example 'Sub Zero?', 'QE – quite extraordinary' and 'Quantitative easing – walking on custard'). It now appears, at least for the time being, to be a part of monetary history in the UK, and more recently the US. However, it is being reapplied in Japan and about to do a grand tour of Europe. Our earlier blogs were an attempt to analyse a new experiment. What do we think now we have had the practical implication of the theory?

Let's go back to basics first. Monetary policy reaches the zero bound, so short-term interest rates can no longer be cut. Therefore it is time to print money. Being prudent, the central bank needs to be able to tighten policy again at some point by destroying the printed money. So it favours purchasing large, liquid, risk free debt and buys government bonds in huge quantities.

This drives longer-term interest rates down to the zero bound, and therefore should encourage long term borrowing, discourage long-term saving, increase asset prices that are a function of long term rates (property and equity), and therefore via the wealth effect, stimulate growth.

The above effects and especially the wealth effect are seen as proof by its supporters that QE has worked via higher asset prices and the following chart is often used as evidence of the correlation between the two.

UK QE and asset prices

Cumulative BoE asset purchases, £m (LHS) — FTSE 100 (RHS)

Source: M&G, Bloomberg, 5 December 2014

BONDVIGILANTES.COM
@BONDVIGILANTES

Asset prices have risen and growth has indeed returned, but where is the inflation?

Inflation has indeed been temporarily induced in countries where the exchange rate has collapsed (for example the UK and Japan). However, this has proved to be a blip in the UK, and will likely be the same in Japan once the yen, which is down more than 50 percent versus the dollar over the past three years, finds a new stable equilibrium.

There are principally two reasons inflation has not returned. Firstly, inflation is not just a monetary creation but is a function of other factors, ranging from the oil price, to productivity, technology, inflationary expectations and free markets. The first of these has been exceptionally volatile, creating cyclical inflation and disinflation spurts, whilst the last four have been a constant driver of structurally low inflation for many years.

Secondly, let's look at what QE actually does from a monetary perspective. The central bank simply exchanges cash for near cash. Holders of government bonds now own cash having sold them, while the central bank now owns government bonds. Interest rates are lower along the yield curve, but there is no actual new money circulating in the economy. Cash that has been created has been exchanged for another form of cash – government bonds.

Central banks have printed money in a very conservative way, so its growth and inflation effects are limited to wealth effects, and a reduction in long-term rates.

The interest rate effect of driving the whole yield curve towards zero will reach its own zero bound, and cease to be effective, like short rates at the zero bound. The wealth effect will diminish as it will reach the bounds of investors' rational market expectations (like inflation expectations) and asset prices will cease to rise as strongly. The assets that do rise are held by individuals who will reduce their marginal consumption as their wealth increases, or those that can't access them as they, for example, are in a pension fund. Therefore QE itself, in its current form, reaches a zero bound.

When we first discussed QE, the great fear was that it would result in an inflationary spiral as money is printed prolifically. However, QE has been done in a responsible fashion so far. If it were to return to its philosophical roots, as outlined by 'helicopter Ben' in his 2002 speech before the National Economists Club, then you would get inflation. Printing money with nothing in exchange for it is inflationary. Printing money and swapping it for near money (ie government debt) is not quite the same.

Fortunately, monetary and fiscal policy has been effective in restoring growth, though inflation remains low. Will the new member of the QE fan club that is the ECB generate any meaningful long-term inflation with its traditional QE programme? I doubt it. No one else has.

2015

Chapter 66

Long US Treasury bonds are overvalued by 250 bps. Discuss.
Jim Leaviss – Friday, 9th January 2015

As we started 2014 the US Treasury market was expecting 10 year yields to be at 4.13% in a decade's time. This 10 year 10 year forward yield, derived from the yield curve, is a good measure of where the bond market believes yields get to if you "look through the cycle", and disregard short-term economic trends and noise. I wrote about it before and suggested that we were approaching the top of the yield cycle. The reason I thought this was that the FOMC members tell us (through a range of point forecasts, one for each FOMC member, known as "the dots") where they think the long term Fed Funds rate will end up – in other words looking through the cycle. As mathematically a long bond yield should equal the sum of all the overnight rates over the life of a bond, the FOMC's long term expected Fed Funds rate should have a good relationship with the long term US Treasury yield. In that blog I did also say that there should then be an adjustment for a term premium – the additional yield that a bond investor would demand for lending to a government for 10 years with all of its uncertainty and credit risk rather than lending overnight. We'll come on to that, but you can see that since January 2014 forward bond yields have collapsed from that 4.13% to around 2.75%.

The start of 2014, 10-year US Treasuries looked cheap
Forward-looking yields were above the Fed's long term expectations

[Chart showing USD forward rate 10y10y from Jun-12 to Dec-14, ranging between 2.5% and 4.25%, with shaded band representing FOMC long-run rate expectations. Median FOMC long-run rate expectation (8 members) shown as dashed line around 3.75%. Highest FOMC long-run rate expectation (2 members) at top of band. Lowest FOMC long-run rate expectation (1 member) at bottom of band.]

But the rally last year makes them unattractive.

BONDVIGILANTES.COM
@BONDVIGILANTES

Source: Bloomberg, Federal Reserve, 31 December 2014

M&G INVESTMENTS

The 10 year 10 year forward yield at 2.75% is below even the most dovish member of the FOMC's expectation of the long-term Fed Funds rate (the lowest forecast is 3.25%). On the face of it we'd suggest that there is little value in long Treasuries at the moment. But it's even worse than that. Let's look at what the typical yield pick-up is between Fed Funds and the 10 year US Treasury. Going back to 1971 the average spread between the two instruments is 1.16%. There have been periods of inversion, where Fed Funds is above longer dated yields, most notably at the start of the 1980s when Paul Volker decided to kill inflation by hiking rates above the CPI rate, and thus made long-dated bonds investable again. The spread between the Fed Funds rate and 10 year bond yields is largely about term/risk premium, but it might at times reflect a central bank regime change (like Volker) or expectations of a turning point in the rates cycle (there's an excellent New York Fed's Liberty Street Economics blog on drivers of the term premium in the US Treasury market). On the whole though the curve is positive, with a 1 standard deviation band of +70 bps to +145 bps.

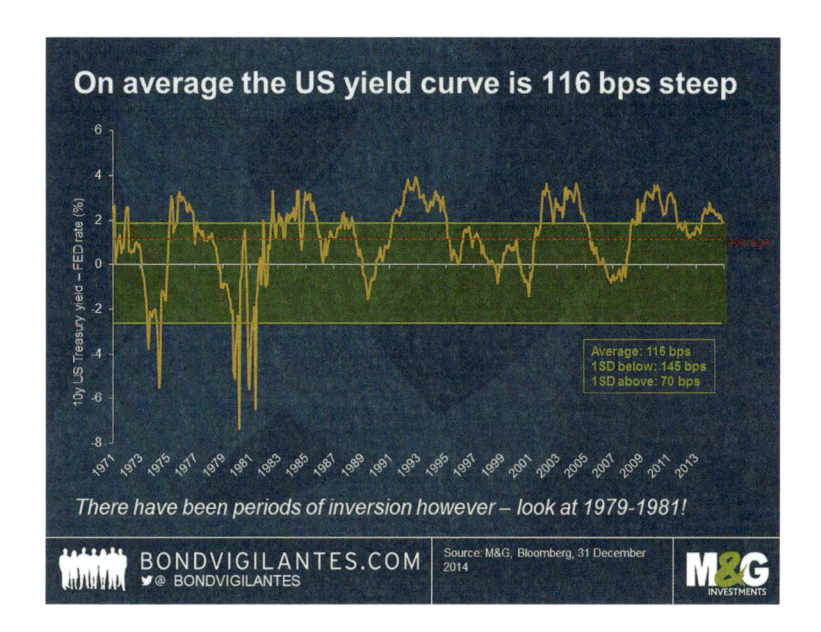

On average the US yield curve is 116 bps steep

There have been periods of inversion however – look at 1979-1981!

Average: 116 bps
1SD below: 145 bps
1SD above: 70 bps

Source: M&G, Bloomberg, 31 December 2014

It therefore follows that as a measure of "value" the Fed's long-term expectation band isn't enough; we should add on the typical curve slope (116 bps) to the FOMC members' expectations to reflect the risk premium. The chart below shows that this obviously makes long-dated US Treasury bonds look even more extremely overvalued – around 200 – 300 bps overvalued. This is a capital overvaluation of somewhere from 15% to 25%.

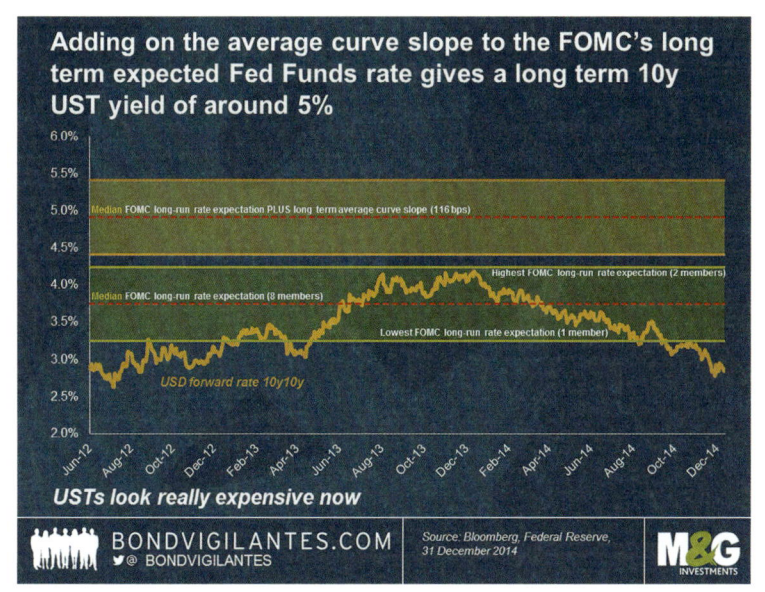

Adding on the average curve slope to the FOMC's long term expected Fed Funds rate gives a long term 10y UST yield of around 5%

USTs look really expensive now

Source: Bloomberg, Federal Reserve, 31 December 2014

So what scenarios make today's forward bond yields look reasonable? Most obviously the Fed could be getting things very wrong. Maybe we are in "secular stagnation" (permanently low growth and inflation due to demographics and the debt overhang) and the Fed Funds rate from 2024 to 2034 isn't going to be 3.75%, but 1.5% or lower. That would work.

Additionally the curve might be much flatter in future than historically – perhaps driven by pension fund demand for long-dated fixed income given the huge hole that has opened up in America's pension schemes. But it's quite hard to imagine the massively inverted yield curves (-600 bps in 1980/81) of the Volker years given the low starting point for yields. Finally – and this is Deutsche Bank's Torsten Slok's most likely explanation – maybe value doesn't matter anymore. The expansion of central bank balance sheets has created more than $10 trillion of new money since the Great Financial Crisis, and it is this money looking for a return of any kind in a zero rate world that has, and could continue to, drive yields down. Of the 5 central banks I've put on this chart only two have called an end to QE, and one – the ECB – has barely got started yet. On most valuation measures though, there's not a lot to like in the US Treasury market. Although I wouldn't go as far as Chinese credit rating agency Dagong on this ("Russian Debt Safer than US").

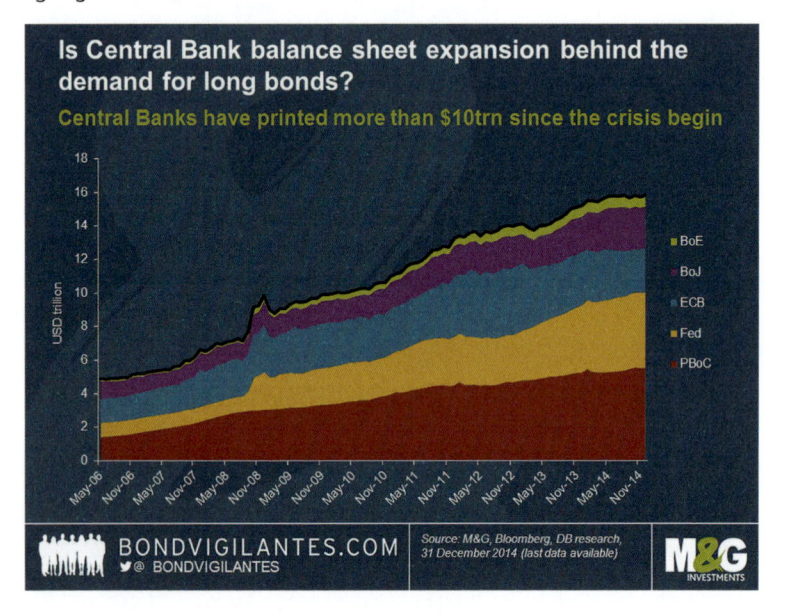

Chapter 67

Europe needs a German fiscal stimulus package but won't get it

Anthony Doyle – Thursday, 15th January 2015

The German government can theoretically borrow at negative yields if it were to issue short maturity debt today. Longer maturity debt is also yielding a record low amount. Could the collapse in yields be a blessing for Germany and Europe? Two economists at the International Monetary Fund (IMF) seem to think so. Indeed, the German government's narrow-minded pursuit of the "black zero" (a balanced budget) could be precisely the wrong thing to do at this point of the economic cycle if the Eurozone is going to continue to move forward with its current membership intact.

In a recent working paper entitled "Das Public capital: How Much Would Higher German Public Investment Help Germany and the Euro Area?" IMF economists Selim Elekdag and

Dirk Muir outline the case for a German infrastructure spending boom. They argue that higher German public investment would not only stimulate domestic demand in the near term, but would also raise domestic output over the longer-run and generate beneficial spillovers across the euro area.

Public investment in Germany is the second lowest in the OECD (1.5% of GDP), while net public investment has been negative since 2003. Years of underinvestment has led to a deterioration of the public capital stock, suggesting that this is a good time to increasingly invest in public infrastructure. And there are areas that a public infrastructure programme would particularly benefit, including aging bridges and roadways. Given that German average GDP rates have been declining since 1980 and has been below trend more recently, the German economy could use a shot in the arm to stimulate economic growth and would benefit greatly from some added stimulus measures. Unlike public consumption – which tends to provide a short-term boost to economic growth if not sustained – an increase in German public investment would raise domestic GDP more durably in both the short and long-term as infrastructure projects become productive public capital.

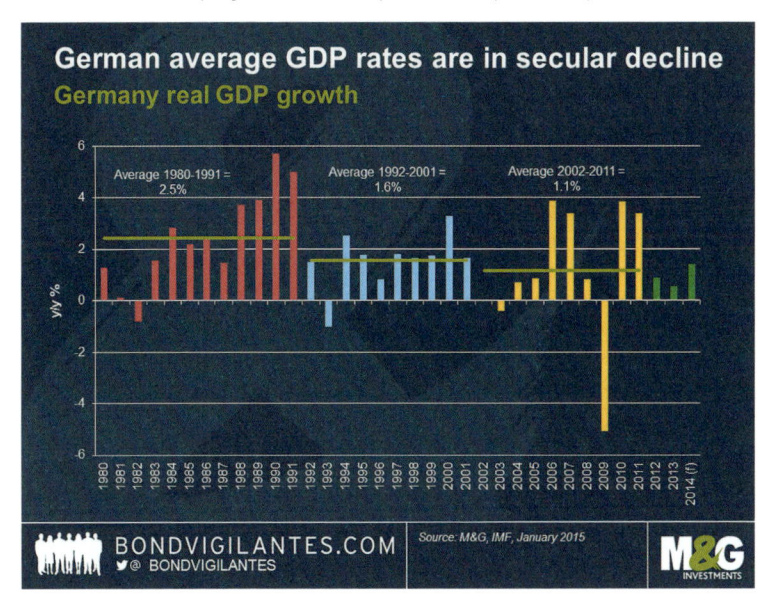

The IMF economists find that a 4 year, 0.5% of GDP increase in German public investment (which is consistent with Germany's fiscal rules) would yield a persistent increase in real GDP of 0.75%. Perhaps equally as importantly, the spending programme would also raise growth in the euro area, with peak effects on real GDP in Greece, Ireland, Italy, Portugal, and Spain (considered together) of 0.3%. The spillover effect into the rest of the euro area is transmitted through a couple of key channels. Firstly, positive effects for other euro area nations are caused by Germany demanding more goods from their euro area trading partners. Secondly, the inflation rate would be higher in Germany as demand increases, resulting in a real effective exchange rate depreciation for the rest of the euro area thereby making these nations more competitive. This is vital at a time when Europe is scrambling to generate any growth it can get.

The decline in inflation expectations across Europe, and some stabilisation in the prospects of the peripheral nations, has seen yields collapse not only for Germany but also the rest of the Eurozone. If European politicians could get their act together and exploit the low yields on offer (as ECB President Mario Draghi has implored them to do) and embark upon a coordinated effort to increase public investment across Europe, this would have some significant results on economic output. A coordinated fiscal stimulus (defined as a 2-year, 1% of GDP debt-financed increase in public investment) across the Euro area would generate a sustained 1.2% and 1.1% increase in German GDP and other Euro area countries respectively. If the economics is sound, why won't the German government act?

The answer lies in the views of the German electorate. There is a fear within Germany that they will end up indefinitely subsidising the whole European periphery (much like the German West has been subsidising the East for the past 25 years with no end in sight). In order to avoid getting into a situation in which the German government has to pick up the bill for European peripheral debt, Germany is trying to enforce austerity on the whole Euro area. The only way Germany can credibly do that is by leading by example, like parents teaching children to eat vegetables. If Germany ramped up public investment and started running deficits now, it would have no (moral) authority whatsoever to make any demands on peripheral countries to keep budgetary discipline.

So at this stage it appears that project "black zero" is all encompassing for the German government and electorate. The type of coordinated effort that Europe needs – a combination of stimulatory fiscal and monetary policy – appears out of reach. Without the coordinated effort of policymakers, it is difficult to see how Europe will generate higher living standards over the longer term for its 330 million inhabitants.

Chapter 68

Coming to a bond market near you: "A Brave New World: Zero Yield Corporate Bonds"

James Tomlins – Thursday, 5th February 2015

Picture the scene: a meeting room, 40 floors up, plate glass floor-to-ceiling windows with views of central London in the background. At the polished mahogany table sits Hans Schmidt, the CFO of a major consumer global goods company. In walks Chad "Ace" Jefferson III, the latest in a long line of investment bankers assigned to cover his company. Behind Chad follows an entourage of five impeccably dressed junior bankers, whose sole purpose seems to be to carry Chad's presentation packs.

"Hans! Buddy! High five!" Chad almost shouts as he bounds across the room with his hand raised.

Hans looks at him blankly, refusing to reciprocate the vulgar greeting. Instead he gets up and offers a handshake.

"Hello Mr. Jefferson," he mumbles, already slightly irritated.

"I love you Swiss guys, so formal! It's awesome!" says Chad beaming widely, shaking his hand.

"Yes, well, I agreed to this meeting because you said you had a once in a generation opportunity for our business Chad, if you don't mind, let's get on with this yes."

"Alriiiight! Let's get to it." Chad turns to one of his entourage. "Jean-Philippe" he barks, "Get your ass in gear, give Herr Schmidt a presentation, chop chop!"

"OK so I'll cut to the chase," he says, pushing aside the presentation that Jean-Phillippe had worked on until 4am that morning. "Now that the ECB has finally got with the programme and done some good ol' fashioned QE, a good chunk of the European government bond market is now trading at negative yields. This means the scope for funding your business on the cheap is better than ever my friend. Here's the thing …"

Chad leans towards Hans and almost inaudibly delivers his killer blow.

"With our help, your company, Hans, could issue a bond with no cost to the company." Chad leaps to his feet and starts pacing around.

"I'm talking no coupon Hans! Free money! No interest rate! This is a thing of beauty. Think about it, a €500m bond issued at zero cost of financing. We can re-finance a big chunk of your debt and reduce the interest costs to zero. This baby feeds straight to the bottom line. I'm talking major EPS benefits buddy. Your board will love you for it Hans. It's a no brainer! BOOM!" To emphasise his point, Chad slam-dunks the presentation into a nearby bin, causing Jean-Phillippe to wince.

Hans turns to Chad and says, "OK, so you have my attention. This sounds interesting. But why would any investor buy my company's bonds without a positive coupon? Does that not defeat the whole point of a corporate bond?"

"Great question Hans! It's a case of choosing the lesser of two evils here. If you are a bond investor, buying a corporate bond from a respected company like yours for zero return, it may well be a better option than buying a government bond with a guaranteed negative return to maturity. You still get a positive credit spread after all. Also, if you think we are going to experience deflation in the Eurozone, a zero return in nominal terms still means a positive real return, either way, you are better off – crazy I know, but true!"

Chad finishes and sits down, smiling even more broadly than before, suppressing the urge to punch the air.

Fin

Now, I hasten to point out that all of the above is total (and poorly written) fiction, but we may be getting closer to the point where such conversations are possible.

In his daily note to investors on 4th Feb, Jim Reid at Deutsche bank pointed out that Nestlé's EUR 2016 bond closed at a yield of negative 0.002%.

The market is essentially sending out an unprecedented pricing signal to highly rated corporate issuers. It's saying "we will not demand a nominal positive return for lending you money."

The immediate consequence of this is a further reduction in potential funding costs for short-term debt, particularly for investment grade companies. This could lead to yet another round of financing cost efficiencies. Additionally, we may even see zero yield short-term corporate bonds being issued for the first time – a brave new world indeed.

Chapter 69

The zero bound debate – are negative rates a tightening of policy?
Richard Woolnough – Tuesday, 10th February 2015

Matt's and James's recent blogs outlined some of the issues markets face when rates go negative. This is obviously no longer just a theoretical debate, but has real investment implications. Why do investors accept sub-zero rates when they can hold cash?

To recap using Swiss Francs for example, it makes sense for a saver from a purely economic view not to deposit a Swiss Franc note into a negative yielding bank account, as it will be worth less when it gets returned, due to negative rates.

However, the saver faces risks by holding physical cash as they don't receive the security benefits from using a bank account (ie paying for an electronic safety box). The use of the old fashioned lock and key is not as convenient as a bank account, but would make increasing sense to use as deposit rates get more and more negative. This demand for owning physical as opposed to electronic cash is not confined to cash accounts. In theory, as the term structure of interest rates falls below zero, bond investors should sell their bonds and own "cash in a box" instead. How efficient is it to do this?

The great problem with using paper money as a saving instrument is that its inherent best in class liquidity also makes it vulnerable to fire and theft. From an individual's perspective, the use of a secure fire proof safe deposit box in a bank or a secure location away from home is the best starting point. The optimum solution however relies on economies of scale. Is this easily achieved?

As an investor, diversity makes sense. Therefore, an individual should spread their cash over a wide selection of safety deposit boxes in a wide variety of very secure locations. An improvement, but currently not that practical. But there could be a way to achieve the above goals relatively efficiently and cheaply.

In a negative interest rate environment there are likely to be enough investors who want to own bearer cash for a network of highly secure safe deposit boxes to be developed by a bank or institution. This means there would be a high degree of security and diversification regarding the location for the cash. In order to make the cash available to the investor easily, certificates of deposit could be issued physically or preferably electronically. This would allow the investor to transfer money easily, as they would only need to go to their nearest depository to deposit or access the cash, or their nearest bank if a bank agrees to physically deposit or withdraw cash for them. Basically this ends up being a bank account where the cash does not get lent, but has a custodian holding charge. In theory, in the extreme, you could even develop markets in exchange traded derivatives issues that are linked to cash held in a depository, to allow individuals and large institutions to manage cash as a saving instrument with no negative yield. A new efficient savings industry could be developed in a negative yield environment, so limiting the downside to the sub-zero bound for short and long-term interest rates.

One side effect would be that all these savings would have to be held in real cash, which will mean an increase in the demand for physical notes. If cash is held in custody and is not lent on then the supply of money in the economy for normal transactions will fall. This begins to sound deflationary, and runs counter to why sub-zero policy is being pursued.

As long as cash exists in a physical bearer form it is hard to see how you can have significant negative rates of interest in an economy where government debt and cash are the obligations of the same entity, as they are truly fungible. At its worst, monetary policy of sub-zero rates could encourage a deflationary spiral. Maybe the only policy left to create inflation is real and not conservative QE.

Chapter 70

The falling US unemployment rate could benefit some emerging markets
Claudia Calich – Wednesday, 11th March 2015

The declining unemployment rate in the US has renewed the debate on the timing and pace of monetary tightening by the Fed. While wage pressures have been muted thus far, the risk is rising that further declines of unemployment will lower the rate below non-inflationary (NAIRU) levels and prompt the Fed to start hiking.

For emerging markets, one of the main transmission mechanisms is through weaker EM currencies versus the US dollar. Additionally, many are concerned about higher funding costs as US Treasury yields rise further. These are significant concerns for EM investors. Despite the recent increase in euro bond issuance (a result of the lower yields on offer in Europe), most corporate external funding is still denominated in USD.

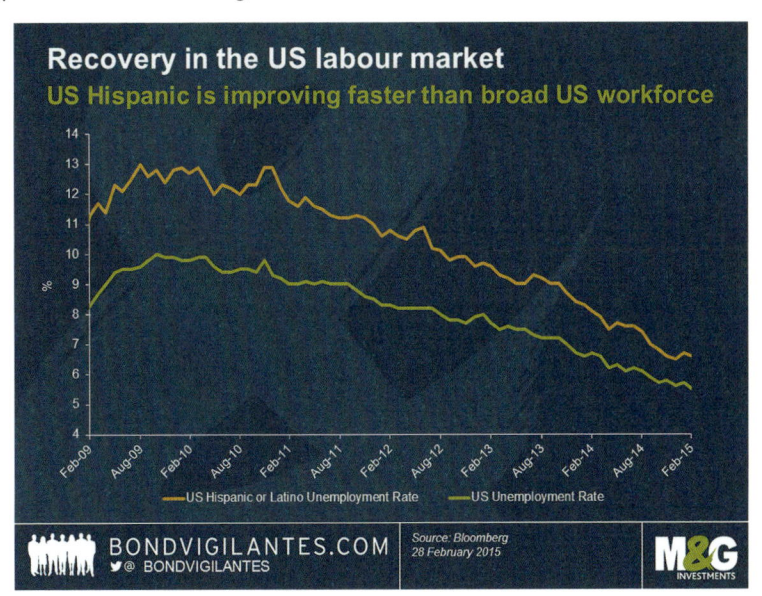

Recovery in the US labour market
US Hispanic is improving faster than broad US workforce

Source: Bloomberg, 28 February 2015

However, another transmission from the US recovery is through remittances. Remittances by US based workers to families in their home countries is highly correlated to economic activity in the US and it can disproportionally benefit a few countries. We can see from the previous chart that the unemployment rate amongst the US' Hispanic population (a proxy for their savings and eventual remittances) is improving at an even faster pace than the broader US workforce, which by itself is recovering at a solid pace. Part of this is because Hispanics are overrepresented in cyclical industries, such as construction.

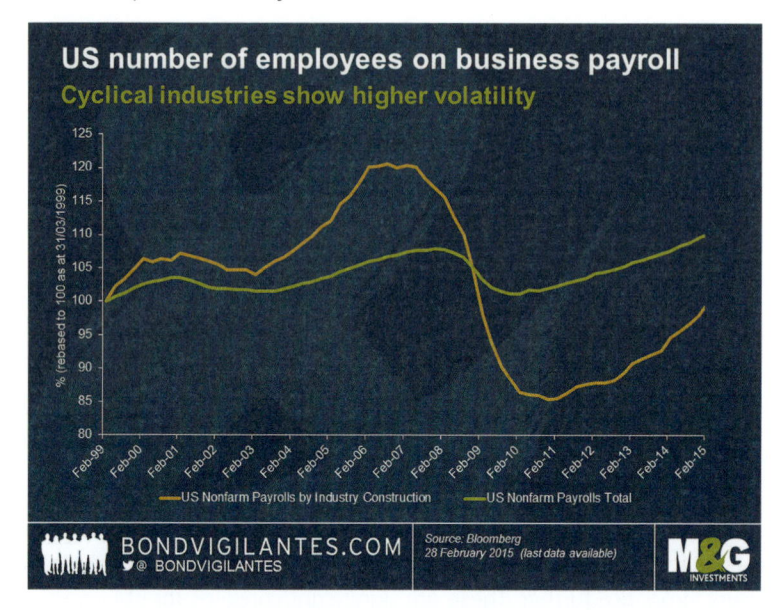

US number of employees on business payroll
Cyclical industries show higher volatility

Source: Bloomberg, 28 February 2015 (last data available)

Remittances have been found to contribute to lower growth volatility in the recipient country (as this recent IMF report pointed out). It also serves as a major social safety net, as the recipient countries generally have very low levels of income and savings and the availability of key services such as health and education is often scarce. Finally, remittances reduce a country's current account deficit and external funding requirements, which is supportive should capital inflows into emerging markets decline.

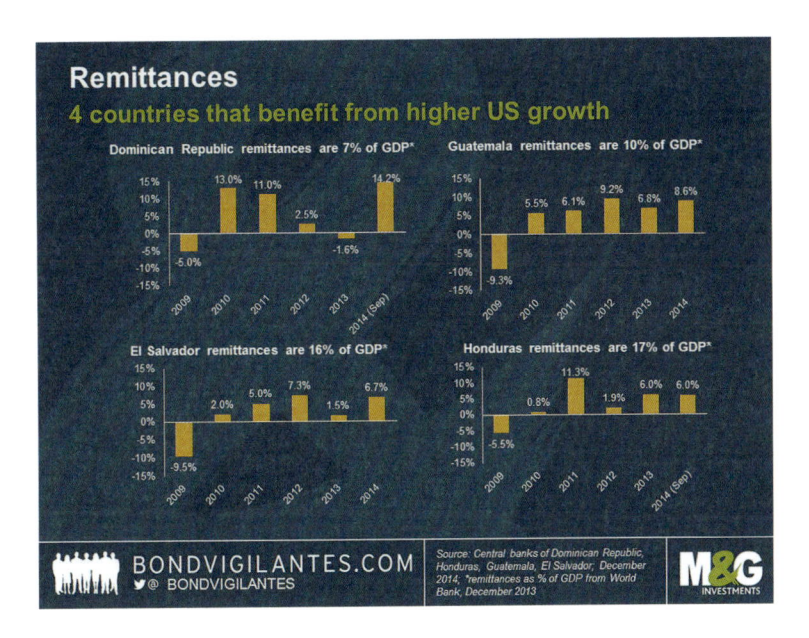

Remittances
4 countries that benefit from higher US growth

Dominican Republic remittances are 7% of GDP*
Guatemala remittances are 10% of GDP*
El Salvador remittances are 16% of GDP*
Honduras remittances are 17% of GDP*

Source: Central banks of Dominican Republic, Honduras, Guatemala, El Salvador; December 2014, *remittances as % of GDP from World Bank, December 2013

BONDVIGILANTES.COM
@BONDVIGILANTES
M&G INVESTMENTS

The eventual Fed hikes will remain a key concern for many emerging markets. However there are countries that will benefit from the stronger US labour market, particularly those that stand to benefit from US employee remittances.

Chapter 71

What are index-linked corporate bonds telling us at the moment?
Ben Lord – Thursday, 16th April 2015

When in past years I have fielded calls from bankers faintly like Chad 'Ace' Jefferson III (A Brave New World: Zero Yield Corporate Bonds) requesting any potential interest in new index-linked corporate bond issues, I have often begun my feedback by pointing to an old maxim. This well-known dogma posits that an index-linked corporate bond should price 25 basis points or so wider than a comparable nominal corporate bond.

So, for instance, were I to have been shown an offer by Ace in the Heathrow 3.334% 2039 index-linked corporate bond at, for example, the beginning of 2012, I would have looked for a comparable Heathrow nominal corporate bond spread, and as a first step checked that we were being paid at least 25 bps more for the linker. At this time, the comparison I would have looked at would have been Heathrow's 5.875% 2041 nominal bond. The spread at this point in time was approximately 255 basis points over the gilt, and Ace was probably showing me the offer at around 270 basis points over for the Heathrow linker. At only a 15 basis point pick-up into the linker, the conversation would very likely have ended there with no purchase made.

Heathrow
Nominal credit spread vs linker credit spread

HTHROW 3.334 12/09/2039 Corp - UKTI 1.125 11/22/2037 Govt
HTHROW 5.875 05/13/2041 Corp - UKT 4.25 12/07/2040 Govt

Source: M&G, Bloomberg, 10 April 2015

Had I got a subsequent offer in the same Heathrow linker at the end of 2013 though, on comparison of spreads between the same bonds I would have been offered the linker on a spread of 150 basis points, when the nominal 2041 bond was offered at about 110 basis points over the gilt. So I was being offered an additional 40 basis points of spread for owning the Heathrow linker versus the nominal. This time, through applying the mentioned dogmatic valuation framework, I would have been much more likely to buy the index-linked bond.

Why might investors seek a higher credit spread for buying the linker over a corporate? First and foremost the additional spread compensates for the relative illiquidity of index-linked corporate bonds compared to nominal corporate bonds. Issue sizes tend to be smaller, owned by a more limited pool of investors, with the majority of corporate bond funds' major investment types being nominal bonds rather than index-linked ones. It is this liquidity premium that gave rise to the desire to receive 25 basis points more than for nominal bonds when buying index-linked corporates, over the long term. Another important factor that could be cited could be that corporate linkers often carry greater default risk, or in particular loss given default risk (the probability of default of the Heathrow linker is identical to the nominal Heathrow bond). As inflation is accrued in the corporate bond, the price rises or the inflation compensation amount grows. But in a default, the investor's claim is the same as a nominal corporate bond investor's – a claim on par. This additional risk needs compensating through additional spread.

So, I am unlikely to buy linkers when I am not being compensated for the relative illiquidity compared to nominal bonds, and I am more likely to buy when the spread over nominal bonds is wider than 25 basis points, such as when the Heathrow linker was paying as much as 50 basis points more than the 2041 nominal. The previous chart also shows, if the pricing history is to be believed, that earlier this year the linkers were trading with tighter spreads than the nominal. In episodes like this, we should be more inclined to sell. After all, investors were effectively paying a premium for illiquidity!

However, secondary factors can drive this premium up or down over time, such as inflation expectations and the related headline levels of inflation, and perhaps this explains the relative tightness in the comparison in early 2012 compared to the divergence in spreads in late 2013. After all, in early 2012 RPI was close to 4% and had only a few months earlier been close to 6%. Wind the clocks forward to late 2013 and RPI was back down to 2.7%, and investors were less concerned about the threat of inflation.

This week, on 14th April 2015, High Speed Rail Finance, which runs the concession on the high speed rail link between St Pancras and The Eurotunnel, brought a tap of its index-linked corporate bond. In February 2013 the entity issued its first corporate and index-linked corporate bonds. Its £610m nominal bond came at 150 basis points over the gilt, and its £150m index-linked bond came at 175 basis points over the index-linked gilt. So, the linker was 25 basis points back of its larger nominal comparable: ring any bells? Yesterday's tap, though, of the linker came at a credit spread of 107 basis points. And as the chart below shows, this is actually pretty much in line with the spread of the larger nominal bond, and so is close to the extreme tights of the linker-nominal relationship.

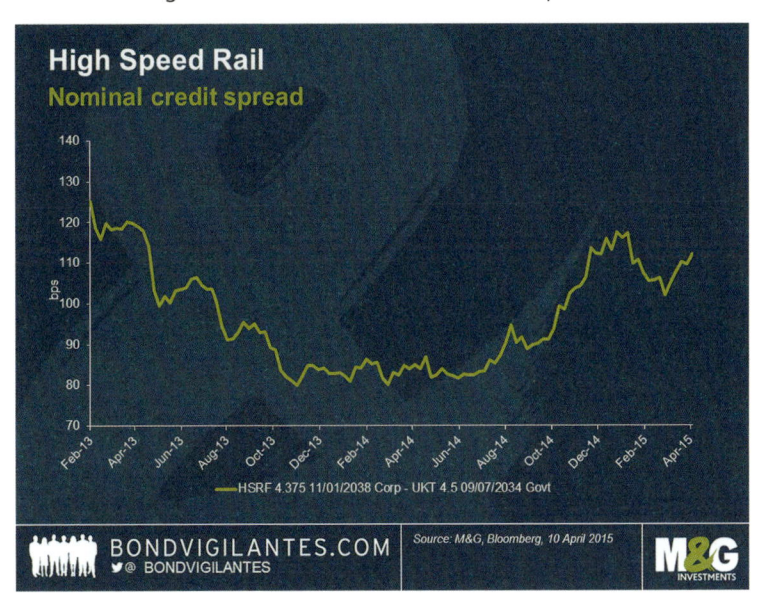

So what might we learn from all this?

Firstly, as the Heathrow chart showed, the spread pick up from selling nominal corporates into linker corporates has been coming down since the start of 2014. And yesterday's tap also suggests that investors are eager to add long inflation protection. One could also cite record lows on long-dated index-linked gilts as further evidence of strong demand for inflation protection, even at low yields. This could be driven by fears of higher inflation in the future, but it could also be driven by expectations that index-linked bonds will do better than nominal bonds, on a relative basis (or in other words, that UK breakevens are too low).

Secondly, it could also be that investors want to remove the uncertainty of higher inflation in the future: if you buy and hold the 30 year gilt linker until maturity, you will get RPI-1% (so you will receive CPI, near enough); whereas if you buy the 30 year gilt, your yield will worsen (improve) if inflation rises (falls) over the next 30 years.

Finally, it could be that investors have taken notice of significant reflation moves in breakevens in the US and in Europe so far in 2015, and are looking for UK linkers to stop lagging and play catch up. 5 year bund breakevens have rallied 100 bps more and 5 year TIP breakevens have rallied 60 bps more than UK RPI breakevens in 2015 so far.

Inflation expectations
Five-year breakeven rates for the UK, US and Germany
Source: M&G, Bloomberg, 10 April 2015

One should mention the possibility that the strength of the inflation-linked bond market, across both gilts and corporates, could be being driven by liability driven investing strategies, who are relatively price insensitive. LDI is certainly playing a part in driving the inflation market in the UK. However, this just adds a technical tailwind to the already supportive arguments I have made. In my opinion, breakevens in the UK look relatively good value, and would justify the early evidence of improving demand for inflation protection.

Chapter 72

Greece, the currency vigilantes and the Expulso solution
Richard Woolnough – Friday, 17th April 2015

It has been a while since we have discussed the economics of the single currency, but once again the issue of its suitability for all its members is at the forefront of economic concerns, as Greece faces some difficult decisions.

The financial crisis has taught us a number of lessons: fiscal policy works, monetary policy works, better regulation is beneficial for the financial sector, confidence is key, and importantly exchange rates matter.

Throughout the crisis, one of the economic mechanisms that aided the economies in most stress was the exchange rate. This can be seen with the collapse in sterling in 2007 on a trade weighted basis, the weakening of the dollar from 2009 until 2011, the yen in 2013 onwards, and the euro of late, see chart below. At the heart of these fx moves lie the currency vigilantes, as we discussed in 2010.

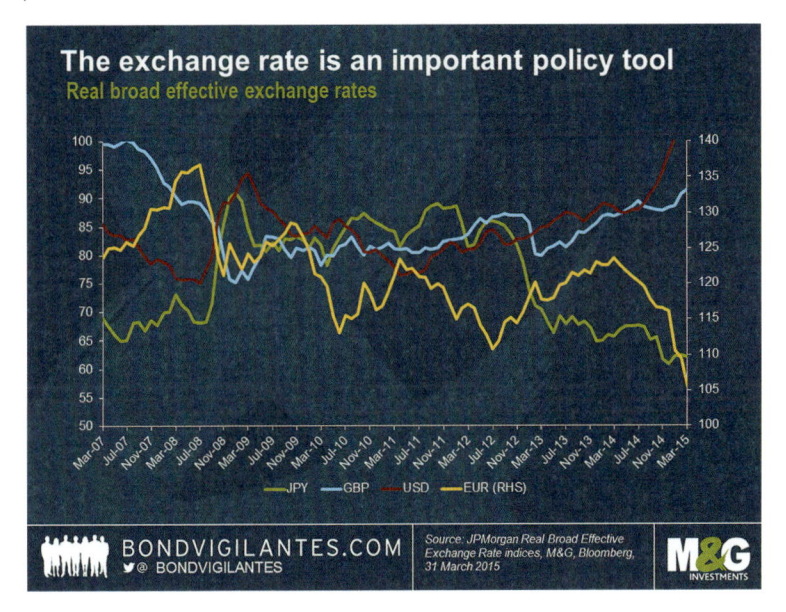

The exchange rate is an important policy tool
Real broad effective exchange rates

Source: JPMorgan Real Broad Effective Exchange Rate indices, M&G, Bloomberg, 31 March 2015

These external foreign exchange rate moves are a textbook play in terms of making labour cheaper and therefore helping economic recovery. However, as we know, in the Eurozone this mechanism does not exist, due to the creation of monetary union. I think exchange rates have become relatively more important in determining national economic outcomes and this is particularly relevant now to Greece.

The three main macro-economic levers are monetary policy, fiscal policy, and the exchange rate. Fiscal policy is still in the hands of politicians and therefore can be used to provide a strong impetus when required to differentiate national outcomes (although less so in Europe). Monetary policy has basically approached the zero bound in the main G7 economies, which means short rates have become hugely correlated. Without room to differentiate economic outcomes by cutting rates, national economic flexibility has been reduced, which means the exchange rate has to play a more important role than has historically been the case.

This is working between the main economic blocks. However, as the need for this most famous "invisible hand" has become greater, it has not been available within the Eurozone. This means that Greece has to somehow adjust with no fiscal room, no monetary room, and no exchange rate flexibility.

It would take at least a generation for Greece to solve its problems via structural reforms given the constraints it sits with. The short-term solution is therefore for Greece to be bailed out via fiscal transfers directly, or in a quasi-manner by allowing a Greek default. These are obviously hard to achieve given the political dilemmas many countries would face in providing this relief.

Greece has faced difficulties before, however we now have further pressure to find a solution as the economic policy options outlined above become more focused on the exchange rate conundrum, and the political environment in Greece points to a government more willing to take radical measures in the face of a great depression. The ability of Greece to provide for its citizens is damaged like the famous Venus de Milo statue. It could well be that politicians recognise the invisible hand of the exchange rate is still an important tool, and a free floating Drachma, the "Expulso" solution (as discussed in a 2011 blog), though painful, might be the best shot at providing an economic solution given the extent of Greece's problems.

Chapter 73

Negative interest rates in European ABS

Anuj Babber – Thursday, 7th May 2015

Negative interest rates have become increasingly prevalent in Europe owing to the expansionary monetary policy measures with a number of central banks implementing negative base rates (Switzerland, and Sweden). Two weeks ago 3 month Euribor, (the reference rate for the majority of Pan-European Asset-Backed Securities (ABS)), followed 1 month Euribor (largely the preserve of most European Auto ABS transactions), into negative territory. Where the reference rate has turned negative, noteholders can expect to receive the net amount (i.e. the positive coupon on the notes offsets the negative reference rate).

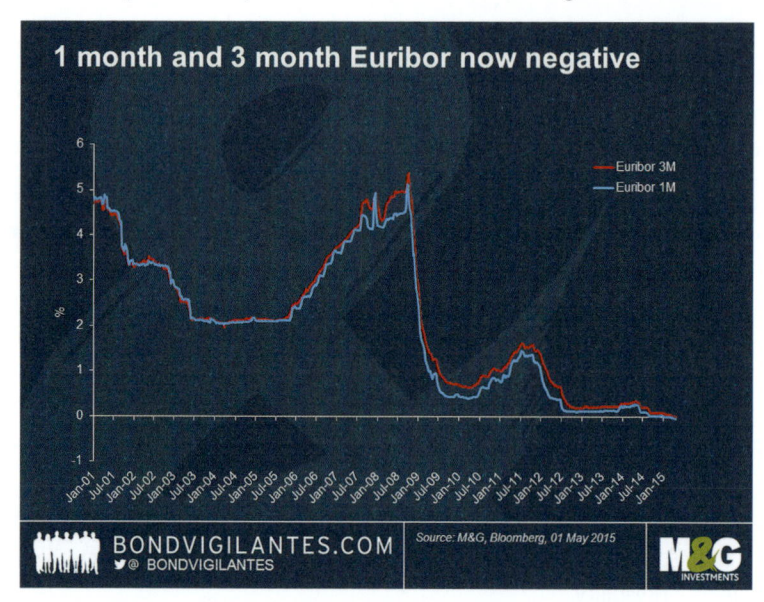

1 month and 3 month Euribor now negative
Source: M&G, Bloomberg, 01 May 2015

The concept of negative interest rates wasn't previously envisaged by the authors of securitisation documentation. The working assumption in the market is that interest payments to noteholders will be floored at 0% – we saw the first confirmation of this theory when issuers of two Spanish transactions issued an investor notice that they will apply a coupon of 0% instead of the negative coupon that would result from applying Euribor. In addition, Moody's canvassed legal practitioners in most European jurisdictions and concluded that the consensus, as far as note interest goes, is that there is a real or effective floor as there cannot be a payment obligation of the noteholders to the issuer implied by negative interest rates on the notes.

In contrast, ancillary monetary obligations (swaps, account banks etc.) are not usually floored at zero. For instance, under a typical fixed floating swap (a derivative instrument that enables the parties involved to exchange fixed and floating rate cashflows), the issuer would pay the fixed rate payments received from the collateral pool and receive floating rate payments from the swap provider (which are then passed on to noteholders). If the 3 month Euribor plus spread becomes negative, the issuer could also end up paying on the floating leg of the swap (which does not typically have floors). The read through to cross currency swaps involving euro liability payments against non-euro denominated assets could result in similar issuer special purpose vehicle (SPV) shortfalls.

This misalignment introduces negative carry whereby the issuer's cashflows are less matched than before the negative rates situation. As ancillary monetary obligations rank as senior costs within a SPV cashflow waterfall (the senior classes have first claim on the cash that the SPV receives, and the more junior classes only start receiving repayments after the more senior classes have been repaid), this therefore reduces cashflows to subordinated noteholders, or at best reduces excess spread which otherwise would flow back to the originator.

On the whole, for legacy transactions with little excess spread and/or credit enhancement, the negative impact can be significant as Euribor gets increasingly into negative territory as the issuer may have no way of recovering shortfalls in cashflows.

For most ABS deals in 2015, new offer documents have seen language inserted to either floor the interest rate at 0% or floor the reference index at a predefined rate.

Chapter 74

The downside of bonds

Anthony Doyle – Monday, 11th May 2015

Government bond yields are extremely low across the globe. The highly unusual phenomenon of negative bond yields – even on debt issued by countries that still face a debt crisis – is now commonplace. In addition, investors are looking to protect themselves from the carnage in bond markets we have seen in recent weeks (for example, the "risk-free" German 2.5% 2046 bond is down 19% since the high price was registered on April 20). The much quoted German 10 year bund yield has risen from a low of 0.075% on April 20th to 0.56% at the end of last week, but to put this in perspective, it has only taken 10 year bund yields back to where they were at the beginning of 2015.

So where should fixed income investors invest, particularly after the moves in yields we have seen in recent weeks? Should they remain in government bonds and enjoy the perceived safety of owning a risk-free asset, or should they be willing to accept higher levels of risk in order to chase the higher returns on offer in investment-grade and high yield corporate bond markets? Perhaps a more relevant question is: what is the potential downside of owning bonds?

Of course, it is not simply a matter of trying to maximise the return on investment. Another major consideration is the volatility an investor is willing to accept in pursuit of higher returns.

The chart below compares the drawdowns (peak to trough movements) in global government and global investment-grade corporate bonds since their respective inception dates (1986 for the government index and 1996 for global investment-grade corporates) and is based on monthly total return data.

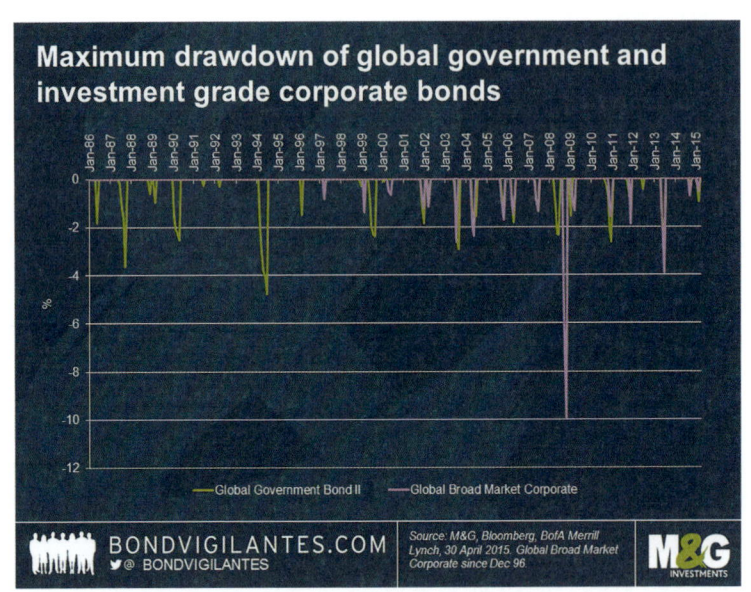

Maximum drawdown of global government and investment grade corporate bonds

Source: M&G, Bloomberg, BofA Merrill Lynch, 30 April 2015. Global Broad Market Corporate since Dec 96

Since 1986, government bond investors have lost money in three calendar years. The magnitude of those losses is as follows: -3.1% (1994), -0.8% (1999) and -0.4% (2013). The reason that total returns have rarely been negative is because investors were receiving relatively high coupons and had a significant income cushion to protect against any capital downside. These days, total returns in government bond markets will largely be a function of capital movements, with income providing little support in a bear market for government bonds. Interestingly, the year after a negative returning year has historically been a fantastic time to own global government bonds with the asset class enjoying a total return of 16.9% in 1995, 8.1% in 2000 and 8.4% in 2014.

Government and investment grade corporate bond investors typically experienced a pretty smooth ride, though many will remember the great bear market sell-off of 1994. Even though there was a sell-off in government bonds in 1994, investors experienced a drawdown of around 5%. A drawdown of this magnitude in government bond markets has only occurred once in the past 29 years. The average maximum drawdown per calendar year since 1986 is only 1.5%. Hence government bonds enjoy a unique position in many investors' portfolios, as they have been viewed as safe, they have been liquid, and they have let many investors sleep well at night.

Investment grade corporates have historically appeared to be a good alternative to government bonds with similar risk and return characteristics. They are more closely correlated to government bonds but are characterised by a lower interest rate risk profile. In addition, the historical default rate on investment grade corporates has been very low. Since 1970, the 5 year cumulative default rate on USD investment grade non-financial corporate bonds has been 1.1%. Given the global macroeconomic backdrop, we continue to believe that investment grade corporate bonds represent good value relative to government bonds, particularly as we think investors in the corporate bond market are being adequately compensated for a) default risk and b) liquidity risk.

Since 1997, the maximum drawdown was 10% in 2008, not helped by the historically very large weighting to financials as the world went into a major banking crisis. The average maximum drawdown since 1997 is 1.9% with an annualised return of 7.7%. Over the same time period, government bonds generated an annualised return of 7.0%.

Looking at the maximum calendar year drawdowns it quickly becomes apparent that high yield corporate bond investors suffer through greater volatility than the more defensive fixed income asset classes. There have been no less than six occasions since 1998 when the maximum drawdown in high yield was over 5% with an average annual maximum drawdown of 5.6%.

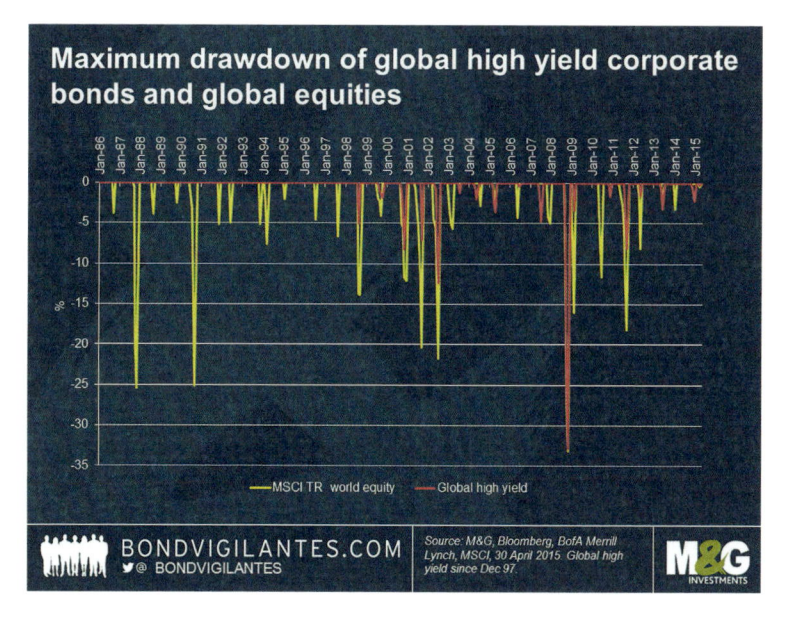

Maximum drawdown of global high yield corporate bonds and global equities

Source: M&G, Bloomberg, BofA Merrill Lynch, MSCI, 30 April 2015. Global high yield since Dec 97.

Over the past 29 years, the average annual maximum drawdown in the global equity market has been 9.4%. In this respect, high yield corporate bonds have a greater correlation to equity markets then traditional fixed income markets. The reason is high yield bonds and equities tend to respond in a similar way to macroeconomic developments, which can lead to similar return profiles over the course of a full market cycle. Equities are obviously a different asset class to high yield corporate bonds, but to a bond investor equities can be viewed as perpetual securities and therefore have a huge amount of credit spread duration. Additionally, unlike bonds, the owner of an equity usually has little or no security over a company's asset base. High yield bonds tend to be less volatile than equities because the fixed income component of the total return provides an added measure of stability and the potential for capital appreciation means that high yield corporate bonds can offer equity-like (or better than equity) total returns in the long-run.

However, during bouts of market risk aversion, high yield bonds generally underperform the broader fixed income market. In 2008, facing a storm of forced selling global high-yield corporate bond investors experienced a 33% decline in the value of their investments. High yield also performed poorly because these highly levered companies have a lot more credit risk than investment grade companies (since 1970, the 5 year cumulative default rate on USD high yield non-financial corporate bonds has been 20.5%), and the macroeconomic outlook in Q4 2008 was the worst it has arguably ever been. Over the same period, government bonds appreciated in value by almost 5%. This highlights a benefit of government bonds – they tend to be uncorrelated with riskier assets.

Those high yield investors that avoided the temptation to sell during the dark days of 2008 have been duly rewarded by the market. From November 2008 until March 2015, global high-yield corporate bonds have generated a total return of 172% in an environment where global high yield default rates have been exceptionally low. Over the same time period, global equities have experienced a total return of 135%. In this sense, high yield corporate bonds have behaved more like equities rather than traditional fixed income assets like government bonds.

For those that are curious, the blue line in the chart below shows the performance of an equally-weighted portfolio of global fixed income assets since December 1997. This portfolio generated an annualised return of 7.9% (similar to global equities) with less than half the volatility of being invested fully in high yield or equities.

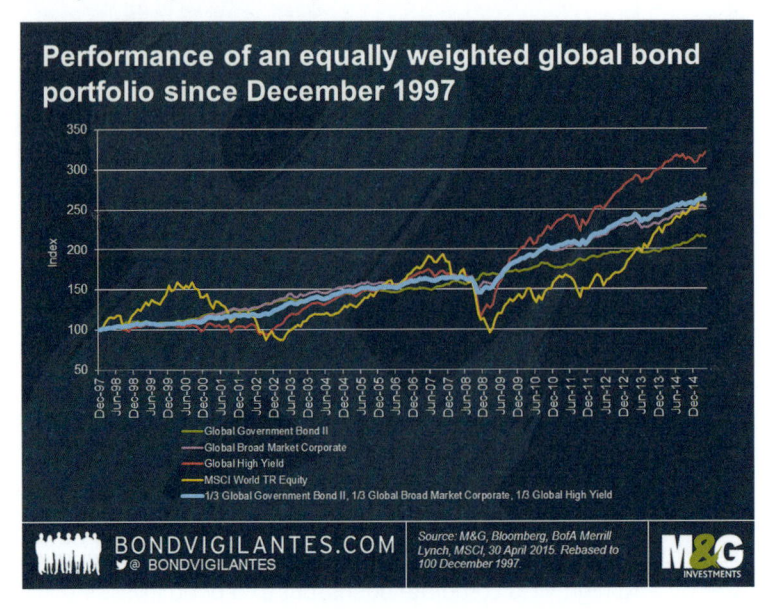

Whilst an historical analysis is interesting, is there anything that can be gained in order to assess potential future returns from fixed income assets?

It is possible to model (with some simplifying assumptions, like any move in rates is a one-off shock and the yields rise across the curve by the same amount and no move in currencies) for any movements of bond yields and corporate bond spreads and compare to the historic return profile for fixed income. It is simplistic but is useful as a rough guide to highlight the impact that lower yields could have on fixed income total returns.

Firstly, assuming that government bond yields and corporate bond spreads do not change and investors receive the current yield to maturity on the fixed income asset classes, the expected 12 month total returns are:

- Global government bonds: 1.0%
- Global investment grade corporates: 2.5%
- Global high yield corporates: 6.0%

Secondly, looking at a scenario where government bond yields increase by 1% but credit spreads remain stable gives the following total returns over 12 months:

- Global government bonds: -6.6%
- Global investment grade corporates: -4.0%
- Global high yield corporates: 1.8%

Given that yields are at historic low levels, there has never been less of an "income cushion" to protect against the possibility of a fall in bond prices. Government bond yields only need to increase by 73 bps in order to match the record drawdown experienced by government bonds in 1994.

Finally, the yield on the Global Government Bond Index rose from January to November 1994 by 219 bps. 1994 was the year that generated the maximum drawdown in global government bonds. An equivalent move today (and assuming no change in credit spreads) would result in the following total returns:

- Global government bonds: -15.5%
- Global investment grade corporates: -11.7%
- Global high yield corporates: -3.2%

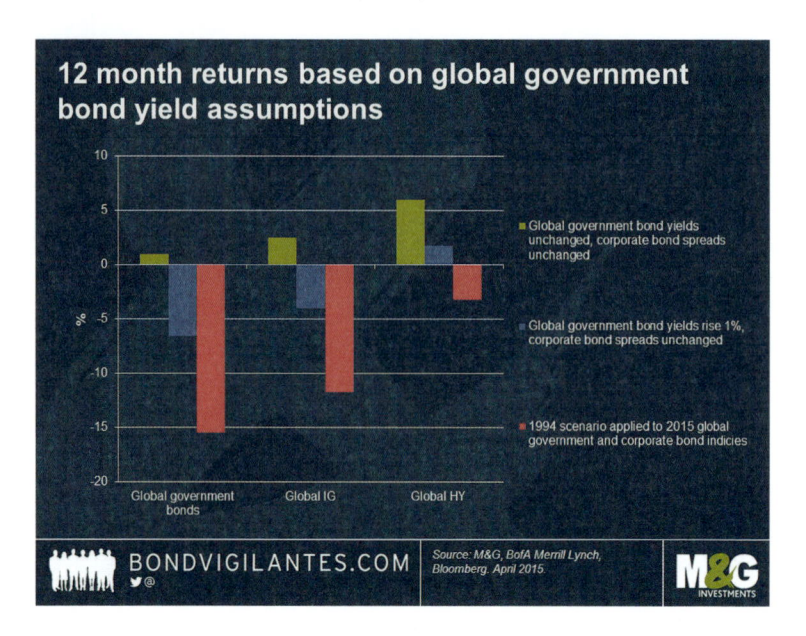

12 month returns based on global government bond yield assumptions

- Global government bond yields unchanged, corporate bond spreads unchanged
- Global government bond yields rise 1%, corporate bond spreads unchanged
- 1994 scenario applied to 2015 global government and corporate bond indices

BONDVIGILANTES.COM
Source: M&G, BofA Merrill Lynch, Bloomberg. April 2015.

The conclusions we can draw from this analysis are:

1. Now more than ever, duration positioning is contributing to bond returns.
2. It would not take much in terms of higher bond yields to cause a record drawdown in government bonds. Interest rate hikes or higher inflation could cause a significant move higher in bond yields.
3. Future returns from fixed income are likely be much lower than investors have historically experienced.
4. Government bonds have and do experience losses. Arguably, the chances of losses have never been greater given the collapse in bond yields around the world.
5. If corporate bond spreads were to rise (due to investors pricing in a higher default premium) in tandem with higher government bond yields the above return scenarios would be optimistic.

Of course, there are some very good reasons to own government bonds which I have previously written about. High global debt levels, structural deflationary forces and the global savings glut mean that over the long term, government bond yields may not increase to levels seen a couple of years ago. As the drawdown analysis above shows, government and investment grade corporate bonds tend to be less volatile, have lower drawdowns and have proven to be less correlated with higher risk assets like high yield corporate bonds and equities.

For those looking at moving out of government bonds given low yields, based on a risk and return basis investors might view investment grade corporates as a good alternative, and historically investment grade assets have shown a relatively low probability of generating a negative return in a calendar year. However, investors should be aware that investment grade corporate bonds have proven to be closely correlated to government bonds.

Subsequently, any sell-off in government bond markets will likely hit IG corporate bond returns as well. The collapse in corporate bond yields to extremely low levels has reduced the income contribution of total returns, though the credit spread on offer is rewarding in an environment of low defaults and solid economic growth.

In a world of ultra-low yields and lower future returns from fixed income, many may be tempted to invest in riskier assets. High yield corporates are more closely correlated but exhibit lower volatility to equities. High yield corporate bonds experience far greater volatility than more defensive fixed income asset classes and hence investors should be prepared to experience drawdowns in their portfolios over the course of a market cycle. That said, the higher yield on offer does protect against any possible increase in yields, as does the shorter duration profile of the high yield asset class.

Looking at historic returns, drawdowns and correlations give a useful guide to how fixed income returns might be impacted in a world of rising yields. However, the collapse in yields across the fixed income spectrum now means that investors are at greater risk of higher drawdowns than ever before, and the income component of their total return is unlikely to adequately compensate for any hits to capital returns like it would in the old days.

Chapter 75

Greece is not Argentina: don't expect exports to drive growth if Greece leaves the euro

Jim Leaviss – Thursday, 18th June 2015

I have heard it said, semi-seriously, that the biggest risk for the Eurozone isn't that Greece leaves the single currency and its economy collapses, but that it leaves and thrives. In this scenario Greece starts again, debt free, able to adapt fiscal easing rather than austerity, and with a devalued "new drachma" encouraging an influx of tourists and a manufacturing and agricultural export boom. When the other indebted and austere European nations see the benefits of leaving the euro, they do so, leaving their debts behind and causing the complete breakup of the European Union as we know it (and the second Great Financial Crisis in a decade?). One parallel that's drawn regularly is that of the 2002 Argentinian devaluation, and subsequent economic recovery. We wrote about the similarities between the two economies a couple of years ago.

From four years of negative annual rates of GDP growth (at worse over -10% per year), Argentina bounced back to see positive GDP growth of high single digits per year for five years when it left its currency straightjacket. Could we expect Greece to experience the same sort of economic rebound if it left the eurozone that Argentina experienced after abandoning its peso-dollar parity peg in January 2002?

Argentina saw a huge rebound in growth when it abandoned its dollar peg

Six years of positive GDP following the devaluation

Argentina Real GDP (annual YoY)

Source: M&G, Bloomberg, 18 June 2015 (last data point 31 Dec 2014)

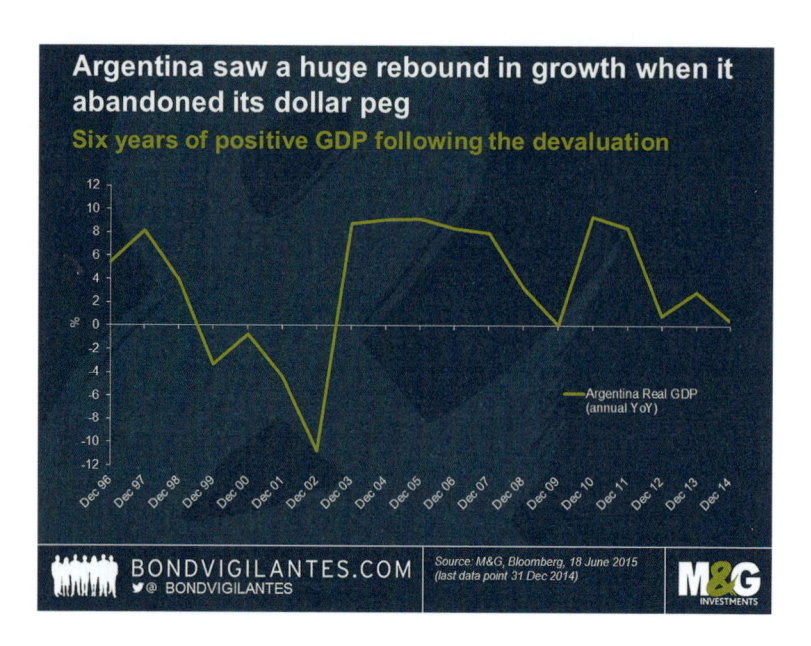

Argentina Real GDP (annual yoy)

There are many economic similarities between the Argentinian and Greek crises; the overvalued currency pegs; unsustainable government debt burdens and IMF involvement; poor tax collection; dubious statistical accuracy and high unemployment. Following the hyperinflation of the 1980s, the Argentinian peso was pegged to the US dollar. Inflation fell dramatically, and this stability and stronger currency led to a boost to domestic living standards and a big rise in imported goods; but there was also capital flight as many realised the peg might not hold forever. The current account deficit soared. In 1999 as the economy slowed from a period of growth, Argentinian unemployment hit 15% and the public debt started to rise alarmingly. External debt hit 50% of GDP, and the IMF told the government that it needed to implement austerity in order to access funds. Market interest rates almost doubled to 16% and Argentina's credit rating was cut to weak junk (there was subsequently a debt restructuring). Eventually the IMF refused to release new funds as the government hadn't kept to its budget deficit targets. By the end of 2001 bond yields were 42% above US Treasuries and bank accounts were all but frozen (the "corralito") to stop bank runs. Amid political chaos and riots (rising inequality had been another feature of the economy) – and the lack of circulating dollars – there emerged alternative IOU currencies issues by municipalities (Claudia Calich here has some "patacons" issued by Buenos Aires, we tweeted pictures on @bondvigilantes if you want to see one). In January 2002 the dollar-peso peg was abandoned, and the peso devalued and floated freely. Dollar bank accounts and investments were forcibly converted into pesos. From 1:1 the exchange rate moved to 4:1. Inflation returned, imported goods became scarce, businesses went bust and the unemployment rate hit 25%, with another 19% under-employed. (Wikipedia has an excellent timeline of Argentinian crisis period for much more detail, and I also recommend Arturo O'Connell's paper "The Recent Crisis – and Recovery – of the Argentine Economy").

But 2003 saw a turnaround; and it's this recovery that gives some hope that Greece might follow the same path if it leaves the euro. Tourism was indeed a contributor to economic growth as the weak currency made it a cheap destination. In 1997 tourism and travel had a total contribution of 7.5% of GDP, and by 2006 it had risen to 12.5%. Greece has a much larger tourism industry already, accounting for around 18% of GDP. I've heard this high level of the Greek tourism industry described as a handicap – perhaps it already is operating at full capacity (airports and transport, restaurants and hotels) and after default there would be little initial appetite to provide capital to ramp up capacity. But it doesn't seem fanciful to expect a devaluation to produce growth through tourism in Greece, even though it's unlikely to be a near doubling as was the case in Argentina.

But Argentina's big win was one of fortunate timing – and Greece won't have this luck on its side. World growth was very strong in the period post the Fed's emergency rate cuts after the 9-11 terror attacks. Global GDP growth was 3.1% pa in the period 1992 to 2001, but for the next ten years it averaged 3.9%. China joined the World Trade Organisation (WTO) in 2001 and there was an explosion of global trade – supplier nations to China did especially well – to Argentina's benefit. Until the ending of the dollar peg Argentina had been extremely uncompetitive, especially once its neighbour Brazil devalued in 1999 (Asian currencies had also devalued – O'Connell points out that only Argentina and Hong Kong had maintained their pegged currencies and suggests that over the 1990s Argentina's Real Effective Exchange Rate had appreciated by 40%). The rapid rise in global trade, and a return to competitiveness post devaluation helped lead to a 120% rise in Argentina's exports from 2002 to 2006. Chinese demand for soybeans are often credited for many of the economic gains, although Mark Weisbrot in the Guardian says that's an exaggeration.

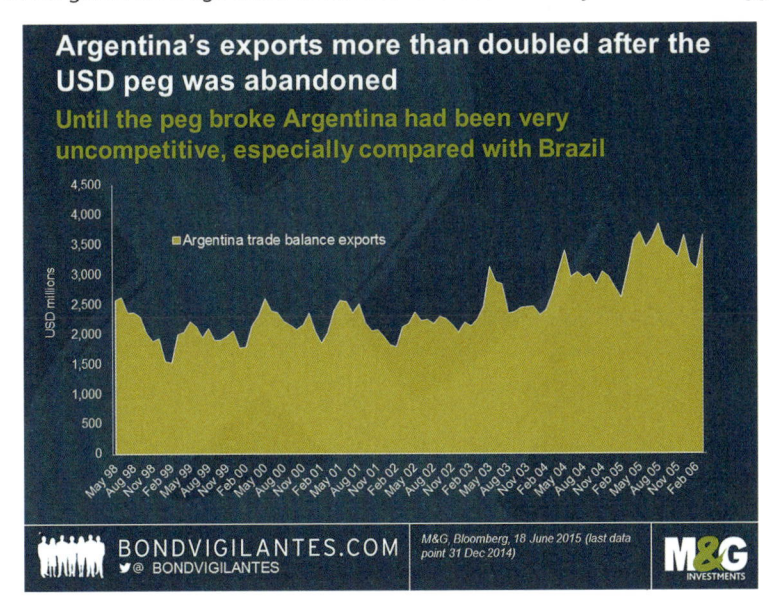

Argentina's exports more than doubled after the USD peg was abandoned

Until the peg broke Argentina had been very uncompetitive, especially compared with Brazil

BONDVIGILANTES.COM
@BONDVIGILANTES

M&G, Bloomberg, 18 June 2015 (last data point 31 Dec 2014)

M&G INVESTMENTS

Does Greece have the potential to export its way out of depression? Perhaps, although the poor quality of its land (most is unsuitable for agriculture) makes it much more difficult. Food and meat make up just 12% of its exports, compared to more than a third in Argentina. Greece's biggest export is refined petroleum, which is a pass-through industry, priced in hard currency in any case, so with no devaluation benefits. Also, its biggest export destination is

Germany – possibly problematic post a debt default...

So to conclude, those nations that have thrived post devaluations (Argentina, Canada, Sweden) have been fortunate in that their trading neighbours had been growing strongly at the time. Greece does not have that luxury, nor an economy that can respond quickly to increased export competitiveness. We should also remember that whilst Argentina grew strongly post devaluation and debt restructuring, its current real GDP rate is just 0.5% and hard currency government bond yields are around 8%. The ending of the dollar peg and debt restructuring did not prove to be a permanent economic panacea – but it is also hard to argue that the status quo was sustainable or desirable. Greek policymakers will be thinking the same thing.

Chapter 76

Mike Riddell's work here is done

Jim Leaviss – Tuesday, 7th July 2015

Mike Riddell, who worked in and around the bond team here at M&G for the past twelve years, has decided to move on. We can't say where to yet, but it's to another big bond fund manager and it's a good move for him. Normally we'd ask the airbrushing team to have him removed from the official histories, but he did a great job for us and we are all sad to see him go.

Mike did a great job running government bond portfolios for clients, as well as writing some of our most popular blogs (lots of good and prescient stuff on China, emerging markets and peripheral Europe).

Apart from declaring that he was a shoe-in to run the 400m for Wales at the 2014 Glasgow Commonwealth Games (coulda woulda shoulda) he never let us down. Journalists and future clients should note however that his famous "Blue Steel" publicity photograph does not reflect the reality of Mike today. See the following.

Good luck Mike!

Chapter 77

Greek debt forgiveness: Where there's a will, there's a way

Pierre Chartres – Monday, 27th July 2015

The Euro Summit meeting in Brussels that took place a couple of weeks ago seems to have finally provided some temporary closure to the Greek debt crisis. The dreaded Grexit scenario was avoided (at least for the moment) and the Greek government was able to repay its arrears to the IMF and the ECB using the €7.2 billion bridge loan provided by the European Council. Looking ahead, this short-term loan gives Greece and its creditors a bit of breathing room to establish a "Memorandum of Understanding" around a more comprehensive bailout package, estimated to total approximately €85 billion over the next three years. In terms of concessions made by the Greek government, Prime Minister Tsipras was forced to cross many of his Party's "red lines" on taxes and spending cuts, and these austerity measures will probably continue to exert pressure on the Greek economy for the coming months and years.

Whereas the lengthy negotiations until now have focused primarily on the reforms to be implemented by the Greek government, I find it quite interesting that **very little progress has been achieved on providing some type of debt relief to the Greek government and its people**. Indeed, despite having already been significantly reduced in 2012, Greek debt to GDP has soared again from less than 130% in 2009 to over 180% today, and according to the IMF should peak at 200% within the next two years. Even more alarmingly, debt dynamics in Greece continue to look extremely worrying, as continued slippage on the fiscal side and disappointing growth numbers (the European Commission recently reduced its growth forecast for Greece for 2015 from 2.5% to 0.5%) mean that **the situation will**

continue to get worse before it gets better. More recently, the forced closure of the banks and imposition of capital controls only exacerbated the country's woes, as a larger than anticipated capital injection in the Greek banking sector will now be required to keep it afloat.

Because of these recent developments, it now seems a widely accepted notion that the Greek government debt is unsustainable in its current form. This was not only mentioned fairly explicitly by the IMF in its update to its "preliminary draft debt sustainability analysis" (published last July 14th) but also by many people involved in the matter, such as the EU's Economic and Financial Affairs Commissioner, Pierre Moscovici. **The crucial and hotly debated issue now is whether relief on Greek debt should be provided via an upfront reduction in the amount of Greek debt** (also known as a "haircut" or "debt forgiveness") as requested by Tsipras and the Greek government, **or through a debt restructuring** (the preferred option for the Eurogroup led by Angela Merkel), which would keep the total value of the debt unchanged but would involve extending the maturities of the debt and lowering the interest costs.

Since the beginning of the crisis, Angela Merkel and her Eurozone partners have always said that debt forgiveness was out of the question for Greece, and this intransigence has caused them to receive quite a bit of criticism from international observers and from the Greek people themselves. To be fair, it is true that the idea of debt forgiveness does have some drawbacks:

- It would, for example, help fuel populist voices in other debtor countries, notably in Spain where the Podemos party would see its position strengthened.
- It would also have an immediate negative impact on the Greek banking sector, which still owns approximately €26 billion of Greek government bonds (although this represents less than 10% of total Greek debt) and would be forced to take further losses.
- The European Central Bank, who purchased over €20 billion in Greek bonds in 2010 through its Securities Market Program, would also be forced to realize losses, and the legal consequences of this are still uncertain.
- Finally, such a move, and this is Angela Merkel's most voiced objection against debt forgiveness, would be impossible because it would go against article 125 of the Treaty of Lisbon (now known as the "no bailout clause") that states that the Union shall not be liable or assume the commitments of other public entities.

Personally I find this argument to be a bit dubious coming from the same Angela Merkel who replied to David Cameron's push for EU treaty reforms last 29th of May "where there's a will, there's a way". Anecdotally, she repeated the same phrase to Tsipras on the 12th of June when negotiations were at a standstill, so she seems to be enjoying this expression at the moment. Nonetheless, **the reality seems to be that the Lisbon Treaty can be amended for David Cameron's reforms on European immigration and pensions, but not for Greece's debt relief requirements.**

I think this a shame because, despite the drawbacks, there are a couple of compelling arguments in favour of a haircut:

1. Given that Greek debt was already restructured first in 2010 and then again in 2012, the average interest rate that the Greek government currently pays on its debt is already quite low (around 2.4% according to the European Commission), only 0.2% higher than France's and Germany's, as the chart below shows:

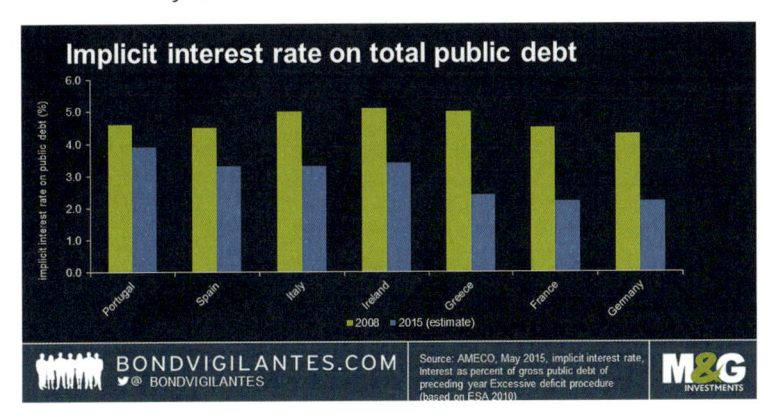

   Implicit interest rate on total public debt

   Source: AMECO, May 2015, implicit interest rate, Interest as percent of gross public debt of preceding year Excessive deficit procedure (based on ESA 2010)

   BONDVIGILANTES.COM / @BONDVIGILANTES — M&G INVESTMENTS

   In addition, the average maturity of the debt is also already quite long, at over 20 years. Because of this, not only would a restructuring only marginally reduce the cost of the debt, but also extend for several decades Greece's financial tutorship and the need for austerity measures. For example, reducing the average interest rate on Greek debt from 2.4% to 1.4% and extending the average maturity of the debt by 30 years (as certain institutions have recommended), would only reduce the net present value of the debt burden by approximately 30%[1]. This would be a step in the right direction, but probably wouldn't give Greece a whole lot of breathing room either.

   And should interest rates be lowered and maturities extended for Greece, what will be the reaction of the populist parties in Europe? Surely their case for debt relief is almost just as strong whether that relief is provided via debt forgiveness or through a restructuring?

2. As we enter the 7th year of the Greek recession, one can argue that the country and its people have reached the end of what they can endure in terms of austerity measures. A Greek haircut would allow for some much needed increased spending in the short term, in view of boosting investment and reducing unemployment.

   Hopefully, Germany and its Eurogroup partners are sensitive to the potential benefits of debt forgiveness, and have refused to consider this option so far because they believe the timing is not right. Indeed, with the upcoming national elections in Portugal, Spain and Ireland, as well as the German federal elections in 2017, now is arguably not the best time to crystallise a loss on loans made to Greece.

   In this respect, Germany's strategy probably makes sense, and one can only hope that in a few years' time –if Greece has demonstrated a strong commitment towards reforms and political pressures have abated in Europe– the idea of debt forgiveness may be back on the table. At this moment, maybe we will even hear Angela Merkel use her favourite catchphrase again... because where there's a will, there's a way... isn't there, Mrs Merkel?

[1] Assuming a flat discount rate of 2.4%

Chapter 78

Covenant case study: Change of Control

James Tomlins – Friday, 7th August 2015

We've written in the past about some of the concerns we have over the gradual weakening of bond covenants (the legal language that protects the right of bondholders) over the past few years. However, today we have seen a real world instance of a bond covenant kicking in to the benefit of existing holders, namely the change of control. This illustrates how and why such covenants can help protect the interests of investors.

It was announced this morning that Lowell Group, a speciality financial services business in the UK, will merge with a German competitor. As part of the deal there will be a change of ownership. Consequently, the "change of control" language will be triggered. This gives the bondholder the right but not the obligation to sell back the bonds to the company at a price of 101% of face value.

The company's GBP 5.875% 2019 bonds have been trading below this level since mid-2014. Following today's news we can see in the chart below that the price has risen up by a little over 3% to this 101 level. As the new combined business will be more financially leveraged, it is fair to say that without this covenant the bonds would most likely have fallen in price to reflect the increased credit risk of the combined entity. This clearly demonstrates the economic value that this covenant can have.

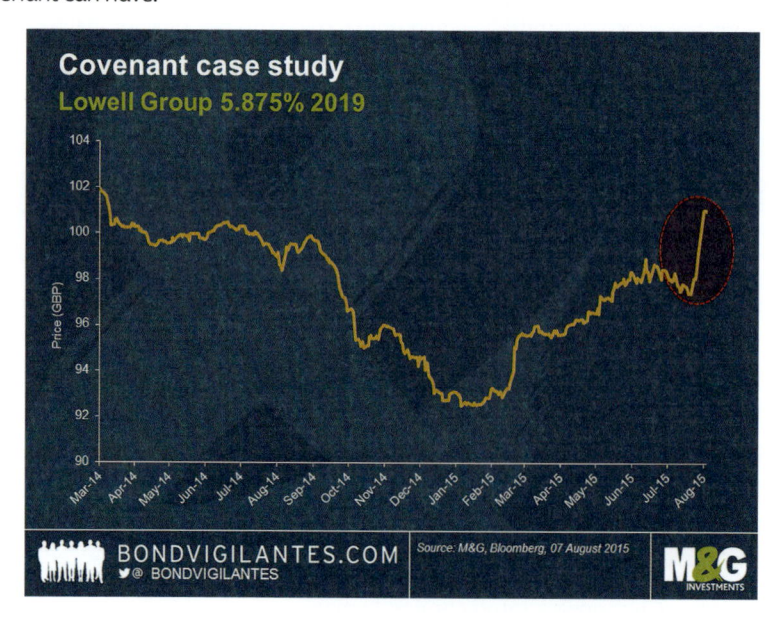

Chapter 79

How bond investors should assess the opportunities in the US high yield energy sector

Luke Coha – Friday, 14th August 2015

U.S. high yield energy bonds have sold off recently, virtually reversing their Q1/Q2 rally. The main culprit is, again, oil prices. The recent re-repricing in oil has led to energy bonds trading at levels worse than the last time oil sold-off at the beginning of 2015. In fact, the BAML U.S. high yield energy index this week reached its widest levels (in terms of spreads) since April 2009 at 1019 bps.

While oil prices were trending lower throughout 2014 on slow global growth expectations, the sharp decline in late 2014 was prompted by OPECs decision to not curb production. Oil prices recovered briefly in Q2 as U.S. production cuts were expected to stabilise supply and support prices in the latter part of the year. So what has prompted oil to sell off this time around? Well, global growth remains subdued and China's outlook has worsened. Additionally, the devaluation of the yuan will exacerbate the pressure on commodity prices. Plus, U.S. production cuts have not been enough to offset unexpected supply from the Middle East including Iraq, while Saudi Arabia and Kuwait both posted record production levels last month. Oil prices also moved lower on the anticipation of new supply from Iran next year (estimates as high as 900k/bbd) on the back of sanctions potentially being lifted following the recent, tentative, nuclear accord.

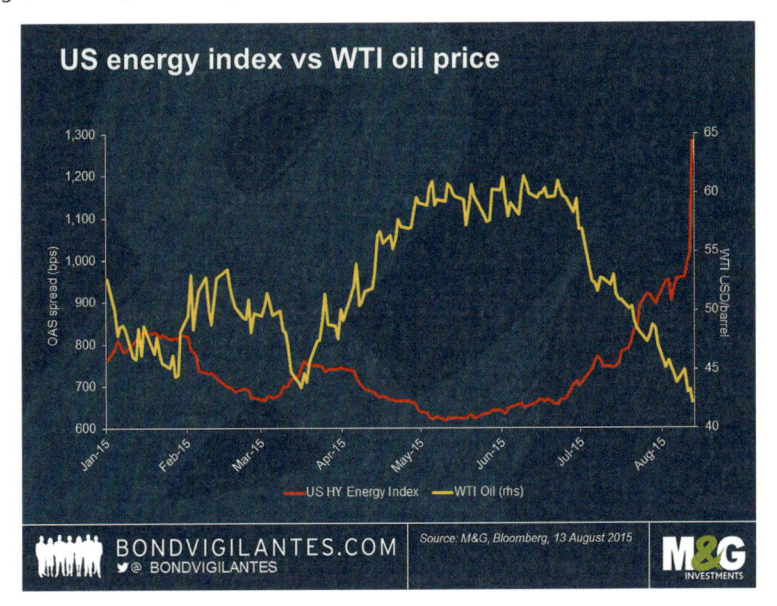

There are a few reasons why high yield energy bonds have sold off more dramatically this time around.

Firstly, several energy companies that issued bonds secured by their assets (called Second Lien bonds) in Q1 and Q2 to extend their financial liquidity profiles have seen these bonds underperform massively. This has scared investors to the extent that this potential source of funding is effectively closed to other companies that would benefit from additional liquidity. This has had a knock-on effect on investor sentiment, with investors even abandoning bonds of companies that were not expected to need this additional liquidity.

Secondly, the forward oil curve has flattened. Previously, the market was expecting a fairly robust rebound in prices in the second half of 2015 and 2016; now forward price expectations are more subdued. With many companies well-hedged for 2015 they were effectively insulated from the drop in oil prices and had time to wait for the oil price environment in improve. However, hedges eventually roll off and the sector as a whole is, generally speaking, less hedged in 2016. This suggests that companies will have to operate in a low-cost environment longer-than-previously expected without the benefit of hedges which is likely to impair earnings and stretch liquidity.

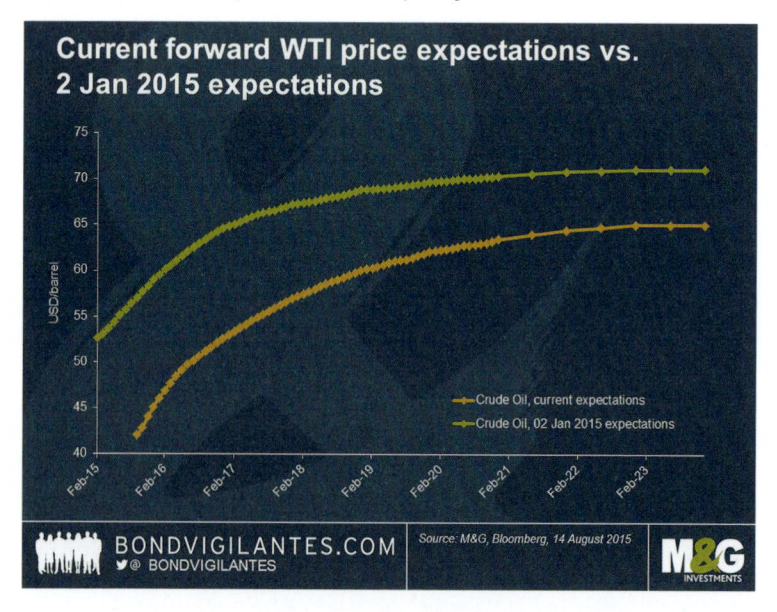

Current forward WTI price expectations vs. 2 Jan 2015 expectations

Source: M&G, Bloomberg, 14 August 2015

BONDVIGILANTES.COM
@BONDVIGILANTES

M&G INVESTMENTS

Finally, with the Second Lien market basically closed barring a rebound in WTI, this places greater burden on companies RBLs (Reserve Backed Lines – their asset-backed bank credit facilities) to provide liquidity. These RBLs are re-valued by the companies' bank groups generally in October; and a lower forward curve suggests that the borrowing capacity of these facilities will be trimmed precisely at the time that earnings and cashflow are under additional pressure, stretching companies' liquidity profiles.

Now to be fair, the market hasn't punished all companies indiscriminately. Service providers, offshore producers and highly-indebted exploration & production (E&P) companies have sold-off more dramatically than stable midstream (pipeline) and E&P companies with sound balance sheets and low operating costs.

The following demonstrates the price action of a few of the bonds within these individual subsectors:

- Crestwood Midstream Partners – stable pipeline company
- Concho Resources Inc. – E&P company with solid balance sheet
- Hercules Offshore, Inc. – an offshore service provider
- Energy XXI Gulf Coast, Inc. – an offshore, Gulf of Mexico E&P company

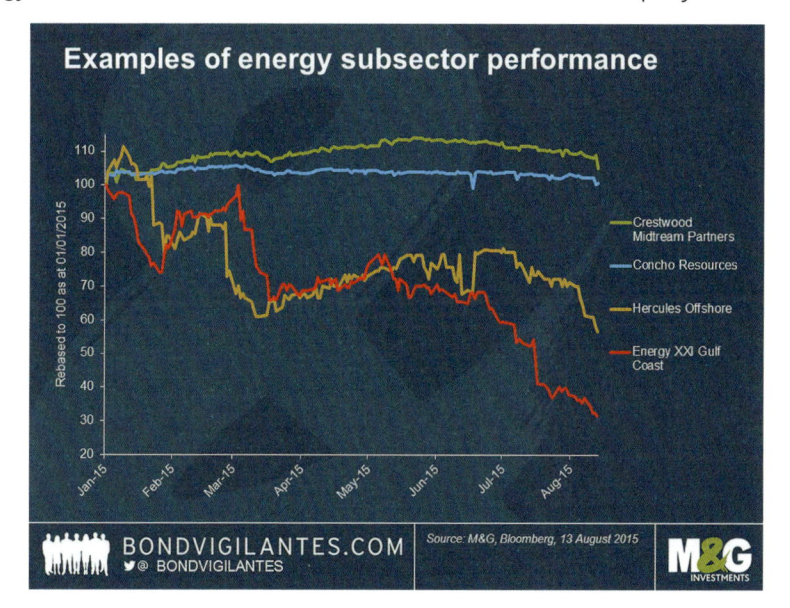

Examples of energy subsector performance

Source: M&G, Bloomberg, 13 August 2015

So how should bond investors approach this space? With energy-related bonds accounting for 13.5% of the broader U.S. high yield index (off from its peak, but still the largest component of the index), it is difficult for investors to completely avoid the energy sector. Shunning it entirely now may result in missing out on any eventual recovery.

Despite the carnage, there is still some opportunity for patient investors to capitalise on those names that have been too severely punished and are likely to survive what now looks to be an extended low oil-price environment. In particular, investors should focus on:

- Low-cost operators capable of continuing profitable production levels at sub $50 (or even lower) WTI prices.
- Producers in good basins (the quality of basin is important as well as its location which limits transport costs).
- Manageable debt levels with limited or no near-term maturities and low financial leverage vis-à-vis earnings.
- Solid financial liquidity – solid cash levels and ample borrowing capacity from bank groups. Note, not all companies are stretched in terms of their liquidity and several were shrewdly proactive during the Q2 recovery in WTI to enhance their liquidity profiles through borrowings, extending maturities and even issuing equity.
- Dry powder regarding cost cuts – virtually all companies have cut costs, some more so than others. Those companies that have cut less but have the capacity to cut more

without too severely affecting production levels have some flexibility to manage the lower price environment.

- Midstream operators with a high percentage of fixed-fee, take or pay contracts with investment grade counterparties are better insulated to manage the low-price environment.

- Identifying possible M&A opportunities. The sector is ripe for consolidation and there have been a few examples of high yield companies being bought by investment grade companies to the delight of those companies' bondholders. Rosetta Resources, for example was bought by investment grade rated Noble Energy, Inc. Similar to bond investors, investment grade companies will look at high yield operators in good basins, with low production costs and solid reserves. Investment grade companies will also look at vertically acquiring distribution and refining assets such as pipeline partners that they already have arrangements, joint ventures or similar relationships with. The chart below highlights the bonds of Regency Energy Partners which is being bought by investment grade rated Energy Transfer Partners.

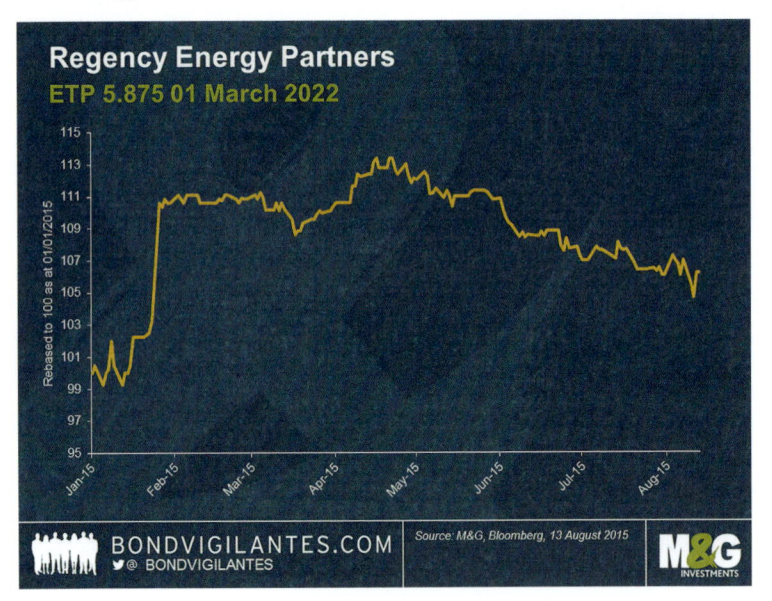

Regency Energy Partners
ETP 5.875 01 March 2022

Source: M&G, Bloomberg, 13 August 2015

We continue to avoid the service and offshore companies as, despite the extremely low prices, the risk of further downside is still high and bond volatility will be exacerbated by the entrance of aggressive, distressed investors playing in these bonds.

Will oil prices recover? It's hard to say, but probably not in the near term; China data, supply levels and the forward price curve suggests that oil prices will remain depressed for some time. One potential positive catalyst could be if the Iranian nuclear deal fails to pass the U.S. Congress (a real possibility), but this is likely to have only a moderate impact on oil prices given the relatively small impact on worldwide production/supply levels.

Chapter 80

Covenant case study – after the good, the bad

Charles de Quinsonas – Wednesday, 19th August 2015

We recently highlighted a bond covenant that benefited fixed income investors. After the good, this week we have seen the bad. In this case, a bond covenant may impact bondholders in a detrimental way. Both examples are evidence of how critical it is to have a thorough understanding of bond documentation ahead of investing in a bond.

Kuwait's third largest bank, Burgan Bank, announced in a regulatory filing that they had received approval from the Central Bank of Kuwait to redeem $400 million of outstanding subordinated bonds. In Burgan Bank's instance, the 2020 subordinated bond – old-style Tier 2 capital – cannot be redeemed prior to 29th September 2015. These bonds were trading at a cash price of 113 as of Monday 17th August 2015.

Approval was granted by the central bank on the "redemption for regulatory capital treatment reasons" covenant. This clause is very common in bank bond documents. It gives the issuer the option to redeem at par or 101 any outstanding bonds that have lost their regulatory capital status in case of a change of regulation.

The Central Bank of Kuwait had announced the transition to Basel III capital adequacy in early 2014, with old-style Tier 2 capital not benefiting of any phase-out period unlike in Europe where there is grandfathering. The implementation of Basel III was effective in June 2014. Hence, nothing new here.

However, the Burgan Bank 7.875% 2020 bond document states on page 25 and 26 that:

REDEMPTION FOR REGULATORY CAPITAL TREATMENT REASONS

IF AT ANY TIME AFTER THE DATE OF ISSUE OF THE NOTES A REGULATORY EVENT OCCURS, SUBJECT TO THE PRIOR WRITTEN APPROVAL OF THE CENTRAL BANK OF KUWAIT, THE GUARANTOR MAY ON OR AFTER 29 SEPTEMBER 2015, BY WRITTEN NOTICE, REQUIRE THE ISSUER TO, HAVING GIVEN NOT LESS THAN 30 NOR MORE THAN 60 DAYS' PRIOR NOTICE TO THE NOTEHOLDERS (WHICH NOTICE SHALL BE IRREVOCABLE), REDEEM IN WHOLE, BUT NOT IN PART, THE NOTES IN ACCORDANCE WITH THESE CONDITIONS AT THEIR PRINCIPAL AMOUNT TOGETHER WITH INTEREST ACCRUED TO THE DATE FIXED FOR REDEMPTION, PROVIDED THAT BOTH AT THE TIME WHEN THE NOTICE OF REDEMPTION IS GIVEN AND IMMEDIATELY FOLLOWING SUCH REDEMPTION, THE GUARANTOR IS OR WILL BE (AS THE CASE MAY BE) IN COMPLIANCE WITH THE APPLICABLE REGULATORY CAPITAL REQUIREMENTS (EXCEPT TO THE EXTENT THAT THE FINANCIAL REGULATOR NO LONGER SO REQUIRES)."

"REGULATORY EVENT" MEANS AN EVENT WHERE, AS A RESULT OF ANY CHANGE OF ANY LAW OR REGULATION OCCURRING AFTER THE DATE OF ISSUE OF THE NOTES, THE LOAN CEASES TO BE ELIGIBLE TO QUALIFY IN FULL AS TIER 2 CAPITAL FOR THE PURPOSE OF THE CAPITAL REGULATIONS, PROVIDED THAT NO REGULATORY EVENT SHALL BE DEEMED TO HAVE OCCURRED IF SUCH NON-QUALIFICATION IS AS A RESULT OF EITHER (A) ANY APPLICABLE LIMITATION ON THE AMOUNT OF SUCH CAPITAL AS APPLICABLE TO THE GUARANTOR, OR (B) SUCH CAPITAL CEASING TO COUNT TOWARDS

THE GUARANTOR'S CAPITAL BASE THROUGH ANY AMORTISATION OR SIMILAR PROCESS OR ANY CHANGES THERETO (INCLUDING ANY AMORTISATION OR SIMILAR PROCESS IMPOSED THROUGH ANY GRANDFATHERING ARRANGEMENTS)"

In light of this clause, Burgan Bank received from the Central Bank of Kuwait the approval to redeem their 2020 subordinated bonds on or after 29 September 2015. The covenant also states that the bonds are redeemable at par, which would result in a potential loss of around 13 points for existing bondholders should the bonds be redeemed.

At this stage, Burgan Bank has not officially announced whether it will or won't call the bond. Given the high coupon on the bond (7.875%) and the current significant cash position of the bank, one might think the subordinated bonds will likely be called as it will materially reduce interest expenses and be in favour of shareholders. As of today, the bond is quoting 105 mid- price (101.3 / 108.7), reflecting a high probability (more than 50%) – assigned by the market – of the bonds being called.

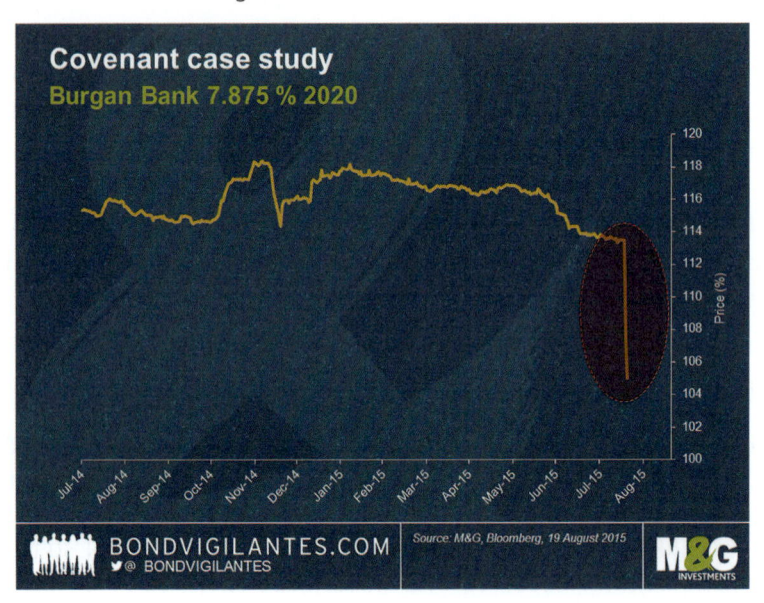

Covenant case study
Burgan Bank 7.875 % 2020

Source: M&G, Bloomberg, 19 August 2015

Existing bondholders will not be happy should Burgan Bank call the bonds at par. This is why other options should not be ruled out. While very unlikely, the bank may choose not to redeem the bond as it has other outstanding bonds, such as a deeply subordinated hybrid security (a 7.25% perpetual), and may fear bondholders' negative reaction. Another more plausible option is to launch a tender offer on the bonds at a price lying between par and where it was trading a few days ago, i.e. 113. In this instance, existing holders would get compensation for the loss of value. Credit Suisse had chosen this latter option when it called its Tier 1 7.875% hybrid in early February 2015. The bank offered to buy-back the notes at 103, while the notes were trading at 107 prior to the announcement.

This Burgan Bank example highlights how important it is to investors to perform covenant and regulatory due-diligence in order to avoid an ugly outcome.

*Please note we have no economic interest in Burgan Bank debt

Chapter 81

Contrary to popular opinion, the Bank of England's next move will be a monetary easing

Matthew Russell – Wednesday, 26th August 2015

On the 7th of September £38bn worth of UK gilts (4.75% 2015) will mature. The Bank of England (BoE) own just under half the issue, having purchased the bonds through its £375bn quantitative easing (QE) programme. At this point in time, the BoE have indicated that they are committed to keeping the size of the QE program at £375bn. As a result of the 2015 bonds maturing, the bank will therefore have about £17bn to invest back into the UK government bond market.

In my view, this is equivalent to an easing of monetary policy. This is because the average duration of the BoE's gilt holdings will increase, and therefore the £17bn reinvestment in gilts will have a larger (downward) effect on gilt yields than it currently does today.

The BoE has helpfully laid out a few rules as to how they execute this sort of reinvestment. Firstly, the cash will be invested equally (£5.6bn) across three maturity buckets; 3-7yr, 7-15yr and 15+ yrs. Secondly, the BoE has stated that they will not purchase more than 70% of an individual bond issue.

All else being equal, an inflow of £17bn into the gilt market will clearly put downward pressure on yields along the length of the curve – and that doesn't even take into account the other £21bn that private investors will have to find a home for. As there are fewer bonds in the 7-15yr bucket than either the short or long-dated buckets my feeling is that the reinvestment should have a disproportionately positive effect on this part of the yield curve.

The individual bonds that the bank will buy and hence which yields could be the most squeezed is –unsurprisingly – something of a debate within the gilt market. Focusing on just the 7-15yr maturity bucket, we can see below that the bank own a substantial amount of the 4.25% 2027's whilst owning a very small percentage (or none at all) of some of the other outstanding gilt issuance.

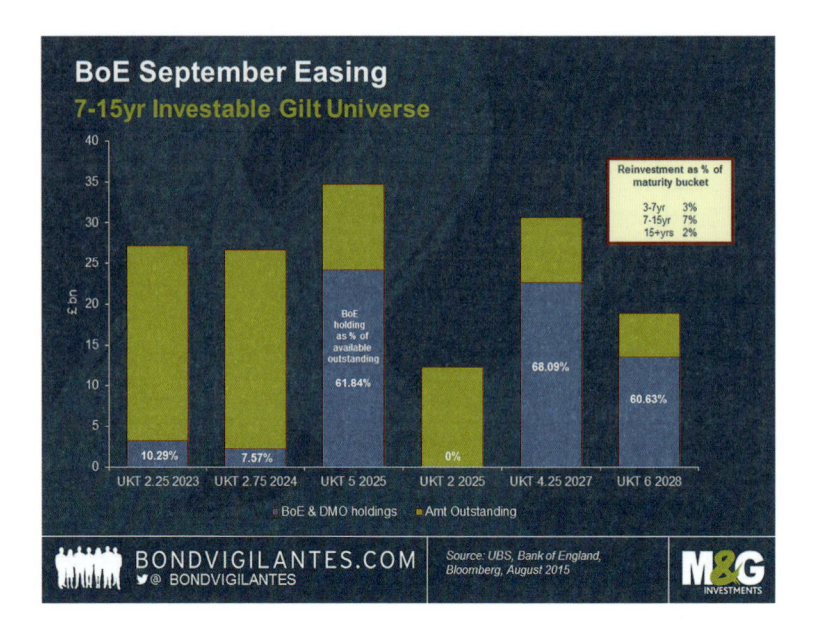

My view is that the gilts that the BoE already has a fairly large holding in (over 60%), but not so large that there isn't much room for them to buy more before hitting their 70% ceiling are likely to benefit the most (such as the 5% 2025s and 6% 2028s). Given these technical dynamics, gilt investors could benefit from lengthening duration and focusing on the belly of the gilt curve in coming weeks.

Chapter 82

The ECB may lower rates, but the Swiss shouldn't follow suit
Mario Eisenegger – Tuesday, 1st December 2015

Expectations are high that European Central Bank (ECB) president Mario Draghi will announce additional easing measures at the next monetary policy meeting on Thursday this week. If the ECB decides to provide further stimulus via extended (or expanded) QE and/or lowers its negative deposit rate further, the Swiss National Bank (SNB) has some thinking to do. I am probably not the only Swiss person concerned that Switzerland faces -1.4% deflation and is struggling to keep its exchange rate competitive. Since the SNB ended its EUR/CHF 1.20 peg in January this year, a sharp appreciation of the safe-haven currency was unavoidable. The EUR/CHF exchange rate is now a bit less than 1.10, still high for the franc if we consider a purchasing power parity of roughly EUR/CHF 1.25. The consequences of this can be seen in Swiss local newspapers, which just reported that another traditional company has gone bust as a result of the strong franc. This is not an isolated case and is not surprising, given that Europe is Switzerland's number one trading partner with roughly half of Swiss exports going to the Eurozone. With that dependency, if the ECB lowers its deposit rate, there are obvious expectations that the SNB would follow suit and further cut its already negative rate of -0.75% on sight deposit account balances for banks and other financial market participants. In my view, though, the following points need to be kept in mind as they make such an SNB move far less certain:

Remember the banking crisis

Switzerland has experienced problems in the past from overly long phases of too loose lending standards. The last scenario that comes to my mind is the banking crisis in the 90s, in years where credit lending increased significantly by historic standards, especially compared to economic activity. A banking crisis is more severely felt in Switzerland compared to other countries because of the size of its banking sector. Around 275 banks have legal status in the country and the sector contributes around 6% to Swiss GDP (with inclusion of the insurance sector this rises to more than 10%). Importantly, regional banks in particular rely heavily on their interest margin business. The SNB has warned more than once in its financial stability report that banks with a focus on their home market may have too little diversification and high interest risk on their balance sheets. The latest SNB financial stability report indicates that direct interest rate risk in domestically focused banking books is at a high level, resulting from a mismatch between the maturities of assets and liabilities. Lower deposit rates make it even more attractive for banks to lend excess reserves on at relatively comfortable spreads instead of holding them at the SNB at negative rates. Based on the aforementioned SNB report, in 2014, for 42% of new mortgages granted by domestically focussed banks, the imputed costs would exceeded the general limit of one-third of gross wage or pension income. This, together with a very high proportion of loans that would be affected in the short or medium term if rates were to then rise, points to affordability risk in the Swiss mortgage market. Too low a deposit rate could encourage more and more private sector leverage and increase the possibility of another banking crisis, a consideration that the SNB will be well aware of.

Banks are starting to pass on negative interest

Whilst the big Swiss banks have already introduced an individual deposit charge for large account balances held by corporate and institutional clients in reaction to the SNB's negative deposit rates, banks so far have been reluctant to pass on negative rates directly to depositors. This may reflect the fear of losing customers in a competitive landscape. However, this trend could be ending given the environment for interest margin business is getting tougher and tougher as margins have shrunk considerably. Indeed, the Alternative Bank Schweiz has just become the first bank in Switzerland to announce negative interest rates of -0.125% on its current accounts for individual personal customers with effect from 1 January 2016. For savings over CHF 100,000, the bank will pass on the whole negative interest rate of -0.75%. Lowering deposit rates further could incentivise other banks to follow, which might encourage people to store their money in a safety box or elsewhere. Would you be happy to pay monthly fees for a bank account that is charging you a negative interest rate at the same time? As Richard has written, storing cash is risky for individuals (money is not insured and can be stolen) and costly for the economy as the money stuffed under the mattress cannot be lent on. The big CHF 1000 Swiss bank note doesn't help either and makes it even easier to store Swiss francs.

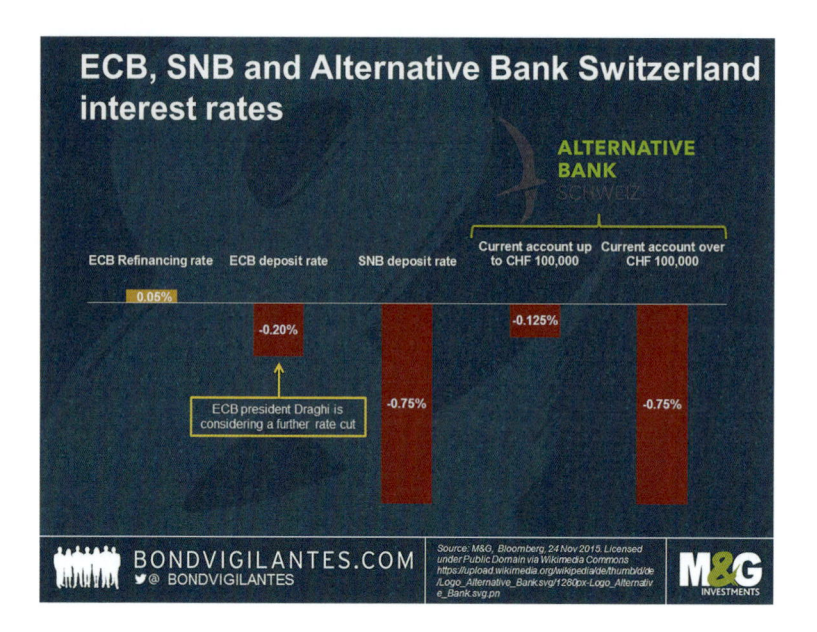

ECB, SNB and Alternative Bank Switzerland interest rates

	ECB Refinancing rate	ECB deposit rate	SNB deposit rate	Current account up to CHF 100,000	Current account over CHF 100,000
	0.05%	-0.20%	-0.75%	-0.125%	-0.75%

ECB president Draghi is considering a further rate cut

Source: M&G, Bloomberg, 24 Nov 2015. Licensed under Public Domain via Wikimedia Commons https://upload.wikimedia.org/wikipedia/de/thumb/d/de/Logo_Alternative_Bank.svg/1280px-Logo_Alternative_Bank.svg.pn

The euro is important, but...

...there are other major currencies for the SNB to focus on as well. It's true that most Swiss exports go to the Eurozone, but an even higher volume is imported every year from Europe. If we consider net exports (exports – imports) the most important countries are China, India and the US. Following a hawkish tone from the US Federal Reserve in October, and recently released FOMC minutes that confirm this stance, market expectations for a US rate hike in December received a sizeable boost. Furthermore, the US dollar has rallied more than 7% vs the Swiss franc since mid-October, making Swiss products cheaper for the US. As the chart shows, the greenback is now back at a level when the SNB abandoned its currency peg. As the Chinese renminbi is closely linked to the US dollar, similar movements have resulted in a CNY/CHF exchange rate that is only marginally lower compared to the start of the year when the Swiss currency peg still was in place. This significant decrease of the CHF exchange rate versus its major trading partners will be welcomed by the SNB as it reduces the need for further stimulus.

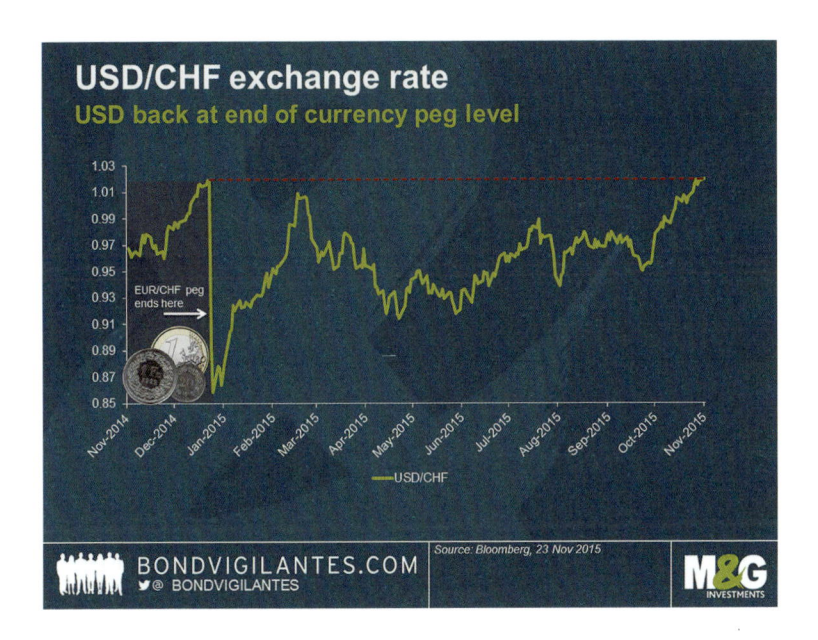

USD/CHF exchange rate
USD back at end of currency peg level

Source: Bloomberg, 23 Nov 2015

Further market interventions more likely than a rate cut

Looking ahead and trying to anticipate the SNB's next steps, it's worth mentioning that despite all the headwinds, the Swiss economy has proved surprisingly resilient with still positive annual growth. I think global growth will help Switzerland get through this difficult time as it reduces the impact of an overvalued CHF. The franc's recent falls versus the USD and CNY also give the Swiss authorities more room to breathe and eases some of the currency valuation pressure. The size of the SNB balance sheet looks quite scary as a result of market intervention, with foreign reserves accounting for more than 80% of Swiss GDP (to put that in context, the UK's foreign reserves represent approximately 6% of UK GDP). However, rather than pure size, diversification remains key as the SNB cannot hedge exchange rate risk against the CHF without neutralising the impact of its monetary policy. In my view, the SNB did a decent job over the past challenging years in managing to diversify its euro currency exposure by reallocating across other currencies.

Foreign currency investment of the SNB as of 30th October 2015
Volume has increased significantly, but remains well diversified

Source: Swiss National Bank, 30 Oct 2015 — BONDVIGILANTES.COM / @BONDVIGILANTES / M&G Investments

That said, I think the SNB can and surely will intervene in the market if necessary, but will do that by further buying of euros rather than lowering its deposit rate more into negative territory. The latter action would expose the Swiss economy to a bigger extent to the widely unproved and unconventional monetary policy instrument of negative interest rates. In addition, I don't think a deposit cut by the ECB in December is a given. Remember the ECB's December meeting will take place two weeks before the Fed decision, and I can see Mario Draghi wanting to keep some powder dry should the euro appreciate versus the dollar in case the Fed decides, against market expectations, to keep rates unchanged. All in all, a busy year-end beckons for central bankers.

Chapter 83

Three reasons why the UK will not raise rates anytime soon

Anjulie Rusius – Monday, 21st December 2015

With the Fed recently raising its interest rates via a unanimous vote, I've been wondering whether the UK will shortly follow suit. The market seems to think not, pricing in the first UK rate rise in Q1 of 2017, compared to two further US rate hikes in 2016. At face value this huge divergence feels strange; both countries are targeting (and undershooting) a 2% inflation rate, both have similar rates of year on year GDP growth and both have seen significant labour market improvements since the onset of the financial crisis (the UK arguably more so as inroads have continued despite the backdrop of an increasing participation rate, in comparison to the US decline in this measure). Indeed, the large reductions in unemployment rates indicate that the economies are at or approaching full employment, which should in turn bring mounting wage pressures and generate domestic inflation. All solid justification for considering a rate hike, which is why the US has done just that.

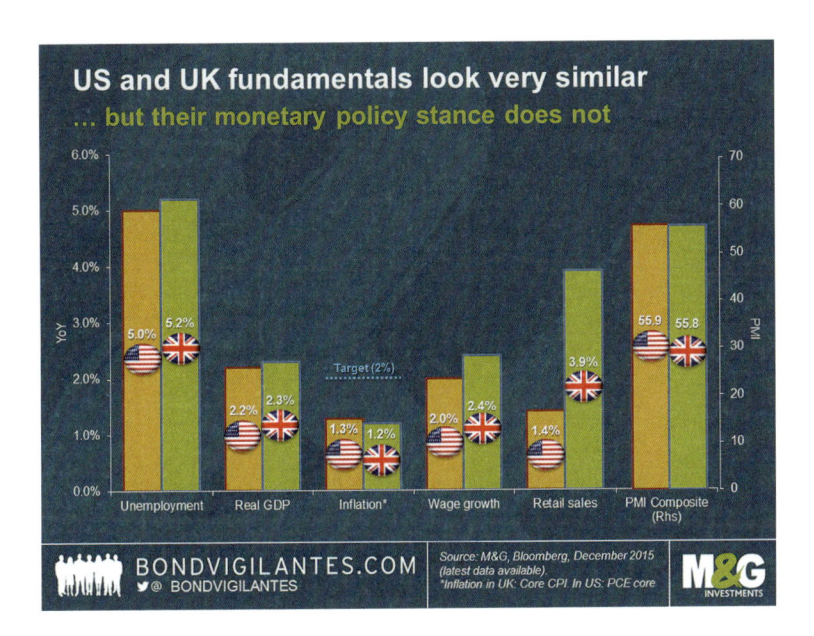

US and UK fundamentals look very similar
... but their monetary policy stance does not

- Unemployment: US 5.0%, UK 5.2%
- Real GDP: US 2.2%, UK 2.3%
- Inflation*: US 1.3%, UK 1.2% (Target 2%)
- Wage growth: US 2.0%, UK 2.4%
- Retail sales: US 1.4%, UK 3.9%
- PMI Composite (Rhs): US 55.9, UK 55.8

Source: M&G, Bloomberg, December 2015 (latest data available). *Inflation in UK: Core CPI. In US: PCE core

BONDVIGILANTES.COM / @BONDVIGILANTES — M&G INVESTMENTS

Looking at the graph below, it is clear that up until the end of last year, the market was predicting that the UK would be the first to raise rates. Even this year there were periods where it looked to be neck-and-neck. With the US recently winning the rate-hiking race, why has the runner-up now fallen so far behind?

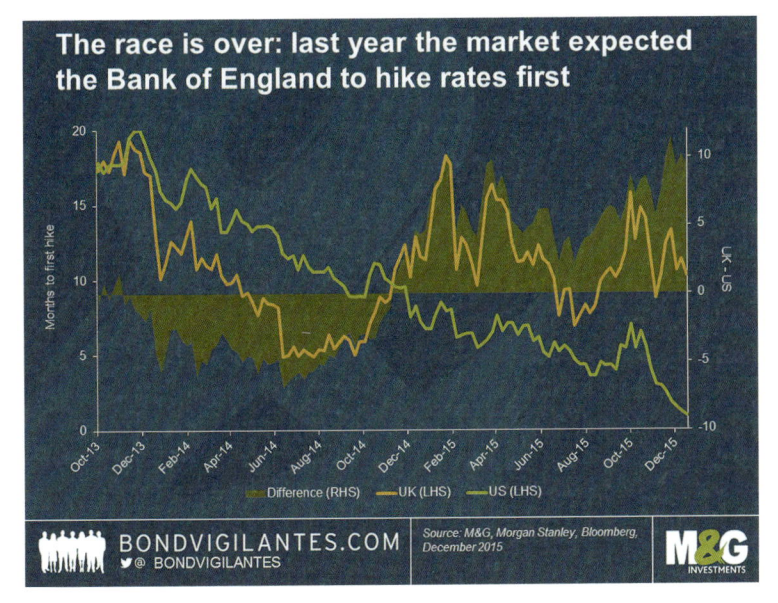

The race is over: last year the market expected the Bank of England to hike rates first

Difference (RHS) — UK (LHS) — US (LHS)

Source: M&G, Morgan Stanley, Bloomberg, December 2015

BONDVIGILANTES.COM / @BONDVIGILANTES — M&G INVESTMENTS

Though the macroeconomic fundamentals may look very similar, the micro factors paint a different picture.

1) WAGES: Last week I saw Minouche Shafik speak in London. As the Deputy Governor of the Bank of England, appointed specifically to oversee markets and banking, her message was clear: she will not be voting for a UK interest rate hike until she has witnessed a sustained pick-up in wages (Shafik is waiting to witness wage growth that is 2-3% above productivity, which is more aligned with the pre-recession years, which she believes will ensure that inflation returns to target). Here's the kicker; the latest data release showed that the UK headline (3 month average) wage growth rate fell from 3.0% to 2.4% in October (excluding bonuses, annual growth fell from 2.5% to 2.0%), while productivity rose at its fastest quarterly rate in 4 years, with output per hour rising 0.9% in Q2. Given these numbers, it's highly unlikely that Shafik will be voting for a rate hike at the next MPC meeting on 14th January.

2) **CURRENCY:** Both the UK and US have experienced trade weighted appreciation, but this has had a larger impact in the UK where imports and exports constitute a higher proportion of GDP (approx. 30% in UK Vs. 17% in the US). The appreciation of the currency makes imports cheaper and exports more expensive which manifests as downwards pressure on growth and inflation. Given this relationship, it is important to consider the UK's trading partners. The US is a relatively closed economy in comparison to the UK, whose main trading partner is Europe, where monetary easing remains on the table for the foreseeable future (some market participants are not forecasting an ECB rate hike until Q4 2018). The Bank of England must therefore be mindful of a divergence in policy which could cause the currency to significantly appreciate, otherwise UK imports invoiced in euros would essentially import deflation. Sterling is already up 6.7% year to date. Further appreciation brought on by a rate hike would harm exporters and hamper growth strategies which pursue diversification away from domestic demand.

3) **POLICY:** It is well known that monetary policy works with a lag, but this tends to last longer in the US due to the greater prevalence of fixed rate mortgages; the UK is therefore granted some leeway with regard to the timing of its monetary policy implementation. Fiscal policy is another consideration, as the Conservative UK government are committed to fiscal austerity while the US are entering a pre-election period and are more likely to see their fiscal deficit increase. The UK policy is likely to be contractionary – which would make the case for further easing rather than hiking– potentially delaying lift-off further. Thirdly, minimum wages in the UK are high compared to its European counterparts and set to increase. If this attracts a greater supply of low-skilled workers via increased migration, wage growth could credibly plateau, ultimately limiting upwards pressure on pay and dashing any hopes of UK inflation hitting its target. Finally, the real possibility of the UK leaving the EU certainly deserves a mention since the referendum – regardless of the outcome – is sure to generate some currency volatility in the build-up and aftermath of the vote (the date has not yet been set, but it has been suggested that this may take place in June or September next year). If the UK does vote to leave the union, this will have wider-ranging repercussions for the economy. This certainly gives the Bank of England reason to pause now, before the referendum result becomes clear.

Despite these three reasons to delay monetary policy lift-off, the UK recovery nevertheless remains robust. Consumption is solid, investment is recovering and productivity is returning. The main piece of the missing puzzle is – as Shafik says – wages. Although UK rate increases may not be immediately trailing the Fed, I wouldn't be surprised if this occurs much sooner than the market expects.

Chapter 84

High Yield Liquidity: 5 ways to help deal with it
James Tomlins – Wednesday, 23rd December 2015

Following the closure of the Third Avenue fund earlier this month, liquidity issues are once again at the forefront of investors' minds when it comes to the high yield market. Ultimately, conditions will only improve with structural changes to the market but in the meantime we think there are several steps that can be taken to help improve the underlying liquidity profile of a high yield portfolio.

Buy and Hold – by keeping portfolio churn low and buying securities with a view to a long-term holding period and accepting that there will be some price volatility, the liquidity needs of a portfolio are automatically curtailed. This also means corporate fundamentals and the underlying creditworthiness of an issuer over the long term are bought more sharply into focus at the point any purchase is made. The question "Would I be happy to hold this bond through periods of market distress" is a good one to ask. If the answer is "yes", then the chances of finding a buyer during such periods are greatly enhanced.

Stick to larger bond issues – The bigger the bond issue, the greater the investor base and the greater chance of being able to match a buyer and a seller (we illustrate by comparing the recorded activity trade activity for a $4.28bn bond, and a $200m bond issued by the same company). However, this can be a double-edged sword. The larger a bond issue, the more likely it is to be a constituent of an ETF portfolio which can be disadvantageous during periods of large redemptions.

Trade History for Sprint 9.25% 2022
December 17th 2015 - $200m outstanding

Source: Bloomberg, TRACE

Diversify by market – Trading environments can and often do differ in different markets. A portfolio that can invest across the range of ABS, financials, corporate, sovereigns, emerging markets, fixed rate or floating rate, Europe or the US can often exploit better liquidity conditions in one market when another is facing difficulty.

Use liquid proxies – The daily volume that trades in the synthetic CDS index market is an order of magnitude greater than the physical cash market. Keeping part of a portfolio in such instruments provides access to a deeper pool of liquidity and can provide a useful buffer in periods when the physical market conditions worsen. However, there is an opportunity cost in terms of stock selection that needs to be considered.

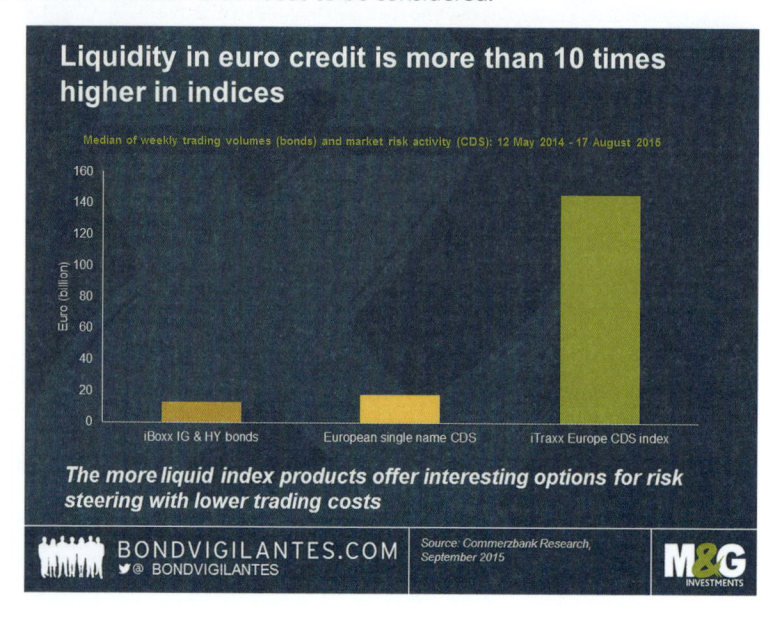

Liquidity in euro credit is more than 10 times higher in indices

Median of weekly trading volumes (bonds) and market risk activity (CDS): 12 May 2014 - 17 August 2015

The more liquid index products offer interesting options for risk steering with lower trading costs

Source: Commerzbank Research, September 2015

Keep cash balances higher – The most effective way to boost liquidity in a portfolio is the simplest: hold more cash. 5% is the new 2%. Again, there are opportunity costs in terms of market exposure and stock selection, but the benefits in terms of liquidity are immediate and tangible.

It's important to stress that none of these measures are a silver bullet, but they are mitigants. They can buy time and help investors tap liquidity. In today's high yield markets, the question of how a portfolio's liquidity is managed has become just as important (if not more so) than its investment position.

2016

Chapter 85

Oil price slump is a drag on emerging markets. But wait, why?
Charles de Quinsonas – Friday, 8th January 2016

Oil price moves and their impacts on emerging markets will continue to be a hot topic in 2016. It is true that economies which rely heavily on oil exports and fiscal revenues, such as Saudi Arabia, Russia or Venezuela, have been facing an extremely challenging macro environment with the decline in oil prices. But, overall, there are more net oil importers than exporters amongst the developing economies. Moreover, at the corporate bond level, the Oil & Gas sector accounts for a relatively small share of emerging market corporate bonds, according to various hard-currency bond indices. So why are sliding oil prices consistently dragging emerging market asset prices down?

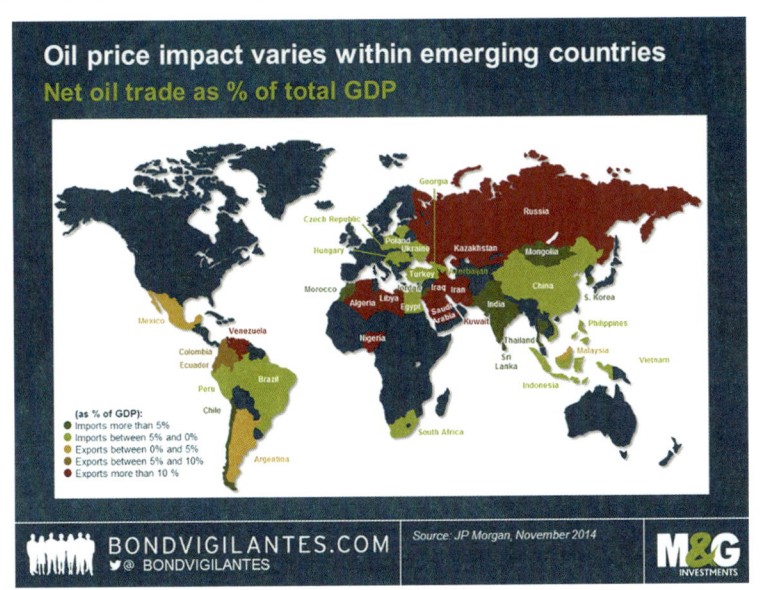

A large number of developing economies directly benefit from lower oil prices.

Asia is the biggest winner of this new oil price environment, with the exception of Malaysia which is a net exporter, as can be seen in the above chart. Within the region, India, China,

Thailand and South Korea are likely to benefit the most, notably via cheaper oil imports, reduced input cost, lower fuel subsidies and/or increased consumer spending. Outside of Asia, some other large developing economies are net oil importers, e.g. Turkey, South-Africa and Brazil. Eastern European countries, in particular Hungary, Poland and Czech Republic, also benefit from lower oil (and gas) prices. Finally, it is arguable that the Caribbean and Central America indirectly take advantage of boosted US consumption through lower oil prices.

Energy names account for 13.6% of the most widely used EM corporate bond index.

Quite counter-intuitively, albeit very much in line with the fundamentals of developing economies, the Oil & Gas sector accounts for only 13.6% of the most widely used EM corporate bond index (JPM's CEMBI BD index). However, the macro factor needs to be taken into consideration because for example financials in the Middle-East are likely to suffer from lower oil prices. Therefore, when looking at oil exposure investors must add another filter to their investment process: looking at corporate bonds that are exposed to countries with oil exposure. According to our calculations, EM corporate bonds in net oil exporting countries account for 30.3% of the index. This leaves two thirds of the index potentially immune to oil volatility... in theory.

Commodities and currencies are the main channels of contagion.

Despite the fact that there are more net oil importers than exporters in the developing economies, falling oil prices continue to drag emerging market asset prices down because commodities ex-oil and currencies act as channels of contagion.

When oil prices started to collapse, countries relying to a large extent on oil revenues saw their currencies depreciating sharply, sometimes by way of devaluations (eg Kazakhstan). The first effect was (and continues to be) technical, with a negative sentiment spillover to all emerging market currencies, as well as commodities. The second effect, more fundamental, was twofold:

(i) oil as a significant input cost influences the breakeven cost of producing metals and food; in an environment of slowing growth and commodity overcapacity, low oil prices therefore put downward pressure on other commodity prices;

(ii) the side effect of currency depreciation was that the oil-exporting countries improved their competitiveness in other commodities exports, e.g. Russia with fertilisers. This resulted in increased pressure on currencies of the non-oil exporting countries as their metal or agricultural commodities had become less competitive.

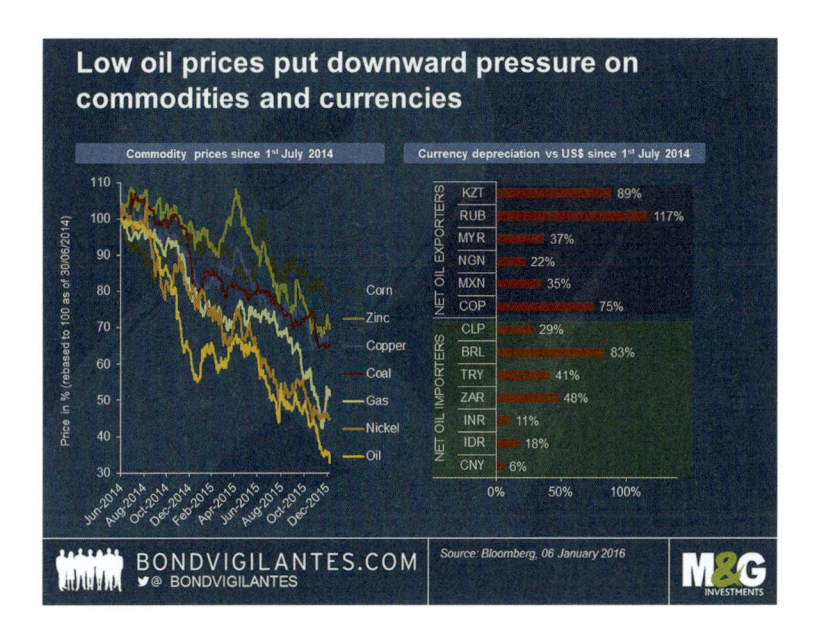

Low oil prices put downward pressure on commodities and currencies

Commodity prices since 1st July 2014 / Currency depreciation vs US$ since 1st July 2014

Source: Bloomberg, 06 January 2016 — BONDVIGILANTES.COM @BONDVIGILANTES — M&G Investments

Oil is everywhere. But what matters most are the idiosyncratic stories.

Within this context, it is fair to say that an emerging market bond portfolio is unlikely to be fully immune to oil. Looking into 2016, this is good news if you are bullish oil: any significant oil price increase will in most cases drive a rally in emerging market assets. If you are bearish oil, you may still find interesting investment opportunities: the Oil & Gas sector in emerging markets generated a negative return of -3.0% in 2015 but the dispersion of corporate bond returns was huge and not necessarily correlated to oil prices. For instance, the fall in Petrobras bonds was more driven by the ongoing corruption scandal in Brazil and the group's debt levels than the actual decline in oil prices. On the other hand, despite their country exposure, PDVSA (Venezuelan state-owned oil company) or LUKOIL (Russia-based oil producer) bonds had double-digit total returns in 2015. In what might be a good lesson for 2016, it shows that in emerging markets, in many cases, macro and credit idiosyncratic stories matter more than oil.

Chapter 86

Need motivation for your New Year diet? M&G's cake index shows that cake is getting more expensive

Anjulie Rusius – Monday, 11th January 2016

I blogged in 2014 with good news for cake lovers; falling soft commodity prices indicated that the cost of baking cakes was getting cheaper. Unfortunately (and in contrast to hard commodity prices, notably oil recently hitting new post global financial crisis lows), the final quarter of 2015 depicted a reversal in trend with soft commodity prices on the rise.

In September we discussed the potential impacts of the El Niño weather phenomenon here. Just a few months later and we're beginning to get a clearer picture as its impact spreads through key crop-growing regions worldwide. Indonesia (globally the largest palm oil producer) and Africa (supplier of cocoa) have experienced droughts, while Brazil (dominant sugar and coffee producer) has been hit by heavy rainfall and the worst flooding in 50 years; all of which has been attributed to El Niño. As a result of weather-induced supply fears and constraints, prices for sugar, palm oil, coffee and cocoa increased by 42%, 18%, 8% and 2% respectively in Q4 2015.

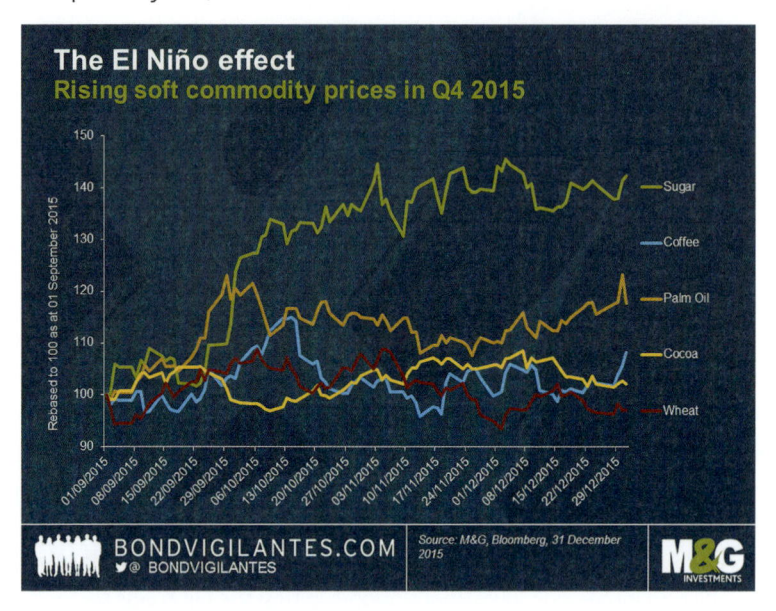

The El Niño effect
Rising soft commodity prices in Q4 2015

Source: M&G, Bloomberg, 31 December 2015

So how does this feed into the M&G cake index?

Due to the surge in soft commodity prices in the final quarter of last year, I have refreshed the M&G cake index. This teams global commodity price data with some basic recipes from the BBC Good Food website, roughly constructing a basket of soft commodities in order to demonstrate the changing cost of baking cakes (palm oil is used as a proxy for butter).

Given that the price of sugar has increased significantly – and that this is the key component of most cakes – it is not surprising that all cake prices have increased. The offsetting impact of wheat however (which has fallen in price) acts to alleviate this, which explains the breakaway of flour-based sweets such as scones and sponge cake. The cocoa and coffee commodity price appreciation thus acts in the opposing direction. It should however be noted that chocolate cake is not simply a proxy for cocoa – for its recipe basket carries the greatest amount of sugar – which explains why chocolate cake is more expensive than coffee cake on this measure, despite the coffee commodity experiencing a greater price increase. Bad news all round for New Year cake consumption and those wanting to see their post-Christmas pennies go further.

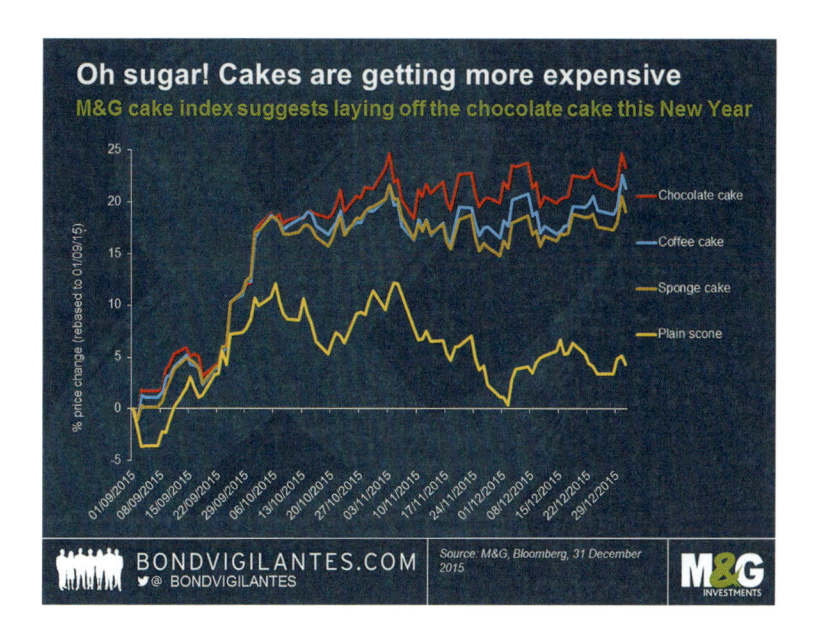

In contrast to the above, last week's United Nations Food and Agriculture Organisation data release demonstrated a fall in its overall food price index for December. This index weights five soft commodity groups: meat, dairy, cereals, vegetable oils and sugar, while the M&G cake index weights only the final two. The decline in the food price index suggests that the El Niño effects are not yet driving or generating headline food price inflation. Weather forecasters have however warned that the current El Niño is the strongest since 1998 and has not yet passed. Though this may or may not ultimately feed through and cause the overall basket of food prices to rise, we've certainly witnessed inflation baked into the cake in recent months.

Chapter 87

Investment grade credit spreads spinning wider

Wolfgang Bauer – Wednesday, 20th January 2016

We recently blogged about the uninspiring performance of many fixed income asset classes in 2015. Investment grade (IG) corporate bonds certainly had a tough year as credit spreads trended wider, both in the USD and the EUR market. Taking a look at option-adjusted spread (OAS) levels, USD IG credit (+29 bps) marginally outperformed against EUR IG credit (+36 bps) in 2015. In both cases periods of spread compression in Q1 and Q4 were short-lived and failed to offset substantial spread widening in Q2 and Q3 (as per the following chart).

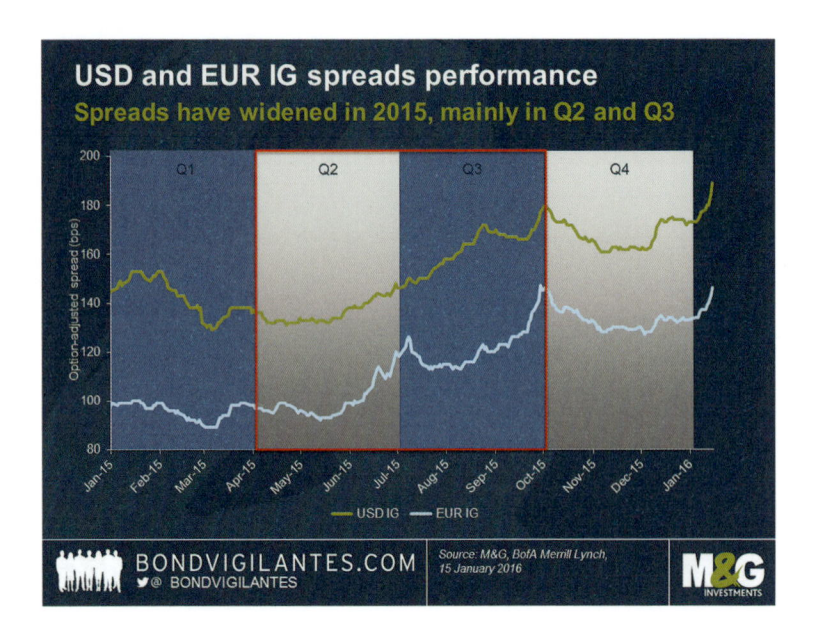

USD and EUR IG spreads performance
Spreads have widened in 2015, mainly in Q2 and Q3

Source: M&G, BofA Merrill Lynch, 15 January 2016

The sell-off in Q2 and Q3 was caused by a combination of heavy new issue volumes and subdued demand for corporate bonds, as investors rushed into safe-haven assets after a string of "risk-off" episodes, mainly the Greek referendum, worries about China and other emerging markets and weakness in commodity prices. The latter two themes have so far been dominating news headlines in 2016 as well, and consequently IG OAS levels have gapped wider again in the first half of January (+16 bps for USD IG and +13 bps for EUR IG).

But is it fair to say that IG corporate bonds as a whole are now more attractively valued than at the end of 2014, or have overall bond index levels merely been driven wider by extreme spread moves within the commodity complex? To answer this question, we have to deconstruct bond indices into industry sectors (see following chart).

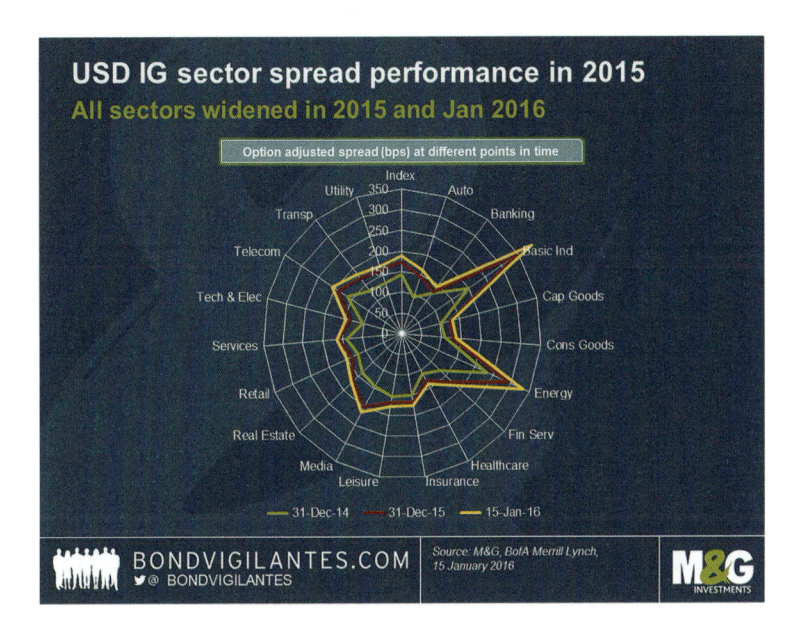

USD IG sector spread performance in 2015
All sectors widened in 2015 and Jan 2016

Option adjusted spread (bps) at different points in time

— 31-Dec-14 — 31-Dec-15 — 15-Jan-16

BONDVIGILANTES.COM
@BONDVIGILANTES

Source: M&G, BofA Merrill Lynch, 15 January 2016

M&G INVESTMENTS

Unsurprisingly, the worst performing sectors in the USD IG universe have been energy and particularly basic materials which have widened on an OAS basis by 101 bps and 191 bps, respectively, from the end of 2014 until mid-January 2016. While these moves are certainly large, it is important to highlight that other sectors have sold off significantly over the same period as well, e.g., media (+72 bps), automotive (+67 bps) or financial services (+54 bps). In fact, the only sector that has widened by less than 20 bps is banking (+18 bps), which reflects that US banks are well-positioned in a rising rates environment. These numbers show that an across-the-board spread widening has taken place affecting every sector within the USD IG universe, albeit to varying degrees.

Just like in the case of USD IG credit, every sector in the EUR IG space (see following chart) has widened from the end of 2014 until mid-January 2016 on an OAS basis, with basic materials being by far the worst performer (+190 bps). This makes basic materials currently the widest sector in the EUR IG universe, even ahead of insurance (+70 bps), which used to trade at distinctly elevated spread levels compared to the rest of the index due to its high share of subordinated bonds and uncertainties around Solvency II legislation. The automotive sector has been the second worst performer (+82 bps), being hit by a slowdown in the Chinese market and the fallout from VW's "diesel-gate" emissions scandal.

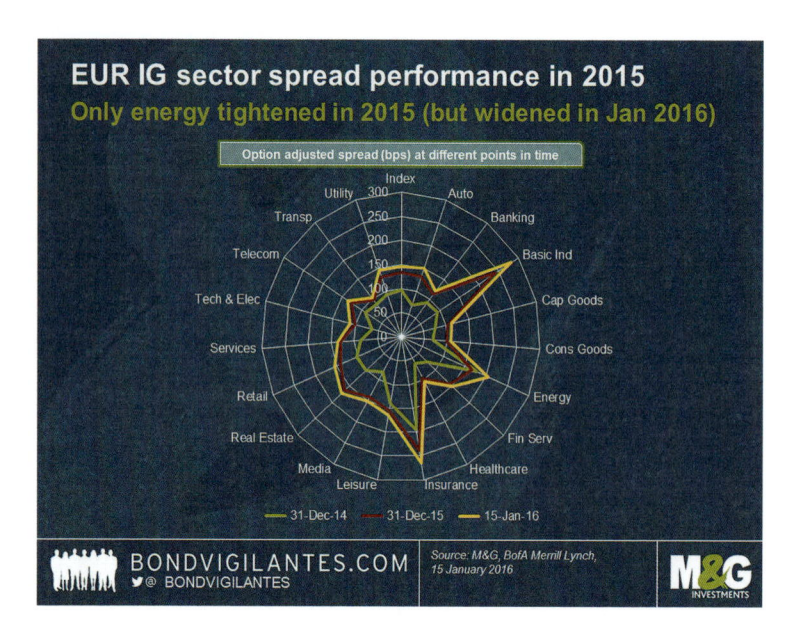

EUR IG sector spread performance in 2015
Only energy tightened in 2015 (but widened in Jan 2016)

Option adjusted spread (bps) at different points in time

— 31-Dec-14   — 31-Dec-15   — 15-Jan-16

BONDVIGILANTES.COM
@BONDVIGILANTES

Source: M&G, BofA Merrill Lynch, 15 January 2016

M&G INVESTMENTS

Interestingly, the EUR IG energy sector has performed very well (+27 bps) relative to its USD counterpart (+101 bps) from the end of 2014 until mid-January 2016. In 2015, it was in fact the only sector in both IG indices that exhibited OAS compression (-10 bps)! The reasons for this are twofold: First, EUR IG energy started 2015 at an already very high spread level (178 bps) relative to the EUR IG index (97 bps), from where it tightened meaningfully when the oil price temporarily rebounded in March and April last year. Second, the average credit rating of EUR IG energy is relatively high as it is dominated by AA and A rated issuers and contains far fewer BBB names than the USD IG energy sector. Thus, the widening of EUR IG energy spreads during the risk-off episodes in Q2 and Q3 2015 was dampened by a "flight to quality" of investors preferring higher- over lower-rated IG credits.

As described above, after a broad-based widening across all sectors, USD and EUR IG corporate bonds offer investors much higher credit spreads than at the end of 2014. In certain pockets of the markets, particularly for long-dated USD BBBs, current spread levels are exceptionally high for non-crisis times. So either we believe that recent market turmoil is just the beginning of something bigger, in which case we would expect IG credit spreads to continue to widen, or even to blow out to 2008/09 levels. Or we think that, despite certain global headwinds currently causing a risk-off sentiment across markets, developed economies are not going to enter a full-fledged recession any time soon. In that case EUR and USD IG corporate bond spreads would offer compelling valuations at the moment. Considering the strength of the US economy in general and as Richard wrote yesterday, its labour market in particular, in combination with modest economic improvements and accommodative monetary policy in Europe, we believe that the latter reading is a lot more convincing.

Chapter 88

Why doesn't the ECB just buy oil?

Wolfgang Bauer – Monday, 8th February 2016

It's pretty clear that the pressure is on the European Central Bank (ECB) to come up with some form of policy response at their next Governing Council meeting in March. Take, for example, the 5-year, 5-year EUR inflation swap rate (i.e., the swap market's estimate of where 5-year inflation rates might be in five years' time), which has taken a nose dive to 1.5% (see chart below). This is remarkable as the current number implies that the market expects the ECB to still be failing quite miserably to bring medium-term inflation close to 2% even in five years, despite negative interest rates and quantitative easing (QE). Not exactly a strong vote of confidence in the ECB's policy tools, I'd say.

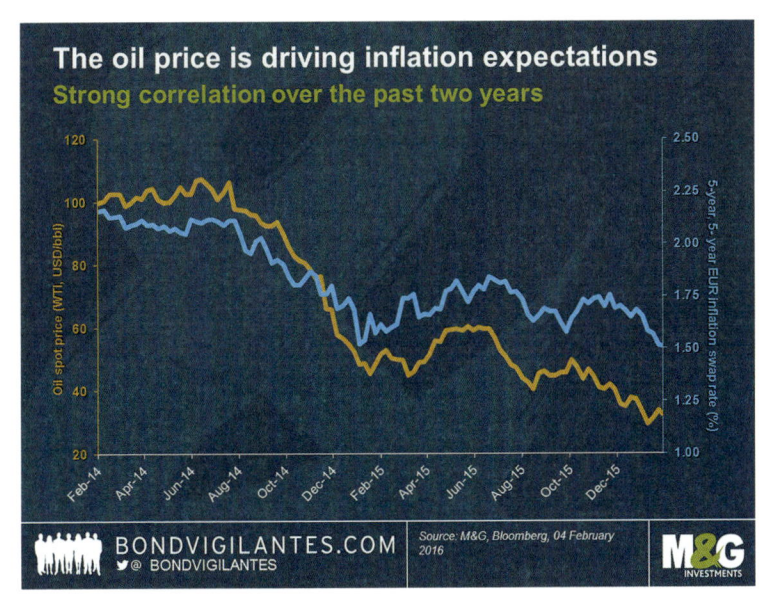

The oil price is driving inflation expectations
Strong correlation over the past two years

It seems that monetary policy is taking a backseat, whereas the oil price is driving market expectations of the future path of inflation rates. This follows some logic, of course, as a drop in oil price has direct deflationary effects on the energy component (and indirectly via lower transportation costs on other components) of the price index. One could argue however that a nearly perfect correlation (+0.9 over the past two years) between the oil spot price and expectations of 5-year inflation rates in five years' time seems excessive. We have, for example, written about base effects (see Jim's Panoramic) and the diminishing downward pressure on petrol prices of any further oil price declines going forward (see Richard's blog). In the past, the correlation between both data series also used to be a lot weaker (+0.3 over the prior two years). Still, market sentiment is pretty unambiguous these days: moves in the oil spot price by and large dictate future inflation expectations.

Adding to the ECB's inflation woes are turbulences in financial markets. "Risk-off" has been the prevailing sentiment in 2016 so far. The Euro Stoxx 50 equity index has lost more than

13% year-to-date and EUR investment grade credit spreads have widened by c. 20 bps. Again, the oil price appears to be the dominating metric driving risk asset valuations. At this point it doesn't seem to matter much anymore whether oil plunges due to sluggish demand (which would indeed be a legitimate concern) or because of growing supply. Remember how markets reacted to the Iran sanctions being lifted surprisingly early. The positive effects for the world economy of opening a country with nearly as many citizens as Germany to international trade and investment flows – the planned purchase of more than 100 airplanes from Airbus to modernise Iranair's fleet is just the tip of the iceberg – were easily outweighed by market expectations of additional crude oil supply.

Markets do not seem to care much either whether a country or an industry is "long" or "short" oil. Germany, for instance, is one of the world's biggest net oil importers (i.e., short oil) to the tune of around 110 million tonnes of oil equivalents per year, according to the Energy Atlas of the International Energy Agency. Cheaper crude oil lowers expenses for German companies and consumers alike, so that money can be invested or consumed elsewhere. All else being equal, the German economy should benefit from low oil prices. Still, on a day when the oil spot price falls for whatever reason, you can be almost certain that Bund yields rally and the DAX equity index finishes in the red. A similar case can be made for many other countries, too (see Charles' blog).

The market's obsession with the oil price is bad news for the ECB which is judged by its ability to deliver inflation close to 2% and promote market stability. So in order to remain credible, the ECB would need to control the oil price. But that's beyond the capabilities of a central bank, or is it? Maybe the ECB should announce at its March meeting that asset purchases will from now on include crude oil. The ECB currently buys assets worth EUR 60 billion per month, so that's around EUR 2 billion every day. If only 1% of this amount, a cheeky EUR 20 million, were invested in oil at a spot price of – optimistically – USD 35 per barrel (bbl), this would translate at an exchange rate of 1.1 USD per EUR into just shy of 630k bbl of sweet, sweet crude per day. The ECB would thus more than offset the proposed 500k bbl per day of additional supply with which Iran is spooking the market.

It wouldn't be the first time either that a European institution props up goods prices by buying up excess supply. Just think about the infamous "butter mountains" and "wine lakes" of the 1980s under the framework of the European Union's Common Agricultural Policy programme. Still, storage of large quantities of crude oil might prove challenging. Let's assume the ECB kindly agrees to convert its shiny new Frankfurt headquarters into a giant strategic oil reserve. We all have to make sacrifices, eh? Applying some basic geometry to the numbers from the ECB's factsheet we can approximate the storage volume: 350k cubic meters for both towers combined, give or take. This reservoir could hold around 2.2 million bbl of oil – not bad. But sadly not good enough as the ECB would run out of storage space after only 3.5 days of oil purchases. Fortunately, there is still the derivatives market. Instead of physically buying crude oil at spot, the ECB might want to consider buying oil futures to intervene in the oil market.

Of course, none of this will happen in reality. But all proponents of the "low oil is always bad" mantra should exactly push for such a, shall we say, unorthodox solution. If you truly believe that falling oil prices will forever squeeze inflation prospects and destroy asset valuations, you should urge Mr Draghi to fill his boots with the unloved commodity.

Chapter 89

How long until China reaches the floor of the recommended reserve adequacy range?

Claudia Calich – Thursday, 11th February 2016

Much has been discussed on the topic of the optimal level of foreign exchange reserves. One of the common methodologies is the IMF's ARA (Assessing Reserve Adequacy) metric, which essentially provides a range based on a country's trade, broad monetary aggregates and external liabilities. How much weight should be given to each factor varies according to the economic structure of each country, including whether it is a relatively open or closed economy in terms of trade and capital flows and whether the exchange rate is floating or not. Based on past EM crises, the IMF has recommended a range which is normally expressed in terms of 100-150% of the metric. The ongoing pressures on the Renminbi and China's attempt to smoothen its depreciation through currency intervention beg the question of how much firepower China has, given declining reserves.

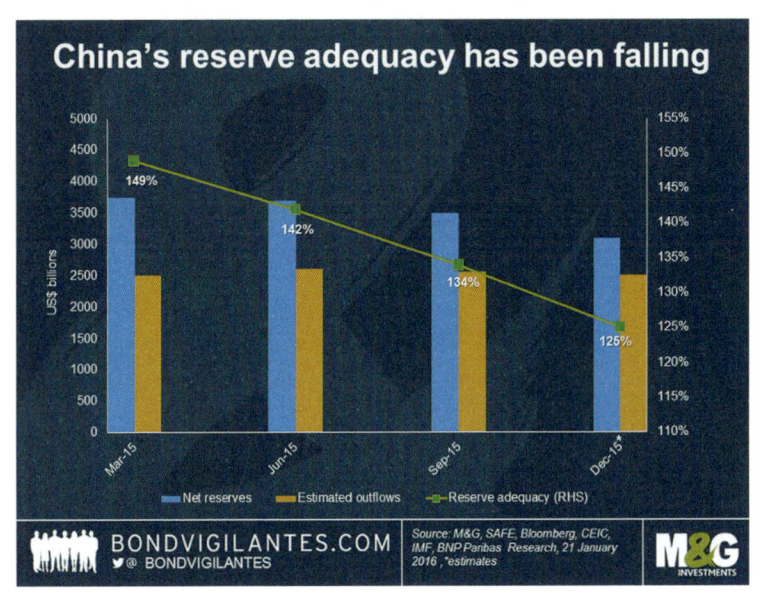

Using the IMF's standard framework, we calculate that China has approximately 6-7 months until it reaches the lower bound of the recommended range (100%). Arguably, this includes several large assumptions, including that the ongoing capital flight and reserve loss (at around $100 billion per month) and current account surplus remain at the same pace. We also do not know how much intervention there actually has been in the currency forward market, and some data, like debt stocks, are reported only quarterly with a lag (the last data is from September).

Estimated lower bound of reserves

China Reserve Adequacy Ratio	IMF recommended	Latest data
Exports (month)	3	$224bn
Broad Money (M2)	20%	$21,461bn
Short-term debt	100%	$1,024bn
Total external debt	15%	$1,530bn
Foreign exchange reserves		$3,231bn
ARA* at 100% (approximate)		$2,510bn**

*Assessing Reserve Adequacy
**Using author's own weights

Source: M&G calculations, Bloomberg, National Bureau of Statistics, SAFE. February 2016

BONDVIGILANTES.COM
@BONDVIGILANTES

Any policy response from the authorities is likely to aim for faster depreciation of the Renminbi than we have seen so far, though we do not expect a large one-off move. That would require a strong coordination with global central banks to minimise financial contagion, given China's systemic impact on global markets, and we do not think we are there yet. Tighter capital controls for residents have been gradually adopted and this is the most likely policy option in the near term, but is never 100% effective. Higher rates and tighter domestic liquidity would be problematic, given China's large domestic debt levels.

In the spirit of the Chinese New Year – and wishing all our readers a rally monkey – we hope that our calculations are wrong and China has far more time than 6 months. For one, the number 6 is thought to be an unlucky number in Cantonese – it has a similar pronunciation to that of "lok6" (落, meaning "to drop, fall, or decline"), quite *apropos*.

Chapter 90

The ECB, negative rates, and the Swiss experience

Mario Eisenegger – Wednesday, 9th March 2016

Ahead of tomorrow's ECB monetary policy meeting, the market has high expectations of rates being cut further into negative territory (consensus is a cut in the deposit rate by 10 to 20 bps). However, a report this week from the Bank for International Settlements (BIS) suggests that cutting rates further could be counterproductive and damaging for the banking sector.

The BIS's quarterly review, points out that negative policy rates either don't work in lowering borrowing costs for households and businesses, in which case why bother cutting; or they are passed on in loan rates, which means they must be passed on to depositors too, otherwise bank profits will fall. And if they are passed on to depositors there will be a risk of cash fleeing the banking system, which is another undesirable outcome. The paper did acknowledge that there was one potential transmission mechanism of further rate cuts without such consequences for the Eurozone – euro depreciation might be desirable, although that comes with geopolitical (currency wars) implications.

The Swiss experience with negative rates demonstrates clearly that negative rates have direct consequences for banks and can actually lead to tightening credit standards. A note published by UBS a year ago (not available in English as far as we know, but to be found here) deserves attention as it shows that 10 year mortgage rates for bank clients have actually risen after the SNB has lowered its deposit rate into negative territory.

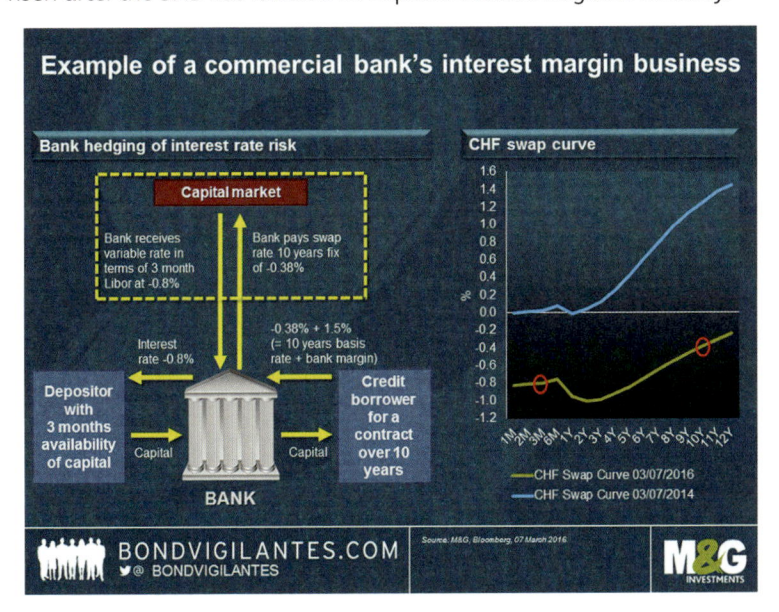

Example of a commercial bank's interest margin business

Let's use a simplified example to illustrate a commercial bank's interest margin business. A major task of a bank is to act as an intermediary of money. Depositors provide their money to the bank on a short term basis, for example, via savings accounts, whereas many investments require longer-term financial commitments. This process is called maturity transformation, which exposes banks to certain risks, one of which is interest rate risk. Imagine interest rates go up significantly. Savers will demand a higher rate on their savings account, but the bank has agreed a mortgage rate of 1.12% for the next 10 years, as illustrated in the example, which then would have a direct negative impact on the bank's margin.

Fortunately, there is a capital market to hedge out the interest rate risk. Looking at the current Swiss swap curve, the bank in our example could hedge their interest rate risk by paying away the 10 year fixed part of the curve (-0.38%) to receive a variable rate, which is currently even more negative at -0.8%. In a negative interest rate environment however this process faces a problem. Banks cannot pass on the negative interest rate of -0.8% to their depositors as there is the immediate danger that savers withdraw their money and store it somewhere else.

So what can Banks do?

Either

1. They accept a smaller margin, which affects their profitability
2. They don't hedge the mismatch between maturities of the assets and liabilities, which would expose them to even higher profitability risks if interest rates go up quickly
3. They hedge the interest rate risk and at the same time try to increase their margin via other revenue streams

The latter point is what happened in Switzerland according to the 2015 UBS report. After the SNB's announcement of negative rates of -0.75% in January 2015, the price for a 10 year mortgage offered by Swiss banks increased. So the banks have increased their margin on long-term mortgages to offset the increasingly negative rates on deposits, which equals credit tightening. In other words, mortgage borrowers are subsidising depositors. Assuming banks have also increased their margin on corporate loans as a result of negative rates it would likely weaken economic growth instead of accelerating it.

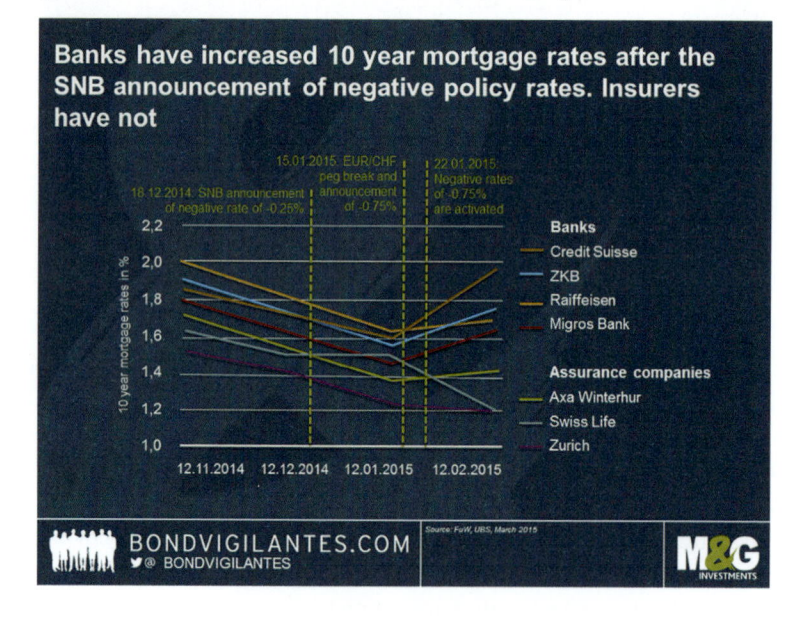

Banks have increased 10 year mortgage rates after the SNB announcement of negative policy rates. Insurers have not

Source: FuW, UBS, March 2015

Swiss assurance companies offer mortgages for clients too, which complicates the situation for banks even more. As UBS points out, insurers have not been forced to increase their margin like banks did, as their deposits are usually long-term investments, e.g. a life insurance contract over 10 years. The chart above shows quite nicely that the relative competiveness of insurers' mortgage offerings has improved compared to banks since the SNB introduced negative policy rates. However, the mortgage business is not a core business for assurance companies, so we can assume they have less information about their borrowers and less extensive credit assessments compared to banks, which according to UBS increases the risk of capital misallocation and higher credit defaults going forward.

Draghi faces a dilemma. Too big a cut of the already negative deposit rates could be perceived negatively by the market as damaging for bank profitability and thus the transmission mechanism to the real economy. He has to live up to his promise of bringing inflation back without breaking the very system that – in the absence of fiscal easing – is needed to spur European companies and households in to growth.

Chapter 91

Has the ECB reached the limits of monetary policy?
Stefan Isaacs – Wednesday, 9th March 2016

The simple answer is a no. Eric Lonergan in a guest blog has already debunked the idea that central banks are at the zero bound. And since then the market has become increasingly confident that the ECB will cut its deposit rate further into negative territory at tomorrow's meeting. And it has reason to do so. Inflation and growth will be lower than the Bank had forecast a mere three months ago with inflation expectations also falling out of bed.

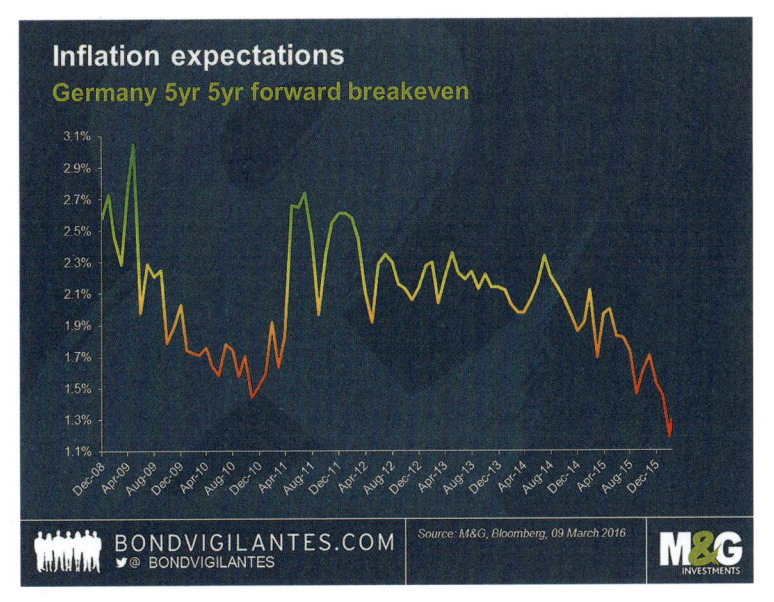

But that isn't to say that there aren't diminishing returns to be had from a further loosening of policy. The reality is that many of the problems holding back the Eurozone are structural in nature. And doesn't the ECB know it. I can hardly remember a press conference when Mario Draghi hasn't failed to mention the need to address these issues. Hardly surprising given that the Eurozone is only represented twice in World Bank's top fifteen 'Ease of doing business survey'. The likes of France at 27, Spain at 33, Italy at 45 and Greece at 60 makes for painful reading.

Ease of doing business
Ranking

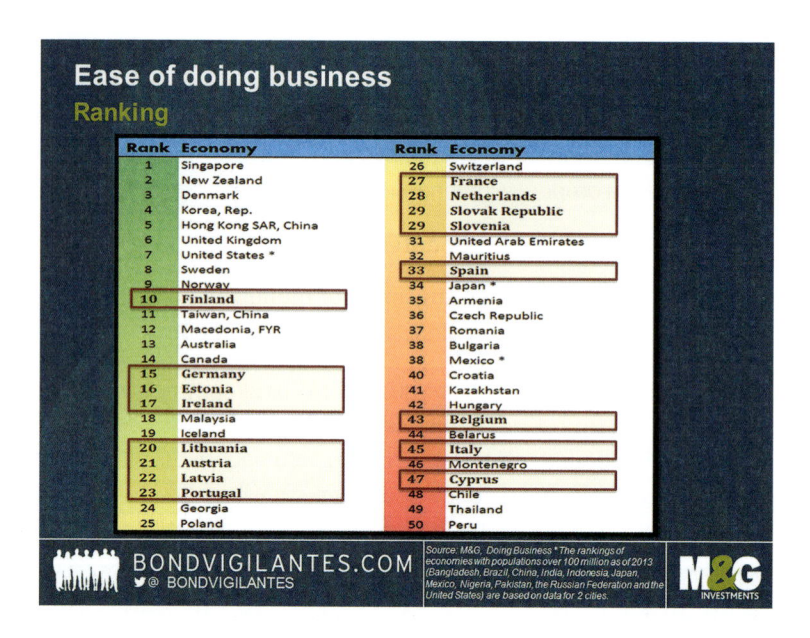

Rank	Economy	Rank	Economy
1	Singapore	26	Switzerland
2	New Zealand	27	France
3	Denmark	28	Netherlands
4	Korea, Rep.	29	Slovak Republic
5	Hong Kong SAR, China	29	Slovenia
6	United Kingdom	31	United Arab Emirates
7	United States *	32	Mauritius
8	Sweden	33	Spain
9	Norway	34	Japan *
10	Finland	35	Armenia
11	Taiwan, China	36	Czech Republic
12	Macedonia, FYR	37	Romania
13	Australia	38	Bulgaria
14	Canada	38	Mexico *
15	Germany	40	Croatia
16	Estonia	41	Kazakhstan
17	Ireland	42	Hungary
18	Malaysia	43	Belgium
19	Iceland	44	Belarus
20	Lithuania	45	Italy
21	Austria	46	Montenegro
22	Latvia	47	Cyprus
23	Portugal	48	Chile
24	Georgia	49	Thailand
25	Poland	50	Peru

BONDVIGILANTES.COM
@BONDVIGILANTES

Source: M&G, Doing Business * The rankings of economies with populations over 100 million as of 2013 (Bangladesh, Brazil, China, India, Indonesia, Japan, Mexico, Nigeria, Pakistan, the Russian Federation and the United States) are based on data for 2 cities.

M&G INVESTMENTS

The ECB is acutely aware of the moral hazard it creates in addressing the Eurozone's troubles purely via the monetary channel. And yet with a sole mandate to hit an inflation target of close to but below 2%, they are once again finding themselves with the unenviable task of having to do the bulk of the heavy lifting. On Thursday we will likely see a cut to the deposit rate with some sort of tiering in an attempt to address some of the challenges faced by the banking system, as well as an extension to the PSPP (QE programme), both in terms of size and duration. We may even see a greater willingness to buy certain corporate bonds – although this will likely be a step too far for the majority on the Governing Council.

But the reality is that increased productivity and greater innovation is much needed to drive the Eurozone. Antiquated bankruptcy regimes need to be radically reformed, red tape needs to be removed and the banking system needs to own up to further loan losses that it has yet to provision for. These changes aren't easily achieved, not least because they require the sort of short term pain that politicians rarely have long run incentives to deliver.

Consider the case of Italy. Since the global financial crisis the Italian housing market has fallen in value by around 19% from its peak. This, combined with recessions that have left Italian GDP around 10% lower than in 2008 and rises in unemployment to around 12%, have conspired to create a large amount of c. €200Bn of non-performing loans (NPL's) in Italy as households and companies have encountered difficulties in servicing their debt.

Unlike in other Eurozone periphery countries such as Portugal and Spain, Italy has been slow in restructuring its banks and addressing the problem with many NPLs still sitting on banks' balance sheets. The Italian banking system is therefore considered to be weak and there have been a wave of recent high profile bank collapses that have resulted in 'bail-ins'. With this in mind the Italian authorities have just set up a scheme to create Asset Management Companies who will then look to securitize these non-performing loans, in theory reducing a bank's balance sheet and allowing them greater scope to lend to the broader economy. As the scheme is very much in its infancy we will have to wait to see whether it can have the desired effect.

Absent further structural change I'm convinced the Eurozone will labour under a cloak of lower potential growth and struggle to encourage investment given the need to earn an attractive rate of return on capital. Yes the ECB can likely drive risk-free rates even lower. Yes they can depreciate the €. And yes they can provide ever more liquidity to the banking system. These may all help near term. But without real reform the market will increasingly worry that we have reached the limits of monetary policy. And at some point if the market cannot be convinced otherwise, then the consequences will be significant.

Chapter 92

Negative Rate World (NRW) – a wiki of unintended consequences

Jim Leaviss – Wednesday, 6th April 2016

The world has seen negative interest rates before – Switzerland set interest rates below zero for foreigners in the 1970s in order to slow flows into the Franc. But today's negative rate environment is far more widespread, with Switzerland, Denmark, Sweden, Japan, and the Eurozone all setting negative policy rates. Lots has been written about the intended transmission mechanisms of negative rates – cheaper direct borrowing costs for households and businesses leading to stronger economic activity, a portfolio rebalance effect in which investors sell low/negative yielding assets to buy riskier instruments, thus reducing funding costs for companies, and, controversially, reducing the attractiveness of an economy's currency in a world in which competitive devaluation is seen as desirable. This blog however hopes to capture some of the other consequences of negative rates, some unintended, and some creating different problems for policymakers.

I've started this list with 10 observations, but I plan to update it periodically as we see how the Negative Rate World (NRW) develops over the months or years ahead. I'd like to ask for your help in spotting any interesting behavioural changes and historically important news stories. Sourced facts are the best facts, but I will also consider anecdata.

1. If you are an organisation that sits on large amounts of cash, negative rates are an unexpected cost. For example, insurance companies have been used to taking premia from customers and making a return on that invested cash. In a negative rate world, early payment of a premium is a drag on your returns. That's true for all companies – late payers become your most valuable customers. It's also true for the tax authorities. In Zug, the Swiss canton, the taxman has asked taxpayers to delay paying their bills for as long as possible. Zug calculates this will save the canton SFr2.5 million per year.

2. Sales of safe deposit boxes are soaring. By removing your cash from a bank account and locking it away at home, or in a secure facility, you can guarantee that zero is the worse interest rate you will receive. You'll also be immune from any bail-in of depositors if a banking sector gets into difficulty (Cyprus for example). Japanese hardware store Shimachu says that sales of safes are running at 2½ times what they were a year ago.

3. It's not just households that are stashing the cash in order to avoid paying to save. German insurance company Munich Re is experimenting with physical storage of banknotes. To start with it will store €10 million in notes.

4. If storing physical cash disrupts the transmission mechanism, what can central banks do to make it difficult to do? Mario Draghi of the ECB has suggested that they might scrap the 500 euro note, which accounts for 30% of cash in circulation. He talked about the note being used as a store of value for organised crime, rather than as an inconvenience in the operation of monetary policy, but it's clearly a factor.

5. Financial authorities might also be preventing – either explicitly through regulation, or through the age old "raised eyebrows" method – the withdrawal of large sums of cash by banks, pension funds and insurers. In Switzerland a bank seems to have refused to allow a pension fund to remove a large sum of cash from its account in banknotes. The SNB has apparently asked banks to be "restrictive" with such payments, to the annoyance of the Swiss pension fund association.

6. There's a technology and administrative burden that comes with negative rates. Financial institutions have had to change computer systems, legal contracts have had to be altered (for example the ISDA swap agreements), bond documentation (floors on FRNs) redesigned.

7. With 12 month Euribor turning negative in February 2016 for the first time ever, Spanish property owners – who generally have mortgage interest payments set on this measure, with no floors at zero – are seeing their outgoings collapse. Spanish Bankinter also offered mortgages linked to Swiss rates, and some customers are due payments from the bank each month (in practise the bank is reducing the principal owed rather than paying over the cash). The Spanish mortgage sector was often quoted as a reason the ECB would never go negative, as it would have a big P&L hit to the banks. A similar reason, related to the UK building society sector, has been used by the Bank of England to justify keeping rates at a relatively high 0.5%.

8. A different scenario has had an impact on the Swiss banking sector. Perversely, mortgage rates in Switzerland offered by banks rose in the aftermath of rates turning negative. Retail banks there realised they would find it difficult to pass on the negative rates to depositors that they themselves were being charged on reserves by the SNB. In order to keep their profits at a similar level they therefore need to charge borrowers more, and lending rates rose. Swiss insurance companies also offer mortgages, and fund through longer dated bond issuance rather than deposits – thus they were able to pass on lower rates to investors, and have become relatively more competitive compared to the banks.

9. As we've seen, the ability to remove banknotes from the official system can interfere with the operation of the monetary policy transmission mechanism, effectively flooring rates at zero for those who do it. This means that the topic of electronic money has become a live one. Modern economies are generally moving in this direction anyway: credit cards, mobile transactions, Paypal, e-banking have developed exponentially in recent years. In Sweden, cash now represents just 2% of the economy compared with 7.7% in the US and 10% in the Eurozone. In part, Sweden's reduction in cash usage was driven by new rules aimed at reducing tax avoidance, although it is also an early adopter of new technologies. The reduction in cash in circulation means that there are fewer hiding places from negative rates. Could the authorities eliminate paper money

entirely? It's even something that the Bank of England's Andy Haldane has discussed in the context of setting negative rates. I'd advise you never to discuss such a thing in public however, as it drives some people absolutely crazy.

10. As mitigants to the unintended consequences of negative rates, most central banks have tried to minimise the damage that negative rates can do to banks' profits by introducing tiered interest rates. Different levels of rates apply to different portions of banks' reserves. In Japan's case, reserves held before rates went negative would still earn 0.1% for example. Banks are generally incentivised not to convert reserves into banknotes as any such reduction is taken from the highest interest rate tier, rather than the most deeply negative. A blog by J P Koning is good on the subject.

What have we missed?

Chapter 93

Negative rates – a tax on saving? Don't forget about actual tax
Richard Woolnough – Tuesday, 10th May 2016

There has been much discussion recently that by introducing negative rates central banks are effectively taxing savings. This is self-explanatory, and is one of the criticisms of how negative rates can distort economic behaviour. This however is not a new phenomenon. Let's not forget that money has always been effectively clipped by the traditional enemy of savers – inflation. Fortunately, holders of cash have traditionally been compensated for depositing it in a bank account by receiving interest payments. But is this something that is now at threat with negative rates?

If you take the Bank of England rate as a proxy for the interest earned on cash and adjust for inflation (i.e. subtracting RPI from base rates), although negative nominal interest rates are a new phenomenon, real negative rates are not. If we expand this thinking to include the historic rate of basic income tax, we can attempt to fully depict what can be considered the real rate of return on cash. This gives a more accurate reflection of what savers have actually earned in real disposable income per annum and as you can see from the chart overleaf, this has been negative in the UK for much of the past ten years.

Annual return on cash after inflation and tax

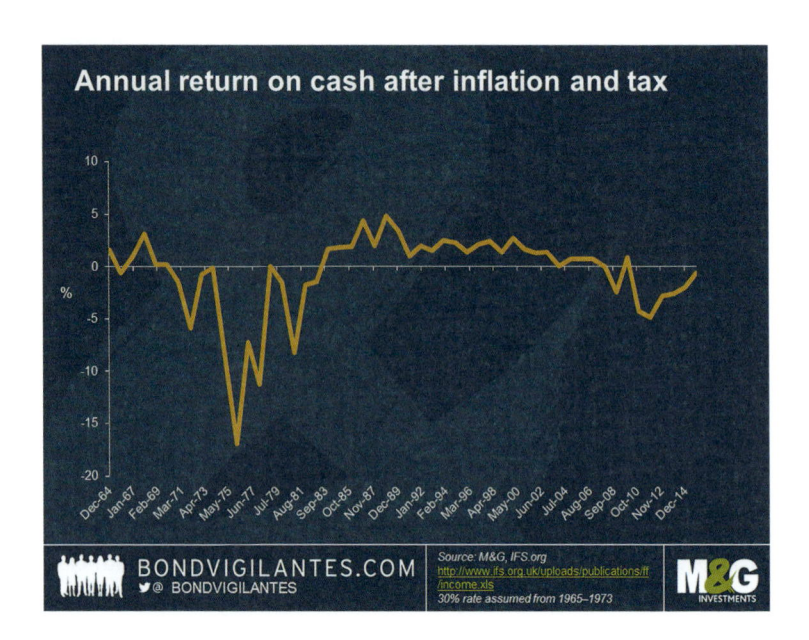

Source: M&G, IFS.org
http://www.ifs.org.uk/uploads/publications/ff/income.xls
30% rate assumed from 1965–1973

Given the recent outcry regarding the effect of negative rates on savers one has to believe that they are suffering from the economic concept of money illusion. This 'savers illusion' is a function of them focusing solely on the nominal rate and ignoring the true level of return after inflation and tax. (Remember that negative interest rates are more likely to occur in a deflationary environment, so it is still possible to earn a positive real return).

Focusing at the extreme and the 45% highest tax rate, the table below helps to illustrate the real return to these savers in various interest rate and inflation rate scenarios. As one would expect, high nominal interest rates and low inflation are beneficial for savers at all tax levels.

Effect on savings of different interest rate and inflation scenarios at 45% income tax rate

45% tax	Interest rate (%)								
Inflation rate (%)	-2	-1	0	1	2	3	4	5	6
-2	0	1	2	2.55	3.1	3.65	4.2	4.75	5.3
-1	-1	0	1	1.55	2.1	2.65	3.2	3.75	4.3
0	-2	-1	0	0.55	1.1	1.65	2.2	2.75	3.3
1	-3	-2	-1	-0.45	0.1	0.65	1.2	1.75	2.3
2	-4	-3	-2	-1.45	-0.9	-0.35	0.2	0.75	1.3
3	-5	-4	-3	-2.45	-1.9	-1.35	-0.8	-0.25	0.3
4	-6	-5	-4	-3.45	-2.9	-2.35	-1.8	-1.25	-0.7
5	-7	-6	-5	-4.45	-3.9	-3.35	-2.8	-2.25	-1.7
6	-8	-7	-6	-5.45	-4.9	-4.35	-3.8	-3.25	-2.7

Source: M&G

But one of the most interesting results occurs at zero or negative rates. The tax rate of the saver becomes irrelevant at this level; as no income is generated, no income tax can be levied. Also, although the tables illustrate a negative rate, in reality savers can get around this by holding physical cash. This is something we have talked about before, along with the elimination of currency and the nature of cash. Negative and low nominal interest rates are new, low and negative real returns both pre and post tax are not.

And whilst we are on the subject of eliminating cash it's worth noting the ECB's announcement about stopping printing the €500 note. By taking this action the ECB is recognising an antisocial demand for its notes (tax evasion, crime), although there remains a strong suspicion that it's also because cash storage disrupts the transmission mechanism of monetary policy at negative rates. The ECB has, however, allowed the notes to continue to be legal tender, and presumably demand for the note will still be strong. If that's the case could we see the €500 note trade at a premium? If so, what would that premium be? There must be some calculation based on the additional storage costs incurred by hoarding cash in lower denomination notes?

Chapter 94

The unintended consequences of Negative Rate World Part II. An update.
Jim Leaviss – Wednesday, 1st June 2016

At the start of April I wrote about some of the unintended consequences of central banks setting negative interest rates. I also promised to update the blog as we spotted more interesting implications, and asked readers to submit examples too. Thanks for those who got in touch. Here are some more of the interesting things that happen when the zero lower bound ceases to exist, as well as links to some theoretical thinking on negative rates.

1. In the last blog we worried that banks would be unable to pass on negative rates to depositors (fearing deposit flight), and therefore could not pass on lower rates to borrowers, and so lending wouldn't be boosted. In fact whilst this remains broadly true we have seen some movement here. The President of the German Sparkassen (savings bank) Association Georg Fahrenschon has said that "the era of free account management is over" and that commercial customers will pay "penalty interest rates". Household rates however will (so far) remain untouched. Germany's Sparkassen are 74% funded by non-MFI deposits. (Story source: FAZ). In Spain, newspaper Cinco Dias reports that banks there are now charging 0.3% interest on deposits for large businesses.

2. The chief executive of UBS Sergio Ermotti has said that the negative rate environment makes his whole industry ask "do we still really want to take on client assets when doing so costs the bank money – and when we have to back up liquid assets with an unreasonably large amount of capital?" He also said that the bank had put up some loan rates as a result of the cost of negative deposit rates. (Source: WBP online)

3. The Eurozone's central banks have been earning millions of euros from deposits on which they would previously have paid interest. The Financial Times reported that, for example, "the Central Bank of Ireland earned €28.5m on deposits from the government and credit

institutions". For the larger European central banks this is presumably far more. (Source: FT via Torben Hendricks)

4. The always interesting Bank of England blog, The Bank Underground, has written about the impact of negative rates on the derivatives market. The industry standard for pricing interest rate options is called the SABR model, and assumes that rates do not go below zero. Fischer Black, who helped develop the thinking about options pricing, had said that "the nominal short rate cannot be negative". Modifications to the model, necessary since rates did go negative, now imply greater uncertainties of outcomes and hence higher hedging costs. The need to hedge some of these risks, and others deriving from the historical sale of structured notes may have increased the demand for physical bonds and hence driven yields even further lower, increasing volatility at the same time.

5. The Japanese Ministry of Finance is printing more of the largest Y10,000 note, to cope with demand. Production will increase to 1.23 billion of the notes per year, up from a typical level of 1.05 billion. Cash held at home has thought to have increased by 14% in the last year. Partly this may be due to negative rates, but it also could be due to the introduction of a new identification number regime ("My Number") linking tax and social security. (Source: Japan Times)

6. Looking at the papers from a 2015 conference by the Centre for Economic Policy Research, the conference was called "Removing the Zero Lower Bound on Interest Rates" and includes not just the economic debates, but discussion of the implications for legal and payments systems.

7. A 2012 post from New York Fed's equivalent of The Bank Underground blog, Liberty Street Economics, is worth a read. Amongst other "disruptions" that might occur from negative rate environments, it suggests that large corporations who can't physically hold enough cash to make it possible to withdraw it from banking systems, might financially innovate. They give the example of a special-purpose bank, with a vault full of physical cash, issuing cheques giving a claim on that cash. At some level of negative rates the SPV becomes able to charge a fee that makes it attractive to corporates to own a physically small cheque backed by cash held in a secure facility, rather than to keep their money in the traditional banking system. They also suggest that people might stop banking cheques – even if you try to pay somebody early, you might find you can't get rid of your cash. In a final great quote the Fed says that "if rates go negative, we may see an epochal outburst of socially unproductive – even if individually beneficial – financial innovation".

Chapter 95

What I am doing to protect against Brexit... or Bremain
Ben Lord – Thursday, 16th June 2016

Over the last few days and weeks, as the odds of a vote to leave in the referendum have moved from a remote possibility to somewhat less so, market participants have spent more and more time wondering about how they are positioned going into the vote, relative to their benchmark, their peer group, or their risk budget. The significant moves that we have seen in recent trading sessions show pretty clearly that many were not content with their positions or risks going into the vote, as evidenced by a pretty clear period of volatility and risk aversion with selling of credit risk and a rally in government bonds.

Only a couple of weeks ago, the credit markets were frantically fighting to get hold of reasonable quantities of the significant amount of new issuance we were seeing from investment grade companies. A few weeks later, issuance has ceased and sellers of these much sought after bonds seem to be outnumbering buyers, given the back-up in credit spreads seen in recent sessions. The simple conclusion is that as the odds of Brexit rise, investors feel the need to reduce risk and are selling corporate bonds.

Playing devil's advocate, let's imagine that a portfolio manager has sold credit risk and raised cash ahead of next week's vote. The portfolio manager is now feeling very satisfied at this moment in time as risk aversion has increased, resulting in a widening of credit spreads. However, the vote outcome is binary: either Britain votes to leave, or to remain. If the vote is to remain, then we can reasonably expect a significant retracement of the spread widening we have seen since fears of a leave vote rose.

If this proves correct then our imaginary portfolio manager is under-invested in credit and the credit risk that he or she sold will now need to be bought back, potentially at more expensive levels. Even if spreads did not rally in the event of a leave vote, then to replace the bonds that were sold, the portfolio manager will have to pay the prevailing bid-offer spread.

In other words, those selling credit risk now are predicting a vote to leave. This decision will benefit a bond portfolio as spreads rise, or as the leave probability increases, or if the leave vote were to occur (at least for a period of time, however long or short). But it does not work in the event of a vote to remain, and incurs costs on the bond portfolio.

Now let's think about what to do with our duration positioning going into the vote. This, in my opinion, is an even harder call to make than with credit. Which way will gilt yields move in the event of a leave vote? On the one hand, the period of economic uncertainty that would result could see growth and inflation fall, which would argue clearly in favour of further falls in government bond yields. On the other, international investors currently own more than a third of the gilt market. What if these investors decide they no longer want to own sterling, or to own the same amount of sterling? Whilst my hunch is that the knee-jerk immediate response to Brexit would be for sterling to weaken and for gilt yields to rally further, how long would these moves last? Could we end the day with higher gilt yields and no change in the pound? Either way, the direction of travel of gilt yields is highly uncertain to me, which makes hedging or positioning duration for the referendum a very tricky call.

In my opinion, owning short-dated breakevens is the most prudent way to go into the vote from the perspective of duration positioning. Firstly, if you believe that the currency is likely to weaken then you should own exposure to inflation linked bonds that will, especially at the front end, see higher inflation expectations from import inflation. This will support index linked valuations relative to nominal bonds. In other words, front end breakevens are likely to rise if sterling weakens. Secondly, putting the currency to one side for a moment, if yields rise (either on a leave vote as foreign sellers of gilts emerge or on a remain as risk appetite recovers and rate hikes are brought forward), then one would typically expect breakevens to rise. In this scenario, index linked bonds also outperform nominal bonds.

If yields fall on the other hand, a scenario most likely to happen in the event of a vote to leave due to risk aversion, then whilst typically breakevens fall, and so index linked bonds are underperforming nominal ones, at least owning breakevens means having a pretty decent link to nominal yields. It is difficult to create a scenario in which nominal yields rally strongly following a leave vote and index linked bonds fall in price (this scenario would be one in which inflation fears aggressively collapse, so it is not impossible, but it is unlikely).

So I believe that given the binary nature of the result, in which we are either in or out (what odds on 50:50, and what happens then?), the best way to be positioned in terms of duration ahead of the vote, outcome and aftermath is to own short-dated inflation linked bonds. It is not binary, as whilst owning breakevens means you are positioned for higher inflation, if breakevens fall following the vote and nominal yields fall, you are still linked to nominal yields and are likely to see the price of your bonds rise.

If the currency weakens after the election result, then import price inflation will lead to rising inflation expectations. And if the currency doesn't weaken following the result, it has still been on a downward trajectory since last November which is yet to feed through into RPI, and the ugly current account deficit suggests on a medium term, fundamental basis, that there is more weakness ahead for sterling.

Finally, there are a number of reasons to choose front end index linked bonds. Firstly, front end breakevens are the cheapest on the curve. Secondly, the front end of the index linked curve is most likely to reflect inflation surprises and outcomes (such as oil base effects, sterling weakness, wage growth in the bonds' prices); and lastly, because with gilt yields at all-time lows, it is prudent to keep interest rate risk at a relatively low level at this juncture.

Chapter 96

Bond market reaction to UK "Leave" vote

Jim Leaviss – Friday, 24th June 2016

The UK has voted to "Leave" the EU. We're seeing some significant moves in fixed income assets first thing this morning as financial markets had very much discounted a "Remain" outcome, in line with the last opinion polls and in particular the betting markets which had heavily backed that outcome. The biggest market movements though have occurred in the FX markets where the pound fell from nearly 1.50 to 1.36 versus the dollar, lows not seen since 1985. The US dollar index has rallied by nearly 3%, and the big winner in this "risk off" scenario has been the Japanese yen, itself now up 3.6% against the US dollar. The Euro is performing badly as both the economic and political implications of the "Out" vote are digested – will European growth be hit, will other EU nations hold their own referendums, what will become of the periphery and the banking sector? The Euro is down by over 3% against the dollar. In a risk off morning, the other big losing currencies are those in emerging markets. The Mexican peso for example is 6% weaker.

Within bond markets themselves, the US 10 year Treasury has rallied by 25 bps (more than two points) overnight, and the 10 year bund has moved sharply back below zero – now trading at a new record low of -15 bps. This follows Thursday's sell-off in government bonds in anticipation of "Remain". Gilt markets will also rally when they open at 8am, and all eyes are on the Bank of England which has committed to keep the banking sector awash with liquidity. I wouldn't rule out a rate cut from the BoE later this morning, perhaps to 0% from 0.5% (although this would likely trigger a further sell-off in sterling). A likely ratings downgrade for the UK has been flagged in advance in the event of a "leave" vote – markets have generally not punished downgrades on highly rated sovereigns (for example the US when it lost its AAA rating). There is no significant default risk for a nation which can print its own currency.

The "losers" in bond markets are the riskier fixed income assets. As further EU break-up fears grow, Italian and other peripheral government bonds are underperforming. Italian and Spanish 10 year bond yields have risen by 30 bps so far this morning. Peripheral financial bonds are perhaps 60 bps wider in spreads at the senior level and up to 130 bps wider at the subordinated level. Banks in general, even in "core" nations, are also performing poorly relative to traditional corporate bonds. Senior bank debt is 50 bps wider, and subs are 100 bps wider. Corporate bonds are anything from 20 bps to 80 bps wider. There has been talk of institutional buying at these lower levels, although we are sceptical that there has been much trading so far today. Emerging market bonds are all much lower. Turkey's US$ debt is off 2 points, South Africa 3 points and Hungary 6 points. The high yield market was extremely weak initially, with the Crossover index at one point 120 bps wider. It's retraced some losses and is "just" 80 bps wider now.

Fundamentally the sell-off in risk assets presents some opportunities for long-term investors. Credit markets were already discounting a much higher level of defaults than we believed likely, and today's moves increase the over-compensation for default risk. However, with liquidity likely to be low today (and potentially for some days to come as the implications of yesterday's vote become clearer) the chance to pick up bargains might be limited.

What about the economy? Well 90% of economists expected a "leave" vote to be negative for UK growth. Some say that even the uncertainty leading up to the vote took up to 50 bps off GDP growth. Certainly investment intentions are likely to be delayed by businesses, and households may become more cautious. A recession can't be discounted. With the global growth outlook also now likely weaker we expect the US Federal Reserve to be on hold. No rate hikes for the foreseeable future. UK inflation is a different matter. A fall of this magnitude in the pound will lead to higher import prices. After years of inflation being below target, it should move higher than 2%. However in the interests of growth and financial stability this is unlikely to provoke a response from the Bank of England: as mentioned earlier a rate cut is more likely in the first instance.

Finally I am cross that there was nowhere open to buy caffeine on Cannon St at 6am this morning.

Chapter 97

Four years of the ECB doing "whatever it takes"
Anthony Doyle – Tuesday, 26th July 2016

Transport yourself back to July 26, 2012. Borrowing costs for the "peripheral" European nations are uncomfortably high. Ireland, Portugal and Greece were in the process of applying for bailouts, while the Spanish banking system was dangerously close to falling over. It wasn't a question of when an EU member would leave the single currency bloc, but who? Step forward ECB President Mario Draghi, who in an address delivered to a room full of business leaders and investors, proceeded to deliver the most important sentence delivered by a central banker in modern times – "Within our mandate, the ECB is ready to do whatever it takes to preserve the euro. And believe me, it will be enough".

The big question at the time was what is it?

Fast forward to today, and we have some understanding of what President Draghi meant. He was referring to a range of conventional and extraordinary monetary policy measures, including a cut in the ECB's main refinancing rate from 1 to 0%, a cut in the deposit facility from 0.25 to -0.40%, long-term refinancing operations that reached over 1 trillion euros in size, emergency liquidity assistance for Greece that currently stands at 54 billion euros, and an asset-purchase programme worth 1.1 trillion euros (subsequently extended, expanded and increased by around a third). As a result, the ECB balance sheet now stands at 3.2 trillion euros (or 131% of Euro area GDP).

That's the *it*. Was it *enough*?

Looking at peripheral bond yields suggests that it was. Investors are no longer demanding the credit premium they once were, resulting in a collapse in bond yields.

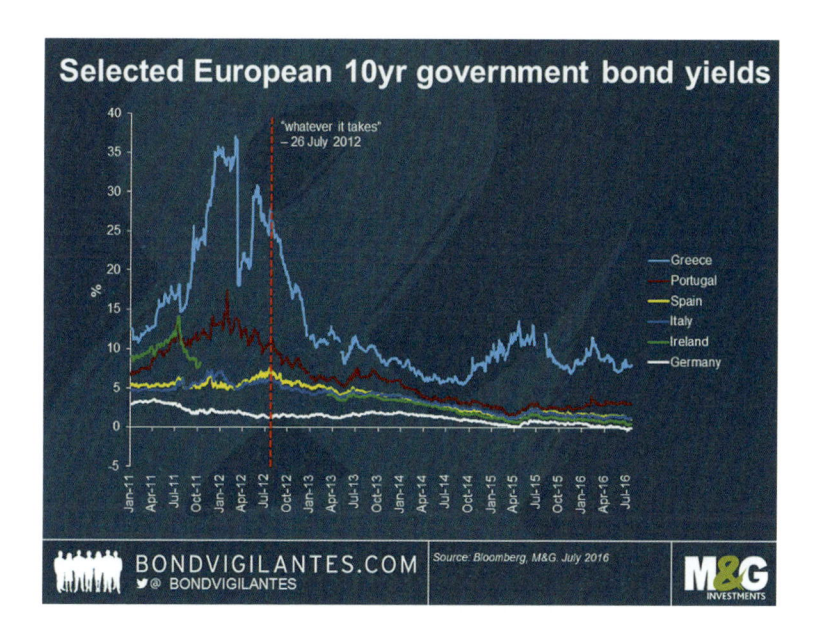

[Chart: Selected European 10yr government bond yields]

In his speech, Draghi referred to the spike in risk aversion being linked to counterparty risk. As shown below, CDS premia have collapsed in the Euro area from 2012 levels but sub-financials have been on a widening trend since Q4 2014. More recently, investors are questioning the amount of bad debts that a number of European banks have on their books and whether these losses can be sustained in some of the more fragile financial systems of the Euro area.

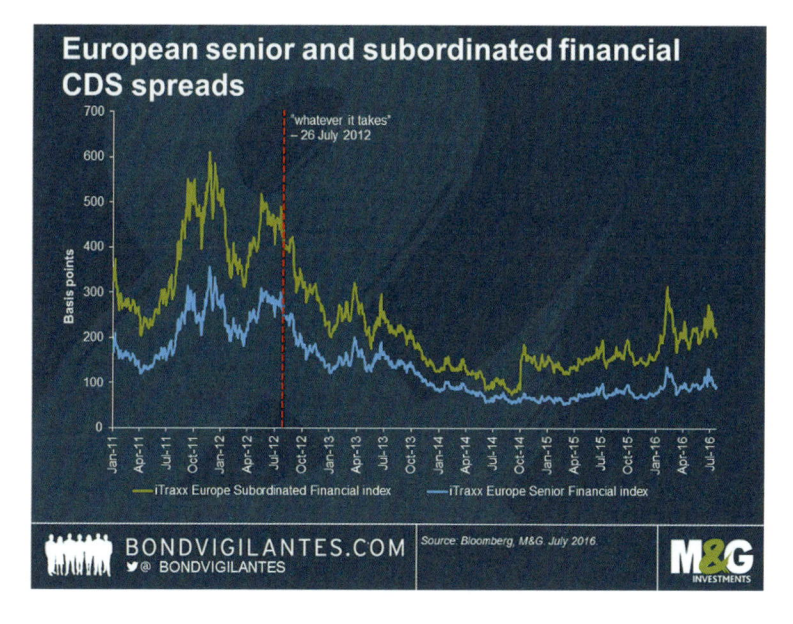

[Chart: European senior and subordinated financial CDS spreads]

Finally, using Google, it appears that people from the US and UK are more worried about a European recession than Europeans themselves over the past two years. The vast majority of searches for "Europe recession" come from the US or UK (I also checked for local language equivalents: there are 7 searches per month on average in Germany for "Europa rezession"; and "recessione Europa" registers 5 searches in Italy for example).

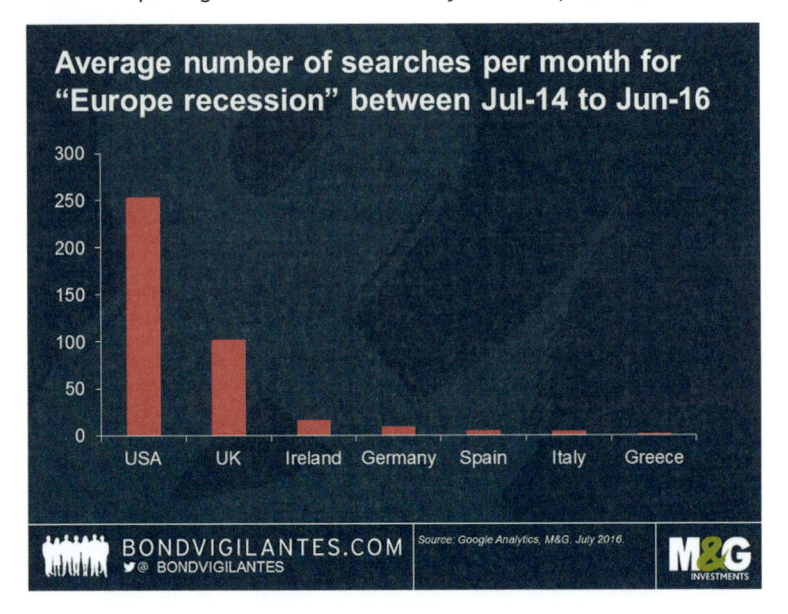

Average number of searches per month for "Europe recession" between Jul-14 to Jun-16

Country	Searches
USA	~250
UK	~100
Ireland	~15
Germany	~7
Spain	~5
Italy	~5
Greece	~2

Source: Google Analytics, M&G. July 2016.
BONDVIGILANTES.COM / @BONDVIGILANTES

President Mario Draghi brought calm and stability to very volatile markets four years ago through his speech. His words acted like a risk-off circuit breaker, and European government bond markets and the financial system benefited from that. It goes to show that a central banker with a mandate does have the ability to heavily influence financial markets. Indeed, President Draghi may have saved the single currency bloc, as it appeared the ECB was the only European institution that had the ability to act quickly, decisively and in a large enough magnitude to support the European economy in the absence of a European fiscal union.

Unfortunately, not much has changed on the fiscal front. Europe still faces some significant structural issues, with a significant divergence in economic outcomes across the Euro area member states. Brexit will also likely prove to be a headwind for economic growth. Economically, Europe is still struggling with high unemployment rates and very low inflation despite four years of extraordinary monetary policy. With the markets expecting more monetary stimulus in September, it appears that the ECB's job of doing "whatever it takes" is still not over.

Chapter 98

The Bank of England could be about to unveil a bumper monetary policy package

Anjulie Rusius – Wednesday, 27th July 2016

Despite keeping interest rates on hold at the 4th July meeting, the minutes of the Monetary Policy Committee indicated that "most members expect an easing in August" (even long-time hawk Martin Weale has shifted to a dovish stance). Subsequently, markets are pricing in a staggering 98.3% probability of a rate cut at the next meeting in 8 days' time. With UK data expected to deteriorate over the next few months, market pricing seems appropriate.

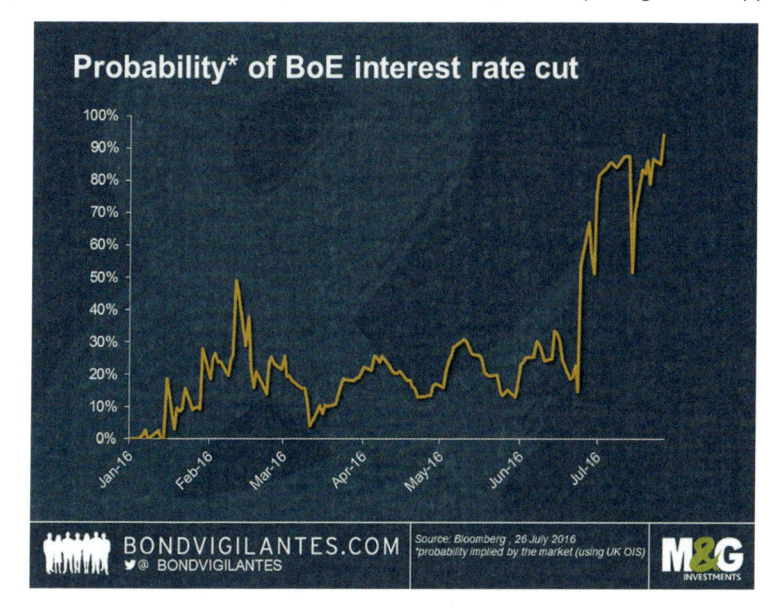

Probability* of BoE interest rate cut

Source: Bloomberg, 26 July 2016
*probability implied by the market (using UK OIS)

However, something else that stood out from Governor Carney's 30th June speech (other than his expectation of some summer monetary policy easing), was this: *"In August, we will also discuss further the range of instruments at our disposal."* With interest rates close to zero, Governor Carney could be indicating that the BoE is limbering up to provide a bumper stimulus monetary package, alongside an interest rate cut, akin to that unveiled by the ECB in March this year.

Here are five options that could be available to the MPC.

1. Quantitative easing

A renewal of the BoE's quantitative easing programme seems the most likely easing measure that the MPC could take outside of cutting interest rates; the ultimate goal of the policy being to facilitate an expansion of private bank lending, via central bank asset purchases. Should this occur, we would expect the belly of the UK government bond curve to be well supported. In particular, gilts with maturities in the 7-15yr range could benefit given that there are fewer bonds in this maturity bucket (assuming the BoE aims to make purchases in line with its QE reinvestment rules which we have discussed here) and this is the duration neutral part of the curve. More pertinent to the UK perhaps would be what Fathom Consulting have coined "Operation Anti-Twist" (based on the FOMC's 2011 "Operation Twist") which would entail selling long dated gilts and buying short-dated gilt issues. This would engineer a steeper yield curve and could support those with longer term pension liabilities looking for higher yields.

2. Corporate bond purchases

In order to improve market liquidity in 2009-2012, the BoE purchased corporate bonds as part of its QE programme. Though this is not necessarily an imminent priority – there does not appear to be a corporate funding crisis; GBP non-financial investment grade corporate spreads did spike up, but have fallen since the referendum – this nevertheless presents a credible policy option.

If the BoE were to resume corporate bond purchases, along the same criteria used previously (which was much stricter than that currently used by the ECB, especially with regards to rules regarding credit ratings), I estimate that the investment universe would be in excess of £100bn, with utility companies representing the lion's share of eligible purchases. Real estate companies also appear set to benefit notably from corporate QE, which could offer some targeted support to a sector that's already been particularly hard hit.

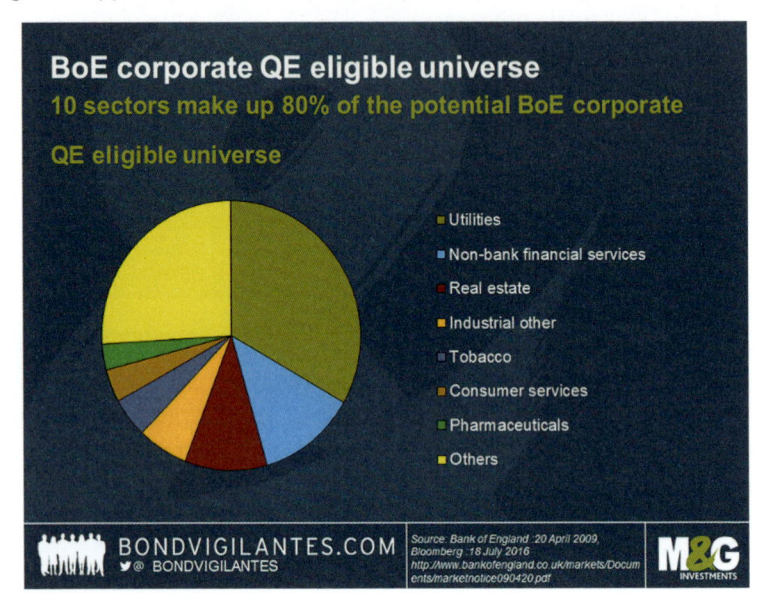

BoE corporate QE eligible universe
10 sectors make up 80% of the potential BoE corporate QE eligible universe

- Utilities
- Non-bank financial services
- Real estate
- Industrial other
- Tobacco
- Consumer services
- Pharmaceuticals
- Others

BONDVIGILANTES.COM
@BONDVIGILANTES

Source: Bank of England :20 April 2009, Bloomberg :18 July 2016
http://www.bankofengland.co.uk/markets/Documents/marketnotice090420.pdf

M&G INVESTMENTS

3. Further support for bank lending

Earlier this month the BoE reduced the UK countercyclical capital buffer rate – for banks, building societies and large investment firms – to zero from 0.5% until at least June 2017. Governor Carney noted that this will lower UK banks' required capital buffers by £5.7bn, essentially freeing up capital for them to lend to the real economy. Should upcoming data warrant it, the BoE could extend its Funding for Lending Scheme (FLS), to further ease credit conditions for households. The current scheme incentivises banks to boost lending, with a skew towards small and medium sized enterprises – arguably those who will be hardest hit from the ongoing uncertain outlook. They could however extend this scheme in a further targeted manner, for example, towards mortgage lending in a bid to subsidise loans for house purchases (should market conditions warrant this). The FLS has been extended many times since it was introduced in July 2012, with the last extension taking place in November. Though we have previously questioned the success of the scheme, we could potentially see another amendment.

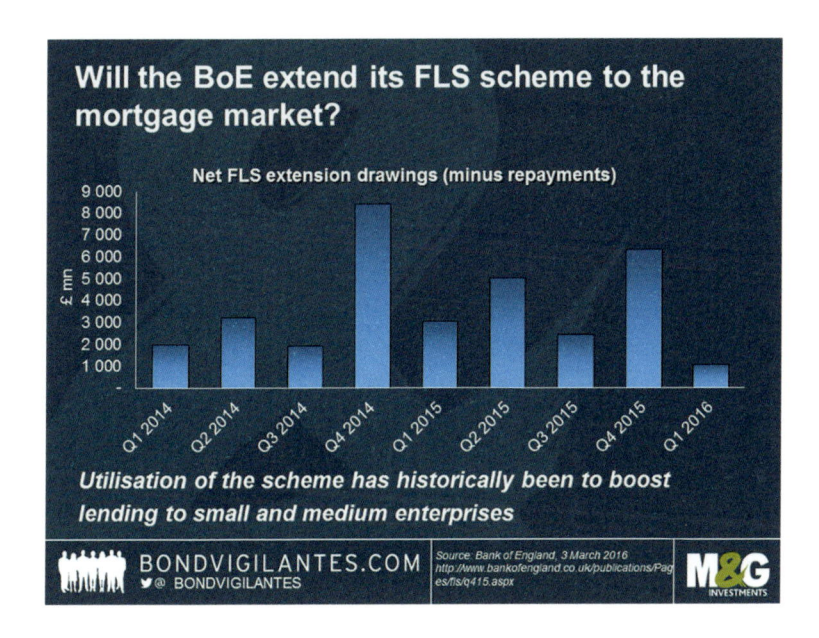

Will the BoE extend its FLS scheme to the mortgage market?

Net FLS extension drawings (minus repayments) by quarter (£mn): Q1 2014 ~2000; Q2 2014 ~3000; Q3 2014 ~2000; Q4 2014 ~8500; Q1 2015 ~3000; Q2 2015 ~5500; Q3 2015 ~2500; Q4 2015 ~6500; Q1 2016 ~1000.

Utilisation of the scheme has historically been to boost lending to small and medium enterprises

BONDVIGILANTES.COM / @BONDVIGILANTES
Source: Bank of England, 3 March 2016 http://www.bankofengland.co.uk/publications/Pages/fls/q415.aspx
M&G INVESTMENTS

4. Joined up fiscal and monetary policy response

Investors and markets are positioned for a low growth, low inflation world, but this could be about to change. With the limits of global monetary policy arguably exhibiting diminishing returns to scale, there is now the potential to see expansionary UK fiscal policy working alongside monetary policy. Given the reshuffling of the cabinet, Osborne's fiscal tightening and austerity budget have fallen by the wayside and it is time for Hammond to show his hand. Given the unusual circumstances, the new chancellor could plausibly move his autumn statement to coincide with the BoE meeting on the 3rd November and offer something original. If he takes the advice of the IMF and OECD, both of which have been calling for a boost in infrastructure spending, we could potentially see the government opting for pro-growth infrastructure projects, funded via bonds that the BoE ultimately buys.

5. Negative rates

Could the BoE introduce negative interest rates, like we've seen in the Euro area and Japan? In theory yes, but in practice I believe that this is some way off. Negative rates are still in their experimental phase (Jim has noted some great anecdotes on this) and the BoE still have some leeway with regards to traditional monetary policy. With interest rates at 0.5%, there is still space for a few cuts before we reach the zero bound and have to contemplate any unconventional measures.

Evidently there are many tools in the toolbox (and I have focused predominantly on the tried and tested), but will the BoE look to use them? Every monetary policy meeting should be noted in your diary, every meeting is 'live'. Roll on the next BoE monetary policy decision.

Chapter 99

Should the Bank of England start buying sterling corporate bonds again?
Jim Leaviss – Thursday, 28th July 2016

When the Bank of England's Monetary Policy Committee meets next week, the market expects that they will cut rates, especially now that even outgoing hawk, Martin Weale (who has been at the Bank for 71 meetings so far, and voted to hike 12 times, and to hold 59 times) says that he will support a reduction. A resumption of the Funding for Lending (FLS) scheme is also a possibility (many economists suggest that this was the most successful policy action taken to stimulate the economy during the UK's Great Recession). The Bank's remit also allows it to reopen Asset Purchase Facility, better known as Quantitative Easing. The BoE bought £375 billion of gilts from 2009 to 2012. It also bought sterling denominated corporate bonds, in the Corporate Bond Secondary Market Scheme. Largely taking place between March 2009 and March 2010, £2.25 billion of investment grade, non-financial, corporate bonds were purchased.

Whilst small in scope compared with the gilt purchases, the impact on credit spreads at a time when investors had already identified post-crisis value, was large. Borrowing costs fell substantially and the new issue market for companies re-opened. The idea that the BoE might start buying sterling corporate bonds again is now being discussed, especially as the ECB is buying euro denominated bonds at a fierce pace as part of its QE programme. On the face of it though, credit spreads are trading near their historical average rather than near Great Depression levels as in 2009, and in the banking market both the availability of credit and the spread costs to large companies – those that could borrow in corporate bond markets – are benign, if not "easy". So why would the BoE want to start buying sterling credit again?

Well although credit spreads have fallen globally, especially post-Draghi's March announcement of corporate bond purchases, sterling credit has definitely lagged. Using BofA Merrill Lynch indices to compare market levels, the UK investment grade corporate bond market trades at a spread of 161 bps over government bonds, compared to 148 bps in the US and 114 bps in Europe. Now there's definitely a compositional bias here – for example the UK corporate bond market is longer dated and you might expect a risk premium as a result. But when you look at spreads on a "same name, similar maturity" basis, the UK corporate bond market is still wide. For example Deutsche Telekom bonds with a 2030 maturity trade with a spread of gilts plus 108 bps in sterling, or bunds plus 90 bps in euros. Johnson & Johnson 2023 bonds trade at gilts plus 40 bps, or US Treasuries plus 19 bps. Tesco 2024 bonds have a spread of 314 bps over gilts, versus the euro 2023s spread at 257 bps over bunds.

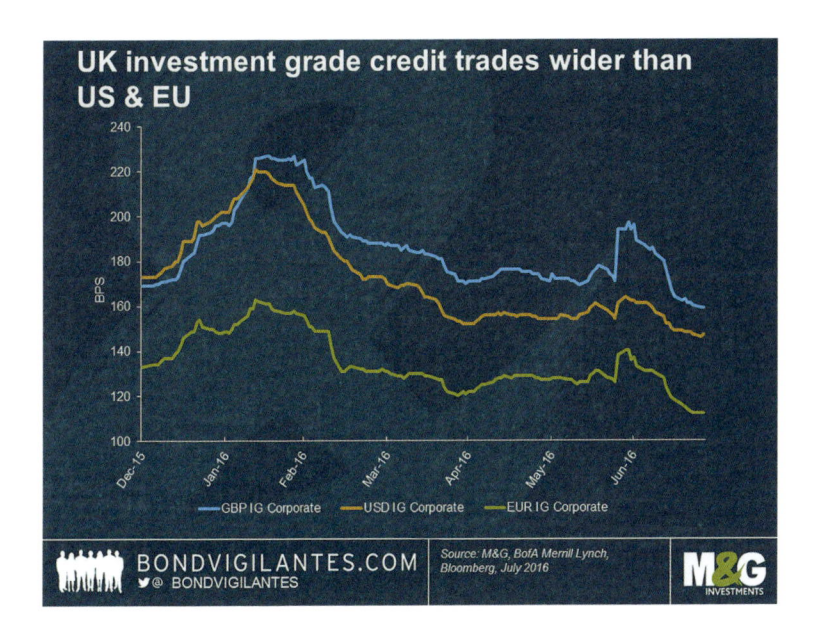

Because the UK credit market trades wider than other big capital markets, it deters corporate treasurers from issuing in sterling. It's more expensive. Most big companies can choose where they issue debt, and they can hedge away the currency risks using swaps, leaving just the "pure" cost of the debt to consider (they must also take into account the cross currency basis swap costs, but that's another story). This has become a vicious circle for the UK debt market. As companies see cheaper funding available elsewhere, they issue in US dollars or euros, which reduces liquidity in the sterling market, which leads to wider credit spreads, which makes it more expensive to issue in sterling. And so on. The BoE examined some of the factors behind the fall in sterling issuance on its excellent Bank Underground blog in April this year. In it they showed that annual gross sterling issuance has almost halved since 2012, and sterling's share of global issuance last year was the lowest on record.

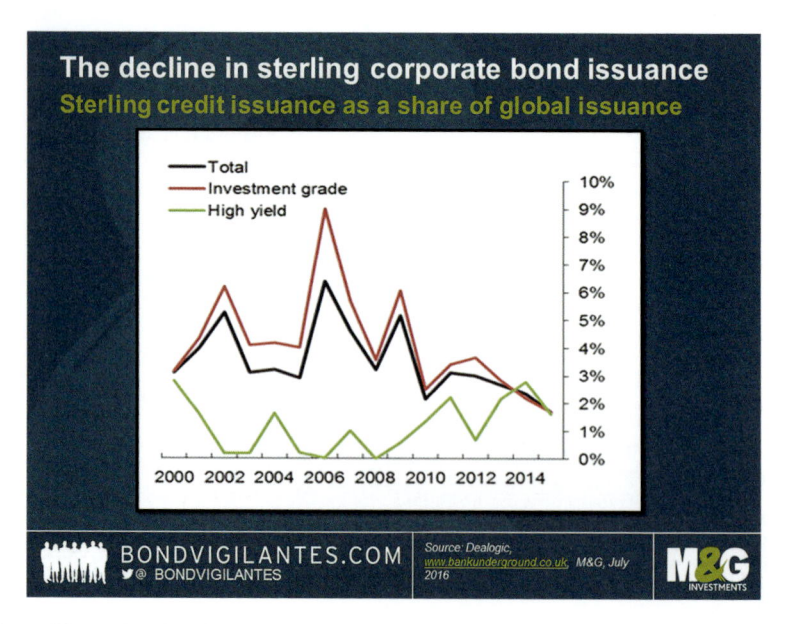

The decline in sterling corporate bond issuance
Sterling credit issuance as a share of global issuance

[Chart showing Total, Investment grade, and High yield sterling credit issuance as a share of global issuance from 2000 to 2014, ranging from 0% to 10%. Source: Dealogic, www.bankunderground.co.uk, M&G, July 2016]

BONDVIGILANTES.COM
@BONDVIGILANTES

M&G INVESTMENTS

The BoE staff ascribe the fall in sterling issuance to three reasons. Firstly, a concentrated sterling investor base and mergers in the industry meant that some large institutions were effectively "full" of some names, and a lower number of participants meant that it could be hard to get deals done, meaning higher yields were required to entice buyers. Secondly, changes in annuity rules reduced the demand for long dated credit. And finally, the growth of the euro denominated corporate bond market since 1999 has led to it gaining "critical mass" for both issuers and buyers.

If the BoE were to restart its corporate bond programme, it could drive credit spreads down to something in line with euro and dollar issuance through ongoing, price insensitive buying. Lower UK credit spreads relative to the other major markets would provide some incentive for corporates (both domestic and global) to start issuing sterling bonds once more.

In a post-Brexit world, with a threat of financial market activity moving away from London, the reinvigoration of a declining UK corporate bond market appears attractive. Whilst the reduction in financing costs for UK based corporates might be marginal, it too would be welcome if the weak post-Brexit survey data is correct in predicting a sharp downturn in economic activity.

Chapter 100

Is QE unquestionably supportive for risk assets? I think not.

Richard Woolnough – Tuesday, 2nd August 2016

We have written about quantitative easing (QE) many times over the years, yet there remains more to be said: the great QE experiment is not yet over. Given the result of the EU referendum, speculation is rife as to whether the Bank of England will embark on another round of QE to stimulate the UK economy; arguably making this a good time to debate the efficacy of such strategies.

It's safe to say that the most surprising aspect of QE has been the lack of inflation, but central banks which have undertaken – or are still undertaking – QE claim that it has worked by preventing deflation through portfolio rebalancing. The shift in funds into riskier assets has led to higher stock markets. My take on this? Central banks are over exaggerating their claims at best, or grabbing at straws at worst.

Let's take the US model experience as an example. I agree that the Fed's balance sheet and S&P 500 index have been positively correlated since 2009, but I would argue that the relationship is casual, not causal. The Fed announced its QE programme only after US stock markets had collapsed to cheap levels, and stopped it only once those markets had recovered. As such, the Fed seemed to use the S&P index as a temperature gauge for the economy ("the share price of the country" as it were), rather than the index appreciation being the direct result of the QE activity undertaken. QE started when stocks were cheap, and finished when they became fair value.

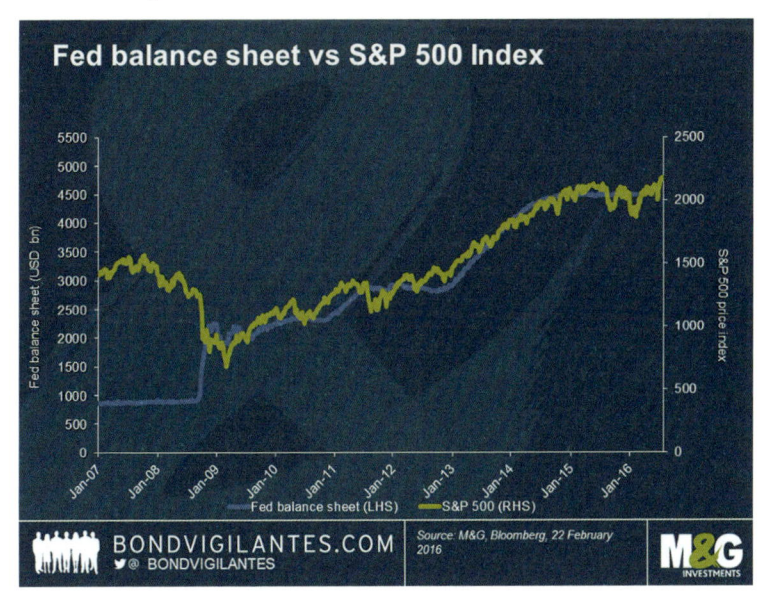

Not yet convinced? The above chart demonstrates a coincidental relationship, but what about other economies? The QE experiment in Europe was initiated in March 2015, a time when the Stoxx 600 equity market was much more buoyant, and not trading at distressed valuation levels. It seems ludicrous to argue that a causal link has been in play in Europe. This is illustrated on the next page.

ECB public sector purchases vs Stoxx 600

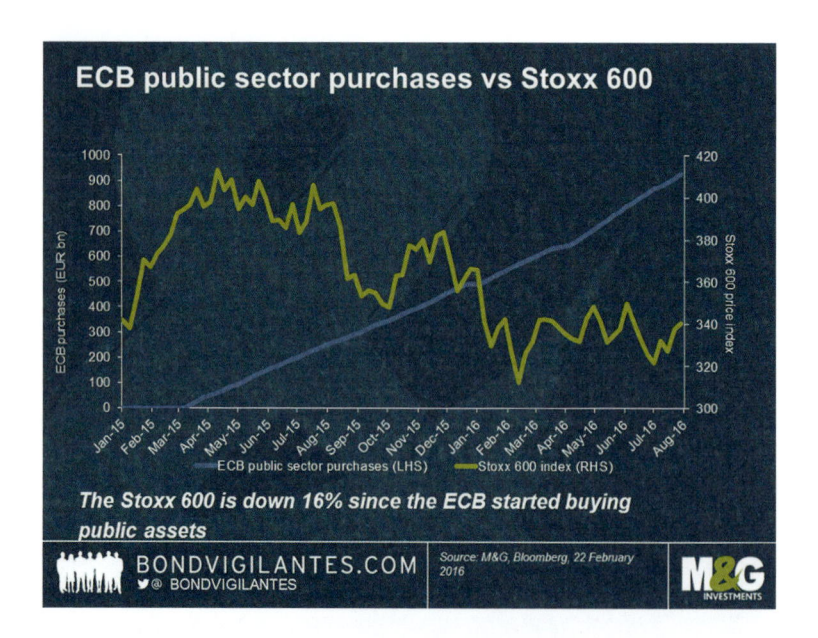

The Stoxx 600 is down 16% since the ECB started buying public assets

Source: M&G, Bloomberg, 22 February 2016

So what have we learnt? QE appeared positive for risk assets when their valuations were depressed in the US, but had little impact when equities were fairly priced in Europe. Because interest rates have already fallen to a large extent (thereby lowering the discount rate that equity investors use), investors will not be able to boost the present value of future cashflows. This means that it is difficult for equity market valuations to increase to the same extent as previously when yields collapsed. Given the sluggish economic outlook and potentially higher interest rates in the US, it is also difficult to argue that profits in the future will be much higher as well.

QE does have some economic effects; it's just (I'm not ashamed to say) still difficult to discern just what these are. It hasn't yet been inflationary (even though the basic principles of QE suggest that increasing the supply of money should reduce its value) and I believe that the link to stock market strength is somewhat illusory. Arguably, the greatest effect of QE has been the reduction in bond yields across the curve and not a portfolio rebalancing into riskier assets. In theory, the portfolio rebalancing effect is most powerful when investors view equities as an alternative to bonds. Given the difference in volatility characteristics of both asset classes, it is unlikely that this will ever be the case (some investors still choose to buy negative yielding fixed income securities for example). If the Bank of England is hoping that QE will prop up the UK economy and inflation through a causal link then the current economic data supporting this theory is mixed at best.

The European Commission
- the executive of the European Union

BRITISH

For Investment Professionals only. Not for onward distribution. No other persons should rely on any information contained within. This information is not an offer or solicitation of an offer for the purchase of shares in any of M&G's funds.

This financial promotion is issued by M&G Securities Limited (registered in England 90776) and M&G International Investments Ltd. Both are authorised and regulated by the Financial Conduct Authority in the UK and have their registered offices at Laurence Pountney Hill, London EC4R 0HH. M&G International Investments Ltd is registered in England, No. 4134655. It has a branch located in France, 6 rue Lamennais, Paris 75008, registered on the Trade Register of Paris, No. 499 832 400 and a branch in Spain, with corporate domicile at Plaza de Colón 2, Torre II Planta 14, 28046, Madrid, Spain, registered with the Commercial Registry of Madrid under Volume 32.573, sheet 30, page M-586297, inscription 1, CIF W8264591B and registered with the CNMV under the number 79.This financial promotion is further issued by M&G Investments (Hong Kong) Limited. Office: Suite 08, 20/F One International Finance Centre, 1 Harbour View Street, Central, Hong Kong

For Switzerland: Distribution of this document in or from Switzerland is not permissible with the exception of the distribution to Qualified Investors according to the Swiss Collective Investment Schemes Act, the Swiss Collective Investment Schemes Ordinance and the respective Circular issued by the Swiss supervisory authority ("Qualified Investors"). Supplied for the use by the initial recipient (provided it is a Qualified Investor) only.

United States: Any information included in this document should be kept confidential and should be used only by the recipient with the purpose of assessing investment options for investors outside of the United States. The funds discussed herein by M&G International Investments Limited have not been and will not be registered under the United States Investment Company Act of 1940, as amended. Shares in the funds discussed herein have not been and will not be registered under the United States Securities Act of 1933, as amended, and may not be offered, sold or otherwise transferred directly or indirectly within the United States or to, or for the account of, US Persons, as such term is defined in the United States Securities Act of 1933, as amended. No public offering of any shares in the company is being, or has been made in the United States. This material is for informational purposes only. It is not an offer to sell or purchase interests in the funds discussed herein. Any purchase of any interest discussed in these materials must be made pursuant to local laws of the relevant jurisdiction in which such interests are offered outside of the United States.

Chile: ESTA OFERTA PRIVADA SE INICIA EL DÍA [01.09.2016] SE ACOGE A LAS DISPOSICIONES DE LA NORMA DE CARÁCTER GENERAL N°. 336 DE LA SUPERINTENDENCIA DE VALORES Y SEGUROS; ESTA OFERTA VERSA SOBRE VALORES NO INSCRITOS EN EL REGISTRO DE VALORES O EN REGISTRO DE VALORES EXTRANJEROS QUE LLEVA LA SUPERINTENDENCIA DE VALORES Y SEGUROS, POR LO QUE TALES NO ESTÁN SUJETOS A LA FISCALIZACIÓN DE ÉSTA; POR TRATAR DE VALORES NO INSCRITOS NO EXISTE LA OBLIGACIÓN POR PARTE DEL EMISOR DE ENTREGAR EN CHILE INFORMACION PÚBLICA RESPECTO DE LOS VALORES SOBRE LOS QUE VERSA ESTA OFERTA; ESTOS VALORES NO PODRÁN SER OBJETO DE OFERTA PÚBLICA MIENTRAS NO SEAN INSCRITOS EN EL REGISTRO DE VALORES CORRESPONDIENTE.

Mexico: The M&G Funds have not been and will not be registered with the National Registry of Securities, maintained by the Mexican National Banking Commission and, as a result, may not be offered or sold publicly in Mexico. The M&G Fund and any underwriter or purchaser may offer and sell the Funds in Mexico, to Institutional and Accredited Investors, on a private placement basis, pursuant to Article 8 of the Mexican Securities Market Law. Please note that each investor into an M&G Fund shall be responsible for calculating and paying its own taxes, receiving any necessary tax advice and that neither the Funds nor M&G shall be deemed to have provided tax advice to a potential investor.

Uruguay: The shares must not be offered or sold to the public in Uruguay, except in circumstances which do not constitute a public offering or distribution under Uruguayan laws and regulations. The shares are not and will not be registered with the Financial Services Superintendency of the Central Bank of Uruguay. The shares correspond to investment funds that are not investment funds regulated by Uruguayan law 16,774 dated September 27th 1996, as amended.

Hong Kong: If you have any questions about this financial promotion please contact M&G Investments (Hong Kong) Limited. For Switzerland, the financial promotion is published by M&G International Investments Switzerland AG, Talstrasse 66, 8001 Zurich, authorised and regulated by the Swiss Federal Financial Market Supervisory Authority. The Portuguese Securities Market Commission (Comissão do Mercado de Valores Mobiliários, the "CMVM") has received a passporting notification under Directive 2009/65/EC of the European Parliament and of the Council and the Commission Regulation (EU) 584/2010 enabling the fund to be distributed to the public in Portugal. M&G International Limited is duly passported into Portugal to provide certain investment services in such jurisdiction on a cross-border basis and is registered for such purposes with the CMVM and is therefore authorised to conduct the marketing (comercialização) of funds in Portugal.